Political Communication in America

WITHDRAWN

**Murdock Learning Resource
Center
George Fox College
Newberg, Oregon 97132**

PRAEGER SERIES IN POLITICAL COMMUNICATION

Robert E. Denton, Jr., *General Editor*

Political Communication in America

SECOND EDITION

Robert E. Denton, Jr., and Gary C. Woodward

Praeger Series in Political Communication

New York
Westport, Connecticut
London

Copyright Acknowledgments

Table 6.3 is from Thomas E. Patterson, THE MASS MEDIA ELECTION (Praeger Publishers, New York, 1980), p. 59. Copyright (c) 1980 by Praeger Publishers. Reprinted with permission.

Library of Congress Cataloging-in-Publication Data

Denton, Robert E., Jr.
    Political communication in America / Robert E. Denton, Jr. and Gary C. Woodward—2nd ed.
        p.   cm.—(Praeger series in political communication)
    Includes bibliographical references.
    ISBN 0–275–93093–9 (alk. paper).—ISBN 0–275–93094–7 (pbk. : alk. paper)
    1. Communication in politics—United States.   2. United States— Politics and government.   I. Woodward, Gary C.   II. Title. III. Series.
    JK271.D46   1990
    306.2'0973—dc20   89–29741

Library of Congress Catalog Card Number: 89–29741
ISBN: 0–275–93093–9
        0–275–93094–7 (pbk.)

First published in 1990

Praeger Publishers, One Madison Avenue, New York, NY 10010
An imprint of Greenwood Publishing Group, Inc.

Printed in the United States of America

The paper used in this book complies with the
Permanent Paper Standard issued by the National
Information Standards Organization (Z39.48–1984).

10   9   8   7   6   5   4   3   2   1

We dedicate this book, as with the first edition,
to our families:
Paula, Bobby, and Chris;
Rebecca, Trevor, and Hilary.

Contents

CONTENTS   ix

CONTENTS

PART III   EPILOGUE

Series Foreword

Those of us from the discipline of communication studies have long believed that communication is the foundation of all other fields of inquiry. In several other forums I have argued that the essence of politics is "talk" or human interaction.[1] Such interaction may be formal or informal, verbal or nonverbal, public or private, but always persuasive forcing us consciously or subconsciously to interpret, to evaluate, and to act. Communication is the vehicle for human action.

From this perspective, it is not surprising that Aristotle recognized the natural kinship of politics and communication in his *Politics* and *The Art of Rhetoric*. In the former, he establishes that humans are "political beings" who "alone of the animals [are] furnished with the faculty of language."[2] And in the latter, he begins his systematic analysis of discourse by proclaiming that "rhetorical study, in its strict sense, is concerned with the modes of persuasion."[3] Thus, it was recognized over 1500 years ago that politics and communication go hand in hand because they are essential parts of human nature.

Back in 1981, Dan Nimmo and Keith Sanders proclaimed that political communication was an emerging field.[4] Although its origin, as noted, dates back centuries, a "self-consciously cross-disciplinary" focus began in the late 1950s. Thousands of books and articles later, colleges and universities offer a variety of graduate and undergraduate courses in the discipline in such diverse departments as communication, mass communication, journalism, political science, and sociology.[5] In Nimmo and Sander's early assessment, the "key areas of inquiry" included rhetorical analysis, propaganda analysis, attitude change studies, voting studies, government and the news media, functional and systems analyses, technological changes, media technologies, campaign techniques, and research techniques.[6] In a survey of the state of the field in 1983 by the same authors and Lynda Kaid, they found additional, more specific areas of concern such as the presidency, political polls, public opinion, debates, and advertising, to name a few.[7] Since the first study, they also noted a shift away from the rather strict behavioral approach.

Then as now, the field of political communication continues to emerge. There is no precise definition, method, or disciplinary home of the area of inquiry. Its domain, quite simply, is the role, processes, and effects of communication within the context of politics.

In 1985, the editors of *Political Communication Yearbook: 1984* noted that "more things are happening in the study, teaching, and practice of political communication than can be captured within the space limitations of the relatively few publications available."[8] In addition, they argued that the backgrounds of "those involved in the field [are] so varied and pluralist in outlook and approach, . . . it [is] a mistake to adhere slavishly to any set format in shaping the content."[9]

In accordance with this assessment of the area, Praeger established the series entitled "Praeger Studies in Political Communication." The series is open to all qualitative and quantitative methodologies as well as contemporary and historical studies. The key to characterizing the studies in the series is their focus on communication variables or activities within a political context or dimension.

We are both pleased and humbled by the response to the first edition of this book. We wanted to provide a systematic and comprehensive analysis of the role of communication in U.S. politics. We also wanted to provide, in a single source, a synthesis of some of the best writings in political communication from the fields of communication, political science, and social psychology. Finally, we wanted to contribute to the growing literature in the area of political communication. Although obviously biased, I think we accomplished these goals. We are delighted that so many fans of politics—young and old, in and out of college—found the first edition of some interest. For us, it is gratifying to see the book in a second edition and as part of the Praeger Studies in Political Communication Series.

I am without shame or modesty, a fan of the series. The joy of serving as its editor is in participating in the dialogue of the field of political communication and in reading the contributors' works. I invite you to join me.

Robert E. Denton, Jr.

NOTES

1. See Robert E. Denton, Jr., *The Symbolic Dimensions of the American Presidency* (Prospect Heights, IL: Waveland Press, 1982); Robert E. Denton, Jr. and Gary Woodward, *Political Communication in America* (New York: Praeger, 1985); Robert E. Denton, Jr. and Dan Hahn, *Presidential Communication* (New York: Praeger, 1986); and Robert E. Denton, Jr., *The Primetime Presidency of Ronald Reagan* (New York: Praeger, 1988).

2. Aristotle, *The Politics of Aristotle*, trans. Ernest Barker (New York: Oxford University Press, 1970), p. 5.

3. Aristotle, *Rhetoric*, trans. Rhys Roberts (New York: The Modern Library, 1954), p. 22.

4. Dan Nimmo and Keith Sanders, "Introduction: The Emergence of Political Communication as a Field," in *Handbook of Political Communication*, Dan Nimmo and Keith Sanders, Editors (Beverly Hills, CA: Sage, 1981), pp. 11–36.

5. Ibid., p. 15.

6. Ibid., p. 17–27.

7. Keith Sanders, Lynda Kaid, and Dan Nimmo, Editors *Political Communication Yearbook: 1984* (Carbondale, IL: Southern Illinois University: 1985), pp. 283–308.

8. Ibid., p. xiv.

9. Ibid.

Preface

Humans are, according to Aristotle's *Politics*, "political beings" and "he who is without a polis, by reason of his own nature and not of some accident, is either a poor sort of being [a beast] or a being higher than man [a god]."[1] And because nature makes nothing in vain, Aristotle continues, a human "alone of the animals is furnished with the faculty of language."[2] Thus, it was recognized over 1500 years ago that politics and communication go hand in hand because they are essential parts of human nature. Both fields claim the subject matter of other fields as part of their own content. Nearly every topic that is fit for comment by someone contains the seeds for political and communication analysis. Neither field can claim an area of interest that is exclusively its own. Each necessarily crosses the boundaries and invades terrain with more neatly defined borders. Advances in medical technology, for example, can be praised or blamed by how they are described. And such descriptions usually have a significant impact on the discussions of the proper role of the state in the control of new technologies. The communication analyst is always a guest (if not an intruder) on someone else's turf. But communication is fundamental to all other fields of inquiry. What we know about events is always revealed first through the communicator's skill and art.

The focus of this edition has not changed from that of the previous one. It concerns the roles and functions of communication in U.S. politics and not on the "politics of communication." In describing the processes common to "political communication," the priorities of the writers would be better reflected if the two terms were reversed. This book is first about the possibilities and problems inherent to public discussion in an advanced industrial society. It is to a lesser extent about political institutions and controversial issues. Although the frameworks for our analysis utilize conventional categories of political activity— for example, activity in Congress, the courts, the mass media, and the presidency—the essential points of our analysis hinge on what we consider to be pivotal communication processes.

We posit that the essence of politics is "talk" or human interaction. Such interaction is formal and informal, verbal and nonverbal, public and private— but always persuasive in nature, causing us to interpret, to evaluate, and to act. Communication provides the basis of social cohesion, issue discussion, and legislative enactment.

As perhaps befits a work on politics, our work is still very much eclectic. The point of view developed in these pages consistently centers on the ideas common to the interactionist and dramatistic perspectives. Both now represent an important tradition in descriptive studies within the social sciences. But we are also indebted to the substantial body of survey research on political attitudes that enriches our knowledge of the polity. Combined with these two broad academic traditions, we have built our case with a variety of firsthand sources, including private memoranda, memoirs, speeches, and journalistic accounts.

Readers familiar with the first edition will notice several changes in this new edition. Wherever possible, we have attempted to condense our arguments and make the book more accessible to general readers. We have also updated many ideas with newer examples drawn from the last years of the Reagan presidency, the elections of 1988, and relatively recent events in Congress. The greatest changes, however, appear in completely new chapters or sections devoted to the courts and to the processes unique to regional and local politics.

Part I focuses on the variables of political communication. The chapters therein attempt to define political communication; to present a systematic, theoretical description of communication's role in society and politics; to investigate the use of the political consultant industry to include the activities, functions, and services they provide in the modern campaign; to identify communication activities in political campaigns; to explore some of the relevant perspectives, problems, and strategies unique to the communication of administrative control; and to investigate the role of the mass media in politics. Part II focuses on communication within the institutions of the presidency, Congress, and the courts. Finally, we conclude with a discussion of communication, politics, and the public trust.

The book reflects a reality that we did not wish to gloss over in deference to the heuristic device of a "single theme." Because the subject matter is necessarily broad, the work as a whole is more horizontal than vertical. While the first two chapters lay useful groundwork for the latter ones, the reader can successfully read the chapters separately as well as in the sequence in which they are published. We made no special effort to weave an artificial thread of continuity in what is a naturally complex and varied range of subjects.

We also resisted the temptation to give our observations and conclusions an air of finality. The reader may be surprised to see that points are argued as much as they are asserted. Many studies of political activity work from a framework of actual (or grammatically induced) certainty. Such certainty is often unjustified. We think the book speaks to a basic reality about politics that needs to be constantly acknowledged, namely, that political communication is about people making choices of indeterminate quality that will produce indeterminate effects. Of this much we are certain: No subject is more worthy of study than the communication processes that can nurture or starve a nation's civil life.

NOTES

1. Aristotle, *The Politics of Aristotle*, trans. Ernest Barker (New York: Oxford University Press, 1970), p. 5.

2. Ibid., p. 6.

Acknowledgments

We are both pleased and humbled by the response to the first edition of this book. To know that the book was useful to friends, colleagues, and students was reward enough for undertaking the revision. We have benefited from comments, suggestions, and reviews provided over the years. To those of you who were kind enough to share your reactions to the first edition, we sincerely hope you will do the same to this one.

As was the case for the first edition, an incalculable number of communication and political writers have influenced our own thinking. Among those to whom we owe the greatest thanks are Kenneth Burke, James Combs, Hugh Duncan, Murray Edelman, Todd Gitlin, Doris Graber, Roderick Hart, Kathleen Jamieson, Harry McPherson, Richard Sennett, and Judith Trent. We have borrowed and adapted material from all of them—we hope with some degree of success. But, of course, any shortcomings in our work are the fault of the ''other'' coauthor.

Although truly a joint effort, each author received help and support from individuals and institutions that deserve special recognition.

Robert Denton wishes to thank his colleagues in the Department of Communication Studies at Virginia Polytechnic Institute and State University and Herman Doswald, Dean of the College of Arts and Sciences, for their personal encouragement and support in completing the revision. Equally important was the typing support of Norma Montgomery. Without her help, he would have missed another deadline. Finally, without the love and support of Robert's wife, Paula, little else would matter.

Gary Woodward is indebted to the generous support of the Faculty and Research and Sabbatical Committee at Trenton State College for several grants that provided time for writing. He also acknowledges the help of the National Endowment for the Humanities for a Summer Study Fellowship at the University of Wisconsin.

PART I

THE VARIABLES OF POLITICAL COMMUNICATION

Chapter One

Political Communication Defined

Within the life of the generation now in control of affairs, persuasion has become a self-conscious art and a regular organ of popular government. None of us begins to understand the consequences, but it is no daring prophecy to say that the knowledge of how to create consent will alter every political calculation and modify every political premise.[1]

TWO CASES OF POLITICAL COMMUNICATION FAILURE

WIN: A Public Relations Disaster

Gerald Ford assumed the Presidency under well known and extraordinary circumstances. To most observers, the amiable Michigan Republican seemed destined to remain in Congress for the rest of his political life, but events quickly changed his political career in 1973. Spiro Agnew resigned from the Vice-Presidency after pleading ''no contest'' to charges of failing to pay taxes on bribes. Richard Nixon immediately appointed Ford to replace Agnew, but this major development was only the prelude to an even bigger disaster for the Nixon administration. By 1974 the taint of political corruption hung over Washington like a summer heat wave. Evidence accumulated indicating that an illegal cover-up was carried out by the President and his staff to protect burglars who had broken into the Democratic Party headquarters at the plush Watergate apartments. What began as a half-hearted attempt to purloin Democratic Party files had snowballed into a scandal that eventually destroyed a carefully constructed political empire. On August 9th Nixon abdicated the office in disgrace, leaving Ford as an unelected heir to the White House.

Ford's leadership helped heal the political wounds that were inflicted during the Watergate scandal, but the turmoil of Nixon's last tortured months in office left a growing legacy of neglected domestic problems. The most pressing need was for federal action to stem the rate of inflation. Economic planning came to a virtual standstill while the Nixon administration unraveled in continuous preoccupation with its own survival. In 1974 prices and wages were increasing at an annual rate of nearly 17 percent, far too high to produce stable growth. Ford knew he had to do something. Acting in response to vocal expressions of concern from the press and Congress, he decided to engage in a major campaign to awaken the nation to the dangers represented by rising prices. It was important for the White House not to allow others to seize the initiative, particularly on an issue that had been traditionally at the heart of the Republican political agenda. The campaign was to end in failure a few short months later.

Ford initially decided to go on the rhetorical offensive by using several well-publicized speeches. His goal was to urge action to control inflation, and to assert his own authority as the newest (and unelected) president. His first major effort was before a joint session of the Congress. It was a nationally televised speech making the case that "we must whip inflation now."[2] That speech was followed a week later with a second televised address detailing the ways the average American might help reduce inflation. Even an advertising agency, Benton and Bowles from New York, had been enlisted to contribute to the effort.[3] Highly publicized plans called for a voluntary "grass roots" mobilization against inflation. Its symbol was the acronym for "whip inflation now." WIN buttons and banners were produced and readied for mass distribution, and industries were enlisted to help publicize the still unformed program.

The first speech initiating the campaign was an attempt at national mobilization. Urging more private-sector jobs, cuts in wasteful government programs, less federal regulation of business, more productivity, and less dependence on foreign oil, Ford requested a broad range of actions from Congress. The bigger thrust of the program, however, was to be based in the voluntary compliance from the American people. The program's urgency was to be generated not in executive acts, but in a rhetorical campaign that was to be initiated by the President, and then carried to the grass roots by labor and business groups. In his televised address to Congress Ford noted that

There will be no big Federal bureaucracy set up for this crash program. Through the courtesy of such volunteers from the communication and media fields, a very simple enlistment form will appear in many of tomorrow's newspapers along with the symbol of this new mobilization, which I am wearing on my lapel. It bears the single word WIN. I think that tells it all.[4]

With echoes back to the war mobilization efforts of Franklin Roosevelt, Ford promised that his next speech would specify "how volunteer inflation fighters and energy savers can further mobilize their total efforts."[5]

That second address was to come on October 15th, before an audience of 13,000 people attending a convention meeting of the Future Farmers of America. As with the first speech, the White House requested full network television coverage. But the broadcasting giants initially declined, sensing that there was little news value in yet another recital of the familiar problems that come with high inflation. Only insistent pressure from the Ford staff forced the three networks to relent into a second clearance of time.[6] After the Nixon years, network executives were beginning to resent demands to replace the lucrative prime-time schedule with presidential addresses.

This address became known among insiders who worked on it as the "lick your plate clean" speech.[7] It proved to be the beginning of the end for the voluntary inflation campaign. "It may not have been news," journalist Richard Reeves recalls, "but it certainly was entertaining."[8] The message turned out to be a litany of what can only be described as "corny" and painfully simplistic suggestions on how to cut waste on the job and in the household. Whatever entertainment value it had for hardened Washington journalists was unintentional. With a WIN button firmly implanted in his lapel, the President enthusiastically suggested remedies for an economy caught in both a recession and incessant wage and price increases:

From Hillsboro Oregon, the Stevens family writes they are fixing up their bikes to do the family errands. They are also using fewer electrical appliances, turning the thermostat down, and the lights off. Bob Cantrell, a 14 year-old in Pasadena California gave up his stereo to save energy. Bob urges the initiation of high school courses that teach students how to conserve energy. He adds, and I quote: "If a kid nags his parents to conserve energy long enough it will help."[9]

To successful "energy efficient" and "inflation fighting" communities the President promised WIN flags. Local municipalities were urged to set up WIN committees. No recommendation was too small for a presidential endorsement:

One friend told me we could probably whip—just understand this—whip inflation with the contents of our trash cans. In your own home, let me make a simple suggestion. Just take one hour to make a trash inventory.[10]

Obviously, something was missing from these statements. Suggestions for better management of life's little domestic problems are not the kinds of utterances that inspire presidential legends. The nation's political cartoonists had a field day sketching the leader of the Western world as a penny-pinching miser. Ford's concerns, however sincere, were measured against the normally majestic presidential *ethos*. In his best moments Lincoln had reshaped the political landscape of the entire nation, setting up a true federal republic. Theodore Roosevelt had staked out a philosophy for an "American Century" that would affect most of the world's populations. Ford, in contrast, seemed to describe big problems while at the same time offering only small solutions. On this particular initiative his indiscriminate enthusiasm contributed to the doomed effort. However well intentioned his attempt, it was widely perceived as hopelessly inadequate in the face of long-term economic changes. He became the victim of a transparent public relations "hype" that ultimately made him seem weaker for not exercising the full extent of his presidential authority. If Richard Nixon exploited and misused the considerable powers of the Presidency, Ford appeared to underutilize them.

The final blow to the effort came less than three months later, when the whole project was suddenly abandoned. White House advisers recommended different remedies based on updated information about the economy's weaknesses. It turned out that the existence of a serious recession made economic *stimulation* rather than *control* the primary economic objective. The WIN campaign had urged the reverse; it was based on the need to save rather than spend.

Ford later recalled: "I didn't mind abandoning the symbol, which was probably too gimmicky."[11] He was equally candid in recalling the press criticism that followed the two speeches:

The Wall Street Journal called my proposals "neither surprising nor bold." The *New York Times*, in a series of editorials, was even more critical. "The overall impact of Mr. Ford's speech was weak, flaccid and disappointing. While some of his measures are good and some are questionable, they in no sense add up to a program for an emergency."[12]

A deeper problem, however, was recognized by Ford speechwriter Robert Hartmann. By demanding national television time for speeches with too many ideas, and by allowing himself to assert more than he could personally deliver, Ford, "made WIN a conspicuous symbol of his leadership."[13] To many Americans, the whole effort probably looked like the degeneration of presidential politics rather than the exercise of decisive leadership. The much publicized "war" on inflation seemed to be fought with the rhetorical equivalent of a toy pistol.

Biden and the Issue of Intellectual Honesty

When he announced his intentions in June of 1987, Delaware Senator Joseph Biden must have known that it was a considerable risk to begin a run for the Presidency. But even he was surprised by the chain of events that doomed his campaign before any of the major presidential primaries had been held. On the eve of the presidential campaign the 44-year-old Democrat emerged as a figure of national prominence. Friends and colleagues in the Senate gave him high marks as a rousing speaker and a telegenic personality. He offered a nondoctrinaire approach to national issues that could attract members of his own party who had defected to President Ronald Reagan. Moreover, he had just taken center stage in the highly charged atmosphere of hearings over the controversial nomination of Federal Judge Robert Bork to the Supreme Court.

Biden's scenario for thrusting himself into the public eye was centered on the congressional hearings. As Chairman of the important Senate Judiciary Committee, he had the access to the political theater from which to press the conservative Bork on a range of issues addressed by the Supreme Court. His position was strengthened even more by surprisingly sharp opposition from many leading Democrats to Reagan's nominee. The air of a showdown with the administration over its choice was so strong that some television and radio broadcasters decided to cover portions of the Senate Judiciary Hearings live.

Biden's plan almost worked out, but not quite. His political enemies gave him high marks in chairing the hearings, which ultimately handed the President and his nominee an unexpected and embarrassing defeat. But Biden withdrew four months after entering the presidential campaign, the victim of earlier statements that came back to haunt him. In the words of Andrew Rosenthal, his attempt became "a textbook case of a campaign gone sour."[14]

The undoing of the Biden campaign began and ended, characteristically for modern politics, with television. At issue at the outset was the content of two videotapes. One recorded his participation in a debate with other Democratic contenders on a warm August evening at the Iowa State Fair. In that joint appearance he ended his remarks with several emotionally charged rhetorical questions. "Why is it," he asked, "that Joe Biden is the first in his family ever to go to a university? Why is it that my wife, who is sitting out there in the audience, is the first in her family to ever go to college?" By themselves these questions were harmless, even eloquent in their implications of unequal access to the advantages of higher education. Biden's problems began when a member of Michael Dukakis' campaign staff secretly passed on a second videotape to several news organizations. It contained a British television commercial from the previous spring—apparently much admired by a number of Democratic Party hopefuls—in which Labor Party leader Neil Kinnock used almost exactly the same rhetoric. In the political commercial Kinnock asked, "Why am I the first Kinnock in a thousand generations to be able to get to university?" Referring to his wife, he asked, "Why is Glenys the first woman in her family in a thousand generations to be able to get to university."[15] The back-to-back running of these two video clips on the major network news programs was riveting television. Although the source of the damaging tape was not made public at the time, it was obvious that Biden had obviously borrowed his own seemingly emotional and personal conclusion from the British politician. As the press first reported it, the instance was a clear but not very shocking case of plagiarism. After all, the construction of campaign rhetoric has traditionally been—to put it generously—a shared process. Yet this event turned out to be only the first of several reports that raised troubling questions about Biden's apparently elastic set of ethics.

Within days, newspapers and television networks reported additional instances of borrowing and truth stretching. Politicians from both political parties told members of the press about other times when Biden had used the specific verbal formulations of others, including John and Robert Kennedy, and Hubert Humphrey.[16] In some instances whole paragraphs were allegedly used without reference to their original sources. These reports were soon followed by still more evidence that Biden's rhetoric was of questionable authenticity. A tape recorded by C-SPAN, the cable television channel devoted to Congress, showed him in a campaign appearance greatly overstating his college academic record. By itself such a boast might have been overlooked, but it was increasingly portrayed as part of a pattern. It took only days for the law school Biden attended to confirm that he had been disciplined for plagiarism in his first year. The cumulative effect of these separate instances began to take their toll. As veteran political reporter R. W. Apple wrote in the *New York Times*, the "news that Mr. Biden appropriated whole sections of a law review article and of other politicians' speeches, without giving credit, seemed to many to substantiate assessments that he was shallow and insubstantial—'plastic' in the lingo of the campaign."[17]

What first seemed to be politically motivated revelations—timed to embarrass Biden in what might have been his triumph in the important Bork hearings— now looked more troublesome. Without doubt some of the information came from people anxious to shoot down this new political star, but the evidence was hard to overlook. Nothing so deflates a politician as to appear to be inauthentic, partly because it is a confirmation of the most elemental of stereotypes. In addition, the cascade of charges that Biden found difficult to refute successfully raised questions that might have been ignored, had he aspired to a lesser office. Campaign specialist William Schneider probably captured the public mood as well as anybody at the time. "I'm not sure that this adds up to a fundamental flaw in character which would be so devastating as to ruin him" he noted, "but what's clearly revealed here is that his intellectual habits are lazy, undisciplined and sloppy."[18]

Biden's withdrawal from the campaign in late September was tinged with conflicting feelings of defeat and victory. He was widely praised for his handling of the Bork hearings, even among his Republican colleagues who were unsuccessful in saving the President's ill-fated nominee. But he also discovered the high price to be paid for relatively minor rhetorical crimes.

GENERAL CHARACTERISTICS OF POLITICAL COMMUNICATION

Even though their failures are now painfully conspicuous, the WIN and Biden campaigns serve as useful illustrations of several fundamental traits of political communication. In a number of ways they share many of the same elements found in messages delivered from the floors of state assemblies, from the hustings of local and national campaigns, and from the offices of countless political lieutenants. To be sure, the many features of messages that we discuss in this book are not exclusive to the political world, but they are more than casual companions to it.

Short-term Orientation

Among the most common realities governing political life is a general pre-occupation with transitory issues and limited time frames. Messages are typically planned, prepared, and delivered with an eye to immediate outcomes. They must enter the continuous flow of public discussion within a period that is beneficial to the communicator and timely for the mass media and their audiences. Gerald Ford seized the topic of inflation when public concern created a naturally receptive environment. Waiting any longer might have risked the impression that he lacked a decisive will to act, or that he was insensitive to the economic dislocations created by an overheated economy. Joseph Biden was under similar pressure to answer charges about his personal credibility before their impact damaged his prospects for defeating Supreme Court nominee Robert Bork. Most political communication benefits from a "window of opportunity" that can pass as quickly as it appears.

Political communicators seek practical and immediate results. Their effectiveness usually hinges on their adaptation to the transient nature of public opinion and the fleeting attention of the mass media. They are often criticized for "rudderless" and "hypocritical" beliefs. Yet, taken on its own terms, political communication can only be understood when there is a willingness to reconstruct the immediate political context—the relevant climate of opinion—that a public figure felt duty-bound to honor. While it may be the case that novels, inspirational speeches, and other forms of communication may permit measurement against "timeless" standards, serious attempts to shape opinion rarely profit from the comparisons against invariant critical yardsticks. Like Ford's quick reversal on WIN, when mere days required a new approach, there may be little sense that an important rhetorical legacy has been abandoned. Even Abraham Lincoln's venerated speeches from the 1858 Senate campaign will appear to the modern reader as dated: intended for a different age with vastly different values and needs.

Communication Based on Objectives

Political behavior is almost always directed to some specific end, even when it takes on the appearance of predictable ritual. What is overlooked in the common complaint that political talk is a "meaningless" substitute for political action is the important fact that it is often intended to increase the prospects of the talker, the agent for the ideas. Every political campaign tries to fulfill this objective, giving credibility to a campaigner by making him or her the vehicle for reasonable proposals and familiar values. Perceptions of a candidate's intellectual honesty and authenticity typically rank high among these values. As amplified by the press, Biden's campaign seemed to violate the very principles that it was originally organized to communicate. Similarly, if the WIN campaign appeared to some as a rhetorical "patch up" of a serious economic problem, the sheer act of talking about inflation and its remedies probably had its public relations advantages.

Importance of the Mass Media

The mass media are basic to the study of politics. No claim about the conduct of modern political life seems more self-evident. Speeches, press conferences, pleas for support, justifications of controversial decisions all imply the presence of constituencies—audiences for those acts. Most of those audiences are only reached by the extended coverage provided by public media.

Political reporting is dedicated—in philosophy if not always in practice—to a "watchdog" role over those public officials that are clearly within their own sphere of influence. In the familiar terms of this philosophy, the free press performs an "adversary" function that provides a check, a "fourth branch of government," to keep a wary eye on the other three. "The only security of all," Thomas Jefferson said, "is in a free press."[19] This role is an obvious and largely undisputed objective of the political press in America. And yet for all of its familiarity, the norm of a constitutionally protected independent press is perhaps the greatest single contribution the United States had made to the lore of democracy.

The mass media function in an important second way, a way that reverses the familiar "reporter"/"subject" relationship. In forms that are detailed more fully in Chapters 6 and 11, the political press "controls" as well as "reports." Especially in this century, journalists have sometimes been able to *lead* rather than just *follow* the course of an unfolding political story. In ways an Eastern European politician perhaps could not grasp—but were probably all too clear to Senator Biden—U.S. politics requires the ability to respond to an agenda of issues and events largely fabricated in America's newsrooms. The political newsmaker still initiates the raw materials for many stories, but the control and management of political information is now largely in the hands of privately controlled news and entertainment enterprises.

When Theodore Roosevelt denounced the "muckraking press" just after the turn of the century, he was not paying a compliment to the new investigative muscle of the William Randolph Hearsts or Ida Tarbells. He was making what has since become a familiar complaint based on the realization that the public media place their own commercial demands on those engaged in political discourse. Like nearly all politicians of his time and later, he savored the attentions of the press, but not their insatiable thirst for stories that intended to capture the public imagination. The narrative thread of political news almost always carries within it popular images of good and evil and national fantasies of justice and injustice. Gerald Ford's lament over the way the *New York Times* and *Wall Street Journal* described his WIN program is recognition of the fact that even the most highly visible politicians are at best only coequals as shapers of American public opinion.

Politics as Audience-centered

Political actors are motivated by the desire to gain the support of specific constituencies. Such an audience-centered approach properly forces the analyst to think in terms of the processes that govern the search for a consensus, or to its unmaking. The arts of compromise, emphasis, de-emphasis, and simplification are all very much a part of this process. Rather than lamenting the avenues for blatant manipulation that are implicit in such a point of view, we prefer to think of an audience-centered activity as wholly natural and nominally democratic. There can be no doubt that politics offers the potential for pandering to the lowest of human impulses. The price we pay for an ''open'' political system is the risk that there will be excesses. We think the greater danger lies not in the manipulation of audience allegiances to political ideas, but in the society that minimizes opportunities for the articulation of such ideas, or gives only lip service to the rhetorical rights of the politically active. At their best, democratic societies are strengthened by exchanges between those in a position of authority, and by citizens with countervailing rights to revoke it.

Generally, then, we conceive of political communication as a practical, process-centered, decision-oriented activity. Because it is dependent on the approval of specific audiences, its utility is strongly restricted by time, and by the willingness of the political media to make its messages accessible. We have necessarily cast our net quite broadly. It includes speeches and addresses, whether heard firsthand or reported in highly edited segments. It also includes many other forms of *public* discussion: reports, ''public'' letters, defenses of administrative action or inaction, hearings, ''mediated'' accounts of events from the press, and even ostensibly ''nonpolitical'' messages such as films and prime-time television. Ultimately, a crucial factor that makes communication ''political'' is not the source of a message, but its content and purpose.

POLITICAL COMMUNICATION DEFINED

Misguided Expectations about Political Life

There is something inescapably seductive about describing political communication so that it is nearly synonymous with ''obfuscation.'' Analysts are frequently tempted to characterize it in terms of the abuse it gives to some set notion of The Truth. This tendency is based in part on what we think is the mistaken assumption that political address is primarily about discovering ''the right'' solution to a problem, or concealing the ''wrong'' one. If an observer believes that one side in a debate has the ''correct'' answer, the only possible way to explain the other side is in terms of the obfuscation of ideas. George Orwell's widely admired description of political address is a case in point:

In our time, political speech and writing are largely the defense of the indefensible. Things like the continuance of British rule in India, the Russian purges and deportations, the dropping of the atom bombs on Japan, can indeed, be defended, but only by arguments which are too brutal for most people to face, and which do not square with the professed aims of political parties. Thus political language has to consist largely of euphemism, question-begging and sheer cloudy vagueness.[20]

In *Political Language and Rhetoric*, Paul Corcoran provides a similar expression of disillusionment that functions implicitly as a kind of operational definition:

Contemporary political language . . . has assumed a peculiar and in some sense an inverted social function as a technique of linguistic expression. This is borne out in the uses to which political language is often put: not to convey information, but to conceal or distort it; not to draw public attention, but to divert or suppress it. In short, contemporary political language may play precisely the reverse role from that classically conceived for political rhetoric. Instead of a rhetorical "method" to inform, persuade and enlighten, contemporary political language aims at an etiolated monologue which has no content, which placates, and which bears no relationship to the organization, coherency and clarification of information and ideas.[21]

These descriptions are superficially likable; criticizing the rhetoric of U.S. political leaders is something of a national sport. But they actually tell us very little because they render political communication deficient *by definition*. The only task that remains for the analyst of a generic rhetoric of camouflage is to point out its inherent irrationality. Not surprisingly, it is much easier to do that than to explain how it works: how audiences are affected by it, converts are made, and how groups and institutions adjust to its more fluent advocates. The counterpart definition for another subject—architecture, to pick an example— might be to label it as the "design and building of what are largely inadequate and deficient structures by people intent on profiting at the expense of others." Without doubt, architects do build ungainly and inhospitable structures. But the essence of architecture, like the essence of political communication, involves more. The problem, of course, is that negative definitions masquerade judgments as descriptions, indicting general processes by inviting consideration of negative examples to stand in for the whole. If one dislikes a policy, the easiest way to attack it is to dismiss the general category of communication used to defend it.

This debate over the nature of practical persuasion is far from new. Aristotle's seminal discussion of public advocacy in *The Rhetoric* over 2000 years ago was a rejection of the low priority to which Plato had relegated it. Plato craved certainty and exactitude from human institutions. Yet, while science and other "hard" subjects might build on such closed systems, audience-centered politics cannot. Aristotle noted that the arts of rhetoric were like many other skills that can be used for evil or beneficial purposes: "A man can confer the greatest benefits by a right use of these, and inflict the greatest of injuries by using them wrongly."[22]

Even so insightful a political analyst as Walter Lippmann at times succumbed to the temptation to find a scientific basis for a "public philosophy." Lippmann was a shrewd observer of the American political scene, yet he sometimes believed that discourse devoid of self-interest could produce something close to universal agreement on many political questions. He wrote—over-optimistically, we think—that "All issues could be settled by scientific investigation and by free debate if—but only if—all the investigators and the debaters adhered to the public philosophy; if, that is to say, they used the same criteria and rules of reason for arriving at the truth and for distinguishing good and evil."[23]

But even in the limited politics of one small group his conditions probably could not be satisfied. It is unrealistic to base an understanding of political debate on the *hope* that there can be a kind of universal standard from which to measure its validity. On most political questions (i.e., questions involving choices with competing advantages to different constituencies) the "Truth" is not easily located. This is because politics is not primarily about truth telling, but consensus seeking. Political conflict typically concerns itself with decisions implying values or preferences rather than determinations of fact, even though there may indeed be relevant facts that should inform political debate. The bulk of most practical discourse is centered on the mobilization of public opinion: a process that involves rationality and fact-finding, but frequently denies a "superior" point of view.

As long as policy lies at the heart of politics, values will have to be discussed rather than precisely reckoned. Values admit to no one standard for judgment. As Lloyd Bitzer has written,

The fact that human valuation interacts with contingent subject matter helps explain why political rhetoric must ever remain unscientific—that is, why it will refuse to be held to statements of the true-false variety. Values and interests will exert such force that persons contending in the same context and about the same subject will disagree in what they perceive and say, a political speaker will be inconsistent from one situation to another, and the perceived truth of political discourse will vary markedly across contexts.[24]

We endorse what seems to be the enlightened distinction made by Chaim Perelman between arguments of all forms that "demonstrate" and those that "argue." The former tend to be analytic, arbitrary, and a priori: as in the synthetic formulas of physics and mathematics where the same conclusions are generated by a wide diversity of individuals. A true demonstration provides no reasonable basis for dissent. On the other hand "arguments"—the ever-present products of what may be legitimate differences of opinion—exist in the realm of preferences.[25] Political conflict is "legitimate" when it originates in pluralist thought about values and priorities. A position put forward in a dispute is necessarily a combination of the individual's own intellectual and social history, and the history of the group that he or she seeks to influence.

Consider, for example, the ongoing politics involved in the federal government's management of national forests. To what extent should the National Forest Service permit the harvesting of timber on federal lands by private companies? Policy for land use may be set by unelected officials in the Forest Service or its parent agency, the Department of Agriculture. But debate may also flare up on this question in Congress and within the President's own staff. Facts will help various interested parties determine a position on this continually renewed debate, but the answer finally depends on how we rank the service's obligations to conservationists, lumber industries and their employees, and to the aesthetics of "harvesting" woodlands. There are clearly moral, logical and evidentiary bases for arbitrating questions like this. But to start from the premise that political address is a form of obfuscation because it fails to tally with some a priori standard is to force it into alien territory. Such a perspective carries a reassuring certainty, but it fails to provide the tools that are necessary to discover the processes and varied perspectives that mediate political decisions.

The Three Concerns of Political Communication

Democratic politics is concerned with the power to decide. Everyday political acts function to influence decisions or defend them. The public communication that accompanies most forms of political activity serves to alter, justify, or clarify the range of choices that are in dispute in the public arena. The more "open" the society and the more active the political press, the better the chances that rhetorical disputes will be productive vehicles for governance.

In concise terms we define political communication as public discussion about the allocation of *public resources* (revenues), *official authority* (who is given the power to make legal, legislative and executive decisions), and *official sanctions* (what the state rewards or punishes). Such discourse make its way into the life of the nation, state, or community when there is conflict between competing interests about what the "official" positions of various agencies of the state shall be. At best, the language of political communication is a valuable mediating agent that replaces sheer violent conflict, and makes orderly change possible. It serves to prepare the way for eventual compromise and acceptance by making arguments, facts, and opinions a part of the public record on an issue. But it is also the language of the faction, of the "friend" and the "foe."[26] It may sharpen differences beyond the point of repair, or it may dull them. It can be a vehicle to mask what should be highlighted, or it may actually repair what has been deeply divisive. One can express optimism for its ability to transform the society for the better; but one can also despair over its widespread abuse. The rhetoric of politics can be many things: therapeutic, divisive, alienating, inspiring, or informational.

Revenue

The much-vaunted cliché that politics is about the exercise and control of power finds it best examples in discourse involving the power to spend. Protracted negotiations over the allocation of scarce resources are common to every society. Potential alterations in the way public money is spent inevitably produce organized advocacy and opposition. Whether to build local baseball fields or repair decaying roads, whether to permit federal funding of abortions for poor women or the leasing of federal lands to oil speculators, all only hint at the broad range of resource-based debates that reach Americans daily. Not all political issues involve conflict over the use of public funds, but the exceptions are rare. Especially in the legislative arena, real commitments to legislative action are revealed more in amendments specifying how a given piece of legislation will be funded than in general endorsements of the legislation. Every city mayor and agency executive that is guided by these actions knows that the intent of most legislation inevitably exceeds what scarce available revenues will actually permit.

Control

The question of *who* decides is the focus of the political campaign. In all levels of government elected public officials are given the power to act as trustees of "the public interest." They may be municipal judges, school board officials, legislators, governors, or presidents. The heart of American faith in republican democracy resides in the assignment of power based upon the "consent of the governed." Unlike any other political event, the political campaign galvanizes the public by giving ephemeral political ideals a universal reference point in the features of a specific personality. Appealing to the electorate's shared vision of its future, the candidate uses real and invented traits of character to enact one part in an ongoing drama of contested leadership. Arguably, the power of the ballot may be overestimated in this age when so many complex bureaucracies and civil service systems have replaced the citizen-politician. But even though decreasing numbers of employees in the public sector are accountable through the electoral process, the chain of responsibility ends most dramatically with the elected leader. He or she is at least nominally accountable for the massive "professional" government that can never be voted in or out of office.

Sanctions

A final class of political discussion arises from official statements that accompany administrative decisions, court rulings, and the consideration of legislation. Political sanctions are typically initiated as governmental actions—either legislated or enforced—which require the compliance of certain segments within the population. Laws defining criminal conduct are the most obvious forms of sanctions, but they may include a presidential decision to the deploy of new weapons systems in a foreign locale, or an attempt by some members of the Congress to forbid it. They are represented by the decision of a big city mayor to give tax incentives to a commercial developer, or the federal judge's award of precious water rights to a state bordering on a river. Because sanctions are governmental and judicial responses to problems that have usually created social conflict, they often set in motion a cycle of public discussion that pit political officials against a range of opposing factions. With the exception of judges, disputes frequently surface between the sanctioning agents of government and a wide variety of traditional opponents, including journalists, corporate leaders, opposing political leaders, academics, and even television writers. Any of these advocates may play for the attention of the larger public by focusing interest on the wisdom or failures of a public policy. In doing so, they frequently initiate public discussion on the wisdom of a sanction's advocates and detractors as well. Some of this discussion creates high political drama, because deep public divisions about where the state should impose its official and moral weight involve the highest of stakes, including fine-tuned feelings of status and well-being.

THE MANIFEST AND LATENT FUNCTIONS OF POLITICAL DISCOURSE

Modern studies of communication fall generally into two fundamentally different approaches. The older and broader tradition is to examine and judge messages largely in light of their publicly stated purposes. These purposes involve the formal and "official" functions of discourse. Our definition of political communication cited above fits into this general pattern. To use the pivotal terms provided by sociologist Robert Merton,[27] the *manifest* functions of communication are objectives that are intended to achieve clearly understood ends. Individuals publicly express their intentions to exert influence, to promote understanding, to educate, and to reinforce. Studies of national figures written by biographers and political journalists largely operate at this level, though the best are not naive about the subtle latent purposes to which an artful political defense can be put.

The newer tradition owes its origins to the social sciences, and to the strong analytical motive to "discount" public actions in favor of concealed or unconscious motives. This pattern did not originate with Sigmund Freud, but it perhaps received its most forceful perspective in the Freudian notion that human expression is a product of the mediation between an instilled sense of public duty, and ego-defensive needs.[28] We speak out to serve ideas and honorable civic goals. But it is also now an unshakable article of faith that we seek to nurture a public regard for our fragile inner selves.

The social sciences are partly built upon this premise. Human behavior with apparently simple motivations signifies infinitely more complex latent objectives: based in the psyche and its inner logic—a *psycho-logic*—rather than on the idealized rhetorical logic of the public forum. For example, Harold Lasswell's *Power and Personality* starts with the hypothesis that an individual's psychology governs some of his political choices. The "power seeker," he notes, "pursues power as a means of compensation against deprivation. Power is expected to overcome low estimates of the self."[29]

The analyst primed for the discovery of latent functions and content profitably considers instances of political communication both for what they say and what they signify. Political language naturally invites consideration of the private "investments," the personal and group needs, that are served under the benign symbolism of "the public interest." Some of the most penetrating political analyses in recent years have explored relationships between personal motives and public rhetoric, or between groups separated and protected by hierarchical distinctions.[30]

To be sure, an interest in exploring private objectives hidden behind the manifest content of language is no guarantee of insight. Freud's own excessively psychoanalytic study of Woodrow Wilson, written with William Bullitt, has the effect of reducing the former president to a one-dimensional caricature whose every decision was apparently the product of earlier discontents.[31] Even so, the study of public rhetoric has been revolutionized in the last two decades by the search for ideological motives underpinning justifications that present themselves as something quite different. Following the lead of Freud and Karl Marx, Kenneth Burke especially influenced a wide range of political communication scholars to search for doctrinal "investments" in all sorts of public discourse.[32]

Our position, however, cannot be reduced to only one approach. Political communication demands analysis and criticism in terms of its own manifest content. But to go no further denies valuable insights about the complex social and psychological processes that contribute to political discourse. We therefore reject a focus that is exclusively centered on structural and social explanations of political acts. We equally reject a purely message-centered view that overlooks the important roles that social and psychological pressures have on political outcomes. It is both a challenge and a source of frustration that even so simple an act of communication as a campaign speech cannot be reduced to a single invariant system of analysis. We believe that the eclecticism that exists in a well rounded study of political communication has an important role. It should help fill the enormous gaps of knowledge left between the time journalists have finished their immediate assessments, and history has had its final say.

Our perspective thus suggests that a good deal more could be asked about the WIN and Biden campaigns than was perhaps initially apparent. For example, why was Gerald Ford's rhetorical offensive developed around a policy that was still in a great deal of flux? Why was he so indifferent to the risk of subjecting the considerable prestige of the Presidency to so ephemeral an effort? Does the WIN campaign itself offer insights into the way Ford perceived his public role? The ill-fated early months of Joseph Biden's bid for the Presidency similarly begs for understanding of the latent functions and effects triggered by his bor-rowed rhetoric. To what extent must a political leader "own" the feelings his rhetoric seeks to arouse in others? What does the presence of a permanent video record of a politician's statements do to enhance or undermine his leadership? These questions all seek to explore the dimensions of decisions taken by a political leader in a specific setting. Many others could be considered from the point of view of the intended audiences. For instance, does the American public believe that campaign speeches are "written" by the candidate? And how do they view the national press when it "unmasks" carefully constructed public personas? In the case of the WIN campaign, is moderately high inflation an issue that can be made salient for a significant percentage of Americans? If so, which groups within the society are best able to control the news agenda on subjects as complex as economic policy?

All of these questions center on the subject matter of this book, and indicate that our goals in these pages are varied and pragmatic. Like most political observers, we are intrigued by the ever-shifting relationships that exist between political agents and their inherited roles, their strategists, and their publics. But our communication orientation leads us to consider politics as an expressive as well as instrumental activity. The subject matter of this book includes more than traditional areas such as policy and leadership it also involves explorations of public communication as the expression of acceptance and rejection, rewards and punishments, threats and reassurances. In these pages we continue to measure political messages against long-honored traditions that foster vigorous public debate in a democratic society. But we are also interested in the ways political values weave themselves into subtle rituals of daily life that have very little to do with formal political structures.

NOTES

1. Walter Lippmann, *Public Opinion* (New York: Macmillan, 1930), p. 248.

2. Gerald Ford, Address to a Joint Session of the Congress on the Economy, October 8, 1974, in *Public Papers of the Presidents, 1974*, August 9 to December 31, 1974 (Washington, D.C.: U.S. Printing Office, 1975), p. 229.

3. Richard Reeves, *A Ford, Not a Lincoln* (New York: Harcourt Brace Jovanovich, 1975), pp. 159–64.

4. Ford, Address to Congress, October 8, p. 238.

5. Ibid.

6. Ron Nessen, *It Sure Looks Different from the Inside* (Chicago, IL: Playboy Press, 1978), pp. 75–76.

7. Gerald R. Ford, *A Time to Heal* (New York: Harper & Row and Reader's Digest, 1979), p. 195.

8. Reeves, p. 161.

9. Gerald Ford, Remarks to the Annual Convention of the Future Farmers of America, Kansas City, Missouri, October 15, 1974, in *Public Papers of the Presidents, 1974*, August 9 to December 31, 1974 (Washington, D.C.: U.S. Printing Office, 1975), p. 308.

10. Ford, Remarks to Future Farmers, p. 310.

11. Ford, *A Time to Heal*, p. 204.

12. Ford, *A Time to Heal*, p. 195.

13. Robert T. Hartmann, *Palace Politics: An Inside Account of the Ford Years* (New York: McGraw-Hill, 1980), p. 300.

14. Andrew Rosenthal, "From Biden's Case, Lessons on Damage Control," *The New York Times* (September 28, 1987), p. B6.

15. E. J. Dionne Jr., "Biden Was Accused of Plagiarism in Law School," *The New York Times* (September 17, 1987), p. B12.

16. Dionne Jr., p. B12.

17. R. W. Apple, "Biden's Waterloo? Too Soon to Tell," *The New York Times* (September 18, 1987), p. A23.

18. Apple, p. A23.

19. Quoted in Douglass Cater, *The Fourth Branch of Government* (New York: Vintage, 1959), p. 75.

20. George Orwell, "Politics and the English Language," in *The Orwell Reader* (New York: Harcourt, Brace, 1949), p. 363.

21. Paul E. Corcoran, *Political Language and Rhetoric* (Austin, TX: University of Texas, 1979), p. xv.

22. Aristotle, *The Rhetoric*, trans. W. Rhys Roberts (New York: The Modern Library, 1954), p. 23.

23. Walter Lippmann, *The Public Philosophy* (Boston, MA: Little, Brown, 1955), p. 134.

24. Lloyd Bitzer, "Political Rhetoric," in *Handbook of Political Communication*, ed. Dan D. Nimmo and Keith R. Sanders (Beverly Hills, CA: Sage, 1981), p. 233. The same point has also been made by John Bunzel in *Anti-Politics in America* (New York: Vintage, 1970). He notes that the "essence of the political . . . situation is that someone is trying to do something about which there is no agreement. He is trying to use some form of government as a means to advance and protect his interest. In other words, politics arises out of disagreement. For politics to exist there must be disagreement over what to do about the particular problem. Where there is perfect agreement, there is no politics" (p. 7).

25. Chaim Perelman and L. Olbrechts-Tyteca, *The New Rhetoric*, trans. John Wilkinson and Purcell Weaver (Notre Dame, IN: University of Notre Dame Press, 1969), pp. 509–14.

26. Carl Schmitt, *The Concept of the Political*, trans. George Schwab (New Brunswick, NJ: Rutgers University, 1976), p. 37.

27. The terms were used in a similar sense by Freud. Merton, however, gave them a sociological context. See Robert Merton, *Social Theory and Social Structure, 1968 Enlarged Edition* (New York: Free Press, 1968), pp. 73–138.

28. See, for example, Sigmund Freud, *A General Introduction to Psychoanalysis*, trans. by Joan Riviere (Garden City, NY: Garden City Publishing, 1938), pp. 102–50.

29. Harold D. Lasswell, *Power and Personality* (New York: Viking, 1962), p. 39.

30. Many are cited throughout this book, including Murray Edelman, *The Symbolic Uses of Politics* (Urbana, IL: University of Illinois, 1967); Claus Mueller, *The Politics of Communication* (New York: Oxford University, 1973); Hugh Dalziel Duncan, *Communication and Social Order* (New York: Oxford University, 1962); Dan Nimmo and James E. Combs, *Mediated Political Realities* (New York: Longman, 1983); and David L. Patetz and Robert M. Entman, *Media Power Politics* (New York: Free Press, 1981).

31. Sigmund Freud and William C. Bullitt, *Thomas Woodrow Wilson* (Boston, MA: Houghton Mifflin, 1967).

32. Perhaps Burke's most influential book in this area has been *A Rhetoric of Motives*, Part II (New York: Prentice Hall, 1953).

Chapter Two

Politics, Communication, and Society

And however important to us is the tiny sliver of reality each of us has experienced firsthand, the whole overall "picture" is but a construct of our symbol systems.[1]

What is government—a set of laws, people, institutions, or specific functions? Is government the White House, Capitol Hill, the Supreme Court, or local town halls? Is politics a social activity, a method of power, a process of government, or a hobby of the idle rich? These questions illuminate the abstract and pervasive nature of the concepts of government and politics. But most books on government and politics focus on specific institutions and functions. Yet government and politics are more than any building, statute, individual, or campaign. Rather, they involve many elements of a process that influences the beliefs, attitudes, values, and behaviors of people. And they encompass more than the end products or outputs of a system.

"Politics," according to Dan Nimmo, "extends to any activity that regulates human conduct sufficiently to ensure that other, non-political activities continue."[2] For him, the purpose of political talk is to "preserve other talk" and thus "the words of politics consist of far more than those listed in any dictionary."[3] Likewise, the functions of any government, democratic or otherwise, encompass more than regulating behavior through the formulation of laws. Other functions include: political socialization and recruitment, interest articulation, the aggregation of interests, political communication, role making, rule application, and rule adjudication.[4] These functions are of a quality nature and demonstrate that specific laws are of lesser importance than trust and confidence in the viability of a system of government.

SOCIETY AS SYMBOLIC INTERACTION

The Concept of Interaction

At the heart of our perspective of government and politics is the notion of interaction. Interaction is not so much a concept as an orientation for viewing human behavior and, ultimately, society. Through interaction, people are continually undergoing change and, consequently, so is society. Interaction is a process involving acting, perceiving, interpreting, and acting again. This interaction among people gives rise to reality which is largely symbolic. Thus, it is through symbolic interaction with others that meaning is given to the world and creates the reality toward which persons act.

Interaction, as a concept, is not limited to spoken and written language. Objects may exist in physical form but they are identified, isolated, catalogued, interpreted, and given meaning through social interaction. For today's yuppies, a BMW is more than a car, a Rolex is more than a watch, Perrier is more than mere water. Thus, artifacts and objects should be viewed as social objects. For the peasant, a rake is a gardening tool as well as a weapon for revolution. Such a transformation results from social interaction. Objects take on meaning for individuals as they interact with others.

Interaction, as a concept, is also not limited to the notion of self-development. It is the very fabric of society. Societies, therefore, should be viewed as consisting of people in interaction. When people interact, they influence the behavior of each other. Behavior, then, is created by interaction rather than simply a result of interaction.

Individuals, of course, interact within larger networks of other individuals and groups. Although many of society's networks are far removed from individuals, the impact of such networks may be considerable. Social networks, formal or informal, social or political, provide a framework within which social action takes place. The networks, therefore, are not determinants of action. Even structural aspects of society, such as social roles or class, should be viewed as setting conditions for behavior and interaction rather than as causing specific behavior or interaction.

Interaction, then, is at the core of human existence. It gives meaning to the self, to symbols and languages, to social networks and societies, to worldviews, and to social objects.

Symbols

It is impossible to talk of human interaction without addressing the symbolic nature of humans. Distinctively human behavior and interaction are carried on through the medium of symbols and their attached meanings. What distinguishes humans from lower animals is their ability to function in a symbolic environment. Humans alone can create, manipulate, and use symbols to control their own behavior as well as the behavior of others. All animals communicate. However, humans are uniquely symbolic.

"An object," according to Herbert Blumer, "is anything than can be indicated, anything that is pointed to or referred to."[5] There are three general categories of objects: physical, social, and abstract. Physical objects refer to concrete objects such as tables, chairs, desks, trees, houses, and so on. Social objects are generally people or positions. This category includes students, teachers, parents, mayors, presidents, and so on. Abstract objects are moral principles. ideas, or philosophical doctrines such as love, justice, freedom, or democracy. Each of these categories has a symbolic dimension or may become a symbol. What an object is depends upon the meaning it has for an individual. The meaning will dictate how the individual sees the object, acts toward the object, and talks about the object. For example, the Democratic or Republican parties will be referred to differently depending upon whether a person favors one or the other, and their degree of involvement with a political party. Common objects result from a process of mutual indications or being seen in the same manner by a given set of people. For Blumer, "human group life is a process in which objects are being created, affirmed, transformed, and cast aside. The life and action of people necessarily change in line with the changes taking place in their world of objects."[6]

George Herbert Mead defined symbols in terms of meaning. A system of symbols "is the means whereby individuals can indicate to one another what their responses to objects will be and hence what the meaning of objects are."[7] The human, as a cognitive creature, functions in a context of shared meanings that are communicated through language (which is itself a group of shared meanings or symbols). Symbols, therefore, are more than a part of a language system. Joel Charon defines a symbol as "any object, mode of conduct, or word toward which we act as if it were something else. Whatever the symbol stands for constitutes its meanings."[8] This definition has important implications for individual action as well as for the nature of society.

We posit that nearly all human action is symbolic. Human action in all its forms, represents something more than what is immediately perceived. Symbols form the very basis of our overt behavior. Human action is the by-product of the stimulus of symbols. Before a response to any situation can be formulated, the situation must be defined and interpreted to ensure an appropriate response to the situation. Meanings for symbols derive from interaction in rather specific social contexts. New interaction experiences may result in new symbols or new meanings for old symbols which may, consequently, change one's understanding or perception of the world. Our view of the world alters and changes as our symbol system is modified through interaction. This process suggests that our reality is made up of symbolic systems.

Social Reality

Simply stated, reality is a social product arising from interaction or communication. Reality for everyone, therefore, is limited, specific, and circumscribed.

Of course, communication can be used to extend or limit "realities." To discover our own reality or that of someone else, we must first understand the symbol system and then the meanings the symbols have for all concerned. Mutual understanding and subsequent action is accomplished through communication or interaction.

The construction of reality is an active process. It involves recognition, definition, interpretation, action, and validation through interaction. Communication becomes the vehicle for the creation of society, culture, rules, regulations, behavior, and so on. From such a chain of actions grows a complex and constantly changing matrix of individual and societal expectations.

The capacity to learn culture (or the process of socialization) enables people to understand one another and at the same time creates behavioral expectations. Consequently, we are in a continual state of orienting our behavior to that of others.

Society

Historically, there have been two dominant approaches to study of society. These approaches, however, are too deterministic for our purposes. The sociological approach emphasizes structure. Behavior results from factors such as status position, cultural prescriptions, norms, values, social sanctions, role demands, and general system requirements. These factors are viewed as causation for behavior while ignoring social interaction which influences the factors. Similarly, the psychological approach emphasizes such factors as motives, attitudes, hidden complexes, and general psychological processes. These factors also attempt to account for behavior while ignoring the effects of social interaction. Thus, rather than focusing on causation factors, the psychological approach focuses on the behavior such factors produce.

As we have already noted, social interaction is of vital importance. Social interaction, as viewed by Blumer, "is a process that forms human conduct instead of being merely a means or a setting for the expression or release of human conduct."[9] Therefore, we emphasize the dynamic, changing nature of society. Individuals are constantly interacting, developing, and shaping society. People exist in action and consequently must be viewed in terms of action. Society may be viewed as individuals in interaction, individuals acting in relation to each other, individuals engaging in cooperative action, and people communicating with self and others.

This interactivist orientation rejects the notion that human society is simply an expression of preestablished rules of joint action. New situations are constantly arising requiring modification or reinforcement of existing rules of society. Even "old" joint action arises out of a background of previous actions of the participants. Participants of any action bring unique "worlds of objects," "sets of meanings," and "schemes of interpretation." In this way all joint action is "new" resulting from interaction although, indeed, from a familiar pattern of action.

Mead identified two levels of social interaction in human society.[10] The most simple he called "the conversation of gestures." This form is nonsymbolic interaction which occurs when one responds directly to the action of another without any interpretation of the action. The use of significant symbols, however, involves the interpretation of an action. Nonsymbolic interaction involves simple reflex responses whereas symbolic interaction demands recognition and interpretation. Blumer illustrates how subtle these may be by discussing the responses of a boxer.[11] When a boxer automatically raises his arms to counter a blow from an opponent, the boxer is engaged in nonsymbolic interaction. If, however, the boxer identifies and interprets the blow from his opponent as a feint to trap him, symbolic interaction has occurred.

This distinction has several implications for viewing the nature of society. Society is people acting toward one another and the interaction is largely on the symbolic level. Group life involves defining what others do, interpreting such definitions, and, consequently, fitting one's activities to those of others.

As already noted, self-control is inseparable from social control. The notion of free well is restricted and limited by the culture of an individual. The interrelationship between social control and self-control is the result of commitment to various groups that produce a self-fulfillment, self-expression, and self-identity. Lindsmith, Strauss, and Denzin argue that there are three forms of group commitment.[12] Instrumental commitment emphasizes material benefits. One's occupational membership is an example. An emotional commitment emphasizes the personal attachment among group members. Such a commitment is best illustrated as that between a husband and a wife. Finally, a moral commitment results from identification of self to the values or principles of a specific group. Social control is not, therefore, a matter of formal government agencies, laws, rules, and regulations. Rather, it is a direct result of citizens identifying and internalizing the values of a group so that the values become essential to their own self-esteem and thus act so as to support the social order. Adherence to the rules of society becomes a fair price to pay for membership in the society.

Dan Faules and Dennis Alexander define regulation as "symbolic processes that induce change or maintain stability in self and others."[13] Of course language provides the major framework dictating ways of thinking and seeing society. Language is certainly more than the vehicle of thought. Rather, language is the thought. There are, however, many types or forms of symbols. Symbols may regulate behavior by: creating expectations, producing negative bias, or by subordinating other considerations by allowing a norm or value to supersede other symbols.[14] In addition to creating expectations of behavior, symbols create social sanctions (i.e., war as God's will) or function as master symbols (i.e., to die for freedom).

Social organization is merely a frame within which identifiable units develop their actions. Structural features of society set conditions for action but in no way determine action.

CREATION OF POLITICAL REALITY IN SOCIETY

When considering politics, it becomes necessary to link the functions and characteristics of government to the general nature of society. Richard Rose identifies three criteria that gauge the impact of governmental actions upon the fabric of society.[15] The first criterion is the scope of a government activity. How many individuals of the population are affected by the action? The second criterion is the intensity of the impact of the government's action. How much importance is attached to the action by the general public? Third, the frequency of impact of governmental decisions is important. Here, the key question becomes how often or how long are people affected by governmental policy or action? These criteria gauge the magnitude of influence of government over society.

Mass support for any individual, institution, or system of government is not automatic. Societal support is a long, continual, and active process. The greatest task confronting any government is to generate enough support for governmental authority and action to meet the needs of all segments of society. David Easton defines political legitimacy as "the conviction on the part of the [citizens] that is *right* and *proper* for him to accept and obey the authorities and to abide by the requirements of the regime."[16] Legitimacy, according to Easton, is a two-way proposition. It is desirable for citizens because it sustains political order, stability, and consequently minimizes stressful changes and surprises. A sense of legitimacy is advantageous for authorities because it becomes the most significant device for regulating the flow of diffuse support.[17]

Political Settings

A political setting, as defined by Murray Edelman, is "whatever is background and remains over a period of time, limiting perception and responses."[18] For him, "it is more than land, buildings, and physical props. It includes any assumptions about basic causation or motivation that are generally accepted."[19] The setting, then, creates the perspective from which mass audiences will analyze a situation, define their response, and establish the emotional context of the act that enfolds. Political actors must carefully assess the situation, calculate the appropriate action, and identify the proper roles to assume. Settings, therefore, condition political acts.

The Reagan administration was especially concerned with political settings.[20] Every major public presentation was carefully orchestrated. In Korea, Reagan, dressed in combat fatigues and standing in front of tanks, addressed the troops. He addressed soldiers of the Normandy invasion surrounded by American flags overlooking the beach and blue sea. Press conferences were moved to the East Room of the White House before an open doorway that revealed the long, elegant corridor. Who can forget the meeting of Reagan and Gorbachev with the Statue of Liberty in the background?

Implicit in the discussion is the need for governments to create appropriate political settings that legitimize a set of values. The assumption is that control over the behavior of others is primarily achieved by influencing the definition of the situation. In a democracy, the secret is to act in such a way that creates an image of the actor or scene that stimulates others to act voluntarily as desired. As early as 1928, W. I. Thomas wrote, "If men define situations as real, they are real in their consequences."[21] Getting others to share one's reality is the first step toward getting others to act in a prescribed manner. This is best achieved by creating or defining reality for others. In turn, the use of potent symbols, rituals, and myths is useful in creating commonalities in the midst of national diversity. The interrelationship of these is succinctly described by Dan Nimmo:

By inducing people to respond in certain ways, to play specific roles toward government, and to change their thoughts, feelings, and expectations, significant political symbols facilitate the formation of public opinion. As significant symbols of political talk, the words, pictures, and acts of political communicators are tipoffs to people that they can expect fellow citizens to respond to symbols in certain anticipated ways.[22]

The entire process, however, yields more than desired behavior. Soon, the process becomes a commitment and total belief in the institutions and system of government.

The principal themes of the Reagan presidency, for example, were heroism, faith, and patriotism. In his first inaugural address in 1981, Reagan claimed that America has a special mission to the world, that individual action is superior to governmental actions, and that governments threaten individual liberty. By 1984, his ads proclaimed that "It's morning again in America" where employment was high and national pride was back. Whereas Carter provided a sense of morality, Reagan provided a strong sense of tradition. His public addresses were national celebrations complete with appropriate national symbols and ceremonial settings. For Carter, the world was one of danger and pessimism. For Reagan, the world was one of hope and opportunity. From this perspective, it is easy to see why the American people preferred Reagan's view of reality to that of Carter.

If settings and situations are created, the next question becomes, how are settings constructed? In properly answering this question, one must consider the role of language, symbols, myths, and rituals. Such considerations are necessary in understanding how the impact of government transcends individual influence to societal influence. Although political symbols, myths, rituals, and talk are all rather commonplace, their implications upon behavior are significant though subtle.

The Role of Language

Socialization depends upon language and is key to the process of creating legitimacy. Language, as the means of passing cultural and political values, provides a group or individual a means of identification with a specific culture, values, or political entity. As people assess their environment, language is created which structures, transforms, or destroys the environment. Words are the molds for concepts and thoughts and become symbols reflecting beliefs and values. Thus, the creation of language, or symbol systems, is required before societies and political cultures can develop. Language serves as the agent of social integration; as the means of cultural socialization; as the vehicle for social interaction; as the channel for the transmission of values; and as the glue that bonds people, ideas, and society together.

Language, therefore, is a very active and creative process which does not reflect an objective reality but creates a reality by organizing meaningful perceptions abstracted from a complex world. Language becomes a mediating force that actively shapes one's interpretation of the environment. "Metaphorically, language and the words embedded in it," according to Claus Mueller, "are posed between the individual and his environment and serve as an invisible filter. The individual attains a certain degree of understanding through the classification made possible by concepts that screen and structure perception."[23]

Political Language

Political consciousness is dependent upon language, for language can determine the way in which people relate to their environment.[24] At the very least, language should be viewed as the medium for the generation and perpetuation of politically significant symbols. Political consciousness, therefore, results from a largely symbolic interpretation of sociopolitical experience. To control, manipulate, or structure the interpretation is a primary goal of politics in general. The language of government is the dissemination of illusion and ambiguity.[25] A successful politician will use rather specific linguistic devices that reinforce popular beliefs, attitudes, and values. Politically manipulated language can promote and reinforce the existing political regime or order.

From this brief discussion, it is clear that what makes language political is not its particular vocabulary or linguistic form, but the substance of the information the language conveys, the setting in which the interaction occurs, and the explicit or implicit functions the language performs. As Doris Graber observes, "When political actors, in and out of government communicate about political matters, for political purposes, they are using political language."[26]

Graber identifies five pragmatic functions of political language: information dissemination, agenda setting, interpretation and linkage, projection for the future and the past, and action stimulation.[27] It is useful here briefly to discuss each of these functions, although they will be discussed in greater detail in other chapters.

There are many ways information is shared with the public in political messages. The most obvious, of course, is the sharing of explicit information about the state of the polity. Such dissemination of information is vital to the public's understanding and support of the political system. This is especially true in democratic nations where the public expects open access to the instruments and decision making of government officials. But the public, being sensitized to uses of language, can obtain information by what is *not stated*, *how* something is stated, or *when* something is stated. Oftentimes, especially in messages between nations, the public must read between the lines of official statements to ascertain proper meanings and significances of statements. Such inferences are useful in gauging security, flexibility, and sincerity. Sometimes the connotations of the words used communicate more truth than the actual statements. Are our relations with the Soviet Union open, guarded, or friendly? There are times, especially in tragedy, that the very act of speaking by an official can communicate support, sympathy, or strength. Thus, the act of speaking rather than the words spoken conveys the meaning of the rhetorical event.

The very topics chosen by politicians channel the public's attention and focuse issues to be discussed. The agenda-setting function of political language primarily occurs in two ways. First, before "something" can become an issue, some prominent politician must articulate a problem and hence bring the issue to public attention. The issue can be rather obvious (poverty), in need of highlighting (status of American education), or created (The Great Society). A major way political language establishes the national agenda is by controlling the information disseminated to the general public. Within this realm there is always a great deal of competition. There are a limited number of issues that can effectively maintain public interest and attention. While certain self-serving topics are favored by a person, party, faction, or group, the same topics may be perceived as meaningless or even harmful to others. While President Nixon wanted to limit discussion and public attention to the Watergate break-ins and tapes, rival groups wanted public debates and revelations to continue. During the Carter administration, rival politicians maintained pressure on the president to resolve the Iranian hostage situation. Carter was unable effectively to address domestic issues during this period. His failure to end the ordeal led to his sound defeat in 1980. In Ronald Reagan's final years in office, the Democratic Congress attempted to discredit his administration by probing into the "Iran-Contra scandal." Investigations and public hearings of the charges of exchanging arms for hostages dominated public attention and restricted Reagan's domestic and foreign policy initiatives for over a year.

The very act of calling the public's attention to a certain issue defines, interprets, and manipulates the public's perception of an issue. Causal explanations are often freely given. Such explanations may be suspect. Control over the definitions of a situation is essential in creating and preserving political realities.

For Ronald Reagan, the rebels in Nicaragua were "freedom fighters" comparable to America's revolutionary war heroes. Some members of Congress, however, called the rebels "common criminals." Participants in election primaries, for example, all proclaim victory regardless of the number of votes received. The top vote-getter becomes the "front runner." The second-place winner becomes "the underdog" candidate in an "up-hill battle." The third-place candidate becomes a "credible" candidate and alternative for those "frustrated" or "dissatisfied" with the "same old party favorites." Political language defines and interprets reality as well as provides a rationale for future collective action.

A great deal of political rhetoric and language deals with predicting the future and reflecting upon the past. Candidates present idealized futures under their leadership and predictions of success if their policies are followed. Some predictions and projections are formalized as party platforms or major addresses at inaugurals or state of the unions. Nearly all such statements involve promises— promises of a brighter future if followed or Armageddon if rejected. Past memories and associations are evoked to stimulate a sense of security, better times, and romantic longings.

No president since Dwight Eisenhower was more successful in projecting a positive future and glorious past than Ronald Reagan.[28] The positive themes of the Reagan presidency, as noted, were heroism, faith, and patriotism. He welcomed heroes, espoused faith in God and country, and surrounded himself with icons of American myth and culture. In the reelection of 1984, his spots proclaimed that "It's morning again in America," showing a wedding, a family moving into a new home, fertile fields, and employed construction workers. His rhetoric provided a sense of momentum, tradition, and historical significance.[29] The characters of his stories were historic and symbolic, reflecting the values of family, freedom, nationalism, faith, to name only a few. Even with real, genuine stories, Reagan made complex operations the story of one person. An important function of political language, therefore, is to link us to past glories and reveal the future in order to reduce uncertainty in a world of ever-increasing complexity and doubt.

Finally, and perhaps most importantly, political language must function to mobilize society and stimulate social action. Language serves as the stimulus, means, or rationale for social action. Words can evoke, persuade, implore, command, label, praise, and condemn. Political language is similar to other uses of language. But is also articulates, shapes, and stimulates public discussion and behavior about the allocation of public resources, authority, and sanctions. Michael Osborn argues that political rhetoric today is dominated by strategic verbal and nonverbal visualizations that linger in the memory of audiences.[30] It functions as presentation, intensification, identification, implementation, and reaffirmation. For him, political rhetoric presents the world, provides emotion, recreates a sense of oneness, sustains action, and reminds us of our history. Osborn's study challenges the notion that political rhetoric is primarily rational. Rather, it "emphasizes instead the symbolic moorings of human consciousness."[31]

Walter Fisher claims that one can identify five motives of political communication: affirmation of cultural images, ideas, and so on; reaffirmation of cultural images, ideas, and so on; purification, a sense of healing and cleansing the polity; subversion by undermining or discrediting political enemies or institutions; and evisceration or nihilism of the political structure or people.[32] From this perspective, Reagan's presidential campaign of 1980 was one of reaffirmation, the restoring of a past America where traditional values reigned and the freedom and independence of the individual were supreme. In 1984, his campaign was one of affirmation, confirming the prevailing cultural myths and desired values. For Fisher, Reagan's appeal derived from "the consistency of his story, . . . the coherence of his character, and the compatibility of his image with that of his constituency."[33]

Before discussing specific aspects of language usage, it is useful to identify Edelman's four distinctive governmental language styles.[34] They include: hortatory, legal, administrative, and bargaining styles. Hortatory language is the style most directed toward the mass public. It is employed by individuals and contains the most overt appeals for candidate and policy support. Consequently, the most sacred of national symbols and values are evoked. Legal language encompasses laws, constitutions, treaties, statutes, contracts, and so on. Legal language compels argument and interpretation. Administrative language is certainly related to legal language. The style usually encourages suspicion and ridicule by the public. Interestingly, administrative language, in its attempts to be clear and concise, is often as confusing to the public as legal language. Bargaining language style "offers a deal, not an appeal" and is acknowledged as the real catalyst of policy formation. Yet, public reaction or response politically is avoided. Once a bargain is created, the rationalization of the bargain often assumes the hortatory language style.

It is important to note that these language styles are content-free and are not limited to certain individuals or government agencies. For example, a president must utilize the linguistic devices in the bargaining style to win congressional approval of favorite legislation; the legal style to draft special legislation; administrative style for enforcing or providing the mechanics for operationalizing the legislation; and the hortatory style for attempting to gain public support for a measure. Each style creates a different reality and subsequent behavior. The realities of crisis, confidence, patriotism, and action may all be created to achieve the final goal. For the basic assumption, as Edelman notes, that the public "responds to currently conspicuous political symbols; not to 'facts,' and not to moral codes embedded in the character of soul, but to the gestures and speeches that make up the drama of the states."[35] The task remains to investigate the types of political symbols and their impact upon societal behavior.

Political Symbols

We have already argued that humans live in a symbolic environment. Our "significant symbols" arise through the process of social interaction. A significant symbol, defined by Mead, is one that leads to the same response in another person that it calls forth in the thinker. Thus, significant symbols are those with a shared, common meaning by group. Consequently, a political vocabulary of significant symbols may evolve which provides common understandings among individuals. They are socially constructed and provide common references for people to engage in more interaction to help solve the problems of the group life.

As a group, there are three ways an individual may respond or relate to a significant symbol. First, there is a content or informational dimension. The content dimension is rather easy to pinpoint and define. Facts can, of course, be manipulated but are rather readily recognizable. There is, second, an affective or emotional dimension to a symbol. Such responses are less predictable and result from years of cultural socialization. Politically, the trick is to use symbols where the affective responses are rather predictable. Finally, there is an evaluative dimension reflecting the importance of the symbol. Each of these dimensions is defined through interaction and hence becomes a rather potent motivator for action.

Hedrick Smith, author of *The Power Game*, notes that Reagan's public power and prestige resulted from his staff's ability to create a "storybook" presidency. "They projected Reagan as the living symbol of nationhood. . . . The more Reagan wrapped himself in the flag, the harder it became for mere mortal politicians to challenge him."[36] Paul Erickson concurs. He argues that we cannot separate Ronald Reagan the individual from Ronald Reagan as a political symbol of the presidency.[37]

There is a large number of significant political symbols in society. They have evolved, according to Dan Nimmo, in five ways.[38] From "authority talk" arise laws, constitution treaties, and so on, which often sanction specific political orientations. "Power talk" usually creates symbols dealing with international politics. Détente, cold war, or perestroika are such significant symbols. In contrast, "influence talk" provides the domestic creation of significant symbols arising from such sources as party platforms, slogans, speeches, or newspaper editorials. Often, "complex issues," when condensed into a single term or phrase, become powerful political symbols. Such symbols include: busing, gun control, abortion, capital punishment, law and order, or civil rights. Finally, significant symbols arise from the "types of objects symbolized" such as democracy or Old Glory. This characterization emphasizes the dynamic, evolving, and emerging nature of political symbols.

Roger Cobb and Charles Elder provide a hierarchical typology of political symbols which is also most useful.[39] They identify four types of stimulus objects as the universe of political symbols. At the top of the hierarchy are symbols of the political community comprising its core values. Old Glory, democracy, equality, liberty, and justice fall within this category. The next type of political symbols is regime symbols or those relating to political norms of the society. These include such concepts as due process, equal opportunity, or free enterprise.

Third in the typology are symbols associated with formal political roles and institutions such as the president, Congress, or FBI. The last type, situational symbols, is comprised of three components. These components include: governmental authorities (Bush, Quayle, O'Connor, etc.), nongovernmental authorities (Ralph Nader, Jerry Falwell, Common Cause, etc.), and the political issues (deficit, gun control, etc.). Those symbols high in the typology are the most abstract and general, whereas those in the lower divisions are more specific in nature. Abstract political symbols are more encompassing, applicable, salient, and less temporally specific. All politicians use abstract symbols, especially during campaigns. Although the typology is clear, the response to the symbols may not be as clear-cut. On the informational level, the same information may be gleaned from the more specific symbols but certainly debatable for those higher in the typology. The affective nature of all the symbol types depends upon the rather unique experiences, culture, and socialization of an individual or group. The same is true for the evaluative dimension. The point is, the classification of a symbol without the appreciation of the social construction and interaction aspects of symbol making is limited in utility.

The next consideration is how symbols are used to structure reality and thus to motivate behavior. For Nimmo, governmental groups and individuals use political symbols to "assure people that problems are solved even if current policies actually achieve relatively little" and to "arouse and mobilize support for action."[40] The use of euphemism, puffery, and metaphor are vital in creating a sense of assurance. During the Ford administration, the word "détente" was avoided because it had become associated with a controversial policy. Carter consistently referred to the Iranian students as "terrorists" in their takeover of the American embassy, and Reagan called the Contra rebels in Nicaragua "freedom fighters." Such uses define the situation and communicate aspects of the informational, affective, and evaluative dimensions of an event. Puffery attempts to exaggerate or to overstate matters of subjective experience. Especially in election years, every issue is of the "gravest importance to the future of our country." Metaphor, as a language device, is useful for explaining the unfamiliar by associating it with something more immediate, clear, or known. A "war on poverty" or a "war on drugs" reveals a degree of seriousness, priority, and intensity. Simply labeling a problem a "crisis" often mobilizes support. Appeals to the "national good" and "self-sacrifice" induce cooperation and support which may restrain free choice. Myth and ritual, which will be viewed later, are potent language forms in arousing public action. Each of these uses of symbols are conveyed through interaction, molded in language, and are more pervasive than any legal power in the Constitution.

How do political symbols work? It is their abstract semantic hollowness that makes symbols so powerful. Although political symbols function as objects of common identification, they simultaneously allow for idiosyncratic meanings to be attacked. Two individuals may disfavor abortion but do so based upon differing—religious or constitutional—arguments. The same individuals may disagree about abortion for rape victims but clearly support congressional or presidential action disavowing the practice of abortion. Political symbols are powerful not because of the broad commonalities of shared meaning but because of the intense sentiments created and attached to them resulting in the perception that the symbols are vital to the system. As elements of the political culture, political symbols serve as stimuli for political action. They serve as a link between mass political behavior and individual behavior.

THE POTENCY OF POLITICAL SYMBOLS

There are three aspects of political language and symbols that endow them with emphasis and power.[41] The content or subject matter of political discourse deals with issues and concerns of the general public. Whether the issue is local in nature or national in scope, the subject matter of political discourse affects large numbers of people. There is no such thing as a neutral political issue. The second consideration is that the communicators involved in political discourse are often perceived as powerful and important individuals. This fact impacts in two ways. First, as highly visible actors, the arguments and messages will gain public attention. Because of their role and status, their credibility may not be questioned and words are accepted as truth. Second, most political officials have easy access to the means of mass communication. In addition, they have access to privileged information. Thus, political actors have resources that aid in evoking and stimulating national debate and issue considerations. Ronald Reagan, for example, was masterful at utilizing the visual dimension of television.

There are aspects, however, unique to symbols that endow them with power whether political or not. Myth, ritual, and ideology are three such symbolic forms. They are especially valuable in arousing public action.

Myth

Myth bridges the old and the new. Myths are composed of images from the past that help us cope and understand the present. Myth functions to reduce the complexity of the world identifying causes that are simple and remedies that are apparent. "In place of a complicated empirical world," Edelman observes, "men hold to relatively few, simple, archetypal myths, of which the conspiratorial enemy and omnicompetent hero-savior are the central ones."[42] Virtually all of our political behavior lies in the realm of myth. For James Barber, myth is the essence of human politics. Barber writes:

The pulse of politics is a mythic pulse. Political life shares in the national mythology, grows in the wider culture, draws its strength from the human passion for discovering, in our short span of life on this peripheral planet, the drama of human significance. Ours is a story-making civilization; we are a race of incorrigible narrators. The hunger to transform experience into meaning through story spurs the political imagination.[43]

Politics, then, relies upon a multitude of images constructed over time comprised of various values, prejudices, facts, and fiction.

Nimmo and Combs provide four views or orientations to social myths.[44] Each view shares insight into the social construction of myths. The "common sense" view of myths perceives them as simple distorted beliefs based more upon emotion than fact. They are dangerous, therefore, because of their falsification of truth. The "timeless truth" view of myths, in contrast, argues that what is important is the fact that people believe the myths. Thus, the issue of accuracy is not important. Myths must be dealt with as true because they are believed to be true by the general public. The "hidden meanings" view of myths is a compromise of the other two. Here, all myths are believed to contain some element of truth of moral principle. Consequently, all myths are grounded in truth. Finally, the "symbolic" view of myths defines myths as "collective representations" of society's beliefs, values, ideologies, cultures and doctrines. "Myths symbolize codes of approved beliefs, values, and behavior and thus function to legitimize authority."[45] Each of these approaches to myths empha-sizes the dynamic and utility aspects of myths. They are constructed through social interpretations of the past and become predictions of the future.

The word *myth* comes from the Greek word *mythos*, meaning "a tale uttered by the mouth," and was generally associated with religious ceremony.[46] Even from the earliest usage of the word, myth had a dramatic quality. Today, how-ever, most people associate myth with illusion and refuse to acknowledge the social utility of myths. We prefer Nimmo and Combs' definition of myth as

a credible, dramatic, socially constructed representation of perceived realities that people accept as permanent, fixed knowledge of reality while forgetting (if they were even aware of it) its tentative, imaginative, created, and perhaps fictional qualities.[47]

This definition satisfies our concerns and acknowledges the dramatic nature of myths.

As one of the most perceptive analysts of American politics, Sidney Blu-menthal argues that elements of American myth and heroic fantasy comprise the essence of the Reagan years.[48] Reagan's mission was simply to make us feel good again. He saved us from the present by evoking the past. Reagan attained the monarchical status denied Nixon and Carter. The result was a presidency that provided a "long national daydream" of righteousness, patriotism, and nostalgic idealism. Wish fulfillment became national policy.

Blumenthal identifies several American archetypes and demonstrates their power to transform presidential campaigns and hence American politics. The Reagan presidency, for example, was just an extension of the Nixon presidency. Unlike Reagan, Nixon always confronted a faceless conspiracy whom we should not trust. George McGovern was the last of the "progressive liberals" who possessed a clear ideology and brought a new generation and class into politics. Reagan used progressive rhetoric against progressive values. He continually evoked the liberals' symbolic heritage in describing America while denying legislative support for such policies. Walter Mondale, in 1984, campaigned as "Prime Minister" and leader of the party. Reagan campaigned as the leader of society. John Glenn was a hero, a superstar who blinded us and scared us. Reagan lacked "star" quality making him ordinary enough to be believable and like us. Jimmy Carter tried to make us act, Reagan tried to make us respond. Gary Hart ran on ideas. George Bush ran on his resumé. Reagan ran on his ideology.

There are several different types of political myths.[49] Master myths are national in scope and encompass the collective consciousness of a society. These are usually utopian in nature. One such prevailing myth in America is the myth of the American dream. We believe that if we work hard, there is no limit to our capacity for success. Such a myth serves to motivate individuals and reinforce societal values. Another prevalent form of political myth in America is myths of "us and them." These myths focus on social structures or collectivities. Specific groups, movements, and governmental institutions encourage myth development in order to generate credibility, to enlist support, and to sustain existence. The myth of American democracy and free enterprise reduces the complexity of our systems of government and economy to rather abstract notions. We all know that our government is a form of democracy and our economy is a variation of free enterprise. Nevertheless, the myths serve to legitimize the governmental institutions. Definitional myths are useful in another way as well. In addition to defining what is preferred, good, and proper, myths can also define what is bad, unjust, and evil. The notions of communism and socialism are fraught with criticism while most of Europe has been more socialist than democratic for many years. In defining, myths sanction and reinforce societal values. In contrast to "us and them" myths, "heroic" myths focus on individuals. Humans need heroes for motivation and emulation. To state that George Washington, our founding father, never told a lie not only adds esteem for the individual but also espouses the virtue of honesty for the citizenry. Finally, an increasing category of political myths are pseudo-myths. They are myths in the making. Most politicians, especially during elections, are attempting to be perceived as "heroic underdogs," the "common man," or the "new maverick." Messages are created and disseminated by the candidate to reinforce desired images. The mass media, which will be investigated in Chapter 6, plays an important role in the development of pseudo-myths.

Within the realm of politics, there are four basic uses of myths.[50] First, and perhaps the most obvious function, myths increase public comprehension and understanding of rather complex notions, theories, or structures. Second, myths function to unite a society and to create common bonds among the populace. Myths can reinforce and articulate common elements within a diversity of social mores. The careful construction of political myths can prescribe proper and legitimate public beliefs, attitudes, values, and behavior. Third, political myths offer unique identities for the citizens. They provide the link between the individual and the polity. Although broad in nature, myths become personalized and the views or morals expressed are internalized. Finally, myths are persuasive. Myths can legitimize, stimulate, and motivate behavior. They can sustain commitments to a specific polity.

Political myths, in summary, are socially conceived, created, permeated, and structured entities and are real. Because they are real, political myths are credible and pragmatic. And because they are socially constructed, political myths are dramatic, involving a story, actors, and morals.

Ritual

Ritual, in many ways, functions in the same way as does myth. Ritual may be defined as "a motor activity that involves its participants symbolically in a common enterprise, calling their attention to their relatedness and joint interests in a compelling way."[51] Ritual is the bridge between the individuality and society. It functions as a leveler providing instant commonality. By allowing one to become a part of a larger entity, ritual promotes conformity in a rather satisfying way. Myths unite people. Rituals also have special significance, for meaning can evoke and reinforce a certain value, belief, attitude, or desired behavior.

Bruce Gronbeck views presidential inaugurals as rituals and "moments of cultural transmission."[52] Inaugurals link past and present in the symbolic acts of remembrance, legitimization, and celebration. Ronald Reagan's first inaugural especially followed this pattern. Although 1981 was not a time for great celebration, Reagan held out hope for future prosperity. He recognized Carter's help in transition of power, a direct appeal to legitimization. He talked of being confirmed by the people and asked for God's help. In terms of remembrance, Reagan went from the difficulties of the recent past to the heroes of the more distant past invoking the names of Washington, Jefferson, Lincoln, and Kennedy.

Ideology

Ideology is a symbolic belief system that functions to turn listeners into believers and believers into actors. Richard Brooks defines ideology as "any set of beliefs about appropriate ways of acting toward the political institution which have been saliently incorporated into the individual's view of himself."[53] From this perspective ideology is more than a set of political norms. Rather, it is linked to an individual's perception of political reality. Ideologies are socially constructed and are in a continual process of definition and interpretation. For the individual, internalizing an ideology requires a continual assessment of political acts based upon norms or values that become a permanent motivation for political action. America, however, is generally characterized as being less ideological than most nations. Our political system focuses on specific issues and personalities rather than political parties and abstract ideologies. Some scholars argue that Reagan's success with the American people had less to do with skills of communication but, rather, his expression of beliefs or political ideology. "Reaganism" came to mean strong defense, less government, patriotism, and family values.[54] In fact, ideology, whether from the right or left, is seldom complicated. Nevertheless, to accept an ideology implies a commitment toward a specific social reality. On a larger scale, the commitment toward an ideology links one to a community of believers who largely share the same interpretation of the world. Thus, such a commonality of viewing reality provides a strong rationale for specific societal behavior or action.

By briefly discussing myth, ritual, and ideology, aspects of the unique nature of political symbols are well illustrated. First, political reality is socially constructed and created through the use of political symbols. There is a participant dimension to political discourse. Second, political symbols are pragmatic in nature. No matter how abstract the idea or concept, the evoking of political symbols affects behavior. Political discourse is persuasive, pervasive, and influences beliefs, attitudes, and values. Finally, political discourse is dramatic. This means that nearly all political discourse seeks to construct a certain reality. Of course, there is usually a great deal of competition in constructing realities. This dramatistic orientation to politics is rather unique and requires further explanation.

A DRAMATISTIC ORIENTATION TO POLITICS

Dramatism, defined and explored by Kenneth Burke, is grounded in the symbolic nature of humans. Burke argues that as a symbol-using animal, one must stress symbolism as a motive in any discussion of social behavior. By 1968, dramatism was promoted to equal status with "symbolic interaction" and "social exchange" as being one of three areas of "interaction" discussed in the *International Encyclopedia of the Social Sciences*.[55] In that article, Burke summarizes dramatism as "a method of analysis and a corresponding critique of terminology designed to show that the most direct route to the study of human relations and human motives is via a methodical inquiry into cycles or clusters of terms and their functions."[56]

He calls his method dramatism "since it invites one to consider the matter of motives in a perspective that, being developed from the analysis of drama, treats language and thought primarily as modes of action."[57]

The heart of dramatism is human action.[58] An "act" is a "terministic center" from which many related influences and considerations derive.[59] Daily actions constitute dramas with created and attached significance. For Burke, drama serves as an analytic model of the social world. As Burke explains,

Though drama is a mode of "symbolic action" so designed that an audience might be induced to "act symbolically" in sympathy with it, insofar as the drama serves this function it may be studied as a "perfect mechanism" composed of parts moving in perfect adjustment to one another like clockwork.[60]

American politics is not a discrete, identifiable phenomenon. Our political process is one of transformation from societal order (the prevailing hierarchy, beliefs, attitudes, and values); division (redefinition of societal attitudes, values, goals, and cessation of identification with the prevailing hierarchy); action (symbolic behavior of articulating grievances, altering perceptions of society, providing courses of action); drama (symbolic acts, events, episodes); conflict (separation, confrontation, violence, tragedy); victimage (identification of the causes of societal evil, conflict, and violence that must be destroyed); transcendence (the purging and removal of social ills while establishing new levels of social identification, cooperation, and unity); redemption (forgiveness of social sins); and order (hierarchy and societal values accepted, sanctioned, and legitimized). Of course, where one phase ends and another begins is often difficult to isolate.

As already noted, leaders and superiors must create and use symbols that unite and transcend individual and collective differences. "The legitimation of authority," argues Hugh Duncan, "is based on persuasion."[61] Leaders, in their struggle for power and attempts to stay in power, must provide integrative symbols for the masses to transcend the ambiguities and conflicts of heroes and villains; of loyalty and disloyalty; of concern and indifference; of confidence and fear; of obedience and disobedience; of hierarchy and anarchy; of peace and violence. On the side of order are notions of faith and reason. Faith is expressed by the acceptance of authority based upon the quality of performance and positive impact upon the quality of life. On the side of disorder are the temptations of the emotions and imagination. Emotions are articulated through dramatic actions, issues, and statements. Imagination creates a new order, governmental system, and social utopia. In simple terms, therefore, when division in society is so great that symbols no longer possess common meanings, people will turn to leaders who will create new symbols. When symbols can no longer transcend differences among people, conflict can only be solved through violence.

Burke states that there are four basic motives arising in human communication: hierarchy, guilt, victimage, and redemption.[62] For him, these motives are revealed in observing human relationships and encompass all human motivation. They also serve nicely to describe the processes of birth, maturation, and ending in political campaigns and movements. Hierarchy, as addressed earlier, stems from human desire of order. Rejection of the established hierarchy, however, produces a sense of guilt. This guilt is relieved through victimage or the sacrifice of a scapegoat that epitomizes the evils of society. In primitive societies, purification came from sacrificing animals to a god. In sophisticated and complex societies of today, however, purification comes from endowing a person, government, idea, or practice with social evils that dictate removal. Removal can range from redefinition to murder. Scapegoats become the sacrificial animal upon whose backs are ritualistically placed all the real or perceived evils.

Redemption follows victimage. Order is restored. Evil is defeated. Sins are forgiven. Mystification returns promoting social cohesion. Symbol users transcend the mysteries of class. The world is redefined. New attitudes and values are tested and legitimized primarily in the symbolic realm.

Sociodramas

Because many aspects of our political process are difficult to isolate, individual episodes or sociodramas can be investigated. Wherever there is action, there is drama. For Duncan, "failure to understand the power of dramatic form in communication means failure in seizing and controlling power over men."[63] It is important to remember that sociodramas are not just symbolic screens or metaphors but they are social reality because they are forms of social interaction and integration.

To analyze a sociodrama one needs to identify some act or action. To focus on dramas of authority one should ask: Under what conditions is the act being presented? What kind of act is it? What roles are the actors assuming? What forms of authority are being communicated? What means of communication are used? What symbols of authority are evoked? How are social functions staged? How are social functions communicated? How are the messages received? What are the responses to authority messages?

The scope of a social drama is prescribed by the investigator. The drama can involve one person or many, a symbolic (rhetorical) event or physical act, one moment or a specific period of time. For example, sociodramas are the acts and scenes that comprise our lives. Individual photographs capture moments and evoke reflection, memories, analysis, and emotions of joy or sadness. Taken together and shown sequentially, the snapshots produce movement, action, and behavior Although drama can be analyzed frame by frame, it is essentially a composite of individual acts.

Politics, in Burkean terms, is a study of drama composed of many acts. They are acts of hierarchy, transformation, transcendence, guilt, victimage, redemption, and salvation. With an act as the pivotal concept, Burke suggests that we investigate scenes that encompass and surround the act, for the scene provides the context for an act. Next, he suggests that we consider the agents involved in an act; the actors who mold, shape, create, and sustain movements. Likewise, consideration of the agency or the channels of communication in an act help reveal the impact of rhetorical activities. And consideration of purpose of an act aids in discovering the ultimate motives or meaning of the act.

Drama is part of the communication process where public issues and views are created, shared, and given life. Ernest Bormann calls this process "group fantasy."[64] A relatively small number of people may attach significance to some term or concept such as the notions of justice, freedom, or the American dream.

These fantasies are shared and passed on to others. Fantasies are contained in messages that channel through the mass media to the general public. When a fantasy theme has "chained through the general public," there emerges a "rhetorical vision." "A rhetorical vision is a symbolic reality created by a number of fantasy types and it provides a coherent view of some public problem or issue."[65] Slogans or labels that address a cluster of meanings, motives, or emotional responses usually indicate the emergence of a rhetorical vision.

There are several useful implications to the notion of fantasy themes. As a result of creating and sharing fantasies, there is a greater sense of community, cohesiveness, and shared culture. "They have some common heroes and villains; they have sympathized and identified with dramatic characters in suspenseful situations; they have come to share the attitudes implied by the theories."[66] There are, then, common beliefs, attitudes, and values upon which to live and act. And communication is the foundation of it all.

THE MANAGEMENT OF IMPRESSIONS

Although this chapter is largely theoretical in attempting to describe the nature and importance of communication in political and social life, we must, nevertheless, address the notion of political manipulation of symbolic reality. Can the creation and manipulation of significant political symbols affect beliefs, attitudes, or values? The apparent answer to this question is yes. To argue that political behavior is a product of individual or collective rationality is, according to Edelman, rather simplistic and misleading.

Adequate explanation must focus on the complex element that intervenes between the environment and the behavior of human beings: creation and change in common meanings through symbolic apprehension in groups of people of interests, pressures, threats, and possibilities.[67]

Thus, the focus becomes one of cognition control and reality.

There is little empirical evidence to support the notion that hard sell media campaigns significantly alter the attitudes of large numbers of people. Much of the research on political socialization and political cognitions, however, has been short-term studies. Cognition dealing with broad, societal concepts develops over long periods of time. The influence of media and official appeals, therefore, may indeed be greater than current research suggests. In addition, most studies do not tend to distinguish between attitudes and cognitions.[68] They focus on clearly persuasive messages while ignoring the subtle effects of educational messages upon attitudes. The assumption often is that cognitions can be isolated and measured separately from attitudes. We, however, disagree and concur with Brecker, McCombs, and McLeod denying any real difference among attitudes, values, and opinions.[69] It is much more useful to understand that cognition and persuasion are complex, interdependent processes of which fantasies, myths, rituals, and symbols are all a part. We argue that people interpret messages in such a way that is compatible with long-term commitments, with the beliefs created by events (or drama), and with the current (that is, believable) reality.

Political impression management takes two basic forms. One form is to control the flow and amount of information. Information is power and the control of information is the first step in propaganda. Certainly, the Vietnam War, spanning from America's initial involvement to the nation's final withdrawal, is a classic case of government controlling information in attempting to create rather specific political impressions (for example, stable regime, protecting democracy, winning, etc.). The second major form of political impression management is the symbolic mobilization of support. Symbolic mobilization of support calls attention to front stage performances where symbols, verbal and nonverbal, are used to strengthen or maintain the position of political actors.[70] This is the most potent form of impression management in America.

Our position is that public views on issues are mobilized rather than fixed. Issues are largely created, identified, and permeated throughout society. Neither issues nor specific positions on issues exist in a vacuum. Even governmental outputs are results of the creation of political followings and mass support.

Public situations consist of many images and perceptions that are created and evolve from interaction among people, government, and political leaders. Political culture is not transmitted like a telegraph message. Culture is taught in human endeavors that are largely created, staged, and performed by people in the community who have been trained and who are, in turn, training others in cultural presentations. Social action and behavior, according to Blumer, is "the establishment through interpretative interaction of common definitions of the situation. Even though much of joint action is in the form of repetitive, patterned responses to common situations, each instance of it has to be recreated, reconstituted, and reenacted."[71] Political contests are really contests of competing definitions of situations. Winners are those who successfully articulate the definition of situation held by the majority or those who successfully create a potent definition of situation held by the majority of voters. Such a view of society and politics is grounded in a dramatistic orientation.

All drama is powerful in the sense that it impacts upon cognitions, perceptions, and hence, behavior. Orin Klapp posits that "the transcending tendency of drama has a creative power to make and break statuses, to give and take prestige, to generate enthusiasm, to involve and mobilize masses in new directions, and to create new identities."[72] Situations provide, then, the boundaries or context for drama. Situations are not or should not be objectively defined but are created. Such creation affects cognitions, impressions, and perceptions of those involved.

POLITICS, COMMUNICATION, SOCIETY, AND SOCIAL ORDER

This chapter has indeed drawn a rather large circle. It began with discussing the inherent symbolic nature of humans and concludes with a perspective or orientation to view politics and society. The nature and role of human communication in the realm of politics was the focus of discussion.

Political symbols are the direct link between individuals and the social order. As elements of a political culture, they function as a stimulus for behavior. The use of appropriate symbols results in getting people to accept certain policies, arouse support for various causes, and obey governmental authority. Political symbols are the means to social ends and not ends in themselves.

There is, however, a long process for creation, definition, acceptance, and subsequent behavior. For implicit in our argument is the notion that successful leadership and control is dependent upon successful manipulation of political symbols. On one level, then, is the competition and manipulation of political symbols for support. On a broader level, however, national symbols are perpetuated in order to preserve the prevailing culture, political beliefs, and values. Roger Cobb and Charles Elder believe that "rather than a value consensus, we suspect that the stability of the American polity has long rested on a rather shallow symbolic consensus. The type of consensus," they argue, "rests upon symbols that are commonly viewed as important and are the objects of relatively homogeneous affective attachments but which lack any commonality of substantive meaning across individuals and groups."[73] Social unrest results in part from poor political communication. For the legitimacy of political order depends upon the articulation of social needs, the satisfaction of social needs, and the transmission of political values that allows for the development of a sense of community among the people. This process, while complex, is primarily one of communication.

NOTES

1. Kenneth Burke, *Language as Symbolic Action* (Berkeley, CA: University of California Press, 1966), p. 5.

2. Dan Nimmo, *Political Communication and Public Opinion in America* (Palo Alto, CA: Goodyear, 1978), p. 66.

3. Ibid., p. 66.

4. Gabriel Almond and J. Coleman, *The Politics of the Developing Areas* (Princeton, NJ: Princeton University Press, 1960), see "Introduction."

5. Herbert Blumer, *Symbolic Interactionism* (Englewood Cliffs, NJ: Prentice-Hall, 1969), p. 10.

6. Ibid., p. 12.

7. George H. Mead, *Mind, Self, and Society* (Chicago, IL: University of Chicago Press, 1972), p. 122.

8. Joel Charon, *Symbolic Interactionism: An Introduction, An Interpretation, An Integration* (Englewood Cliffs, NJ: Prentice-Hall, 1979), p. 40.

9. Blumer, *Symbolic Interactionism*, p. 8.

10. The discussion of these two levels of social interaction occur throughout Mead, *Mind, Self, and Society* but especially see pp. 13–18, 61–68, 253–60.

11. Blumer, *Symbolic Interactionism*, p. 8.

12. Alfred Lindsmith, Anselm Strauss, and Norman Denzin, *Social Psychology* (Hinsdale, IL: Dryden Press, 1975), p. 430.

13. Don Faules and Dennis Alexander, *Communication and Social Behavior* (Boston, MA: Addison-Wesley, 1979), p. 130.

14. Ibid., p. 140.

15. Richard Rose, *People in Politics* (New York: Basic Books, 1970), pp. 196–97.

16. David Easton, *A Systems Analysis of Political Life* (New York: John Wiley and Sons, 1965), p. 279.

17. Ibid., p. 249.

18. Murray Edelman, *The Symbolic Uses of Politics* (Urbana, IL: University of Illinois Press, 1964), pp. 102–3.

19. Ibid., p. 103.

20. See Robert E. Denton, Jr., *The Primetime Presidency of Ronald Reagan* (New York: Praeger, 1988), especially pp. 63–80.

21. As quoted in Peter Hall, "A Symbolic Interactionist Analysis of Politics," *Sociological Inquiry* 42: 51.

22. Nimmo, *Political Communication*, p. 69.

23. Claus Mueller, *The Politics of Communication* (New York: Oxford University Press, 1973), p. 16.

24. The strongest statement of this notion is provided by Benjamin Lee Whorf. For him, "If a man thinks in one language, he thinks one way; in another language, another way." The structure of language "is itself the shaper of ideas, the program and guide for the individual's mental activity, for his analysis of impressions, for his synthesis of his mental stock in trade." See John Carroll, ed. *Language, Thought, and Reality: Selected Writings of Benjamin Whorf* (New York: John Wiley and Sons, 1956).

25. Murray Edelman, *Politics as Symbolic Action* (Chicago, IL: Markham Publishing, 1971), p. 83.

26. Doris Graber, "Political Languages," in *Handbook of Political Communication*, ed. Dan Nimmo and Keith Sanders (Beverly Hills, CA: Sage Publications, 1981), p. 196.

27. Ibid., pp. 195–224.

28. See Denton, *The Primetime Presidency of Ronald Reagan*, especially pp. 63–80.

29. Roderick Hart, *Verbal Style and the Presidency* (Orlando, FL: Academic Press, 1984), p. 65.

30. Michael Osborn, "Rhetorical Depiction," in *Form, Genre, and the Study of Political Discourse*, ed. Herbert Simons and Aron Aghazarion (Columbia, SC: University of South Carolina Press, 1986), p. 80.

31. Ibid., p. 97.

32. Walter Fisher, *Human Communication as Narration* (Columbia, SC: University of South Carolina Press, 1987), pp. 144–145.

33. Ibid., p. 156.

34. Edelman, *The Symbolic Uses of Politics*, pp. 133–46.

35. Ibid., p. 172.

36. Hedrick Smith, *The Power Game* (New York: Random House, 1988), p. 419.

37. See Paul Erickson, *Reagan Speaks* (New York: New York University Press, 1985).

38. Nimmo, *Political Communication*, pp. 67–68.

39. Roger Cobb and Charles Elder, "Individual Orientations in the Study of Political Symbolism," *Social Science Quarterly* 53 (June 1972): 82–86.

40. Nimmo, *Political Communication*, pp. 83–86.

41. Graber, "Political Languages," pp. 196–97.

42. Edelman, *Politics as Symbolic Action*, p. 83.

43. James David Barber, *The Pulse of Politics* (New York: Norton, 1980), p. 20.

44. Dan Nimmo and James Combs, *Subliminal Politics* (Englewood Cliffs, NJ: Spectrum Books, 1980), pp. 9–13.

45. Ibid., p. 13.

46. Lee McDonald, "Myth, Politics, and Political Science," *Western Political Quarterly* 22 (1969), p. 141.

47. Nimmo and Combs, *Subliminal Politics*, p. 16.

48. See Sidney Blumenthal, *Our Long National Daydream: A Political Pageant of the Reagan Era* (New York: Harper & Row, 1988).

49. Nimmo and Combs, *Subliminal Politics*, pp. 26–27.

50. Mainly based upon ibid., pp. 20–23.

51. Edelman, *The Symbolic Uses of Politics*, p. 16.

52. Bruce Gronbeck, "Ronald Reagan's Enactment of the Presidency in His 1981 Inaugural Address" in *Form, Genre and the Study of Political Discourse*, ed. Herbert Simons and Aron Aghazarion (Columbia, SC: University of South Carolina Press, 1986), pp. 226–45.

53. Richard Brooks, "The Self and Political Role: A Symbolic Interactionist Approach to Political Ideology," *The Sociological Quarterly* 10 (Winter 1969): 23.

54. For example, see Blumenthal, *Our Long National Daydream;* Richard Reeves, *The Reagan Detour* (New York: Simon and Schuster, 1985); Gary Wills, *Reagan's America* (New York: Doubleday, 1987).

55. Kenneth Burke, "Interaction-Dramatism" in the *International Encyclopedia of the Social Sciences* (New York: 1967), pp. 445–52 (hereafter cited as IESS).

56. Ibid., p. 445.

57. Kenneth Burke, *A Grammar of Motives* (Berkeley: University of California Press, 1969), p. xxii.

58. Michael Overington, "Kenneth Burke and the Method of Dramatism," *Theory and Society* 4 (Spring 1977): 129–56.

59. Kenneth Burke, "Dramatism" in *Communication Concepts and Perspectives*, ed. Lee Thayer (Rochelle Park, NJ: Hayden, 1967), p. 332.

60. Burke, *IESS*, p. 449.

61. Hugh Duncan, *Symbols in Society* (New York: Oxford University Press, 1968), p. 200.

62. Kenneth Burke, *Permanence and Change* (New York: Bobbs-Merrill, 1965), p. 274.

63. Duncan, *Symbols in Society*, p. 25.

64. For a good and simple explanation of the fantasy process see Ernest Bormann and Nancy Bormann, *Speech Communication: A Comprehensive Approach* (New York: Harper & Row, 1977), p. 306–17.

65. Ibid., p. 311.

66. Ibid., p. 308.

67. Edelman, *Politics as Symbolic Action*, p. 2.

68. See W. J. McGuire, "The Nature of Attitudes and Attitude Change" in the *Handbook of Social Psychology*, vol. 3, ed. Lindzey and Aronson (Reading, MA: Addison-Wesley, 1969).

69. Lee Becker, Maxwell McCombs, and Jack McLeod, "The Development of Po-

litical Cognitions'' in *Political Communication: Issues and Strategies for Research*, ed. Steven Chaffee (Beverly Hills, CA: Sage Publications, 1975), p. 26.

70. Peter Hall, ''A Symbolic Interactionist Analysis of Politics,'' *Sociological Inquiry*, 42 (1972): 58.

71. Ibid., p. 41.

72. Orin Klapp, *Symbolic Leaders* (Chicago, IL: Aldine, 1964), p. 257.

73. Cobb and Elder, ''Individual Orientations,'' p. 6.

Chapter Three

The Professionalization of Political Communication

Whoever causes another to become powerful is ruined because he creates such power either with skill or with force; both these factors are viewed with suspicion by the one who has become powerful.[1]

Without doubt, the king makers of contemporary politics are the new breed of political and media consultants. A decade ago, Larry Sabato asserted that "there is no more significant change in the conduct of campaigns than the consultant's recent rise to prominence, if not preeminence, during the election season."[2] David Chagall predicted at the same time that consultants "are the Merlins of the electronic age, the Vince Lombardis of modern electioneering. And, like it or not, they are here to stay."[3] Today they are the new power in U.S. politics. In the days before consultants, the old party bosses served as the link between electoral politics and campaigns. Their job was to generate support, control conflict, and reinforce party discipline. Today, political consultants have access to the candidate and develop local campaign strategies and tactics from offices miles away. The focus of their attention is primarily on uncommitted and independent voters. "Whereas traditional campaigns concentrated on mobilizing the faithful," according to Sidney Blumenthal, "modern campaigns ignore them."[4]

In this chapter we investigate the use of the political consultant industry to include the activities, functions, and services it provides in the modern campaign.

THE PROFESSIONAL POLITICIAN

When the general public speaks of a politician they are usually referring to an elected official or a candidate running for an elected office. Others may also include visible party leaders who serve over a period of time in various administrations. Few, however, consider the new campaigners as professional politicians. The new campaigners include consultants, pollsters, television producers and directors, fund-raisers, speechwriters, and direct marketers—all professionals who shape the true character of modern political campaigning in America.

Sabato defines a political consultant as "a campaign professional who is engaged primarily in the provision of advice and services (such as polling, media creation and production, and direct mail fund raising) to candidates, their campaigns, and other political committees."[5] He identifies two kinds of consultants: a generalist advises candidates on all phases of a campaign as well as serves as coordinator of special technical services provided to the candidate; a specialist concentrates only on a specific activity of the campaign. Because of the sophistication and technological advancement of mass communication and persuasion techniques, the trend is toward segmenting campaign activities into areas of specialization. The professional politician today, then, is more likely to be a specialist focusing on one activity of a campaign endeavor.

The number of firms and individuals who earn a living working on campaigns is increasing. Most firms, however, are rather small, often employing five to seven people. During a campaign the more specialized tasks of polling, advertising, fund-raising, are subcontracted to firms specializing in such activities. Most political consulting firms are owned and operated by a well-known successful professional. Being associated with winning campaigns is vital to the professional political consultant. Matt Reese, a well-known consultant, states that the "trinity of necessity" for a political consultant consists of winning (or the reputation of winning), working for people whose names are well known, and winning when you're not supposed to.[6]

Political consulting can be a profitable venture. Most successful consultants or firms require an upfront flat fee to secure their services. Of course, all incurred costs and expenses are paid for by the candidate. In addition, most consultants and firms charge a commission of 15 percent on top of all fixed costs. Sabato reports that about 20 percent of a candidate's campaign budget goes directly to consulting fees, expenses, and commissions.[7] This equates to several million dollars for presidential elections and hundreds of thousands of dollars for various state electoral contests.

At the beginning of the political consulting industry there was a general lack of commitment to any political party or cause. Peter Hart, Walter Mondale's pollster for the presidential campaign of 1984, conducted surveys for the 1976 Republican senatorial nominee John Heinz. Independent presidential candidate John Anderson, in 1980, received help from David Garth, a noted liberal, and from the liberal Democratic firm of Craver, Mathews, Smith, and Company.[8]

Today, however, many of the firms specialize in working with one political party or the other. Vincent Breglio, founder of Decision Making Information, Inc., was active in all three of Ronald Reagan's presidential campaigns and wrote much of the winning strategy for the 1980 contest. Breglio is also a former executive director of the National Republican Senatorial Committee. Jay Bryant, a partner in Research/Strategy/Management, Inc., a Republican campaign consulting firm, has served as the media consultant to more than 20 Senators and Congressmen. Both Breglio and Bryant worked on the Alexander Haig presidential nomination campaign of 1988. Thus, most political consulting firms work for candidates of a particular party handling multiple races. The staff of the firms are "seasoned" political pros with long-term party connections.

Beyond "big name" consultants are literally thousands of "political junkies" who work on numerous campaigns and staffs of elected officials. Within a political season, such people may change jobs and titles many times. Senator Paul Simon of Illinois, in his Democratic presidential nomination bid for 1988, hired Terry Michael who was serving as information director for the Democratic National Committee and was then to become communications director for his campaign. Michael had previously served as Simon's press secretary from 1974 to 1979 when Simon was in the U.S. House of Representatives. After Simon's brief campaign, Michael returned to work on the senator's staff—until after the election, when he changed jobs again.

Today's professional politicians are politicians only insofar as they earn their living working for political candidates and campaigns. They are professionals in the sense that they possess unique skills and knowledge relevant to human motivation and mass communication technology. They are experts and specialists first, and political in the traditional use of the word second. One cannot properly consider the functions and impact of contemporary political consultants without first considering the growth of mass media in America and the changing nature of political campaigns.

THE BIRTH OF THE POLITICAL CONSULTING INDUSTRY

The forefathers of our government laid the groundwork for what they believed to be a dignified, rational electoral process. But the first real presidential contest between Jefferson and Adams resulted in a campaign marked by name-calling and heated debate. In newspapers and pamphlets, Jefferson was called an atheist and enemy of the Constitution. Adams was described as a monarchist and aristocrat.[9] "From the country's first contested election," notes Kathleen Jamieson, "strategists have offered voters advertising that venerated their candidate and vilified his opponents."[10]

Dan Nimmo effectively asserts that today's political consulting industry is a direct descendant of the public relations profession that matured during the 1920s.[11] Their task was to "propagandize" the activities of U.S. business. It is not surprising that the skills and techniques of advocacy became the mainstay of U.S. politics.

Edward Bernays, cited in *Time* magazine as "U.S. Publicist Number One," is considered the father of public relations, In the 1920s, Bernays introduced the "engineering of consent," scientific approach to public opinion formation and dynamics. President Calvin Coolidge was the first president to benefit from his skills. The press of the day portrayed Coolidge as "cold and aloof." To counter this image, Bernays invited Al Jolson and 40 other vaudevillians to a White House breakfast. The next day the *New York Times* headline read "Actors Eat Cakes with the Coolidges . . . President Nearly Laughs." This was, according to Blumenthal, the "first overt act initiated by a media advisor for a President."[12] A decade later, Bernays called for the creation of a cabinet position titled secretary of public relations.

The first political consulting firm was created by Clem Whitaker (a newsman and press agent) and Leone Baxter (a public relations specialist) in 1933.[13] In that year the California legislature passed a bill authorizing a flood control and irrigation project. Pacific Gas and Electric Company viewed the project as a direct threat to the company and thus initiated a campaign to reverse the decision. In turn, proponents of the project hired Whitaker and Baxter to develop a campaign that would defeat the electric company's effort. With a budget of $39,000 the team was victorious in stopping the opposition. Soon after the effort, Whitaker and Baxter formed Campaigns, Inc. Between 1933 and 1955 they won 70 out of 75 campaigns they managed. Their last campaign was the congressional race of Shirley Temple Black in 1967. They developed many of the techniques and strategies that are used in political campaigns today.

Whitaker believed that most Americans do not seek information during a campaign and have no desire to work at being good citizens. Thus, he argued that "there are two ways you can interest [citizens] in a campaign, and only two that we have ever found successful. Most every American loves a contest. He likes a good, hot battle, with no punches pulled. So you can interest him if you put on a fight! Then, too, most every American likes to be entertained. He likes fireworks and parades. So if you can't fight, put on a show."[14]

By 1950, advertising agencies handled national election campaigns. But by 1970, advertising agencies realized that handling campaigns was not as profitable as other products. A political campaign ends in a few months whereas selling soap, cars, or clothes goes on for years. And selling soap is less stressful. The last advertising agency campaign was Nixon's 1968 presidential race, well documented in Joe McGinniss' *The Selling of the Presidency*. He writes of the role advertising played in creating and recreating a "new Nixon."[15]

Public relations specialists were a permanent part of every campaign effort by 1960. Between 1952 and 1957, about 60 percent of all public relations firms had some kind of political account.[16] Part of John Kennedy's campaign staff included a research group, speech-writing group, and publicity group all comprised of public relations personnel.[17] At first, however, Republicans used public relations specialists in campaigns more than Democrats because of their natural ties to business firms, publicity firms, and available money.

Today, campaigns are run by professional consultants who coordinate the activities of media, advertising, public relations, and publicity. They understand both the new technologies and the unique requirements of campaigning. It is that blend of expertise and experience that makes them a sought-after commodity, even after the campaign is over.

THE CASE FOR THE USE OF POLITICAL CONSULTANTS

There are several reasons why political officeholders and candidates need the services of campaign specialists. The modern campaign requires the performance of many specialized tasks to include advertising, issue research, strategy development, polling, and fund-raising. Each of these tasks is complex, requiring training, experience, and knowledge of the industry. It is unrealistic to expect a candidate for public office to have the technical expertise in each of these areas or even to have the time to manage these activities in addition to campaigning or governing.

Another reason for campaign specialists is the impact of behavioral and social science concepts and theories of human motivation. The scientific approach to opinion formation and dynamics has become an essential element of every campaign. Predicting public attitudes and behavior is key to the development of campaign strategy. The measurement, tracking, and analysis of demographic and psychographic data forms the bases for issue positions and public appeals. Social science has provided the necessary tools and methodologies monitoring public beliefs, attitudes, and values.

The electoral process itself places unique requirements upon candidates and campaigns. Historically, Americans value the notion of candidates meeting the public and discussing issues. But as our society has become larger, more diverse, and complex, the requirements of campaigning have become more complex. For most campaigns, extensive direct voter contact is impossible. At the national level, each primary becomes an individualized contest requiring professional help and analysis. American electoral politics is a unique process.

But, of course, the greatest reason for the need of consultants is the role of mass media in our society. Every requirement and characteristic of the mass media impacts upon the nature of political campaigning. To reach the public through the media requires money, news exposure, and 30-second discussions of issues. Actions and statements are carried beyond the immediate audience. Television especially likes drama, a contest, and often favors an underdog. A mistake is recorded forever and subject to instant replay without contextual explanation. The media serve as a source of information, persuasion, and presentation of reality. To use a medium requires knowledge of the medium—its strengths, weaknesses, and nature.[18] The growth and necessity of political consultants and professional politicians are directly related to the growth of the mass media and communication technologies.

Political consultants are also needed today because of what Blumenthal calls "the permanent campaign." The permanent campaign, a direct result of the new technology in the age of information, has become "the steady-state reality of

American politics. In the new politics, issues, roles, and media are not neatly separate categories. They are unified by the strategic imperative . . . the elements of the permanent campaign are tangential to politics: they are the political process itself."[19] The political consultants are permanent, the politicians ephemeral. With the decline of party structure, discipline, and workers, television commercials and media appearances not only serve to mobilize voters but for governing the nation. Governing the nation, then, becomes a perpetual campaign where "the public is constantly roiled and its support continually demanded."[20] Ronald Reagan brought into the White House some of the most sophisticated marketers, pollsters, and media advisors to ever work for a president. Much of his success in opinion formation, information control, and law enactment is a result of Reagan's use of the new technologies. While the "permanent campaign" is a recognizable and dominant aspect of presidential politics, Blumenthal contends that the "permanent campaign will permeate politics down to the most remote legislative district as politicians feel the need to retain consultants to give them the advantage."[21]

FUNCTIONS OF POLITICAL CONSULTANTS

Political consultants are concerned with five broad areas of campaign endeavors: management, planning and strategy, research, and candidate image, and personality. With the election of Jimmy Carter, campaign consultants often became administrative staff members continuing their work in areas of expertise. We first investigate these broad areas and then focus on specific services offered by political consultants.

Campaign Management

An important function of a political consultant is the management of an entire campaign. They first establish the campaign organization consisting of professionals, committed party regulars, and citizen volunteers. Complete campaign management requires the implementation of campaign strategies and the allocation of candidate time, money, and talent.

Today, even in congressional races, campaigns employ a team of consultants.[22] Some are strong in media like Charles Guggenheim or Matt Reese, and some in organization like Doug Bailey or John Deardourff. Campaign management involves paying attention to the greatest of details. Chagall reports that consultant David Garth manages, coaches, and even dresses his candidates. He has even been known to put some clients on a diet.[23]

Campaign Planning and Strategy

Strategic considerations are an important part of the consultant's duties. In planning a political campaign, the consultant considers the candidate's personality, temperament, experience, strengths, and weaknesses. The basic themes, slogans, issues, and modes of attack are created and the game plan is formulated. The scheduling of campaign appearances and activities is also an important part of the total planning of a campaign. Strategy development, refinement, and execution is a continual process. Its success or failure directly impacts upon the reputation of the consultant and future jobs. This function, then, is critical to both the candidate and consultant.

Although campaign planning and strategy is a multifaceted task, nearly every consultant has a noted strategy or pattern of conducting campaigns. Joe Napolitan, a consultant who works primarily for liberal democrats, is noted for the strategy of suddenly stepping up a campaign late and hitting the opponent hard at the end.[24] This strategy almost worked in the presidential election of 1968. Hubert Humphrey, however, did not want to insult Lyndon Johnson and thus was unwilling to be as bold on Vietnam as Napolitan desired. Nevertheless, most analysts agree that given an extra week or so, Humphrey would have soundly defeated Richard Nixon.

Campaign Research

Campaign research is a highly specialized function and provides the basis for strategy development and execution. Campaign research includes investigating voting patterns, voter turnout, demographic correlates of voting, voter attitudes, opinions, issues, registration, and election projections. Most campaigns prepare a "bible" that summarizes the relevant issues of the campaign, profiles "friendly" voters, analyzes opposition strengths, weaknesses, and strategy, and provides local data for campaign stops.[25] Like campaign planning and strategy development, research is a continual process, especially as election day approaches.

It was Stuart Spencer who introduced "tracking research" to political campaigns.[26] This marketing technique of taking frequent voter attitude measurements allows a consultant to isolate specific cause-effect relationships. Thus, the impact of various campaign events, such as radio or television commercials, is identified and adjustments are made.

It is the dimension of scientific research that has impacted the nature of contemporary campaigns the most. For some, as campaigns have become more scientific, they have also become less human and substantive in issue debate.

Candidate Image and Personality

A major task of the consultant is to assist in the development of the candidate's public image. Images are the conceptions of qualities people associate with certain objects, products, or individuals.[27] The consultant's job is to design and stimulate favorable associations so that the voters believe the candidate fulfills their wishes, desires, and needs. The candidate's personality is a composite picture presented to the voters of the candidate's political views, roles, and personal characteristics. During the 1980 presidential campaign, Reagan was presented as "tough"—equal to the task of facing the Soviets and believing in a strong defense. Once in office, he was presented as a nice guy, humble, and easygoing unless pushed into a corner.

In 1988, George Bush worked hard to get rid of his "wimp" image and Dukakis his image of being cold and emotionless. During the campaign, Bush was shown fishing and hunting. He used a more aggressive style and "tougher" language with reporters and in references to Michael Dukakis. One of Bush's most memorable lines during the campaign was at the Republican National Convention when he borrowed some lines from the film character "Dirty Harry," "Read my lips, no new taxes!"

Candidate image and personality are important features of every campaign. After an extensive investigation of mass media and elections, Thomas Patterson reported that images are easily acquired by the voters and once developed, they are not likely to be altered even with the presentation of new information and efforts.[28] In fact, Patterson found that the impressions acquired during the 1976 presidential campaign between Carter and Ford tended to be more stylistic, focusing on candidate mannerisms and campaign performance, rather than on issue propositions or leadership qualities.[29] Unfortunately, this trend continued through the Reagan years. The polls showed, in the 1984 presidential election, that voters favored Reagan based on elements of his persona and charisma but disagreed with his issue positions.

The fact is that today images cannot be taken for granted. They must be built, reinforced, and polished. The electorate forms numerous images of candidates based upon perceptions, attitudes, and emotions. Candidate images are short-term factors subject to creation and impact. A study by Scott Keeter and Cliff Zukin found four major categories of reasons for favorable and unfavorable impressions of candidates.[30] In order of importance they were: personal qualities and characteristics, executive capacities, issues, and partisan references. Generally, a candidate is helped by being thought of as trustworthy, reliable, mature, kind but firm, a devoted family man, charismatic, and in every other way normal. It is because image and personality are conveyed primarily through the visual media that consultants and specialists are essential to any campaign.

WHITE HOUSE PUBLIC RELATIONS AND COMMUNICATIONS MANAGEMENT

Of course, concerns over image and personality do not end on election day. Many have a continuing need to reinforce the properly defined image—especially in today's mediated environment. Elected officials bring their consultants with them once elected.

Today we have what many scholars refer to as "a public presidency."[31] Samuel Kernell makes the argument that presidents "going public" is a strategic adaptation to the information age. "Going public," Kernell calls "a leadership style consistent with the requirements of a political community that is increasingly susceptible to the centrifugal forces of public opinion."[32] Thus, he predicts that "going public" will occupy a prominent place in the strategic repertoire of future presidents and thus require special attention and help.

Today the press and the president desperately need each other. In the 1960s televised coverage of the presidency and political campaigns became a primary occupation of the news media. Since that time, words like "image," "audience share," "targeting," "packaging," "teleprompter," and a host of others have become a part of the political lexicon. Presidents and potential presidents, since Theodore Roosevelt turned the White House into the "bully pulpit," need to link their public persuasive efforts with the media. But today, the media equally need presidential "bits" of exposure and information to satisfy the public's curiosity and preoccupation with our chief executive. And the White House provides many services for the press. It provides background briefings, "off the record" comments, transcripts, daily handouts and grants access, and interviews.

The result of this symbiotic relationship is a constant battle of presidential access and control. To use a medium effectively implies control, planning, and proper execution. For presidents, each category is a challenge, struggle, and process of adaptation. Perhaps the greatest challenge is to control news coverage to ensure that it is favorable to the incumbent. The president's press secretary is the immediate link with the press. Although his or her function is to serve as a conduit of information, an attempt must be made to control the agenda as well as what is said and is not said.

Several scholars have argued that no presidency recognized the need and value of projecting the proper image more than Ronald Reagan.[33] From the beginning, Reagan's staff, as media professionals, recognized that the public has less and less of a historical memory. This requires a daily concern rather than a long-term perspective for impression management. They also recognized that the mass media expected a steady and constant "din" from the White House. And, as Rod Hart confirmed in a recent study, just "talking" provides a president with media access and coverage.[34] Finally, the staff knew that television could be managed because of what Gerald Pomper refers to as its limitation: "reporters can comment only in the context of a picture; the medium is impotent without 'photo opportunities' and cannot easily resist a story with good visual possibilities."[35] As a result, Martin Schram argues that "night after night, Reagan had his way with the television news. He had succeeded in setting their agenda and framing their stories by posing for the cameras in one beautiful and compelling setting after another."[36] The key, therefore, was not to control what the news correspondents would be saying but to control what America was seeing.

Upon his election, Reagan created the Office of Planning and Evaluation. The sole job of presidential aide Michael Deaver during the first term was to present the "right" image of the president. Reagan retained Mark Goode, a media consultant and television producer, who was to make sure that nothing was left to chance and every public appearance was fully orchestrated. The staff's strategy throughout Reagan's eight years in office was to develop a "story line of the day" picking one message per day to make the evening news and newspaper headlines. The general success of this strategy has led Robert Denton to argue that the legacy of Ronald Reagan is in the institution of the "primetime presidency."[37]

In today's mediated environment, it is not enough simply to get the message out. It must be sold and protected. Media consultants and specialists are strategic in terms of selling programs and generating support and defensive in terms of damage control and explaining failures. Presidents need public relations people to ensure that their side is presented, to keep exposure before the public, to maintain popular support, and to begin "positioning" for reelection or their "place in history."

MAIN SERVICES OFFERED BY POLITICAL CONSULTANTS

In executing the functions described above, political consultants provide many services for candidates and elected officials. These countless services, ranging from day-to-day campaign operations, to fund-raising, to image definition depend upon three main services: advertising, public opinion polling, and direct mail. Each of these services is communication-based and has become the bread and butter of the industry.

Advertising

Political advertising is the most recognized and controversial service provided by consultants. It is also, perhaps, the most important. In the 1988 presidential election campaign, Bush and Dukakis spent over $85 million on television advertising with the national parties spending another $14 million for their candidates.[38] Their impact was noted in a *New York Times*/CBS poll, where one-fourth of the voters in the campaign claimed that political ads had influenced their choice of candidate.[39] As Tony Schwartz, a long-time media consultant known for his powerful political commercials, is fond of saying, "the political parties today are ABC, NBC, and CBS."[40]

The media adviser was once primarily a technical adviser not privy to the overall strategy and tactics of the campaign. Today, however, the media consultant is a key member of the staff often responsible for a campaign's total advertising and communication strategy.[41]

According to Richard Armstrong, nothing has changed the "business" of political advertising more than the advent of video.[42] Video allows for quicker spot production as well as lower cost. The result is more different ads, more ads running, and because of the fast turnaround time, there are more reactive or response ads to counter opponents or to reflect a change in voter attitudes.

Tony Schwartz, for example, leases four hours of satellite time every day to produce and distribute advertisements.[43]

Of course, modern political advertising is a far cry from the distribution of flyers and campaign buttons of the 1800s. As radio and television became the primary means of communicating to a large number of people, it was natural for politicians to seek access to the media. But utilizing the commercial, business format of advertising as a way to gain voter acceptance was an evolutionary process. For Joe McGinniss, the process was also a natural one. He wrote in 1968 that "politics in a sense, has always been a con game. . . . Advertising, in many ways, is a con game too. . . . It is not surprising then, that politicians and advertising men should have discovered one another. And, once they recognized that the citizen did not so much vote for a candidate as make a psychological purchase of him, not surprising that they began to work together."[44]

Although in 1948 only 3 percent of the population owned a television, Harry Truman produced a spot encouraging citizens to vote. It wasn't until 1952 when about 45 percent of the nation owned a television set that political ads became commonplace events.[45] In that presidential contest, the Republicans spent $1.5 million and the Democrats only $77,000. Eisenhower's advisers felt television spots could be more controlled and counter his "stumbling press conference performances."[46] Accounting for inflation, Eisenhower's television budget was greater than that spent in the 1980 presidential campaign.[47]

It was also in that year that Richard Nixon, Eisenhower's vice-presidential running mate, took to the airwaves to deny charges of maintaining a slush fund of $18,000 and to save his spot on the ticket. The advertising agency of Batten, Barton, Durstine, and Osborn purchased 30 minutes of network time for $75,000 for Nixon to answer charges. The presentation was carefully constructed, rehearsed, and successful. The medium was not only a way to communicate to an audience but was also a means to persuade them. This key incident is investigated further in Chapter 6.

The dominant format of early political ads featured the candidate speaking directly to the camera. For media specialists, this format was lacking. It did not utilize the full capabilities of the medium and was certainly boring to the general public. Later, in a more creative use of the medium, campaign events were broadcast live. Live events are, however, difficult to control and staged interactions soon followed. In addition to 30- and 60-second spots, extended half-hour documentaries and telethons were a popular format from 1960 to 1972 but are much too expensive to broadcast today.

Since the advent of television, numerous types and formats of ads have evolved and are used in local, state, and national campaigns.[48] "Primitive ads," those of the campaigns of 1952 and 1956, were simple in concept and production consisting of announcers asking questions and candidates responding. As already noted, such spots do not utilize the benefits of television as a communication medium.

"Talking heads" is a popular advertising format that started in 1960 by both

John Kennedy and Richard Nixon. These ads, with the candidate speaking directly to the voter, are successful for incumbents or candidates of high credibility and allow for addressing important issues. Many candidates use this format in the last few days of a campaign to bolster support.

"Negative ads" did not begin in 1988. In fact, they were equally prominent in the 1964 presidential campaign between Barry Goldwater and Lyndon Johnson. Such ads attack opponents by playing upon voter prejudice and emotions.

As appropriate to the medium of television, "visual ads" were a part of the 1952 presidential campaign. With the advent of color, they became more prominent in 1960. A strong visual hook in an ad increases impact and recall. As will be discussed later, George Bush's ad of the revolving door of criminals going in and out of prison and the visual of Michael Dukakis riding in an army tank are attributed as providing the death blow to the Dukakis presidential campaign.

The category of "Production idea" spots may overlap with other formats or types. The critical element in these commercials is the presentation of a memorable and powerful idea. Nearly every presidential campaign has at least one, such as Reagan's "Bear in Woods" spot in 1984 or Bush's "Willie Horton" spot in 1988.

"Cinema verité ads" utilize a documentary technique of capturing a candidate in real life situations interacting with people. This approach was most popular in the 1972 George McGovern campaign and the 1976 Jimmy Carter campaign. The goal was to present unstaged, spontaneous interactions.

"Documentary ads" are primarily biographical stressing candidate experience and national service. They are used most often early in a campaign. They also tend to be longer than a 60-second spot.

"Person-in-the-streets ads" consist primarily of everyday citizens expressing positive feelings and views about a candidate or negative feelings and views about an opponent. Although used in most all contemporary political campaigns at all levels, Jimmy Carter relied heavily upon this type in the 1980 presidential campaign. Such ads are especially good at reinforcement but are less effective in changing attitudes.

"Testimonial ads" offer endorsements by well-known people. Such ads have greater impact during primary campaigns in building name recognition and credibility. More recently, however, entertainment personalities are more likely to provide public endorsements rather than appear in televised spots.

Finally, "independent ads" are those financed by individuals or groups separate from the campaign organization of the candidate. Political action committees (PACs) spend millions of dollars on such ads. Ronald Reagan made extensive use of this type during both of his presidential campaigns. These ads tend to be more negative thus allowing the candidates to deny control of or responsibility for the ads.

After nearly every election, members of Congress express concern about the costs and nature of contemporary political advertising. In 1984, a bipartisan group of congressmen sponsored legislation that would limit political ads to a "tombstone" formula where candidates are "talking heads" only.[49] However, the odds of such legislation becoming law is low. Incumbents benefit most from few restrictions on campaign rules and finance.

Although specific ads may serve a variety of functions or purposes, there is generally a strategy or chronology to their use as identified by Diamond and Bates.[50] Early in a campaign, advertising seeks to create name recognition and candidate identification. Biographical spots are most common as already noted during this phase. The next strategic use of commercials is to generate argument detailing the candidate's themes of the campaign often targeted to a particular demographic voting group. Issues here are treated in emotional terms seeking the approval and interest of voters. Following argument ads are attack commercials or what some call negative commercials. The focus of these ads is on the opponent and they are seldom delivered by the candidate. Finally, by the end of the campaign, ads of resolution appear. In these spots candidates attempt to sum up the issues, their positions, and provide reasons for voting for them. Usually these ads are in the last week of the campaign and have the candidates speaking directly to the audience.

Lynda Kaid and Dorothy Davidson, in their study of political ads, found two very distinct videostyles.[51] The incumbent videostyle uses longer commercials, more testimonials, more candidate positive focus, more slides with print, more formal dress; stresses competence; and is usually represented by an announcer. The challenger videostyle uses more opponent negative focus, talking head ads, cinema verité style, more eye contact with audience, more casual dress; and most often speaks for him- or herself in the ads.

Richard Joslyn argues that the primary appeal made in political commercials is the "benevolent leader" which focuses on candidate personality rather than issues or policies.[52] In fact, after analyzing over 500 commercials from 1960 to 1984, he found that only 15 percent of the ads had a policy dimension. A study by Donald Cundy revealed that once created, candidate images in the media lessen the impact of subsequent messages.[53] Thus, the establishment of an early positive candidate image is key to the entire campaign. Bruce Gronbeck concurs and his analysis of the commercials during the primary season of the 1988 presidential campaign revealed themes of mythic portrayals of the candidates such as Dukakis as a "miracle worker," Bush as the "presidential messiah," Bruce Babbitt as the "frontier sheriff," Robert Dole as the "heroic everyman," and Paul Simon as "the gunfighter."[54]

Practitioners and scholars agree that the key to successful political commercials is impacting voter emotions.[55] The form and content of an ad must be designed to create an emotional response in the viewer. We vote with our hearts, not our minds.

There are several functions of political ads: to create interest in a candidate, to build name recognition, to create, soften, or redefine an image, to stimulate citizen participation, to provide motivation for candidate support, to reinforce support, to influence the undecided, to identify key issues and frame questions for public debate, to demonstrate the talents of the candidate, and to provide entertainment.[56]

The content, approach, and thrust of an ad are based upon several considerations: the strengths and weaknesses of the candidates, the strengths and weaknesses of the opponent, available funds, the nature of news coverage of the candidate, public information and views of the candidate, and the general artistic and aesthetic inclinations of the consultant.[57]

Many journalists and scholars argue that there seems to be an increasing trend towards negative campaigns in recent history at all electoral levels. Negative and "hard hitting" ads have become the focus of many campaigns. Although there have always been negative ads, Richard Armstrong argues that the elections of 1986 marked a new stage in electoral politics, a stage he calls "reactivity."[58] New technologies allowed candidates to respond to opponents, public attitudes, and situations much faster, thus becoming more reactive, resulting in what appears to be more negative campaign activities. Today's technology has developed a kind of "punch/counterpunch" campaign. For Tony Schwartz, today's media campaign is like guerrilla warfare. "Someone takes a shot at you, you move aside and take a shot back."[59]

The popular press proclaimed that the 1988 presidential campaign was the most negative in U.S. history. Of Bush's 37 ads, 14 were negative and he spent 40 percent of his budget airing six of the best negative ads.[60] However, nearly everyone agrees that Bush conducted a more efficient media campaign than Dukakis. His campaign was more organized, paid and free media efforts were better coordinated, and the issues were more salient to the voting public. Bush's ads played upon the emotions while Dukakis's early ads were more discursive featuring statistics, charts, and bar graphs.[61] The Bush campaign spent $47.5 million on advertising compared to Dukakis's $30 million.[62]

Roger Ailes served as Bush's media consultant who is known in the industry as "the prince of negative advertising." His strategy for Bush's ads were to make Bush a more warm and personable candidate, to make him a more expressive candidate, and to portray Bush as an experienced leader. The Bush campaign also wanted to attack Dukakis on four issues: crime, environment, defense, and taxes.[63]

Janet Mullis, media director for the Bush campaign, argues that although everyone dislikes negative ads, the fact is that they are effective primarily because they do not have a long-term effect. "It is kind of like birth pains. Two days later, you forgot how much it hurt."[64] Even with Dukakis's one hundred ads, the most made by any presidential candidate in U.S. history, Patrick Devlin concludes that his main mistake was that "he did not initially want to use negative ads, later grudgingly used them, and then had very few good ones."[65]

Campaign ads from any election, whether a mayoral race or a presidential race, provide in a capsule form the basic issues, strategies, and tactics of a campaign. Together they provide the psyche of the public—their likes and dislikes, their concerns and worries, their hopes and dreams. They indeed provide future historians snapshots of American politics.

Political advertising, however, is and will continue to be controversial. Even David Ogilvy, cofounder of the advertising agency Ogilvy and Mather, in an interview of 1984 stated that "political advertising ought to be stopped. It's the only really dishonest kind of advertising that's left. It's totally dishonest."[66]

Public Opinion Polling

The *Harrisburg Pennsylvanian* published in 1824 contained the first political opinion poll in America.[67] It consisted of a survey of presidential preferences of the constituents between Andrew Jackson and John Quincy Adams. Jackson won the straw vote two to one. But scientific polling did not begin until the 1930s. Mrs. Alex Miller was the first candidate to use polling by her son-in-law George Gallup. She became the first female secretary of state in Iowa by utilizing sampling techniques that Gallup developed in his doctoral thesis. He founded the polling industry in 1935. Franklin Roosevelt's use of public opinion polls was to gauge his popularity and not to form issue or policy. Although Eisenhower's advertising agencies consulted Gallup in the development of themes to use in the 1952 television ads, extensive use of polling did not begin until 1960. John Kennedy used Louis Harris to analyze public opinion in key primary state. Upon Harris's urging, Kennedy entered the West Virginia primary—and West Virginia is a heavily Protestant state. Kennedy nearly lost the primary and lost faith in Harris's predictions. The pollster was no longer used in strategic campaign decision making.

Pollsters Patrick Caddell and Richard Wirthlin signaled a new trend in electoral politics in the early 1970s. Because of their knowledge of computer technology and scientific marketing techniques, they became the principal strategists for the Carter and Reagan presidential campaigns. What made them unique was they did more than simply report polling results. They interpreted the data, developed models and theories of voter behavior, and were dedicated to one candidate. They, rather than the candidate, became the "field marshalls" of the campaign.

Patrick Caddell enjoyed the closest relationship with a presidential candidate and subsequent president than any pollster in history. He was a vital member of not only Carter's campaign staff, but also a member of the president's inner circle. Consequently, Caddell influenced most decisions of the administration. As noted, Caddell did more than simply report results. He developed a worldview and a theory of voter motivation. According to Caddell, voters are volatile and feel alienated. He operates from the assumption that politicians generally lack the public's confidence. Voters are primarily motivated by self-interest. He uses polls extensively to note subtle changes in the mood of the electorate. For example, Caddell noted that young mothers were unsure of Carter in terms of "stability"—control and evenhandedness. Caddell instructed Carter to smile more during an upcoming presidential debate and not to get excited.[68] For Caddell, there is little difference between governing and campaigning. "Essentially, it is my thesis that governing with public approval requires a continuing political campaign."[69]

If Caddell is known for his interpretation of complex data, Richard Wirthlin is known for his pioneering work of statistical modeling of survey data to discover scenarios of how changes in campaign emphasis may affect the outcome of an election. His computer program called the "Political Information System" (PINS) was perfected in the Reagan presidential campaign of 1980 and fully guided the near perfect campaign of 1984. Wirthlin developed a 120-page strategy for Reagan's reelection effort that reviewed issues, themes, and appeals for all voter groups and electoral precincts. The daily and weekly gathering of polling data became the basis for every decision and public statement or action.

Wirthlin joined Reagan in his California gubernatorial reelection campaign in 1970. Reagan's staff was impressed by Wirthlin's ability to determine public support at any given moment in the campaign and the predictability of impact of issues upon public support. Because Reagan conformed to the computer model's guidance, Wirthlin soon became a strategist rather than a pollster-adviser for the campaign. Wirthlin knew from this experience that Reagan would be a great presidential candidate. The team of Reagan-Wirthlin has enjoyed the greatest political success in U.S. politics.[70]

Today, polling is a multibillion dollar industry. It used to be that a major candidate would conduct three polls during a campaign. In the presidential race of 1988, over 144 polls were released to the general public.[71] Today's computers allow candidates to conduct daily canvasses of voters to track even the slightest changes in support.

There are literally hundreds of polling organizations. But, for political purposes, there are three major Republican firms, (Lance, Tarrance & Associates; Market Opinion Research; and Decision Making Information, Inc.) and three Democratic firms (Caddell's Cambridge Survey Research; William Hamilton and Staff, Inc.; and Peter Hart Research Associates). Some consultants maintain their own polling services. David Garth's research staff works year-round and all polling is done in-house. By doing his own polling he controls the interpretation of data.

During elections, political polls play an important role in the electoral process. Many political action committees now require a candidate to demonstrate viability in the polls before making a financial contribution to a campaign. Some candidates base their decision whether or not to run for office on their showing in the polls.

Political polls most often focus on three major variables: the candidate, the public, and specific issues or topics. In terms of the candidate, polls assess electoral viability, strengths and weaknesses of personality characteristics, profile matches with voters or specific voter groups, and current status of the election. In terms of the public, polls seek to identify what kinds of people plan to vote for the candidate and against the candidate, what they are thinking, why they are thinking the way they are, and how their thinking will impact the election. Finally, polls attempt to reveal issue positions in terms of support, strategy development and electoral impact. For example, focus group research was used extensively by the Bush campaign not only to ascertain which issues generated the most support but also to develop ways to attack the opposition without suffering a public backlash. The research revealed that calling Dukakis a liberal would not be as effective as presenting Dukakis's "liberal" positions on issues and letting the public label Dukakis as a liberal.

Nearly everyone in the industry denies the fact that poll results cause candidates to change their views on certain issues but there is no doubt that such results impact the language and nature of promises made during a campaign. Polls released by the Presidential Hotline conducted by Richard Wirthlin, Peter Hart, and the *Washington Post*/ABC in the last week of September, 1987 predicted the strategies and issues of the final campaign over a year later.[72] Nearly half of the voters felt that a "great deal more" needs to be done in "increasing the resources for feeding and sheltering the homeless" and in "working to improve preschool education for children." In addition, 69 percent of the voters believed that more should be done to "help senior citizens." Thus, it is not surprising that Bush talked about a "kinder, gentler, more caring nation" and wanting to be the "education president," or that both Bush and Dukakis developed specific proposals for child care and the homeless. With 41 percent of the voters favoring the need "to keep the country moving in the direction of Ronald Reagan" and 46 percent believing that taxes should be "kept at the same level," little wonder Bush praised Reagan's leadership and told us to read his lips—"no new taxes." The examples could continue but the point should be obvious. Polling plays an essential role in developing campaign strategy.

Although polling has become very sophisticated and scientific, it still remains problematic despite its popularity. Critics claim that polls do not distinguish between awareness of an issue and intensity of opinion. There is often no link between an attitude and subsequent behavior. In the closing days of a campaign, public attitudes, desires, and motivations may change too frequently for pollsters to monitor and predict. After all, in October of 1975, Carter had only a 3 percent support rating according to a Gallup poll, yet still became president a year later. And Dukakis had over a 15 percent lead over Bush after the Democratic convention and lost the election. Polls alone should not, then, become the basis for decision making. But perhaps most alarming is the fact that despite the current science of opinion polling, they are often wrong. In January 1984, the *New York Times* CBS poll showed Reagan a 16-point favorite over Mondale while at the same time a *Washington Post*/ABC poll reported Reagan only a 3-point favorite.[73] In the 1988 presidential primaries, Jesse Jackson won in Michigan and Paul Simon in Illinois despite poll predictions to the contrary. Political opinion polls, unlike public polls of Gallup and Harris, are more tools of persuasion, image control, and creation, than reports of information. They are, simply, an important element of a consultant's service arsenal.

Direct Mail

Of all the services provided by consulting firms, the public is probably less aware of the importance and role direct mail plays in a campaign. As a relatively new industry, direct marketing has rapidly become the cornerstone for mounting a political campaign. Richard Armstrong claims that direct mail "has utterly revolutionized American politics . . . it has drastically changed the role of the national parties . . . created an enormous shadow government of special interest groups . . . completely revolutionized the nature of campaign finance . . . abetted the rise of political action committees . . . created a new form of political advertising . . . changed the way incumbents communicate with their constituents . . . and dramatically altered the nature of lobbying."[74] Direct mail specifically is a powerful and persuasive communication medium. Larry Sabato refers to direct mail as "the poisoned pen of politics" and Armstrong writes, "like a water moccasin, persuasion mail is silent, it is poisonous, and it has a forked tongue."[75] As the fastest growing advertising industry, direct mail utilizes the latest technology and theories of social science research.

In terms of politics, it was the 1972 presidential campaign that demonstrated the power and effectiveness of direct mail.[76] George McGovern was generally unknown and had great difficulty obtaining endorsements from party regulars, wealthy supporters, or organized groups. He was forced to use direct mail to generate funds from individual citizen supporters. Even in a difficult campaign, by 1972 direct mail was bringing in over $200,000 a month.

But Republicans have benefited most from direct marketing. In 1974, following Nixon's resignation, Congress enacted legislation that set a $1000 limit on individual political contributions. The Republicans immediately began developing a sophisticated direct mail program utilizing the latest technology; they now consistently raise four or five times more money using direct mail than Democrats.[77] But the main problem for Democrats, according to Richard Viguerie, a conservative and political direct mail consultant, is that they view direct mail as only a fund-raising activity and not as a form of advertising. He further argues that conservatives were forced to use direct mail because of the need to bypass the "liberal mass media." It became, for them, "a way of mobilizing our people, it's a way of communicating with our people; it identifies our people, and it marshals our people. It's self-liquidating and it pays for itself. It's a form of advertising, part of the marketing strategy. It's advertising."[78]

Viguerie discovered that direct mail responders are more interested in principles than in winning elections. During the 1980s, he churned out direct mail solicitations concerning one hot issue after another. The "new right" began to generate more and more money. The topics ranged from the prevention of the ratification of Salt II to the retention of the Panama Canal. In politics, a hot issue is the "goose that lays the golden egg."[79] Conservative causes used direct mail to finance campaigns and sympathetic PACs. Professional consultants, of course, prefer to work with PACs and advocacy groups because campaigns are seasonal but special causes are year-round. Armstrong even suggests that consultants in Washington looking for work to tide them over between elections played a major role in the growth of the public opinion and special interest politics.[80]

Thus, fund-raising is the primary function of direct mail in political campaigns. Candidates use direct mail to supplement federal financing of elections. Fund-raising objectives include reaching new contributors as well as continual contact with previous ones. Republicans in 1984 generated nearly $100 million from direct mail solicitation.[81] They compiled a list of 2.2 million donors and the average contribution was $26.00. A letter devoted solely to Reagan's reelection effort produced an average contribution of $55.00. The National Republican Committee utilized two direct mail membership programs. Sustaining membership required a contribution of at least $25.00 and for a contribution of $10.00 a month, one could belong to the Republican Presidential Task Force.[82] The National Committee tests about 600 mailing lists each year and conducts about 18 mailings to the "house list" each year.[83]

Other uses of direct mail include targeting voters, developing issues, recruiting volunteers, molding opinions, getting out the vote, and laying the groundwork for future campaigns by establishing a list of donors and supporters. Such organizations as the National Conservative Union, Young Americans for Freedom, and the Moral Majority use computerized mailing lists and letters to identify and organize supporters as well as to solicit funds. Direct marketing techniques have strategic implications. Richard Parker predicted in 1982 that "the computer will be central to the 1980s. Without mastery there's no reason to express a coherent position. For this period, direct mail is appropriate technology. It's a qualified way of reaching people. It makes you think strategically. You have to decide which people will respond to which issues. You have to identify constituencies. You have to identify questions of timing and geography."[84]

Direct mail is powerful because the package is carefully constructed. Starting with the envelope, there is some teaser or attention-getting statement that leads the reader to open the correspondence. The letter usually begins with a startling or dramatic statement by the politician or a celebrity. The letter is conversational and personal using a lot of *I*'s and *you*'s. There is an early identification of an enemy which is either the opponent, a group, or an issue position. The situation is described as being critical, desperate, and urgent. Of course, most letters conclude with an appeal for support and financial assistance. In short, the copy must get attention, arouse interest, stimulate desire, and ask for action.

At the heart of political direct mail is "emotional isolation." The target is an angry person who is politically frustrated. Direct mail acknowledges the anger and shows that someone or some group cares.

Techniques of emotion and motivation are well known by the professionals. They know that a letter is more likely to generate a response for funds if the letter is very specific as to what the money will be used for. A direct mail piece for gubernatorial candidate William Clements included a list of all the reserved television advertising spots by city, station, and program so that each person could see what they would be "purchasing."[85] Experts know that participation devices stimulate interest and focus concentration upon the issues or action discussed. Many mailings include opinion surveys, boxes required to be checked, or sample ballots to be marked. In terms of fund-raising, the size of a contribution will be greater if not only the amount is specified but also if the suggested amounts start with the largest (i.e., $500, $250, $100, $50, rather than $50, $100, $250, $500). Ironically, a two-page letter is more likely to be read than a one-page letter, and the signature should be in blue ink and appear to be personally signed. The timing of a mailing is critical to its impact and success. Generally, it is best to mail just before or after an announcement of candidacy, before a primary or general election, and to coincide with a major media blitz. The day Reagan announced the formation of a committee to explore his reelection, 600,000 letters were mailed and generated $3 million in contributions. A massive mailing to 2.2 million people was timed so that the people would receive the letter the Monday after Reagan's Sunday announcement of seeking reelection.[86] And finally, experts know that direct mail donors are more committed to the candidate and issues than single-event donors. Single-event donors are usually one-shot contributors who like being near the candidate or at a party whereas the direct mail donor will be responsive even in tough times. Thus, the list of contributors is a valuable commodity.

There are several advantages to the direct mail medium. There is more complete control not only over the construction of the message but also over who receives the message and where the message will be sent. The message appeals can be tailored and targeted and tell the full story and present a detailed issue position. The message is not limited to 30 seconds. In direct mail there is wider coverage, personalized and guaranteed contact, and the ability to capitalize on current events. It is also less costly and very effective. The importance and impact of direct marketing techniques will continue to be a factor in every campaign endeavor.

NEW TECHNOLOGIES

There are several new technologies that are playing an increasing role in campaigns. The state of the art in telemarketing was reflected in the Jesse Jackson presidential nomination campaign of 1984.[87] He used a computerized interactive system that would automatically dial random numbers and in his voice would inquire, "How are you doing?"; "Are you registered to vote?"; "Give us your name and telephone number,"; and "Remember, you are somebody and your vote counts." The impact was almost as if Jackson had called the person directly.

With this system, everyone hears the same message contacting thousands of people. Thus, increased productivity and quality control are guaranteed. In addition, telemarketing is more aggressive than direct mail and generally produces a much greater response rate. The key is to personalize, dramatize, and create the illusion that the donor is talking to a high ranking member of the campaign.

As cable television increases segmenting audiences, it becomes an important tool for reaching specific audiences at a reasonable cost. For the first time in our history, Bush and Dukakis spent more in spot and cable buys than on general network advertising. In short, cable television allows geographic, demographic, and psychographic targeting. It also provides much more time flexibility in terms of spot or programming format.[88]

The proliferation of satellites has provided yet another tool for communication specialists. Frank Greer was the first political media consultant to use communication satellites.[89] He argues that they can be used in four ways: for remote press conferences, to feed news stories to local media, for fund-raising, and for local coordination and organization. During the 1984 presidential primary campaign, Walter Mondale used satellites to conduct multistate interviews and feeds to local television stations. Although there was little network exposure, Mondale became the lead story on many local news programs.

The Senate Republican Conference has established a miniature news bureau. It covers statements and activities of party senators. Every afternoon, while the Senate is in session, footage of various senators is sent to hometowns on Westar IV or Galaxy I satellites. Both the Democratic and Republican conferences receive approximately $600,000 each from the federal government for these video press releases.[90]

Computers, of course, are the nervous system of any campaign. They are involved in all forms of research, polling, data collection, voter registration, strategy selection, and so on. As communication technology grows, so too will the need for even more campaign satellites. In 1964, there were about 15 people working on the Lyndon Johnson presidential campaign. In 1988, the number increased to about 5000 per candidate.[91]

THE PROFESSIONAL POLITICAL CONSULTANT: CONSEQUENCES AND IMPACT

One cannot consider the role of the new politician without also considering the impact upon our political process of new technologies and media consultants. Although Jamieson views media consultants as "persons of good will and human failings and as such are neither as innocent as their mothers believe nor as invidious as their doubters aver"; the fact is that now they are "king makers" and are at the heart of our electoral process.[92] James Gannon, editor of the *Des Moines Register*, argues that candidates have become invented and merchandised by a "mercenary army of campaign consultants, advisers, pollsters, and fund-raisers."[93] An industry has developed, according to Nimmo and Combs, to communicate "political celebrities" much like the Hollywood star system and movie gossip magazines.[94] Politicians have become fantasy figures and symbolic leaders because they represent more than politics but also values, life-style, visions, and glamor.

There are two factors that have contributed to the development of today's political celebrity. First, historically Americans have believed in democratic politics which implies that the best, most qualified individual will rise to lead the people representing their desires and reflecting their values.[95] To succeed, politicians must honor their illusion. The public has a host of expectations relevant to behavior, beliefs, and values for those in public life. Second, what most Americans know about politics comes from the media. Few citizens experience the process of politics through direct experience. Thus, political realities are mediated through group and mass communication activities.[96] As a result of Patterson's study of presidential campaigns, he concludes that "it is no exaggeration to say that, for the large majority of voters, the campaign has little reality apart from its media version."[97] Thus, mediated politics give media consultants a great deal of influence and power. This fact alarms Herbert Schiller, who believes that when media people "deliberately produce messages that do not correspond to the realities of social existence, the media managers become mind managers."[98] The ultimate danger is that by "using myths which explain, justify, and sometimes even glamorize the prevailing conditions of existence, manipulators secure popular support for a social order that is not in the majority's long-term real interest."[99]

But are the dangers that great? Consultants, of course, believe that they are actually making the electoral process more democratic. They claim that they cannot control votes as the old political bosses did through the patronage system. Also, consultants can't enforce voter discipline or the voting behavior of elected officials. There is even no empirical evidence of a direct causal relationship between watching a commercial or series of commercials and voting. Consultants further argue that they make elections more open and provide access for reporters to candidate strategy, views, and campaign information.

At worst, Caddell believes consultants are serving as preselectors of candidates. "We decide who is best able to use the technology, who understands the technology. It's a self-fulfilling prophecy.[100] Of course there is nothing inherently wrong or evil in the new technologies or even the desire of politicians to present their best attributes to the public. But the pressure of winning for both the candidate and the consultant cannot be ignored. Therein lies the potential for abuse. For consultants to get business, they must continue to win elections. They are more likely, then, to accept only sure bets and once in the battle, they may not recognize any limits to winning. The fact is, most candidates are willing participants. They seldom question the advice or strategy of consultants. Candidates are paying a great deal of money for consultant services, seldom understand the new technologies nor have the time to develop the necessary expertise to become a full partner in media decisions. The epitome of consultant manipulation is presented in the movie *The Candidate*, which is reported to be based upon the experiences of David Garth.[101] In the film, a consultant takes a good-looking nobody (Robert Redford) and leads the individual to electoral victory. Upon election, the candidate can only ask "What do I do now?" Garth was even offered the role of the consultant but turned it down because it represented "every [deleted] cliché in the book."[102]

In the demise of political parties, consultants have taken their place in generating supporters, motivating voters, and raising money. For major elective offices, consultants rather than parties have become the intermediaries between politicians and the public and the press. The consequences, according to Sabato, are the continuing decline of party organizations; emphasis of images over issues; candidate independence from party ideology; more narrow elections with focus on single issues that can be packaged; dissemination of communication tools and techniques to political action committees or issue groups that greatly influenced the 1980 and 1984 elections; resorting to factual inaccuracies, half-truths, and exaggerations; using deceptive and negative advertising resulting in voter distrust and apathy; emphasis on emotional themes over rational discussion of issues, and drastically increasing the cost of elections.[103] Finally, and perhaps of most concern, David Chagall observes that while journalists view elections as morality plays, political consultants view them as games.[104]

CONCLUSION

The professional politicians of today are not the political officeholders, for the latter are paid for governing while the former are paid for managing and winning elections. For professional politicians, politics is a permanent, continual campaign and not the process of governing. Political consultants possess the tools, skills, and techniques of mass communication and human motivation. As argued in Chapter 2, the basis of politics is human interaction. Communication is the vehicle for the sharing and creation of human beliefs, values, and goals. Elections are primarily mass communication events carefully orchestrated to produce a desired result. In Marshall McLuhan's phrase, it is impossible to separate the "medium" from the "message" or results from motives. But this chapter has recognized the role of the mass communication specialist in American electoral politics. As communication became more complex, sophisticated and technological, the need for assistance was natural. The functions and services of political consultants, while communication based, have indeed had a profound effect upon our electoral process. Consultants influence more than just *how* we elect officials, but *whom* we elect as well.

NOTES

1. Machiavelli, *The Prince*, trans. and ed. Mark Musa (New York: St. Martin's Press, 1964), p. 25.
2. Larry Sabato, *The Rise of Political Consultants* (New York: Basic Books, 1981), p. 3.

3. David Chagall, *The New King-Makers* (New York: Harcourt Brace Jovanovich, 1981), p. 400.

4. Sidney Blumenthal, *The Permanent Campaign*, 2d ed. (New York: Touchstone Books, 1982), p. 22.

5. Sabato, *The Rise of Political Consultants*, p. 8.

6. As reported in ibid., p. 18.

7. Ibid., p. 52.

8. Ibid., p. 30.

9. Kathleen Jamieson, *Packaging the Presidency* (New York: Oxford University Press, 1984), p. 5.

10. Ibid., p. vii.

11. Dan Nimmo, *The Political Persuaders* (Englewood Cliffs, NJ: Spectrum Book, 1970), p. 36.

12. Blumenthal, *The Permanent Campaign*, p. 40.

13. See Sabato, *The Rise of Political Consultants*, pp. 11–13 and 161–65; and Nimmo, *The Political Persuaders*, p. 36.

14. As quoted in Blumenthal, *The Permanent Campaign*, p. 164.

15. See Joe McGinniss, *The Selling of the President: 1968* (New York: Trident Press, 1969).

16. Sabato, *The Rise of Political Consultants*, p. 12.

17. See Melvyn Bloom, *Public Relations and Presidential Campaigns: A Crisis in Democracy* (New York: Thomas Crowell, 1973), p. 86.

18. For a detailed discussion of how the form and content of political messages conform to the requirements of a communication medium, see Robert E. Denton, Jr., *The Primetime Presidency of Ronald Reagan* (New York: Praeger, 1988), especially Chapters 3 and 4.

19. Blumenthal, *The Permanent Campaign*, p. 10.

20. Ibid., p. 311.

21. Ibid., p. 18.

22. Chagall, *The New King-Makers*, p. 297.

23. Ibid., p. 180.

24. Ibid., pp. 31–39.

25. Nimmo, *The Political Persuaders*, pp. 70–71.

26. Chagall, *The New King-Makers*, p. 63.

27. Nimmo, *The Political Persuaders*, p. 144.

28. Thomas Patterson, *The Mass Media Election* (New York: Praeger, 1980), pp. 135, 142.

29. Ibid., p. 134.

30. Scott Keeter and Cliff Zukin, "New Romances and Old Horses: The Public Images of Presidential Candidates" in *The President and the Public*, ed. Doris Graber (Philadelphia, PA: Institute for Study of Human Issues, 1982), p. 67.

31. For example see Robert E. Denton, Jr. and Dan Hahn, *Presidential Communication* (New York: Praeger, 1986); Michael Grossman and Martha Kumar, *Portraying the President* (Baltimore, MD: Johns Hopkins University Press, 1981); Roderick Hart, *Verbal Style and the Presidency* (Orlando, FL: Academic Press, 1984); Roderick Hart, *The Sound of Leadership* (Chicago, IL: University of Chicago Press, 1987); Samuel Kernell, *Going Public* (Washington, DC: Congressional Quarterly Press, 1986); Theodore

Lowi, *The Personal President* (Ithaca, NY: Cornell University Press, 1985); and Jeffrey Tulis, *The Rhetorical Presidency* (Princeton, NJ: Princeton University Press, 1987).

32. Kernell, *Going Public*, p. 212.

33. See Denton, *The Primetime Presidency of Ronald Reagan*; Hedrick Smith, *The Power Game* (New York: Random House, 1988); and Martin Schram, *The Great American Video Game* (New York: William Morrow, 1987).

34. Hart, *The Sound of Leadership*, pp. 32–39.

35. Gerald Pomper, et al., *The Election of 1984* (Chatham, NJ: Chatham House Publishers, 1985), p. 162.

36. Schram, *The Great American Video Game*, p. 23.

37. See Denton, *The Primetime Presidency of Ronald Reagan*, especially Chapters 1 and 4.

38. Patrick Devlin, "Contrasts in Presidential Campaign Commercials of 1988," *American Behavioral Scientist* 32, no. 4 (March/April 1989): 389–414.

39. As reported in M. Oreskes, "TV's role in '88: The medium is the election," *New York Times* (October 30, 1988) pp. 1 and 19.

40. He begins nearly every interview with this comment on the power and importance of political commercials and is repeated in numerous places.

41. See Jamieson, *Packaging the President*, especially pp. 3–38.

42. Richard Armstrong, *The Next Hurrah* (New York: William Morrow, 1988), p. 18.

43. Ibid., p. 20.

44. McGinniss, *The Selling of the President: 1968*, pp. 26–27.

45. Sabato, *The Rise of Political Consultants*, p. 113.

46. As reported in ibid., p. 113.

47. Patrick Devlin, "An Analysis of Presidential Television Commercials: 1952–1984" in *New Perspectives on Political Advertising*, ed. Lynda Kaid, Dan Nimmo, and Keith Sanders (Carbondale, IL: Southern Illinois University Press, 1986).

48. Ibid., pp. 25–32.

49. "This Idea Deserves a Tombstone," *Advertising Age*, April 16, 1984, p. 16.

50. Edwin Diamond and Stephen Bates, *The Spot* (Cambridge, MA: The MIT Press, 1984), pp. 303–45.

51. Lynda Kaid and Dorothy Davidson, "Elements of Videostyle," in *New Perspectives on Political Advertising*, ed. Lynda Kaid, Dan Nimmo, and Keith Sanders (Carbondale, IL: Southern Illinois University Press, 1986), pp. 199–208.

52. Richard Joslyn, "Political Advertising and the Meaning of Elections," in *New Perspectives on Political Advertising*, ed. Lynda Kaid, Dan Nimmo, and Keith Sanders (Carbondale, IL: Southern Illinois University Press, 1986), p. 179.

53. Donald Cundy, "Political Commercials and Candidate Image," in *New Perspectives on Political Advertising*, ed. Lynda Kaid, Dan Nimmo, and Keith Sanders (Carbondale, IL: Southern Illinois University Press, 1986), p. 234.

54. Bruce Gronbeck, "Mythic Portraiture in the 1988 Iowa Presidential Caucus Bio-ads," *American Behavioral Scientist* 32, no. 4 (March/April 1989): 351–64.

55. See Kaid and Davidson, "Elements of Videostyle," p. 208; Diamond and Bates, *The Spot*; Sabato, *The Rise of Political Consultants*; Tony Schwartz, *The Responsive Chord* (New York: Doubleday, 1972); and Chagall, *New King-Makers*, pp. 14 and 57, for examples.

56. This list is compiled from Jamieson, *Packaging the Presidency*, p. 37 and Devlin, "An Analysis of Presidential Television Commercials, 1952–1984," pp. 22–24.

57. Jamieson, *Packaging the President*, p. 37.

58. Armstrong, *The Next Hurrah*, p. 18.

59. As quoted in ibid., p. 23.

60. Devlin, "Contrasts in Presidential Campaign Commercials of 1988," p. 406.

61. Edwin Diamond and Adrian Marin, "Spots," *American Behavioral Scientist* 32, no. 4 (March/April 1989): 383–85.

62. Devlin, "Contrasts in Presidential Campaign Commercials of 1988," p. 391.

63. Ibid., pp. 391 and 394.

64. As quoted in ibid., p. 407.

65. Ibid., p. 407.

66. James Forkan, "Political Ads Are Dishonest: Ogilvy," *Advertising Age*, June 7, 1984, p. 3.

67. Sabato, *The Rise of Political Consultants,* p. 69.

68. Blumenthal, *The Permanent Campaign*, p. 55.

69. As reported in ibid., p. 56.

70. For a fascinating look at Caddell and Wirthlin see Roland Perry, *The Programming of the President* (London: Aurum Press, 1984).

71. Scott Ratzan, "The Real Agenda Setters," *American Behavioral Scientist* 32, no. 4 (March/April 1989): 451.

72. See "Presidential Campaign Hotline," September 23, 25, and 30, 1987, copyright American Political Network, Inc.

73. "Are Pollsters Getting Out of Hand?" *U.S. News and World Report*, May 7, 1984, p. 30.

74. Armstrong, *The Next Hurrah*, p. 28.

75. Sabato, *The Rise of Political Consultants*, p. 220 and Armstrong, *The Next Hurrah*, p. 60.

76. See Blumenthal, *The Permanent Campaign*, pp. 242–44.

77. Richard Edel, "GOP Leaves Democrats In the Dust," *Advertising Age*, April 16, 1984, pp. 52–53.

78. As quoted in Blumenthal, *The Permanent Campaign*, p. 245.

79. Armstrong, *The Next Hurrah*, p. 116.

80. Ibid., p. 118.

81. Richard Edel, "Direct Marketing Gets Politician's Vote," *Advertising Age*, April 16, 1984, pp. 52–53.

82. Ibid., p. 53.

83. Ibid.

84. As quoted in Blumenthal, *The Permanent Campaign*, p. 254.

85. As reported in Sabato, *The Rise of Political Consultants*, p. 238.

86. Edel, "Direct Marketing Gets Politician's Vote," p. 52.

87. Armstrong, *The Next Hurrah*, pp. 139–48.

88. Ibid., pp. 165–90.

89. Ibid., pp. 196–98.

90. Ibid., p. 198.

91. Diamond and Marin, "Spots," p. 387.

92. Jamieson, *Packaging the President*, p. viii.

93. "Presidential Campaign Hotline," October 5, 1987, copyright American Political Network.

94. Dan Nimmo and James Combs, *Mediated Political Realities* (New York: Longman, 1983), p. 96.

95. See Robert E. Denton, Jr., *The Symbolic Dimensions of the American Presidency* (Prospect Heights, IL: Waveland Press, 1982).

96. For a detailed discussion of "mediated political realities" see Nimmo and Combs, *Mediated Political Realities*.

97. Patterson, *The Mass Media Election*, p. 3.

98. Herbert Schiller, *The Mind Managers* (Boston, MA: Beacon Press, 1973), p. 1.

99. Ibid., p. 1.

100. As quoted in Blumenthal, *The Permanent Campaign*, p. 74.

101. Ibid., p. 111.

102. Ibid.

103. Sabato, *The Rise of Political Consultants*, p. 313.

104. Chagall, *The New King-Makers*, p. 16.

Chapter Four

Political Campaigns

Every four years a gong goes off and a new Presidential campaign surges into the national consciousness: new candidates, new issues, a new season of surprises. But underlying the syncopations of change there is a steady, recurrent rhythm from election to election, a pulse of politics, that brings up the same basic themes in order, over and over again.[1]

Much has already been written about political campaigns. The classic "limited effects model" of campaign communication research dominated scholars' views of the impact of campaigns upon voters for nearly 40 years. The model was based upon data from the 1940 elections presented by Lazarsfeld, Berelson, and Gaudet in *The People's Choice*.[2] They found that most voter decisions were based upon attitude predispositions, group identification, and interpersonal communication. Thus, mediated messages would contribute little to the actual conversion of voters favoring one candidate over another.[3]

But today, in terms of voter behavior and campaigns, political outcomes are less predictable than in previous decades. With the decline of political parties, the increase of single issue politics, the prominence of mass media, and the sophistication of social science research, the studies of the 1940s and 1950s are no longer apropos of today's electoral campaigns. Scholars are now recognizing the variety of factors that influence voter preferences. The "uses and gratifications model" of campaign effects is increasing in popularity. This model basically argues that campaign effects upon voters depend upon the needs and motivations of the individual voter. Voters may turn to campaign messages for information, issue discussion, or pure entertainment.[4] There are a variety of motives, therefore, for exposure to campaign communication.

A COMMUNICATION APPROACH TO CAMPAIGN ANALYSIS

Gary Mauser has identified four basic approaches to campaign analysis.[5] The academic perspective is grounded in behaviorism. The goal of most of this research has been to understand individual voting behavior. Within this perspective is a sociological emphasis that attempts to identify the factors that influence *how* people decide to vote and a psychological emphasis that attempts to understand *why* people vote as they do.

The positive approach to campaign analysis based on the rational choice theory of human behavior attempts to explain how voters make decisions based upon personal goals of economic and social well-being. From this approach, elections are merely instruments to obtain group and subsequently individual goals.

The pragmatic approach focuses on the day-to-day decisions and choices confronting the politicians. There is a tremendous difference between being a student of politics and a practitioner of politics. Except for aspects of the popular press, there are few systematic analyses from the perspective of campaigners.

A communication approach to campaign analysis, the perspective of this book, takes issue with the basic assumption of the behaviorists that political campaigns really do not play a major role in election results. Communication scholars argue that too much emphasis of campaign research has been focused on voter conversion. Such research tends to ignore the long-term, subtle effects or cumulative effects of politics and political campaigns. As argued in Chapter 2, political reality is created, manipulated, and permeated. Campaigns are exercises in the creation, recreation, and transmission of significant symbols through communication. Communication activities are the vehicles for action—both real and perceived. It is true, however, as Samuel Becker argues, that "any single communication encounter accounts for only a small portion of the variance in human behavior."[6] He characterizes our communication environment as a "mosaic."[7] The mosaic consists of an infinite number of information "bits" or fragments on an infinite number of topics scattered over time and space. In addition, the bits are disorganized, exposure is varied and repetitive. As these bits are relevant or address a need, they are attended. Thus, as we attempt to make sense of our environment, our current state of existence, political bits are elements of our voting choice, worldview, or legislative desires. As voters, we must arrange these bits into a cognitive pattern that comprises our mosaic of a candidate, issue, or situation. Campaigns, then, are great sources of potential information and contain, however difficult to identify or measure, elements that impact decision making. Information bits can replace other bits to change or modify our worldview, attitudes, or opinions.

Jonathan Robbin, chairman of the Claritas Corporation, a marketing firm that specializes in geodemographics, recognizes the important role of communication in successful campaigns. "The essence of political campaigning is communications. A majority is built by repeatedly contacting voters and persuading them to register, turn out, and cast their ballot for the 'right' candidate or side of an issue.''[8] For him, market data alone will not guarantee electoral success. How the market data is applied is critical to the campaign process. "The efficiency of a campaign depends on *accurate* delivery of *effective* communications.''[9]

FUNCTIONS OF CAMPAIGNS

From a communication perspective, Bruce Gronbeck has constructed a "functional model of campaign research.''[10] The model, consistent with the uses and gratifications model, assumes that "receivers are active human beings who are subjecting themselves to communicative messages because certain needs can be satisfied and hence certain gratifications can be gained from exposure to those messages.''[11]

In campaigns, there are both instrumental functions and consummatory functions. One of three instrumental functions is behavioral activation. Campaigns serve not only to reinforce voter attitudes or convert voter preference but also to motivate voters actually to vote or help in a campaign. Another instrumental function of campaigns is cognitive adjustments. Campaigns, by discussion issues, may stimulate awareness of issues, reflect upon candidate views, or result in voter position modification. Finally, campaigns function to legitimize both the new leadership and the subsequent rules, laws, and regulations.

Consummatory functions are those embodied in the communication processes that go beyond candidate selection and legislative enactments. They help create the metapolitical images and social-psychological associations that provide the glue that holds our political system together.[12] Campaigns provide personal involvement in many forms: direct participation, self-reflection and definition, social interaction and discussion, and aesthetic experiences of public drama and group life. And campaigns provide the legitimization of the electoral process, reaffirming commitment to *our* brand of democracy, debate, and political campaigning.

Campaigns, then, communicate and influence, reinforce and convert, increase enthusiasm and inform, and motivate as well as educate. As Gronbeck argues, campaigns "get leaders elected, yes, but ultimately, they also tell us who we as a people are, where we have been and where we are going; in their size and duration they separate our culture from all others, teach us about political life, set our individual and collective priorities, entertain us, and provide bases for social interaction.''[13]

PRESIDENTIAL CAMPAIGNS

There are numerous channels of campaign communication to include: public appearances (speeches, rallies); interpersonal (luncheons, meetings with opinion leaders); organizational (party machines, workers); display media (buttons, posters, billboards); print media (campaign literature, ads, newspapers), auditory media (radio, telephone); and television (advertising, new coverage, programs). Campaigns are complex communication activities. In the last chapter we noted the growing influence of communication specialists in every level of political campaigns. Some local campaigns are as complex, long, and expensive as national campaigns. Rita Whitlock, an academic who also works as a campaign consultant, confirms the notion that the steps for even a small mayoral race are the same as in presidential elections. There is heavy dependence upon organization, strategy development, media, and special events. Local campaigns differ only in scope and money spent—not in basic task requirements.[14] But the U.S. presidential contest is the most unique in the world. Because of the magnitude of the office, every presidential election is historical and impacts upon the rest of the world. It is for this reason that we chose to investigate the overt and subtle role communication plays in the realm of presidential election campaigns. Many of the general notions explicated here are indeed true for all campaigns. To appreciate and understand a presidential contest is to also understand the nature of American electoral politics.

The formal criteria for becoming president as set forth in Article II, Section 1 of the Constitution are threefold: natural born citizen, at least 35 years old, and a resident of the United States for 14 years. But the informal criteria are numerous and include: political experience, personal charisma, fund-raising, and audience adaptation. Today, the presidential contest extends beyond the traditional three-month campaign between Labor Day and November every four years. In fact, the contest has become continual and, for some participants, a matter of lifelong training and maneuvering. A "good man" for the job is not just found but is created, demonstrated, and articulated to the American public. The distinction between being a president and being a presidential candidate has virtually disappeared. Godfrey Hodgson even argues that the presidential election campaign is no longer simply the way a president is chosen but it actually influences the *kind* of person chosen and the priorities they will have as president.[15] Thus, the strategies and tactics presidential candidates use to present themselves and to communicate with the American public are of vital importance and are the focus of this chapter.

The Process

Since World War II, our political system has undergone a fundamental change in how candidates for the presidency have been selected. In fact, one of the most striking features of our presidential nomination process is its constant change of rules, financing regulations, and primaries. As Rhodes Cook observes, "each presidential nominating campaign is a trek into the unknown."[16] Less than one year after the 1988 election, Democrats passed changes that will impact the process in 1992. The focus of the changes has been on the role of the public in the process. The citizenry rather than party activists increasingly determine which candidates will meet in the general election. Since 1968, presidential primaries have become the critical factor in capturing nominations and the public has become the true power brokers. We have, in effect, blurred the distinction between nominating and electing candidates.

By 1976, with the Carter campaign, Larry Bartels claims we witnessed the strategic success inherent in the contemporary presidential nominating process. The key to success is not "to enter the campaign with a broad coalition of political support, but to rely on the dynamics of the campaign itself . . . to generate that support."[17] The new system is dominated by the candidates who seek public support. A critical issue becomes, of course, whether or not the increased roles of the public and media have resulted in better candidates.

Historically, we have experienced three presidential nominating systems.[18] The congressional caucus system existed between 1800 and 1824. Successful candidates had to appeal to congressmen and the national political elite. Party congressmen controlled the nomination and the role of party grassroots voters and the press was minimal.

The brokered convention system, 1832 to 1968, emerged as a result of the deaths of the founding fathers, general population growth and movement to the west, and the initiation of more democratic political customs. During this system, nominations occurred at national conventions involving a great deal of bargaining. Popularity with state and local officials as well as with major office holders was critical for the successful candidate. Although presidential primaries began in 1908, regular party leaders and national office holders controlled the nomination. As late as 1968, Hubert Humphrey won the Democratic party nomination without contesting in a single presidential primary. Once again, party grassroots voters and the press had little influence upon candidate selection.

The system of popular appeal began with the 1972 presidential election. The old systems functioned under the philosophy of "consent of the governed" and the new under the auspices of "government by the people." Conventions formally ratify state primaries, conventions, and caucuses. Candidates have to maintain popularity with party voters, activists, and media representatives. The new system, initiated by the Democratic party, was heralded as open, democratic, deliberative, and responsive to popular preferences.

Many political scientists are alarmed at how we nominate and elect our presidents. They challenge Al Smith's maxim that "the cure for the ills of Democracy is more Democracy." Scott Keeter and Cliff Zukin argue that the new system of presidential nomination makes for uninformed choice both by the individual and for society as a collectivity.[19] For them, quality of citizen input is not a function of the capacity of the public to participate but the nature of citizen input is a function of the structure and environment in which it is made. Keeter and Zukin conclude "that the contemporary system of presidential nomination presents a most inhospitable climate for rational and informed participation."[20]

The presidential nomination system of popular appeal raises several concerns and issues:

a. Officeholders are at a disadvantage seeking nominations because of the need for full-time personal campaigning for years prior to a general election.

b. The role of political parties decreases, diminishing peer review of candidates and weakening the ties between campaigning and governing.

c. Some states' primaries are more important than others based upon such factors as size, time of primary, and so on.

d. Rules for delegate selection vary from state to state.

e. Voter eligibility rules differ among states.

f. Sequencing of primaries changes the number and candidate choices in later primaries.

g. Most citizens learn very little about the candidates during the primary process.

h. General public opinion seldom corresponds to those of specific or important state primaries.

i. Convention delegates are not representative of the general public.

j. Journalists play a major role in the campaigns.

k. The current system favors people who have a burning desire for power, who can campaign full time, and who have a clean image.[21]

The presidential election of 1988, for some scholars, marked a new system of presidential nominations. The changes revolved around three areas: more involvement by party elites, standardization of state delegate selection practices and primary events, and reduction of the primary season.

There are four important phases to a presidential campaign: preprimary, primary, conventions, and general campaigns.

Preprimary Period

A run for the presidency has become a long, expensive, and complicated process. The period between elections is vital to the success of any presidential campaign.[22] During elections, voters are bombarded with persuasive appeals. The salience of politics is high and campaign persuasion is aimed primarily at reinforcing the perceptions and commitment of the electorate to a candidate. Therefore, the period between elections is ideal for issue and image development when political awareness is low and partisan appeals are less salient. During this time, potential candidates cultivate contacts in the media, write books or have them ghostwritten (Kennedy's *Profiles in Courage*, Nixon's *Six Crises*, Carter's *Why Not the Best?*, Reagan's *Where's the Rest of Me?*, Bush's *Man of Integrity*, or Dukakis' *Creating the Future*). Candidates also start syndicated radio programs and national news columns. Such activities serve to advance the views of the candidate as well as keep the individual before the public. And the public is more susceptible to the views and the candidate than in periods immediately preceding the election.

No one was more successful at maximizing the political potential of this period than Ronald Reagan. In 1976, Reagan believed that there was a large conservative constituency in the nation. By expressing this belief publicly, he was able to identify supporters, demonstrate a continuing interest in politics, and show a commitment to an ideology. Such an approach allowed Reagan to campaign for an idea rather than himself, thus resulting in greater media success and name recognition.

Late in 1976, Reagan started a radio show broadcasting to over one hundred stations and a newspaper column that was syndicated nationally. This allowed Reagan to keep his views before the public as a "working citizen."

After the 1976 presidential campaign, Reagan had over $1.2 million left over. He used these funds to help "friendly" Republican candidates in the 1978 midterm elections as well as as a base for his 1980 presidential contest. In 1977 alone, Reagan visited 75 cities, delivered over 150 speeches, and always avoided any hint of running in 1980. Also, speaking as a "noncandidate," Jimmy Carter could not respond to Reagan's numerous attacks. Thus, by 1978, Reagan had nurtured a constituency, enlarged his political base, cemented relations with the media, and collected many political I.O.U.s. By 1980, of course, Reagan had become the man to beat. His image and issue concerns were firmly established in the minds of the public.

The lesson is clear—start early, organize early (in every state), and try to be so far ahead that no one can reach you. Only two weeks after Reagan's inauguration in 1981, former Vice-President Walter Mondale formed a political action committee and began raising funds for the 1984 contest. Although most of the candidates for both parties had standing fund-raising committees, exploratory presidential committees started as early as 1986 for the 1988 campaign. For example, Bush's committee was created in February 1987; Dukakis's in March 1987, Du Pont's in June 1986; Kemp's in December 1986; Robertson's in August 1986; and Hart's in December 1986, to name a few.

This "exhibition season," according to Cook, begins the day after the general election to the start of the primary and caucus season some three years later. The primary activities include organization, fund-raising, and addressing various interests groups.[23] Those candidates of national stature can raise money quickly, thus allowing more time for campaigning. In terms of money, the 1987 front runners were Bush ($18.1 million), Robertson ($14.2 million), Dole ($13.2 million), and Dukakis ($10.2 million).[24]

Late in the preprimary period, Judith Trent recognized the ritualistic and crucial first act of "presidential surfacing."[25] For Trent, presidential surfacing is a series of rather specific, predictable, and planned rhetorical transactions that serve both consummatory and instrumental functions during the preprimary phase of a presidential campaign. Surfacing activities include: building state organizations; speaking before public groups and formal gatherings; conducting public opinion, attitude, and issue research; developing a formal campaign strategy; raising money; and maintaining media contacts for early exposure. Such activities become even more pronounced from the first day of the election year to the New Hampshire primary.

During the surfacing period, many of the activities are symbolic and ritualistic in nature. It provides the candidate an opportunity to appear presidential, confront various groups and issues, and to demonstrate fitness for the office. Ritualistically, every candidate must call a press conference, make an official public announcement of his intention, and officially embark on the campaign trail to capture the party's nomination. But there are equally important instrumental or pragmatic functions during the surfacing period. The mass media are introduced to the candidate, public expectations are established, campaign issues and themes emerge, and serious contenders are identified.

There are several essential factors or elements that are common to all candidates and cut across all phases of a presidential campaign.[26] The elements are: opinion polls, media, image, electoral rules, organization, and finance. These common elements, however, differ rather dramatically in terms of rhetorical functions and impact across the preprimary, primary, and general election phases of a presidential campaign.

Public Opinion Polls

As noted in Chapter 3, public opinion polls have become a permanent feature of U.S. electoral politics. For candidates in the preprimary period, they are used to determine voter attitudes and candidate image. They provide the primary guidance, especially on the local level, for candidate issue and image development. Thus, they are conducted frequently and are highly personalized. During this period, a disproportionate share of funds is used for polling than for media commercials and organization. The media's use of the polls during the preprimary period will be discussed in the next section.

Media

Because voter resistance to political messages is low, the media may well play their most important role during this phase of a campaign. At no other point of the campaign are attitudes and opinions more vulnerable to change.

There are three elements of media that impact the candidates during the preprimary period. First, because the media have so little time or space to report the news, they use labels to define candidates and their campaign. These labels appear early in a campaign and seldom disappear. The use of labels can either help or hurt the image or reputation of specific candidates. Second, the media play the very important role of "the great mentioner." Candidates need free coverage at both the local and national levels. Staffs expend a great deal of energy devising tactics to create media attention for their candidate. Of course, past reputation and recognition make the job easier. Finally, public opinion polls provide the basis for media coverage of the various candidates. These early polls conducted by the news organizations or provided to them by candidates help set the agenda for the campaigns. Specifically the media use them to determine issues for story development, to create voter expectations about candidates (which influences voting), and to create the drama of the "horse race" by identifying the front runner.

Image

Robert Savage identified five areas essential to the creation and maintenance of a "presidential" image.[27] The role of "timing" the preprimary period focuses on emerging and announcing the candidacy. There is always the risk of entering the race too soon or too late. In the former case, public apathy may result and in the latter there may be too little time to raise funds and generate adequate support. In creating a "rhetorical vision," the candidate must develop and articulate the theme for the campaign. The "campaign theme" extends beyond specific issues and allows the candidate to share his or her vision of America and the American dream. The "rhetorical agenda," which is part of the rhetorical vision, consists of key issues the candidate will focus on during the campaign. These issues, of course, are based on polls and in the early campaign are localized to maximize impact. "Campaign rituals" during this period include fund-raising events. The rituals function to create media attention, meet the voters and build group support, and actually help the candidate to sharpen skills for the primary period to follow. Finally, perhaps the most difficult element of candidate image to define and demonstrate is that of "presidential timber." It is essential that the public perceive the candidate to be a "statesman" and a credible candidate. This is done by exhibiting knowledge and expertise as well as taking trips abroad or introducing special legislation. Thus image in the preprimary period is one of creation, definition, and demonstration, rather than reinforcing as we will see in the later stages of the campaign.

Electoral Rules/Reforms

Many of the above elements function the way they do because of the rule changes and party reforms for presidential nomination. For Democrats, there were no winner-take-all primaries in 1988. Candidates could win delegates in every state but had to establish an organization and conduct an active campaign in all primary states. This required an early start, volunteer recruitment, and money. Also, with the increase of official delegates, candidates appealed to and dealt with independents and established party bosses for control of delegates. And, of course, the Super Tuesday Southern Primary greatly influenced the preprimary campaign. Because of the number of delegates at stake and the timing of the primary, it was argued that all candidates had to start early, address southern issues and concerns resulting in a more conservative southern agenda, run national network commercials, and rely upon PACs for support. A poor showing early meant difficulty in raising funds and maintaining supporters later. The rules of the game obviously impact rhetorical strategies and tactics.

Organization

As already implied, rule changes impact campaign organization formation. In the preprimary period, organizations need to be established whose task is primarily fund-raising in every state. Although campaign organizations need to be established very early, there is little time to conduct a grass roots campaign. It is difficult for candidates to build support throughout the entire primary season. There is too little time between major primaries. Thus, the early organization and staff must be sophisticated and professional. Critical skills are organization, fund-raising, canvassing, and media relations. Public volunteers are not as critical as in past primary elections. In short, one must win the early primaries, not just participate to receive name recognition.

Finance

As with most other things in life, campaigns have become very expensive. But what is important to recognize is the fact that the preprimary period has become more critical and expensive than the primary period and, in some cases, even the general election. The rule changes have not only increased the length of campaigns but also the costs. Organizational demands require great sums of money. The battles for money are conducted in the preprimary period rather than the primary period. Thus, political action committees (PACs) are the most important source of revenue for candidates. Citizen grass roots fund-raising requires too much time to be effective and meet the funding demands of campaigns.

Much of the preprimary campaign is not seen by the average citizen but begins two to three years before the first primary. In fact, the presidential contest is an ongoing process. To become president takes both time and money. For some scholars, this is not a cause for alarm. An individual who wishes to be president must demonstrate desire, determination, sincerity, and fortitude. But much of the process is false. The issues, image, and person are created in carefully prescribed and predetermined ways. Nevertheless, the preprimary period is a vital part of the total campaign and serves both symbolic and pragmatic purposes.

Primary Period

Presidential primaries, in terms of number and importance, are a rather recent phenomenon. In fact, prior to 1972, running in too many primaries was considered a sign of weakness rather than strength. In 1952, Democratic Senator Estes Kefauver entered 13 primaries, won 12 of them, but was still denied the nomination. John Kennedy, in 1960, ran in only four primaries to demonstrate that he could draw Protestant voters. And even as recently as 1968, as already noted, Hubert Humphrey won the Democratic nomination without entering a single primary.

Today, of course, primaries are a vital part of the total presidential campaign.

In fact, it is virtually impossible today to only enter a few select primaries and be successful. By 1980, according to Bartels, the concept of momentum, "the demonstration effect of important primary victories," was institutionalized.[28] Al Gore learned the importance of this lesson in the 1988 presidential campaign. His primary strategy was to bypass Iowa and New Hampshire and wait until "Super Tuesday" in March to test his strength. Although he won six state primaries in early March, it was too little, too late. He was perceived as only a regional candidate. Dukakis won 19 out of the 34 primaries.

Primaries, according to Kathleen Kendall, are "rituals of rebellion" which ultimately serve to release conflict and emotions that will result in cohesion and consensus.[29] Each primary is a localized contest with a national audience observing the game. Primaries define issues, identify groups, and test the fabric of the individual candidate. Although there are numerical winners and losers, it is the process of the symbolic battles that defines the candidate and creates public expectations of behavior. From a communication perspective, then, it is not the specific issues or general strategies used to win the localized contests that are most important. Rather, it is how the candidates position themselves in relation to the outcomes of the contest. Are they winners or losers? Front runners or also rans? Gaining momentum or declining in appeal? Achieving upsets or predictable levels of performance?

Thus, there is a rather specified ritual associated with each primary contest. The candidates must confront each other (either rhetorically or face-to-face), meet the public (to press the flesh), predict the outcome of the immediate and ultimate contest, and interpret the results. Each aspect is very important in creating and reinforcing the image of the candidate. The first two elements are obvious in terms of their importance. The importance of the latter two elements is perhaps less obvious.

Predicting the outcome of a primary contest has several functions. It gives the candidate exposure to the press and allows the candidate to reinforce desired image perceptions of winner, presidential material, front runner, and so on. It also gives the candidate the opportunity to predict modestly and then to look better than predictions. In short, it allows the candidate the opportunity to shape preprimary election expectations. Finally, predicting the outcome helps to generate interest in the election and, it is hoped, increase voter turnout.

Dwight Freshley argues that there are three "rhetorical laws" of primaries.[30] First, candidates will play down their chances for winning a primary or their take of the vote so if they receive more than predicted, candidates can claim victory regardless of the results of the primary. The second rhetorical law of primaries is what Freshley calls the "40 percent law." The underdog candidate will be declared a winner if he receives over 40 percent of the vote in a two-person race. Finally, Freshley argues that the postprimary comments will take one of four positions. The specific interpretation of the win depends upon how many primaries won or lost, time of primary season, margin of victory, and number of delegates at stake. A second position a participant can take is to make it appear that the winner fell short of goal and prediction. Another position a candidate can take is to confirm preprimary predictions and stress that the candidate is viable, successful, and gaining momentum. Finally, if a candidate comes in third or greater, some explanation of losing must be provided. Usually such an explanation is one of "can't win them all," "expected all along to lose," or complete candor that one did not do well and congratulate the winner.

Postprimary comments and interpretations of results are another way of getting voters involved in the election. By completing the immediate event they also set the stage and tone for the next contest or rematch. Postprimary comments also provide additional media coverage for candidates to make national proclamations.

Of course, the timing of the primary influences the rhetorical stance a candidate takes. The Iowa caucus and the New Hampshire primary, as the first popularity contests, are most important. To survive, candidates must either win, place, or show in the events. In recent history, the New Hampshire primary has served as the springboard for long-shot candidates such as McGovern in 1972, Carter in 1976, and even Dukakis in 1988. It can make candidacies credible, as in the case of Hart in 1984 and Gephardt in 1988, or, if candidates receive more votes than expected, make candidates moral winners as were McCarthy in 1968 and McGovern in 1972. However, the New Hampshire primary has an impact far out of proportion to its size and demographics. In 1988, New Hampshire only provided 22 out of 4162 convention delegates for the Democrats and 23 out of 2277 Republican convention delegates; a combined total of less than 1 percent of the nation's delegates. In addition, only 276,634 people voted in the New Hampshire primary, about a third of those eligible to vote. In fact, only 24 percent of the eligible voters took part in all the national primaries. Thus, the importance of many primaries is not in terms of actual numbers of voters or delegate counts but in the national exposure, public posturing, and perceptions of winning and momentum.

For each presidential election there appears to be an increasing number of candidates—especially in the party not in the White House. In 1980 there were four Republican candidates and in 1976 four Democratic candidates. In 1984, there were seven Democratic candidates. Actually, by December of 1983, over 125 candidates had filed with the Federal Election Commission. For the 1988 contest, there were six Republican candidates and eight Democratic candidates. Nevertheless, such large numbers of candidates require them to differentiate themselves based upon aspects of personal image rather than issues. The simple truth is that there are not enough issues or positions on issues to separate a wide field of candidates. Carter, in 1976, was masterful at projecting a personal image of honesty, goodness, and the common man. Even in the 1980 primaries Carter stressed character in his ads as "husband, father, president." Edward Kennedy stressed leadership—not his controversial liberal views on many domestic issues.

Within the primary period, there does exist a unique situation when an incumbent is challenged for the nomination. The incumbent usually emphasizes the fact that he represents the party and to deny him the nomination would indeed divide the party and hence jeopardize the election. The incumbent also usually argues that severe attacks upon the president are, in effect, attacks upon the nation. This is indeed a strong appeal. Not since 1856 when James Buchanan replaced Franklin Pierce has a president who sought renomination failed to receive the approval from his party. The power of the incumbent cannot be overestimated. On the eve of the New Hampshire primary in 1980, Carter had the U.S. Olympic hockey team that defeated the Soviet team visit the White House. Much favorable press resulted. In addition, for example, on the mornings of the Wisconsin and Kansas primaries, Carter made a public announcement of a "positive step" toward the release of the U.S. hostages in Iran—a very hot political problem for Carter.[31]

Challenges to the president will usually claim that the incumbent is not providing the leadership needed by the nation. They will also argue that the president is so weak that all the party candidates will go down in defeat in the November election. Finally, most challengers will also charge that the president did not keep promises made in the last election. In 1980, this charge was consistently made by Kennedy against Carter.

It is useful once again to view the roles and functions of the elements identified earlier in the primary campaign period.

Public Opinion Polls

Instead of issue formation and candidate positioning, public opinion polls in the primary period are the means of monitoring the various races. They are conducted with greater frequency and provide the appearance of a fluid, dynamic, and everchanging public. Polls, however, have a significant impact upon the specific primaries. A change in the polls directly correlates with the media's verdict of winners and losers. Candidates must now play to the polls even more than to the public. They must explain, justify, and even counter poll results. Media labels and the daily rankings make it essential for candidates to run well in the polls during this period.

Media

Media's role is greatly expanded during the primary period. Major candidates no longer must actively seek media to gain access or coverage. They now must be more concerned with presentation and media portrayal. Candidate coverage consists of three dimensions. First, the media focus on the style and personality of candidates. Public demeanor and presentation becomes equal in importance to message content. Second, the media focus more on human interest stories of the candidates than issue debate and exploration. The rituals of campaigning are followed because they are dramatic, colorful, and simply make for "good television." Finally, while media coverage is expanded; stories, issues, and primary results are simplified. As the pace of the period increases, the focus is on campaign activities rather than issue analysis and candidate comparisons.

The media also become much more judgmental during the primary period. As winners and losers are identified, the media provide momentum for some candidates and political death for others. The front runner emerges more quickly through media coverage than through actual votes cast in the primaries. By focusing on certain primaries, the media enhance the victory or loss of candidates. Thus it is more important to win in publicized primaries than in primaries that receive little attention. A vicious circle emerges: lose media coverage and lose primaries; lose primaries and lose media coverage. The task becomes, therefore, to create strength in the polls during the preprimary period to gain media attention during the primary period that will hopefully translate to victories.

Image

Image maintenance and exposure become the goals of the primary period. Television is the best medium to portray the presidential image. It can, however, distort or even destroy a carefully nurtured image. Public presentations as shown on television become critical in maintaining the desired image. Winning, as already mentioned, provides favorable and frequent media coverage which also attracts campaign funds. Thus, the winner image is as valuable as the presidential image during this period.

Electoral Rules/Reforms

For politicians, rule changes impact the preprimary period more than the primary period. Front runners are favored. Early winners are virtually guaranteed the nomination. In terms of the public, candidate explanations of performance are critical. Candidates now demonstrate their vote getting strength and personal popularity.

Organization

Certainly by this time, candidate organization must not only be well established but also running at full speed. The tasks remain of "damage control" and "getting out the vote." In contrast to the preprimary period, the candidates' organizations should not be a major concern because it is too late to make major changes in staff without severe consequences. The various strategies and tactics are implemented with little time for testing. Strong staff personalities become the key decision makers. Volunteer help now plays an important role in getting people to the polls.

Finance

As the primary season begins, the emphasis for raising funds shifts from candidate political action committees to the public sector. Because of finance spending regulations, the major concern during this period is the strategy of funding allocations. Is the decision to spend nearly all funds on the early primaries hoping that winning will generate more funds or save funds for later primaries with fewer competitors assuming a strong showing in the earlier ones? This question illustrates how various strategies impact funding decisions. Big winners have little difficulty in raising funds. Thus financial concerns during the primary period are strategic and internal rather than public and corporate fund raising appeals.

The presidential primaries today are most important. They make or break a campaign. The rhetorical strategies are vast, but the structure and stance of the ritualized conflict are predictable and prescribed. Election interpretations and presentations are most important during this period.

The Conventions

Political conventions really serve three functions. They, of course, officially nominate the party's candidate. Conventions also unify the party for both local and national candidates. And, perhaps most importantly, conventions provide a free forum to present the candidate's issues and image to those watching the proceedings on television. With the increase in the number of primaries, the convention is no longer a political party affair but a candidate's bash. The nominee is the star and focus of attention. The entire convention serves as center stage for the nominee and can provide a good beginning for the official campaign. Thus, a deadlocked convention may be a spectator's dream, but it is a candidate's nightmare. Division, debate, and controversy may provide excitement but contribute little to unity, loyalty, and the reinforcement of candidate image. In 1988, both Bush and Dukakis delivered the speeches of their careers securing lifts in the polls and favorable media reports. Thus, from a communication perspective, the more the eventual nominee of the party can control the agenda, speakers, rallies, and so on, the better the convention serves the candidate.

The Campaign

At the microscopic level, each presidential campaign is a unique historical event. Each possesses its own cast of characters, issues, conflicts, and contexts. A presidential campaigned, according to James Barber, "is a rousing call to arms. Candidates mobilize their forces for showdowns and shootouts, blasting each other with rhetorical volleys. It is a risky adventure; its driving force is surprise, as the fortunes of combat deliver setbacks and breakthroughs contrary to the going expectation, and the contenders struggle to recover and exploit the sudden changes."[32] Yet, from a macroscopic level, modern presidential campaigns are all very similar. There are a limited number of issues, images, tactics, and strategies available for any campaign. In fact, Barber even argues that "from the turn of the century to present day, three themes have dominated successive campaign years: politics as conflict, politics as conscience, and politics as conciliation. That sequence runs its course over a twelve year period and then starts over again."[33] Thus, there are strong similarities in all presidential campaigns. The role and nature of communication is the structure that provides for the commonalities. In this section we will consider the role of communication in determining candidate campaign strategy and techniques.

The Role of Marketing

In Chapter 3 the importance and role of the political consultants were discussed in great detail. Suffice to say that presidential politics are big business, complicated and high tech. Politics has changed from an art to a science. Especially with the supreme importance of the mass media, politicians are utilizing marketing techniques and research tools. Gary Mauser argues that candidates and marketers have the same basic problems and goals. They both are competing for the support of a specified, target group under the constraints of time, money and personnel.[34] It is rather natural, then, for politicians to utilize the techniques of product marketing for election campaigns. This development, according to Jack Honomichl, reached a new high during Ronald Reagan's 1979 presidential campaign.[35] It was, from a marketing standpoint, the most sophisticated and well-funded research program in the history of U.S. politics and provided the blueprint for the 1984 election and Bush's 1988 campaign.

Reagan's 1979 presidential bid was based on a marketing plan developed by Richard Wirthlin, president of the firm Decision Making Information (DMI). He developed a 176-page strategy statement that became the bible of the campaign.[36]

In addition to the normal national polling of attitudes, DMI budgeted $1.5 million for four major national studies and continual tracking studies in nine pivotal states.[37] As early as June 1979, a major psychographic study was conducted to help understand the motives underlying people's attitudes and opinions.[38] Until this time, most politicians relied upon simple attitude surveys, voter characteristics, and demographics for voter profiles. The main conclusion of the study was that Reagan voters obtained high scores on the scales for: respect for authority, individualism, authoritarianism, and a low score on egalitarianism. Also, the study revealed that Democrats over age 55 shared the same characteristics and thus were a prime target for conversion. The study also identified three groups of people Reagan should address: employed head-of-household Democrats, 35 years of age, earning less than $15,000 a year; voters who prefer Reagan over Carter and Edward Kennedy; and voters who switched to Edward Kennedy in the Democratic presidential primaries. This last group would, on the surface, appear to be nonsense. Why would anyone who would vote for a Democratic liberal ultimately vote for a self-professed Republican conservative? Actually, the study revealed that people who vacillated between Carter and Kennedy really did not have strong ideological positions since the two were so different themselves.

Although traditional polling identified a list of pressing national problems, DMI early ascertained that the electorate really wanted a positive view of the future. In order to win, the candidates had to change the electorate's perceptions of the future. Thus, when Carter chose to make Reagan the main issue, he

virtually lost the election. This conclusion was based on a study of voter expectations conducted in June prior to the conventions and main campaign period.[39] The study revealed that when voters were asked to name something bad
that would happen if Reagan were elected, 72 percent named something, but in
terms of Carter, 83 percent named something. If people, then, simply voted
based upon their expectations of the future, Reagan would win the election.

The point is rather obvious. Often it is not concrete issues that win elections
but the images, visions, and persona communicated to the electorate. And the
use of marketing techniques goes beyond the simple identification of key issues
or public concerns. Rather, they help to focus on the subtle likes and dislikes
as well as motivations for human behavior in rather quantifiable terms.

Channels of Communication and Communication Strategy

There are four basic communication channels: the electronic media, the print
media, display media (i.e., billboards, etc.), and personal contact. It is a most
difficult task to determine the best combination of media to reach the potential
audience and that which best communicates the desired theme. In addition, the
factors of timing, money, and distribution are also important considerations.
Candidates must decide when and where they will concentrate their communication efforts making sure that they do not peak too soon or spend too much in
areas of little consequence.

To determine the communication strategy, the target audience must be identified and segmented. This includes both committed loyalist and potential voters.
Next, most campaigns attempt to "map" voter perceptions. The goal here is to
identify the ways voters classify the candidates and issues viewed as important
in the decision process.

A great deal of time is also spent on identifying and characterizing the competition. By mapping voter preferences, candidates can better identify specific
strengths, weaknesses, and likely patterns of competition. From all this information, various strategies can be identified, discussed, and evaluated. Ultimately,
a budget is allocated, a strategy determined, time and content of appeals isolated,
and a detailed media and marketing plan established.

But despite all this activity, there is a high degree of homogeneity in the
political perceptions of the American people.[40] It is difficult for well-known
politicians to radically alter their image once it has become fixed in the minds
of the public. There is little advertising can do to drastically change or convert
voter perceptions, beliefs, and attitudes. Thus, most strategies seek to reinforce
and link campaigns to existing perceptions, beliefs, and attitudes.

There is a standard, well-known marketing and advertising dictum. Products
compete best against each other as long as they are perceived as being similar
to each other. As Mauser observes, "the patterns of competition for any new
product can be predicted from its pattern of perceived similarity with the other
products in the markets."[41] Thus, challengers must appear presidential, and

presidents must act presidential. With this in mind, Mauser argues that the
following communication strategies are probably most effective.[42]

1. Stress importance of features that are most attractive to target electorate.

2. Avoid, or state euphemistically, the features that are deemed to be undesirable.

3. Coordinate all information and advertising to reinforce the most important features of
   the candidate.

4. If possible, attempt to move the candidate along those dimensions that can place him
   in an advantageous position.

Campaign Strategies

Public Statements about Strategies

There is a rather clear distinction, as Henry Ewbank observes, between campaign strategies and public statements about campaign strategies.[43] Public statements about campaign strategies come from three sources: the candidate, the
candidate's spokesperson, or from an opponent. Often strategy statements result
from a direct challenge by an opponent, the media, or a specific voting bloc of
citizens. Sometimes, in an effort to gain media attention or redefine the campaign
issues, a candidate will provide a statement articulating a position or campaign
strategy. Most public strategy statements deal with specific actions to be taken
if elected, feelings or emotions relevant to the current state of affairs, and
intentions relating to the execution of the campaign. The latter serves to establish
appearances of fairness, openmindedness, and honesty. The themes of most
public statements about strategy are twofold: consistency and uniqueness. Consistency is related in terms of how the candidate will meet the needs and expectations of the public, and uniqueness is related in terms of how the candidate
will provide new leadership and new solutions to old problems.

For Ewbank, strategy statements can be classified in five ways according to
apparent intent:

1. offering an interpretation of a past great event,

2. offering an explanation of current campaign events,

3. offering a description of the future,

4. soliciting reaction to some aspect of the campaign that may serve as a "trial balloon"
   for future reference, and

5. construction of a desired perception of an event or issue position that is about to
   become a visible part of a campaign.

The most public view of strategy, from a communication standpoint, is candidate discussion of issues. Critics and scholars claim that with each contemporary campaign, true issues become less salient and less understood. For some,

1988 was the epitome of the "issueless" presidential election.[44] Peter Jennings proclaimed that "the circumstances of history made this a campaign of no issues, no passion and no substance and thus inevitably a campaign of little verve. . . . To be sure, there could have been real issues, even in a period of peace and prosperity . . . but the political realities are such that none of these issues was addressed with anything more than rhetoric, rhetoric which all but the most naive could immediately spot as empty."[45] Bush was largely accused of campaigning on emotional appeals such as prison furloughs, the Pledge of Allegiance, and abortion. Dukakis promised to protect the homeless, to provide jobs, to provide educational opportunities, to protect the environment, and to provide affordable day-care without ever addressing the scope and source of funding for such endeavors.

But issues, from a communication perspective, should not be viewed as abstract or complicated constructions. They are simply what concerns the voters illustrated in concrete examples. Jean Elshtain is correct when she argues there is no real difference between "real" or "symbolic/rhetorical" issues. "To claim, then that candidates are trafficking in nonissues because they immerse themselves in weighty symbolism is to presume that which does not exist—a clear-cut division between the symbolic and the real, between issues and emotional appeals. . . . Thus, the speeches and symbols and rhetorical acts of our presidential candidates are co-authored by 'we the people,' depending upon how we receive their efforts."[46] And one cannot distinguish between "rational" issues and "emotional" issues because even the issue of abortion may be based upon the tenets of a religion or interpretation of the Constitution. Audience response is the key. The real question may be whether or not citizens understand the scope, complexity, or relevance of some issues like the Minute-Man missile, Star Wars, support of the Contras, and so on. Perhaps, as Elshtain observes, the way issues are constructed becomes the issue.

A strategy is a way to achieve an objective or goal. In politics, the goal is to win the election. To do this, of course, requires getting individuals to become committed to one's candidacy, and then, of equal importance, to actually vote in the election. This is indeed a long, complicated process. No single variable, issue, event, or personal characteristic can motivate enough people to become committed and to vote in sufficient numbers to win an election. Likewise, no single strategy can win an election. But we argue that there are a limited number of communication approaches or strategies in which to articulate and motivate voters. Thus, to a large extent, specific issues, candidates, and elections are not of great importance. What is important is whether or not the candidate is an incumbent or challenger.

Incumbent Strategies

Judith Trent and Robert Friedenberg have identified several incumbent campaign strategies.[47] It is useful to review those strategies. An incumbent has many more strategy options than challengers. Some of the strategies involve maximizing the symbolic, subtle aspects of the office. Incumbents are certain to surround themselves with the purely symbolic trappings of the office. Such trappings include the use of the presidential podium and seal, "Hail to the Chief," and various official backdrops. Such devices communicate the strength and grandeur of the office. They serve to remind the audience that they are listening to the President of the United States and not just an average citizen. It is not surprising, therefore, that in April of 1984, President Reagan changed the location of his televised press conferences. He stood before an open doorway in the East Room of the White House that reveals a long, elegant corridor. The cameras record a majestic setting and a stately exit that dramatizes the importance of the office. In addition to the physical artifacts that enhance the prestige of the incumbent, the office itself evokes a sense of legitimacy, competency, and charisma to its occupant. Any individual who holds the office is perceived as rational, intelligent, and is granted deference. The pageantry, history, and majesty of the office is transferred to its occupant. In a campaign, such perceptions are worth a great deal.

Presidents have immediate and almost total access to the media. It is very easy for them to create pseudoevents for the purpose of gaining favorable media exposure. Such pseudoevents include making special announcements, appointments, or proclamations that have more political impact than policy impact. When Reagan visited South Korea, his aides ensured that he was surrounded by barbed wire and sandbags. In fact, they had an armored vehicle placed in the background when he spoke to the troops.[48] Although Reagan stayed for just one inning at the opening day of the baseball season in Baltimore, he was seen the next day in the media throwing a ball and eating a hot dog in the dugout.

During the campaign period, presidents make many appointments to jobs and special committees. This is a way to line up supporters early in the campaign, tap talent for the reelection bid, and identify people for key positions after the election. Also reports of special task forces are usually revealed during the campaign period. Task forces are effective ways to address special issues or concerns of the voters without committing resources or personal support. The very act of forming a task force communicates concern about an issue and the promise of future action. Actually, it allows the candidate to postpone taking a stand on controversial issues while at the same time making an appeal to a particular group of voters.

An incumbent president will appropriate billions of dollars to "cooperative" public officials for cities and projects in return for support. By the 1980 election, Carter had given over $80 billion in the form of federal grants.

Without doubt, incumbent presidents will visit world leaders during an election year. Such trips provide great drama and show the president as a world leader respected by other countries. The foreign visits also provide a repertoire of future references that can be worked in debates and discourse to reinforce notions of leadership and experience. How ironic indeed in 1980 when President Reagan, who spent most of his political career opposing the Chinese Communists, not only visited mainland China but offered U.S. economic and technological assistance. But most important, the trip was a television spectacular. Michael Deaver, a presidential aide, spent nine days in China scouting locations for the president to visit.[49] The Republican National Committee sent a special film crew to record footage to be used in political commercials. Even Reagan's itinerary was influenced by the potential of media coverage. A trip down the Yangtze River was canceled because there was no way to get the tapes to the networks for showing.[50]

Incumbent presidents have the opportunity to manipulate domestic issues. This is done in two ways. First, presidents can divert or lessen the impact of news by creating competing pseudoevents. For example, the day unemployment climbed to 10 percent in 1982, Reagan called a press conference to announce the suspension of Poland's status as a most-favored nation. Another way to manipulate domestic issues is to take short-term actions that will provide at least a temporary impact. This is especially true in the economic realm. Usually, by election time, interest rates and inflation are down. In fact, the stock market has gone down only six times in the 21 years in which presidential elections were held since 1900.[51] The reason is fairly simple. Administrations in the final two years of a term focus on economic expansion to enhance the party's reelection endeavors.

A strategy that is especially useful for incumbent presidents is to obtain the public endorsements of local respected, successful, and well-liked politicians. Here the candidate is trying to link himself with already established leaders.

Presidents can also use surrogates to campaign for them. Popular members from the administration or locals who are part of the administration can have a very positive effect upon a campaign. Simply because of the daily job requirements, nearly all presidents are forced to rely upon the help of others during the campaign season. In 1972, Nixon used over 50 surrogates, and in the midterm elections of 1982, the Republican National Committee developed a program called "Surrogate 82" where all cabinet members were required to give 15 days to campaign activities. During the 1980 presidential campaign, Carter was forced to use surrogates because of his statement that he would not campaign while Americans were still held as hostages in Iran. As their length of captivity lengthened, Carter had to rescind his statement. There is a limit to the use of surrogates. The American public expects candidates to travel and press the flesh—up to a point. An incumbent president must not appear to be neglecting the job of running the country. Thus the use of surrogates best complements the campaigning of an incumbent president rather than replacing it.

Somewhat related, most incumbents try to create the image that they are above the political battle and removed from the day-to-day charges and countercharges of politics. Early presidents, as already noted, seldom actively participated in campaigns or even attended the party conventions. Such participation appeared undignified and unstatesmanlike. In contemporary times, the extreme of such a strategy is called the "Rose Garden" strategy. Very strong candidates can stay at the White House appearing presidential, committed, and serious. Gerald Ford used this strategy in 1976 until it was clear that he faced stiff competition from Jimmy Carter.

Nearly all presidents claim that reelection will communicate to the world a sense of stability. Most incumbents intensify their description of foreign policy problems to create an illusion of crisis to motivate voters to rally around and support the administration. Franklin Roosevelt was most successful using this strategy. History has shown that regardless of the crisis, Americans offer support to their leaders rather than condemnation.

Finally, the major strategy of every incumbent president is to emphasize administration accomplishments. They must demonstrate tangible results to promises made or problems solved. If not, they must deny problems are problems or clearly place blame on a single individual or group. Actions often speak louder than results. To propose a constitutional amendment to balance the budget even though such a proposal would never be taken seriously is to at once fulfill a campaign promise and to place blame if not accepted. For every action, there is an official interpretation that must be provided.

In 1988, Bush enjoyed many of the advantages of an incumbent. Of course, there was established name recognition, plenty of money, and the support of a popular president who campaigned for him. In addition, Bush was visible in official capacities during the long election campaign. We saw him appearing in ads with foreign dignitaries and the dramatic appearance of Bush with Reagan and Gorbachev at the steps of the Statue of Liberty. And, of course, no one could deny his governmental experience.

Despite the appearance of an almost limitless number of strategy options, Trent and Friedenberg are correct in claiming that there are several major dis-advantages of incumbency campaigning.[52] First, as already mentioned, every president must run on his record. All actions or interactions must be explained and justified. Naturally, the challenger will blame the incumbent for all ills and problems of the nation. As the total presidential campaign period lengthens, challengers literally have years to question, second-guess, and negate the efforts of the current president. In the real world and especially in politics, there are seldom complete victories. Most victories are partial and it becomes demoralizing for every effort to be criticized or questioned. Finally, the media create a climate of expectations, conflict, and excitement during a campaign. There is a great deal of pressure associated with being the incumbent. America traditionally favors the underdog and a good fight. Thus, there are more restrictions on behavior and performance pressure associated with the incumbent than with the challengers.

Challenger Strategies

When campaigning against an incumbent president, challengers must take the offensive position in a campaign. Every action, issue, and stance of the president is questioned, challenged, and sometimes ridiculed. This often goes beyond simply attacking the record of the incumbent. The probing and questioning seldom results in the presenting of concrete solutions. John Kennedy never provided the details to the New Frontier nor Nixon on how he would end the war in Vietnam nor Reagan on how he would end inflation. In fact, being too specific can lead to counter-questions and attacks. For example, in 1972 McGovern provided the details of a tax plan and guaranteed income that caused many problems. Mondale's call for higher taxes virtually ended any hopes for a close race in 1984.

Most of the time, challengers call for a change—a change in direction and leadership. They emphasize optimism for the future and share a vision of future prosperity and peace. Challengers focus their appeals on traditional values as Carter did in 1976 (honesty, self-rule, humility, morality) and Reagan did in 1980 and 1984 (free enterprise, capitalism, democracy, and moral courage).

Challengers must create constituency groups and will always claim to speak for the forgotten American, the silent majority, and middle America. This transforms into a strategy of articulating the values and feelings of an average American. The philosophical center is the road to follow.

The importance and functions of the essential elements of a campaign change again rather drastically during the general election phase.

Public Opinion Polls

There are two types of polling done during the general campaign phase. The various media polls are primarily concerned with the "horse race" of who's ahead. For the candidate, however, the tracking polls are important in terms of directing where to campaign. Key regions and states may be critical to electoral success and thus where to spend time campaigning is more important than the overall picture. Also, the polls continue to monitor strength and weaknesses of various events, appeals, and issues.

Media

A great deal of attention was given to this element in Chapter 3 from the candidate perspective. The political advertising during the general election is focused on issues and salient appeals. Toward the end of the campaign there will be a personal appeal for votes by the candidates. The candidate seeks to give reasons for voters to vote for the candidate and attempts to maintain those committed to the candidate.

The popular media is primarily concerned with who is winning and covering the daily events of candidates and running mates. Candidates, of course, are mindful of getting the right sound bites for the evening news. The pending election dominates media attention.

Image

At this phase of the campaign, candidate image and perceptions are set. At best all activities and paid media attempt to reinforce the desired image. Public events, such as debates, can impact image now more than advertising. Although a great deal of effort is placed on maintaining a consistent and clearly defined image, the possibilities of great change are slim.

Electoral Rules/Reforms

Both candidates now play under the same rules. The major impact upon strategy is the electoral college which, depending upon candidate strengths and weaknesses, will dictate where each candidate will spend most of his or her time. In 1988, for example, Bush wanted to hold the Republican base in the South and Mountain West as well as campaign hard to win the states of Ohio, Michigan, Illinois, and California. Dukakis wanted to capture Texas, contest the border states, win the Pacific Coastal states, and secure the Northeast and upper Mid-west.

Organization

As was the case in the primary campaign period, candidate organization must be well established and running at full speed. Momentum carries the organization during this phase. Internal cooperation and coordination are critical during this period. Staff indecision and conflict can be most harmful. Many attribute such difficulties to the Dukakis staff in 1988. As noted in Chapter 3, there was much disagreement as to how to answer the Bush campaign attacks. Dukakis, after the campaign, admitted that he probably waited too long to answer Bush's charges and negative ads.

At the state level, the key activity is getting out the vote.

Finance

By this time there is very little fund-raising activity. The political parties may continue to solicit funds but the budget is set and allocated. Thus, the primary activity is where to spend the money. In 1988, each candidate received $46 million from the Treasury and another $8.3 million from their respective party. Each candidate received over $30 million additional funding from various groups as permitted under federal election laws.

The 1988 Campaign

Bush's election in 1988 was the first time in 152 years that a sitting vice-president was elected president.[53] In fact, only four sitting vice-presidents were elected without first succeeding the incumbent (John Adams, Thomas Jefferson, Martin Van Buren, and George Bush). This election was only the twelfth time we elected a new president who was of the same party as the outgoing one. Thus, in many ways, the 1988 election was special and unique.

On the other hand, it was less than spectacular. Bush got 53.4 percent of the popular vote tying Franklin Roosevelt's percentage for his last election in 1944. Ronald Reagan, as few will recall, only got 50.7 percent of the popular vote his first election against Jimmy Carter.

The actual number of voters decreased by a million, the first time this has happened since 1944. The turnout nationwide of 50.2 percent was the lowest since 1924. In fact, only 26.8 percent of the voting age population selected Bush for president which is about the same as in 1976 and in 1980. So much for the myth of majority rule.

According to the ABC News exit polls, Bush won the election because most voters were happy with the status quo. Of those who voted, 52 percent thought the nation should continue on the Reagan course. Of those who voted for Bush, 47 percent claimed his experience was the reason. Only 14 percent said leadership motivated them to vote for him. For Dukakis, only 28 percent, the highest of all the reasons given, said they voted for him because he cared for people. Clearly these data suggest that Dukakis did not generate a clear image of leadership, competence, or experience to warrant votes. And Bush was successful in highlighting his experience and defining Dukakis as incompetent.

Perhaps most revealing is the fact that, again according to the ABC News exit polls, nearly 50 percent of Bush and Dukakis backers voted the way they did to "stop the other candidate." Indeed, both candidates had high negatives and were less than desirable by the public.

Finally, it also appears that Americans are less than satisfied with the campaign process. Seventy percent of Americans think that a shorter primary campaign would improve the process and 76 percent think that candidates should spend less.[54]

The Campaign Promise

An important feature of American politics is the campaign promise. In theory, an elected official is obligated to fulfill promises made during a campaign as a result of the electoral mandate. Despite jokes about campaign promises, each election generates countless promises from candidates. To demonstrate the seriousness with which they are made, Carter's transition team compiled a 114-page listing of his 1976 campaign promises. But promises are difficult to keep or fulfill. In 1980 Reagan promised to reduce federal spending, to cut federal taxes, to reduce inflation, to balance the federal budget, and to increase defense spending. By 1984, Reagan's federal budget had the highest deficit in American history. Some would argue that the fulfillment of three out of five major campaign promises is not a bad record.Of course, for test purposes that represents a score of 60 percent—a failing mark by most standards. Others would argue that even to promise reduced federal spending and a balanced budget reflects supreme naiveté. But keeping campaign promises is a difficult task and their fulfillment depends upon the cooperation of others. Few promises can be met with a simple presidential declaration.

From a communication perspective, there are four observations about campaign promises. First, the degree of importance attached to a promise depends upon how much the fulfillment of the promise affects each of us. Thus, of the promises made during a campaign, only those relevant to us as a group or as individuals are to be remembered. Second, what constitutes fulfillment of a promise is likely to be an attempted action rather than a complete fulfillment of the promise. To lower inflation by 1 percent is to fulfill the promise of lowering inflation but may be of little real value in real economic terms. The issue of what determines fulfillment of a campaign promise, then, is a matter of interpretation and campaign debate. Third, it is best not to make specific promises that may come back to haunt the candidate in future elections. That's why *value* statements are better than *issue* statements. Finally, there is indeed a rhetoric of campaigning that differs from a rhetoric of governing. One is the rhetoric of hope, promise, and certainty. The other is one of negotiation, persuasion, and compromise.

The Basic Campaign Speech

Local appearances by candidates demand a few appropriate remarks. With the frequency of travel and the nature of national campaigning, candidates develop a set speech that becomes the basis of their remarks for every speaking situation. The basic campaign speech has four purposes.[55] First, the basic speech defines the crucial issues of the campaign. Most issues fall within the areas of policy issues, personal issues, or leadership issues. Issues in campaigns also display similar characteristics. They tend to be very broad, be small in number, lack definition, and are seldom defined in terms that will arouse controversy. Also, campaign issues are often linked to claims about the personal qualities of the opponent. Finally, some issues are indeed localized as education for the South, unemployment for the Northeast, farming for the Midwest, and environmental protection for the West.

The second purpose of a basic campaign address is to identify and emphasize the failures of the opposition. Here past issue positions, actions, and voting records are used to demonstrate either a lack of ability to lead by the opponent or a lack of proper position on the issues by the opponent. The speech must at least attempt to show why the opponent should not obtain the office. Statements concerning actions, positions, or personal characteristics are offered as evidence of failure.

Another important purpose of the basic campaign speech is to appeal to the audience. This is achieved through style and substance of the address. Stylistically, the candidate hopes to use common words and phrases unique to the area. The goal is to give the appearance of being one of the locals, sharing their concerns and speaking their language. Dress is also a part of this process. When speaking to farmers, candidates often wear jeans and open shirts.

Finally, the basic campaign speech offers a vision of the future. The vision is usually a carefully constructed articulation of the American dream: a world of peace, prosperity, justice, and equality. The vision often involves evoking a sense of duty and obligation to make the future better than the present for the sake of our children and grandchildren. The vision portion of the speech need not be logical but rather uplifting and inspiring.

The structure of the basic campaign speech also follows a rather fixed pattern or formula. The speech describes, in general terms, "the problem," fixes blame for "the problem," calls for change, and promises that change will indeed improve the future. Thus, each candidate defines the current state of affairs as one of crisis and blames the current situation on the opponent. The candidate calls for change and the change is, of course, the election of the candidate who will provide a glorious future.

For the basic speech, the writer will depend upon poll data or identified intended audiences for guidance to determine the "hot" issues. Focus groups can be used to test key ideas and phrases as well as to discover the best ways to handle certain issues rhetorically. Often the speech-writing staff will include an audience analysis unit and a research unit.[56]

The basic stump campaign speech is truly a localized affair. The major issues of the campaign have long been decided. But the candidate meeting the public face-to-face has become an important part of presidential politics. Such events, however, hold little interest for the national newspeople traveling with the candidate. They hear the basic speech hundreds of times. What interests them most are the question-and-answer exchanges that follow most addresses. Here the candidate may show unexpected emotion, share a new statement or position, or stimulate some newsworthy event. With an eye toward the evening news, the candidate may begin the address with a timely retort or challenge to the opponent. Thus, although the basic speech is given over and over again, the national audience is unlikely to have heard the speech. The campaign event is new and appears spontaneous to those hearing the candidate in person.

Presidential Campaign Debates

Presidential debates are becoming an expected element of presidential campaigns. Historically, the Lincoln-Douglas debate of 1858 provided the precedence for the debating of political issues. But the Kennedy-Nixon debates of 1960 firmly established the debates as a part of presidential politics. In fact, the 1960 presidential debates attracted the largest television audience (at that point in history) of over 100 million viewers.[57] Incumbent presidents view debating opponents as too risky. Gerald Ford became the first incumbent president to debate his opponent, Jimmy Carter. Four years later, Carter also debated his challenger. In both cases, however, the incumbent lost the election.

Today, not only are debates expected but their format is virtually ritualized. "The moderator introduces. The candidates stand behind podiums. The panel of questioners is seated. Questions will not be timed; answers will be brief. Some provision will exist for rebuttal. Topics will shift drastically from questioner to questioner."[58] Television has had the greatest impact upon the form and content of presidential debates. It made debates less expensive, provided a larger audience, and free media or exposure for the candidates. As a result, debates have become an essential part of a candidate's overall campaign strategy.[59] Thus, today's debates, according to Kathleen Jamieson, are an interesting combination of the old and the new.[60] The common audience, opposing candidates, time limits, right to rebut, and agreed upon rules are vestiges of traditional debate. Multiple topics, question-and-answer formats, and use of "interrogating" reporters are contributions from press conferences. Television technology has contributed various production techniques and time constraints.

Debates have several benefits for the electorate. They provide an opportunity to compare the personalities and issue positions of the candidates in a somewhat spontaneous setting. They also invite serious consideration and attention to the campaign and the candidates, thus stimulating voter interest in the election. And finally, they certainly increase candidate accountability. What they say, support, and promise become a matter of record for future evaluation. But contemporary presidential debates are not as freewheeling or spontaneous as most voters think. They are as planned, rehearsed, and constructed as any other speech, commercial, or public presentation. The candidates place a great deal of importance on the debates. Image definition and confirmation is supreme to issue development and debate.[61]

To get candidates to even debate requires a great deal of negotiation. In the debates of 1976, the issues of lighting, staging, position of cameras, use of reaction shots, camera movement, and the height of the podiums became major points of discussion and negotiation between the candidates prior to agreeing to debate.[62] In the 1980 debates, an issue of discussion was whether or not the candidates would sit or stand. Carter favored sitting while Reagan favored standing. The compromise was to have stools for both candidates such that if seated the candidate would still appear to be standing. Are such issues, totally irrelevant to running the nation and current problems, really important? Most campaign organizations believe so and there is a growing body of research to support such conclusions.[63] For example, one study of the 1960 presidential debates reports that those listening to the debates on the radio thought neither candidate won the debates but those watching the debates on television thought Kennedy clearly won the debates.[64] Robert Tiemens, in investigating factors of visual communication in the 1976 presidential debates, found that differences in camera framing and composition, camera angle, screen placement, and reaction shots seemingly favored Carter.[65]

The 1980 debates, according to Myles Martel, represent the ultimate in candidate planning and preparing for presidential debates.[66] Reagan's preparation for the debates was much more elaborate than Carter's preparation. As early as August, Reagan developed a Debate Task Force that would perform the following tasks: negotiate the formats, prepare briefing materials, conduct research, develop debate strategies and tactics, and provide professional consultation on presentational aspects of the debates. Reagan spent three intense days prior to the debates practicing before knowledgeable panelists. In addition to strategy, they discussed such things as how he should arrive at the debates (they chose by airplane because it would appear more presidential), whether or not he should shake hands (they decided to shake hands first to give appearance of friendliness), and when to smile.[67] The Reagan campaign even had a Debate Operations Center where 50 researchers carefully monitored the debates to see if Carter committed any errors in statements so they could contact the media immediately.[68]

Edwin Diamond and Kathleen Friery argue that perhaps the media coverage is more important than the actual debates.[69] They attract a large quantity of news coverage and analysis. Diamond and Fiery identify five media themes of debate coverage. First, the media begin weeks in advance "signaling the big event." Issues, strategies, preparation, and negotiation are discussed in print and broadcast. There is a great deal of speculation as to the role and importance of the debates. The week before the event all the networks engage in a lot of self-promotion in coverage and analysis. The countdown begins and dominates all newscasts and front pages of national and local newspapers.

Second, the media spend a great deal of time "picking the winners and losers." They speculate on who won and why to what impact. This analysis function has led to the development of the use of "spin doctors," campaign professionals who attempt to shape media interpretation of campaign events. After debates, each candidate has their "doctors" before the cameras proclaiming victory and points scored.

The third media theme is that of "assessing the candidate's appearance." This includes special stories on the candidates' performances on such items as oral competence, personality, and image. Even such aspects as candidate nervousness and ability to handle questions are noted. The focus of such stories is on the style of performance rather than the issues discussed.

Another theme tends to focus on the "debate as theatre." Journalists want excitement, drama, and confrontation. The language of reporting the event reflect the need for "color" commentary. Comments of "stinging-attacks," "dullness," "striking a death blow," are common. The athletic, fight image of the event pervades most commentary.

Finally, the authors would add the theme of "avoiding the facts." The press is too concerned with reporting impressions of the debate and not enough facts of the debate. Television is an especially poor medium for the presentation of facts and "pure" information. Their general concerns about the coverage of debates include the inability of reportage to advance knowledge of what is said, they often serve to separate viewer from the central enlightening purpose of debates, and a general lack of balance coverage.

Current research on the impact of debates upon voters suggests that they plan more of a confirmatory than persuasive role in voter decision making.[70] Predebate preferences tend to crystallize opinions and confirm voting decisions. Thus, the greatest potential for debate impact is for one of the candidates to commit a blunder or make a mistake in answering a question. A strong performance, of course, can provide that final momentum necessary to lock a victory. Bush's performance in the second debate against Dukakis in mid-October is credited with ending any hope Dukakis had of catching Bush in the polls. It did, in effect, seal the victory for Bush. It was now his election to lose.

There are numerous strategies and tactics one can use during debates. Each one must be carefully analyzed to assess the potential gain or loss for the candidate. Many decisions are based upon the perceived image or approach by the opponent. The simple point is, there are many communication variables involved in any presidential debate. The strategies and tactics are carefully planned and rehearsed.[71]

Post-Campaign

Ruth Weaver argues that there are rather strong rules that govern victory and concession statements made by candidates on election night.[72] Acknowledgment of victory and defeat have almost become a ritual of American politics. There are three rules that govern postcampaign statements. The loser of the contest must concede before the winner can claim victory. The loser reads the congratulatory telegram sent to the winner and the winner rereads the telegram before supporters. The loser appears before supporters surrounded by family. Thus, the sequence of messages, the reading of loser's telegram, and personal appearances of candidate surrounded by family members provide the contextual expectation associated with victory and defeat statements.

But the content of such statements is also familiar. Losers usually, first of all, offer thanks for family, friends, workers, and supporters during the campaign. They often then provide a statement of support for the newly elected president. Such support, depending upon the margin of defeat, may make reference to the notion of loyal opposition. Weaver observes that the greater the margin of defeat the more prevalent the theme of continual challenging of the opponent becomes in the concession statements.[73] Support statements often contain explicit offers of help and direct assistance to the newly elected president.

Victors also thank their supporters, workers, and family. In addition, they are often laudatory in the comments about their opponents. They acknowledge a good campaign and express respect for their opponent. Next, the winner must make overt appeals for national unity. He is and will be president of all the people regardless of issues or views. Most of these statements are less policy-oriented and more general in nature. The victor, without doubt, expresses humility and offers a pledge to all the citizens that he is dedicated to the principles that make America great. Finally, most winners reassure the public that there will be a continuity in the transition of power or, if an incumbent, a continuation of the administration without an interruption of government.

Election night statements of victory and defeat are only the first elements of the process that ultimately unites the citizens behind the reign of a new president or the continuation of an old one. In the months prior to the inauguration, the media floods the nation with background information about the new president. The person is set within a historical perspective of the office. Anticipation of the members of the new administration mounts. The newly elected leader, when speaking before groups, makes appeals to national unification, support, and rearticulates a vision of the future that inspires hope, confidence, and excitement. By inauguration day a candidate has emerged as president. A tremendous transformation, at least in the eyes of the public, has occurred. The citizens are committed to the democratic process and notion that one of them has been elevated to the position of leader fully deserving a chance of success. In fact, a large majority of citizens will report voting for the new president regardless of the actual size of electoral victory.[74] The inauguration activities and speech culminate the process of acknowledgment and acceptance of the new administration.

CONCLUSION

Political campaigns are long and expensive. They offer numerous messages about our past, future, and current situations. As primarily communication phenomena, they influence and impact our behavior in both obvious and subtle ways. Their importance transcends the preference of one individual over another.

Although many countries have elections, U.S. presidential elections are most unique. Political campaigns are truly communication events: communication of images, characters, and persona. Presidential campaigns are long, nearly continuous events. The burden is on the candidate to appear presidential, capable, and worthy of trust and confidence.

The preprimary is when most of the candidate creation takes place. During this period the public is more susceptible to the ideas and arguments of future candidates. The groundwork for the campaign is carefully planned and constructed during this period.

For most Americans, the political season really begins during the primary period. The period tests the fabric of the candidates, the depth of their views, and the dimensions of their persona. Election interpretations and presentations are most important during this period.

Presidential campaigns follow rather predictable patterns. There are a limited number of issues, images, tactics, and strategies that are available for any campaign. Today, as never before, the tools of marketing and research are the instruments of electoral victory. American presidential politics is not based upon issue development as much as specified images, visions, and persona targeted to identified and segmented audiences.

Most campaign strategies are designed to do more than get votes. They are designed to project a certain image, alter a perception, or counter the opposition. Communication is at the heart of every campaign strategy. Strategies can be grouped based upon whether the candidate is an incumbent or challenger. In terms of American presidential politics, the incumbent has many more strategy options than challengers. From the strategies, the promises, the basic speeches, and even the acceptances of victory and defeat, the rhetorical patterns are predictable in both form and content. In the end a president is elected who must confront new communication challenges.

Paul Quirk argues, especially in light of the 1988 election, "there is a poor match between what a campaign must accomplish to strengthen democratic government and what a candidate must do to win the election."[75] For him, strengthening democratic government includes candidates stating their positions on the major issues facing the country, confining their campaigns to responsible positions and essentially honest, if debatable claims, conducting a wide-ranging debate throughout the campaign, and campaigning primarily on rational appeals and issues relevant to the presidency. Quirk does not think campaigns in their current state reflect his criteria for three major reasons. First, voters spend little time studying and understanding issues. Consequently, they tend to vote on candidate personality. Second, the news media offer limited information about a campaign. They focus on the "horse race" aspects more than issues, ideology, and candidate positions. Finally, according to Quirk, there is a real lack of independent commentary on the issues of a campaign. Candidates follow the path of least resistance and the one that "works."

The challenge for the future was clearly articulated in a press conference the day after the landslide defeat of Walter Mondale in 1984.[76] In running against Reagan, Mondale acknowledged that he was at a distinct disadvantage in the television age. "Modern politics requires mastery of television. I think you know that I've never warmed up to television, and it's never warmed up to me. By instinct and tradition I don't like these things [twisting the television microphones in front of him]. I don't believe it's possible to run for president without the capacity to communicate every night." Mondale continued his observations about the impact of television upon the quality of a presidential campaign. "American politics is losing its substance. It is losing the debate on merit. It's losing the depth that tough problems require discussion. More and more it is those 20-second snippets. I hope we don't lose in America this demand that those of us who want this office must be serious people of substance and depth and must be prepared not to handle the 10-second gimmick that deals with things like war and peace."

Despite the problems and ills of our presidential election process, it's still important for citizens to participate and vote. Whether we like it or not, the results of every election impact the future. Just consider the lasting legacy of Reagan's Supreme Court. Every election is important. As Peter Jennings observed, "yet it could be 1988 served us better than we realize. If the candidates had no real solution to our problems, need they pretend otherwise? Perhaps part of the wisdom of democracy is to accept inaction as well as action."[77]

NOTES

1. James Barber, *The Pulse of Politics* (New York: W. W. Norton, 1980), p. 3.

2. P. Lazarsfeld, B. Berelson, and H. Gaudet, *The People's Choice* (New York: Columbia University Press, 1984).

3. See Also Garrett O'Keefe, "Political Campaigns and Mass Communication Research," in *Political Communication: Issues and Strategies for Research*, ed. Steven Chaffee (Beverly Hills, CA: Sage, 1975), pp. 129–64, and Garrett O'Keefe and Edwin Atwood, "Communication and Election Campaigns" in *Handbook of Political Communication*, ed. Dan Nimmo and Keith Sanders (Beverly Hills, CA: Sage, 1981), pp. 329–58.

4. For a full explanation of this approach, see R. Sanders and L. Kaid, "An Overview of Political Communication Theory and Research: 1976–1977," in *Communication Yearbook II*, ed. Brent Rubin (New Brunswick, NJ: Transaction Books, 1978), pp. 375–89.

5. Gary Mauser, *Political Marketing* (New York: Praeger, 1983), pp. 31–50.

6. Samuel Becker, "Rhetorical Studies for the Contemporary World," in *The Prospect of Rhetoric*, ed.Lloyd Bitzer and Edwin Black (Englewood Cliffs, NJ: Prentice-Hall, 1971), pp. 21–43.

7. Ibid., p. 33.

8. Jonathan Robbin, "Geodemographics: The New Magic" in *Campaigns and Elections*, ed. Larry Sabato (Glenview, IL: Scott, Foresman, and Co., 1989), p. 106.

9. Ibid. p. 107.

10. See Bruce Gronbeck, "Functional and Dramaturgical Theories of Presidential Campaigning," *Presidential Studies Quarterly* 14 (Fall 1984): 487–98 and "The Functions of Presidential Campaigning," *Communication Monographs* 45 (November 1978): 268–80.

11. Gronbeck, "Functional and Dramaturgical Theories," p. 490.

12. Gronbeck, "The Functions of Presidential Campaigning," p. 271.

13. Gronbeck, "Functional and Dramaturgical Theories," p. 496.

14. See Rita Whitlock, "Political Empiricism: The Role of a Communication Consultant in One Mayoral Election," *Southern Communication Journal* 20 (Fall 1989).

15. Godfrey Hodgson, *All Things to All Men* (New York: Touchstone, 1980), p. 211.

16. Rhodes Cook, "The Nominating Process" in *The Elections of 1988*, Michael Nelson, ed. (Washington, DC: Congressional Quarterly Press, 1989).

17. Larry Bartels, *Presidential Primaries and the Dynamics of Public Choice* (Princeton, NJ: Princeton University Press, 1989). p. 3.

18. See Thomas R. Marshall, *Presidential Nomination in a Reform Age* (New York: Praeger, 1981), pp. 58–59.

19. For their complete argument see Scott Keeter and Cliff Zukin, *Uniformed Choice: The Failure of the New Presidential Nominating System* (New York: Praeger, 1983).

20. Ibid., pp. vii-viii.

21. For these criticisms and more see George Grassmeichk, ed. *Before Nomination: Our Primary Problems* (Washington, DC: American Enterprise Institute, 1985); Keeter and Zukin, *Uniformed Choice: The Failure of the New Presidential Nominating System*; and Marshall, *Presidential Nomination in a Reform Age*.

22. James Cantrill, "Reaching the People When They Least Expect It: The Role of Inter-Campaign Communication" (paper presented at the Annual Convention of Eastern Communication Association, Hartford, Connecticut, May 8, 1982). This paper provided a good discussion of this notion.

23. Cook, "The Nominating Process," p. 31.

24. Ibid., p. 31.

25. See Judith S. Trent, "Presidential Surfacing: The Ritualistic and Crucial First Act," *Communication Monographs* 45 (November 1978): 281–92 and Judith Trent and

Robert Friedenberg, *Political Campaign Communication* (New York: Praeger, 1983), pp. 25–35.

26. The analysis for this argument and subsequent ones in the phases are part of a larger project under development entitled *A Communication Model of Presidential Campaigns* (Praeger) by Robert E. Denton, Jr. and Lisa Goodnight.

27. Robert Savage, "Statesmanship, Surfacing, and Sometimes Stumbling: Constructing Candidate Images During the Early Campaign," *Political Communication Review* 11, 1986, pp. 43–57.

28. Bartels, *Presidential Primaries and the Dynamics of Public Choice*, p. 26.

29. Kathleen Kendall, "Fission and Fusion: The Primaries and the Conventions" (paper presented at the Annual Convention of the Central States Speech Association, Chicago, Illinois, April 11, 1981).

30. Dwight Freshley, "Manipulating Public Expectations: Pre- and Post-primary Statements in the '76 Campaign" (paper presented at the Annual Convention of the Speech Communication Association, Minneapolis, Minnesota, November 4, 1978).

31. As reported in Richard Watson, *The Presidential Contest* (New York: John Wiley & Sons, 1980), p. 34.

32. Barber, *The Pulse of Politics*, p. 3.

33. Ibid.

34. See Mauser, *Political Marketing*.

35. Jack Honomichl, *Marketing/Research People: Their Behind-the-Scenes Stories* (Chicago: Crain Books, 1984), p. 67.

36. Ibid., p. 70.

37. Ibid.

38. Ibid., pp. 69–70.

39. Ibid., p. 74.

40. For a good statement and rationale provided see Mauser, *Political Marketing*, especially pp. 266–68.

41. Ibid., p. 267.

42. Ibid.

43. Henry Ewbank, "Public Statements Concerning Campaign Strategies" (paper presented at the Annual Central States Speech Association Convention, Lincoln, Nebraska, April 8, 1983).

44. For example, see Thomas Patterson, "The Press and Its Missed Assignment" in *The Elections of 1988* and Paul Quirk, "The Election" in *The Elections of 1988*.

45. Peter Jennings, "Introduction" in *The '89 Vote—ABC, News*, ed. Carolyn Smith (New York: Capital Cities/ABC, 1989), pp. vi and vii.

46. Jean Elshtain, "Issues and Themes in the 1988 Campaign," in *The Elections of 1988*, pp. 117–18.

47. Trent and Friedenberg, *Political Campaign Communication*, pp. 83–105.

48. "It's Show Time for President in China," *U.S. News and World Report*, May 7, 1984, p. 23.

49. Ibid.

50. As reported in Ibid.

51. As reported in *U.S. News and World Report*, January 16, 1984, pp. 60–61.

52. Trent and Friedenberg, *Political Campaign Communication*, pp. 104–5.

53. The election data presented in this section comes from *Vote '88—ABC News*, ed. Carolyn Smith.

54. Patterson, "The Press and Its Missed Assignment."

55. Lenny Reiss and Dan Hahn, "The Dichotomous Substance and Stylistic Appeals in Kennedy's 1980 Basic Speech" (paper presented at the Annual Convention of Eastern Communication Association, Pittsburgh, Pennsylvania, April 24, 1981).

56. Craig Smith, "Speechwriting: An Acquired Art" in *Campaigns and Elections*, ed. Larry Sabato (Glenview, IL: Scott, Foresman and Co., 1989), p. 40.

57. Myles Martel, *Political Campaign Debates* (New York: Longman, 1983), p. 1.

58. Kathleen Jamieson and David Birdsell, *Presidential Debates* (New York: Oxford University Press, 1988), p. 118.

59. Joel Swerdlow, "History of Presidential Debates in America," in *Presidential Debates*, ed. Joel Swerdlow (Washington, DC: Congressional Quarterly Press, 1987), pp. 13–14.

60. Jamieson and Birdsell, *Presidential Debates*, p. 118.

61. Martel, *Political Campaign Debates*, p. 2.

62. Robert R. Tiemens, "Television's Portrayal of the 1976 Presidential Debates: An Analysis of Visual Content," *Communication Monograph* 45 (November 1978): 362–70.

63. See Martel, *Political Campaign Debates*; Sidney Kraus, *The Great Debates (Carter vs. Ford)* (Bloomington, IN: University of Indiana Press, 1976); Sidney Kraus, *The Great Debates (Kennedy vs. Nixon, 1960)* (Bloomington, IN: University of Indiana Press, 1962); Early Mayo, *The Great Debates* (Santa Barbara, CA: Center for the Study of Democratic Institutions, 1962); *Report of the Commission on Presidential Campaign Debates* (Washington, DC: American Political Science Association, 1964).

64. Elihn Katz and Jacob Feldman, "The Debates in the Light of Research: A Survey of Surveys," in *The Great Debates*, ed. Sidney Kraus (Bloomington, IN: Indiana University Press, 1962), pp. 173–223.

65. Tiemens, "Television's Portrayal," p. 370.

66. Martel, *Political Campaign Debates*, p. 7.

67. Ibid., pp. 12–76.

68. Ibid., p. 27.

69. Edwin Diamond and Kathleen Friery, "Media Coverage of Presidential Debates" in *Presidential Debates*, ed. Swerdlow, pp. 43–51.

70. See George Gallup, "The Impact of Presidential Debates" in *Presidential Debates*, ed. Swerdlow, pp. 34–42 and Gregory Payne, et al., "Perceptions of the 1988 Presidential and Vice-Presidential Debates," *American Behavioral Scientist* 32, no. 4 (March/April): 425–35.

71. For the best identification and description of political debate strategies and tactics, see Martel, *Political Campaign Debates*, pp. 62–76.

72. Ruth Ann Weaver, "Acknowledgment of Victory and Defeat: The Reciprocal Ritual" (paper presented at the Annual Convention of the Central States Speech Association, Chicago, IL, April 1980).

73. Ibid., p. 10.

74. William Mullen, *Presidential Power and Politics* (New York: St. Martin's Press, 1976), pp. 2–3.

75. Quirk, "The Election," p. 64.

76. See comments reprinted in "He Keeps Chin Up, Bows Out of Politics," *Chicago Tribune*, Thursday, November 8, 1984, Section 1, p. 1.

77. Jennings, "Introduction," p. vii.

Chapter Five

Dimensions of Administrative Rhetoric

Washington, June 22 (AP)—Tourists at the Washington Monument flinched in surprise Tuesday as Federal safety officials blew two turkey carcasses to bits in a demonstration of the dangers of fireworks. A pair of watermelons also met their end as the Consumer Product Safety Commission used the monument grounds to conduct its annual pre-Independence Day demonstration for the news media.[1]

The difficulty with many career officials in the government is that they regard themselves as the men who really make policy and run the government. They look upon the elected officials as just temporary occupants. Every President in our history has been faced with this problem: how to prevent career men from circumventing presidential policy.[2]

The Treasury is so large and far-flung and ingrained in its practices that I find it is almost impossible to get the action and results I want. . . . But the Treasury is not to be compared with the State Department. You should go through the experience of trying to get any changes in the thinking, policy and action of the career diplomats and then you'd know what a real problem was. But the Treasury and the State Department put together are nothing compared with the Na-a-vy. The admirals are really something to cope with, and I should know. To change anything in the Na-a-vy is like punching a feather bed. . . .[3]

In this chapter we explore some of the relevant perspectives, problems, and strategies that are unique to the communication of administrative control. We treat the topic broadly, but by no means comprehensively. Our goal is to offer both historical perspectives to administrative communication, and a variety of insights from participants and observers concerned with understanding the dynamics of leadership from the executive side of government. Two general orientations are examined. One is analytic and critical: how the process of "ruling" affects the rest of the polity for good or ill. The second—which opens and closes the chapter—examines the human and structural constraints that elected executives and their staffs must master. Our concerns are not about the development of an administrative style, but the communication of administrative competence. And, though we dwell on the nature of modern executive branch departments at various governmental levels, our concern is less for how bureaucracies work than how they communicate internally and to others.

ADMINISTERING POLICY: DILEMMAS OF COMMUNICATING ADMINISTRATIVE CONTROL

The "Interests" and the "Bureaucracy"

In a perceptive study of the American Presidency, British journalist Godfrey Hodgson puzzles over the question, "Why are the President and his men so powerless when it comes to carrying out their policies, even within their 'own' government?"[4] This query is a perennial one. It is asked not only about the Presidency, but about a wide range of elected executives faced with the task of implementing policy.

Part of the answer, of course, is that the reality of government is much more complex than is first apparent. Official authority in the United States is not simply vested in three coordinated institutions. Executives must do more than master the hurdles thrown up by the legislators and the courts. Some of the most penetrating studies of the political process have focused on the partially invisible barriers that render traditional organizational charts inadequate as maps to guide the observer through the varied political terrain.[5]

The most formidable barrier is the presence of large bureaucracies that political leaders find indifferent to vulnerable elected executives. It is a first principle of governmental life that high-level professional managers see their elected or politically appointed superiors as far more transient and vulnerable than themselves. Recognition of that fact makes these managers far more immune to the pressures and directives from "the top" than in a comparable private organization. For instance, when a bill becomes law—the official policy of the state or municipality—its administration typically passes to an agency under nominal supervision of a mayor, governor, or president. But in actual fact the law is essentially in the hands of civil servants who are removed from the political process. To politicians these careerists are frequently unresponsive and conservative—out of touch with public sentiment, and unmoved by the political pressures that perhaps guided a program down the rough road to enactment. The elected official is perforce a communicator, guiding opinion while at the same time attempting to adapt to it. All but the very top officials of most agencies are comparatively immune to the ebb and flow of public opinion. In a study of the State Department, for example, Smith Simpson points with some disdain to the vastly differing objectives that separate a president from the bureaucracy that is supposed to serve him.

The politician keeps one eye on the next election, which the Department ignores. The politician keeps tab on votes in Congress, not only on foreign issues but on the whole range of his program, while the Department assumes the high ground of what is best for the country. The politician is also sometimes involved in situations which make him appear to act the clown with redskin headgear . . . while the other, too far from domestic politics to view such spectacles with understanding, only shudders to think how such tomfoolery will appear abroad.[6]

Differences in constituencies also create natural tensions. Executives must be more or less continuously available to the members of the mass media that offer access to the constituency they are trying to serve. Ostensibly representing the whole, their appeals must be inherently universal rather than specific, designed to serve at least some vague sense of the public interest rather than the more specialized needs served by specific state or federal agencies. A president or governor cannot seem to have "clients" who receive favored treatment at the expense of other constituents. But most agencies clearly do have limited con-stituencies with strong interests in their actions. A significant number of Fortune 500 companies would lose their corporate clout without their carefully nurtured ties to the Department of Defense and its Pentagon consultants. Similarly, im-portant clients to the Federal Communications Commission include broadcasters, cable television operators, the major networks, and a comparatively small number of consumer action groups. Agencies like the FCC are frequently staffed by people fundamentally sympathetic to fostering the growth of the private industries they do business with or "regulate." "The permanent bureaucracies," notes Morton Halperin, "tend to define issues in terms of the organizational interests of the career group to which they belong. They easily come to believe that the well-being of their group is a necessary precondition for the prosperity and security of the country as a whole."[7] As a result, they may delay and temporize when asked to carry out an administrative order. They may also compete for turf with other agencies, creating a partially submerged level of bureaucratic politics that even a popular president may find difficult to handle.

The battles within the Carter and Reagan administrations over health-related issues have been representative. Surgeon General C. Everett Koop was often at odds with the Reagan White House over his activism in attempting to curb the sale of tobacco products and his promotion of condoms to reduce the spread of AIDS. Similarly, Jimmy Carter's Health, Education and Welfare Secretary Jo-seph Califano wanted a much tougher administration stand on smoking, in line with the disturbing findings of the Surgeon General and other research organi-zations. However, Califano's counterpart in the Department of Agriculture had a different constituency to consider. Tobacco is a major cash crop for thousands of American farmers. A serious offensive against smoking, from agriculture's perspective, would weaken the administration's avowed commitment to strengthen American farming. To further complicate matters on what first seemed an uncomplicated objective, Califano was reminded that the President's own state of Georgia was dependent on the tobacco industry.[8]

New York Mayor Edward Koch likes to tell similar stories about the organizational labyrinths that exist between a decision and its enactment. When the city decided to build fences around its heavily vandalized subway yards, for example, the Mayor encountered endless red tape from the Metropolitan Transportation Authority, a fact that he was only too happy to relay to a receptive audience. With a New Yorker's fine-tuned sense of the daily compromises required of urban life, his demonstration of the MTA's largess made a salient political point about the limits of his own power:

We are building the fence. But with the MTA, do you know what they have to do *before* they build the fence? They have to have an R.F.P.—Request for Proposal. Any place else you go out and buy a fence. Not in the city of New York. This fence, before it will be built, I will be in my third term.[9]

The "Interests" and Policy Formation

A policy may surface for the first time in a city council, state legislature, or the Congress. What is less widely known is that it may have been written by interested private parties rather than legislators or elected officials. Not infrequently a bill *cum* policy—or a key amendment to a bill—will originate from the legal staff of a special interest group. The first draft of a number of legislative efforts at administrative oversight have been constructed by those who will ostensibly be regulated. Their motives are obviously to gain the adoption of legislation favorable to their commercial interests, or detrimental to the interests of their competitors. In recent years, for example, consumer protection legislation and antitrust policies have been successfully amended or redrafted in part with the help of a powerful "Business Roundtable" based in Washington.[10] Similarly, the long-term battle over funding of the expensive B–1 bomber in the mid–1970s created a massive alliance between Rockwell International and the Air Force. The goal of the Pentagon/corporate lobby was to silence congressional critics, even though members of an executive agency are prohibited by law from lobbying Congress. With components from over 5000 companies located in 48 states, the B–1's appeal was eventually communicated to members anxious to secure jobs and federal money for their districts.[11]

The process of policy formation thus involves a wide range of interests and needs, many of which are well beyond the control of the elected leader who will be charged with administration of the final legislative product. From the elected executive's view, the complexities of administering a government charged with enforcing decisions that have been made both in and out of one's own control raise many logistical communication questions. Has the input of other interests—private and political—made the proposal untenable? Will the typically slow process of policy implementation dissipate the carefully orchestrated support that accompanied the introduction and passage of the legislation? Will new circumstances arise that make identification with the policy a political liability?

And will an unfriendly bureaucracy—or "bad press"—sabotage implementation of a worthy program?

A rhetoric of administration must therefore take into account the varied and often private audiences that are affected by the necessity to "enforce" or administer a public policy. In theory, the elected executive may have a clear mandate to carry out what officially designated deliberative bodies have decided: to administer the law for the benefit of the general public. In practice, however, the leader is frequently left with the enforcement of decisions that are, in the end, only partially of his or her own making.

The Expressive Function of Policy Advocacy

The enforcement of a policy or initiative necessarily carries the obligation to give an acceptable public accounting of governmental decisions in a way that does not bring discredit to the process or the key participants. Such an accounting involves a carefully constructed expression of an action's intent: a summation of the motives behind what are often the obscure elements that go into the literal "enforcement" of an initiative. This is the *expressive* (as opposed to the *instrumental*) function of a policy. Policy discussion symbolizes the motives, intentions, and character of those who intend to enforce it. We may not be able to see a policy "at work," but we can witness the visible symbols of its enactment that reassure us of its existence. With regard to regulation of industries in the "public interest," for example, Murray Edelman argues that the result is a process of mediation among special interests and is an expressive rhetoric of the "public interest":

Administrative agencies are to be understood as economic and political instruments of the parties they regulate and benefit, not of a reified "society," "general will," or "public interest," At the same time . . . they perform an equally expressive function as well: to create and sustain an impression that induces acquiescence of the public in the face of private tactics that might otherwise be expected to produce resentment, protest, and resistance.[12]

With few exceptions, public sentiment is quicker to grasp the expressive elements that accompany change than the specific social consequences that genuine reforms create. The romance of politics resides in simple evocations of a "better life," a "more just society," and the enactment of shared ideals. It is rarely so interesting in the subtle effects that specific reforms may produce.

Trading on the Imagery of Change

Democracies are commonly judged by their abilities to foster stable institutions within a framework that allows for individual advancement and progressive change. For decades, as historian Daniel Boorstin notes, American institutions have justified their worth by their "missions," by the belief that individual and collective initiative can overcome the constraints of class and wealth.[13] The ethic of work and enterprise thrives on the belief in the possibility of improving one's lot in life. "People came to America," Richard Nixon once recalled in a State of the Union Address, "because they wanted to determine their own future rather than to live in a country where others determined their future for them."[14] Although this view is not necessarily taken naively, in contrast to most Europeans, Americans largely minimize the constraining effects of class. It is a widespread article of faith to believe in the possibility of political redress of injustices. Belief in the responsiveness of political institutions and in the possibility of constructive reform are still key American commonplaces. The idea of a "land of opportunity" makes Americans less deterministic about the influences of class than their European counterparts. We therefore bank on the possibility of change (and the problem-solving rhetoric that accompanies it), but change per se rarely occurs in ways that are anticipated or wanted. We honor the idea of reform—of the pending legislative remedy—far more than the specific political manifestations those reforms usually take. This fact is perhaps one reason so many politicians seem to be better campaigners than administrators; the function of a political campaign is almost totally expressive.

The Problem of Sustaining Attention

The amount of time that is devoted to the public discussion of an issue is often shorter than the time it takes to produce concrete legislative results. The transient focusing on new initiatives is frequently "out of sync" with the necessarily delayed and incremental solutions that political institutions are capable of putting in place. Over the years increasingly sophisticated forms of newsgathering and dissemination have combined to give unprecedented exposure to selected issues, but usually in the absence of sustained attention. Major forms of national news media rarely allow for an accumulated understanding of a problem. The fickle nature of the television audience, for example, requires a news delivery pace that approximates the variety and scattershot approach taken in the remainder of the entertainment schedule. So, while presidents may be encouraged to "do something about the flood of imports to the United States," the initiatives that are negotiated and eventually put in place may be judged a "failure" by the same media well in advance of a date in which it would be reasonable to look for actual changes in import-export ratios. Implementation of a policy is now often totally out of phase with public consciousness of the policy itself. This leaves the political process without the sustained attention it frequently needs to ultimately achieve long-term objectives.[15]

To cite one instance, few middle-aged Americans will forget the serious gas shortages that developed in the late 1970s. Many care owners waited in long lines for very limited supplies, sometimes witnessing fistfights between irate drivers and beleaguered station owners. As it turned out, every action taken by the government, and every major change in public opinion was seriously out of step with unfolding events. Jimmy Carter finally secured funds for the development of "alternate" forms of energy, but only after oil supplies had again become plentiful in 1978. Predictably, public interest had diminished. At the same time the federal government adopted guidelines to encourage U.S. automobile companies to give up the ubiquitous "land cruiser" in favor of lighter fuel-efficient cars. But these actions took effect after gas prices actually began to drop, and after mass media attention began to wane. So lower prices and a lost sense of urgency allowed consumer interest in larger cars once again to develop.

There was an unanticipated irony in this rapid change of fate. By the time gas prices had again dropped, U.S. auto makers had already made irreversible changes in order to produce smaller cars. Moreover, in the belief that Japan's inexpensive "econo-boxes" were going to ruin America's car industry, the automakers and the unions had succeeded in getting government-negotiated quotas placed on Japanese imports. So the market was made unintentionally ripe for the Japanese again. Their response to a policy of strict quotas was to export fewer but more expensively equipped cars: larger automobiles that catered to the American sense of luxury, and allowed profits to be made from "extras." They achieved this goal just in time to benefit from the short public memory of gas shortages, and from favorable comparisons with unsold stocks of newly "stripped down" American small cars.

A pessimist might come away from such an episode of missed opportunities with the feeling that the only political certainty the politician can count on resides in the *rhetoric* of policy enactment, not policies and administrative acts. Public opinion is more clearly created by the former, and is often hopelessly out of touch with the latter. In terms of attitude-centered effects, an administrative decision or a statute can often be reduced to what is *said* rather than what is *done*. A president's civil rights enforcement record, for example, is popularly measured by what has been promised—what goals have been set and what passion has been demonstrated—than by the inevitably selective enforcement of various civil rights statutes by the attorney general or the Department of Justice. For this reason there is no consensus from professional historians on the civil rights legacy left by the tragically incomplete Presidency of John F. Kennedy. An important part of what the Kennedy administration "did" was what the President "said." His words were the more accessible representations of his policy than the occasionally erratic civil rights actions of his administration.[16]

Shifting Fashions in Leadership Styles

Another dilemma inherent to administrative leadership is what has become a pronounced ambivalence Americans feel toward a strong executive. With regard to the Presidency in particular, two attitudes toward executive power have been increasingly embraced since the invention of the office.

On one hand, as we note in Chapter 7, we often view the Presidency as an "imperial" office. Its perks and prerogatives seem enormous, and have been dramatized by a wide range of observers.[17] There is almost an irresistible urge to characterize the position as the preeminent seat of power occupied by "great men" performing "great acts."[18] This was the model embraced by Alexander Hamilton, and opposed by Jefferson, when the designers of the Constitution tangled with both the unhappy memories of the English monarchy and the need for centralized authority.[19] The "great man" idea leads us to expect activism and dynamism from a leader. The proud and activist Kennedy, for example, seemed genuinely frustrated by the slow pace that the various federal agencies held him to. But the most he would admit was that "it is a much tougher job from the inside than I thought it was from the outside."[20] It was only later that we learned that some presidential orders—such as his explicit request that missiles be removed from Turkey—were routinely delayed or ignored.[21]

The second model builds on knowledge of the complex nature of bureaucracies, and presents a sharp contrast to the image of decisive executive power. This view is of a bureaucratized executive whose powers are greatly circumscribed by an inert and apolitical establishment. Politicians make up a decreasing percentage of the public sector. Repeated civil service reforms have had the effect of limiting the role of political appointees in many government units, particularly at the local and state levels. Many cities, for example, are virtually run by a professional class of managers who are not elected, and are often insulated from political officeholders. The same fact is evident in federal agencies. A president may be unable to locate let alone replace a desk officer in the State Department responsible for "leaking" an administrative secret. He may find it equally difficult to determine why a specific order has been delayed, or why an agency continues to perform services seriously at odds with the stated objectives of the administration. The possibilities for bureaucratic delay are almost endless: a fact that Jonathan Lynn and Antony Jay have demonstrated to hilarious effect in their whimsical diaries of a British cabinet member who was no match for the entrenched civil service.[22]

To seasoned aides and departmental staffers, the President frequently appears as a well pampered and powerful leader, but hardly the counterpart to even the corporation executive who holds much more decisive control over his own extensive domain. It is thus only partially true to conclude that a state or federal executive's power comes from the constitutional imperative to administer the government. As we have seen, the administrator is constrained by countless forces that have the ability to render him ineffective: by the occasionally aroused public, opposing party leaders, congressional potentates and their jurisdictional committees, and the massive permanent government of nonpolitical careerists.

In the remainder of this chapter our task is to explore both general and specific explanations of how support for existing policy and leadership is maintained. For now we leave our contemporary focus on the constraining characteristics of modern bureaucracies. In the following section the emphasis is primarily on theories and tactics that account for the communication of administrative authority. Although it has been traditional to analyse the process of political *change*—for example, elections and legislative debate over controversial new proposals—it is obvious that politics is more frequently the activity of maintaining *stability*. No single thread extends so continuously into the history of political thought than explorations into how the political process secures social order, how political systems maintain their credibility as well as their occasional venality. The essence of the political process at all levels of government is in the maintenance of continuity. All governments—even the most authoritarian—seek to maintain a semblance of approval, or at least the creation of a climate of indifferent acceptance.[23]

THREE BASIC DOCTRINES FOR ASSESSING THE ROLES OF ADMINISTRATIVE RHETORIC

It is worthwhile momentarily to divert our attention from modern problems of civil administration to review some of the pivotal ideas from some major early contributors. Three classic representations of the ways administrative rhetoric can be studied are found in Plato's *Republic*, Machiavelli's *The Prince*, written in 1532, and *The German Ideology* written in the late 1800s by Karl Marx and Friedrich Engels and first published in 1932. Each theorist wrote from a distinctly different point of view. Plato was generally prescriptive, offering a visionary's summation of how leaders should be trained, and how they should function. Machiavelli was a dramatist. His format for political analysis is now well known: He used satire—the characterization of very human and sometimes very "raw" political impulses—to show how administration could be reduced to a pattern of techniques and calculations. And Marx and Engels sought to explain an entire organic system, tying politics to the "fetish" of money and the exploitation of labor. They not only thought they had found some iron laws of political development, but that these laws explained how political power was maintained in the industrial state.

Plato and the Idea of Administrative Elites

Plato's thought, echoed intentionally or unintentionally by virtually every critic of political life, emphasizes the moral and rational responsibilities of the leader. *The Republic*,[24] *Phaedrus*,[25] and other tracts on politics are accounts of an idealized civil life. Plato instructed his students that political agents were to discount for their own interests in favor of the good of the state. He wanted policymakers to be epistemologists, in other words, seekers of true knowledge. The ideal society was a world that was immune from the impulses of the frail ego, imperfect knowledge, and the urge to "pander" to popular beliefs.

In many ways Plato's proposals for the ideal state today look distinctly unpolitical, and clearly undemocratic.[26] His conceptions were not particularly people centered; nor were they "ideological" in the modern sense. Instead, his was a world of ideas rather than policies. He expressed contempt for the arts of securing popular approval for civic decisions. Because most public debate was hopelessly inadequate and ill-informed, politics was an obligation for the philosopher—for those specifically trained to be agents in the search for enduring Truth and carefully considered Justice. It was not an enterprise open to endless public participation and speculation. The decisions made by the state were too important to be left to people turning their backs on Truth, and engaged in the demeaning art of "brokering" conflicting interests. Indeed, the opinions of most were unworthy of any kind of serious consideration. Politics was a duty. The brightest and the best, trained to place their sights higher than the opinions of the crowd, were to serve as trustees of the community. "Most of the time," Plato noted, ideal leaders' efforts "must be spent in philosophy, but when their turn comes, they must labor hard yet again in politics; rulers they must be for the city's sake, doing it not as a beautiful thing but as a necessity."[27]

Plato saw himself as a dialectician, not a politician or rhetorician. The leader first had to ascertain what was right—what was True, what was best for the state—and then implement decisions based on "the good" even if the resulting courses of action were unpopular. The ruler was to seek out "the best" rather than the feasible, the "ideal" rather than the acceptable. His vision of government was clearly not to implement the ideal of "the consent of the governed," but to put the polity under the benign control of "guardians" with greater knowledge and wisdom. This contempt for public opinion still haunts contemporary political analyses today, torn as many observers are between the imperative (dismissed by Plato, but accepted by many of his philosophical heirs) to honor the judgments of public opinion, and by the contradictory impulse to assess political courage as something that implies a willingness to rise above the limited understandings of the popular mind.

Through the ages the major criticisms that have been made of Plato's idealization of political life has not been that it is "wrong," but that it is largely irrelevant to the ways in which human institutions work. Many have pointed out that our reasoning is situational rather than absolute: largely determined by contingent and tentative claims rather than eternal "deductive" first principles.[28] Our politics is governed to a great extent by egocentric needs and the attitudes of reference groups, rather than consistent altruism.[29] It might be possible to make a logic or a science that contains its own certain rules and procedures. But the governing of people with inherently different priorities and values requires a willingness to start from what is "possible"—what attitudes will permit— rather than what is "perfect."

Plato was obsessed by his educational competitors, the so-called "Sophists," who provided rigorous and respectable training in the arts of democratic leadership, often emphasizing political skills based on a pluralist outlook that fits in with contemporary notions about the variability of perceptions, values, and beliefs.[30] In his dialogue, *Gorgias* he made the Sophists out to be slow-witted and manipulative, concerned with efficient persuasion over solid rational methods. He thought they were indiscriminate teachers of the political arts (including political persuasion) without a political epistemology—a method to determine what was proper to advocate. In actual fact, they were probably far more effective and rigorous than Plato's view of them would suggest. Indeed, the Sophists were centuries ahead of their time in anticipating what are today considered the legitimate situational constraints that govern almost all forms of political action.[31]

Protagoras' famous aphorism that "man is the measure of all things" was an explicit affirmation of the importance of human attitudes that was totally at odds with the absolutism of Plato.[32] Anticipating the tradition of democratic pluralism, Protagoras and other Sophists properly directed attention to political dialogue as debate over judgments rather than unshakable truths. Along with Aristotle, they noted that public debate sometimes depended less on a simple discovery of the "facts" than on the imperative to cultivate allegiances from citizens with legitimate but differing priorities. W. K. Guthrie describes Protagoras' subjectivism as a position whereby "the standard of truth or falsehood is abandoned, but replaced by the pragmatic standard of better or worse. 'Some appearances are better than others, though none is truer.' "[33] Ultimately this was precisely the view that was to dominate the tone of calculation and moral indifference in Machiavelli's *The Prince*.[34]

Machiavelli: The Administrator as Pragmatist

If Plato fought against what he considered to be the corrosive effects of political relativism, the Florentine aristocrat signaled a willingness to *account* for political success from the dispassionate perspective of the careful observer (though the contrived pragmatism was clearly intended to prick the reader's critical sensibilities). In its short space it sets out the unremarkable and sometimes ordinary principles for effective governance of the state. If its flagrant opportunism offends, it is perhaps because readers tend to forget that Machiavelli was a comedian and dramatist; the work was at least partially intended to give local politicians their due. As Kenneth Burke has noted, the lessons in *The Prince* offer a virtual catalogue of communication-based administrative techniques. Burke's own summary of them is useful:

[E]ither treat well or crush; defend weak neighbors and weaken the strong; where you foresee trouble, provoke war; don't make others powerful; be like the prince who appointed a harsh governor to establish order (after this governor had become an object of public hatred in carrying out the prince's wishes, the prince got popular acclaim by putting him to death for his cruelties); do necessary evils at one stroke, pay out benefits little by little; sometimes assure the citizens that the evil days will soon be over, at other times goad them to fear the cruelties of the enemy; be sparing of your own and your subjects wealth, but be liberal with the wealth of others. . . .[35]

Machiavelli's world was light years away from Plato's. The Italian was totally oriented to ways in which administrative rhetoric can control a docile public.

Hugh Dalziel Duncan surmised that he was "concerned with how the ruler can address the people to make them want to do what they ought to do in a republic."[36] What changed significantly in Machiavelli's work was his perspective. The tone of the study—written in the form of a handbook for the leader set on maintaining his control is descriptive rather than evaluative. Compared to Platonic theory, the arrows are reversed. The study takes human nature as a "given," rather than a collection of imperfect traits in need of extensive remediation. It requires the leader to choose courses of action in terms of their acceptability and credibility to the public. In short, it remains a classic statement on the durable principles for keeping and maintaining political control. One cannot read it without noting how universal many of its recommendations still are, even in the context of its crafty opportunism:

Thus it is well to seem merciful, faithful, humane, sincere, religious, and also to be so; but you must have a mind so disposed that when it is needful to be otherwise, you may be able to change to the opposite qualities. . . . [The Prince] must have a mind disposed to adapt itself according to the wind, and as the variations of fortune dictate, and, as I said before, not deviate from what is good, if possible, but be able to do evil if constrained.[37]

Machiavelli's tract remains as one of the strongest early statements of the importance of *appearances*—symbolic political gestures—in the process of governance. The denigration of a political act as "Machiavellian" stems from the awareness that political processes are known more through the outward rituals than more substantive changes. When he educates the reader with the observation that "Everybody sees what you appear to be, few feel what you are, and those few will not dare to oppose themselves to the many,"[38] he makes observations at several important levels. On one hand he recognizes the multiple roles that make the public figure necessarily a "different" individual in private than in public. The public figure has expectations to fulfill, roles to play well or badly, audiences to please. In addition, he gives weight to the truism of democratic life that widespread popular support produces a kind of momentum of its own, a form of general acceptance that may produce acquiescence in the critical minority.

Ironically, his explicit suggestions of the frailties of the audiences to political acts leads many to condemn the opportunistic advice written into every page. But in fact the mock dispassionate style of explaining the world of real politics has the effect of rendering the analysis "moral" as well. When he writes that "the vulgar is always taken by appearances . . . and the world consists only of the vulgar" he has clearly implied that bogus political justifications come from regrettably low levels of political sophistication.

Machiavelli at least pretended to separate description from judgment, leaving an invaluable account of administrative control bereft of the usual layers of Platonic incantations for a nobler style of politics. We are given a description of politics that is also a handbook of administrative justification. We are told that there are conventions for winning the assent of loyal followers, that political authority must be displayed as well as earned, and—most importantly—that politics is an audience-centered activity even when it is clearly coercive and undemocratic. Politics is represented as it is: a very human form of interaction.

MARX AND THE STUDY OF ADMINISTRATIVE MANIPULATION

The uses to which political control could be put received a far more detailed theoretical framework under the evocative analyses of the German writer and scholar, Karl Marx. Marx's contributions can be measured in many ways. He was an essayist, social critic, social theorist, and—obviously—a political theorist.[39] He even served a stint as correspondent for Horace Greeley's *New York Herald Tribune* in the mid–1800s. In reality all of these roles are inseparable, requiring the careful reader to adapt what is useful and discard what is not.

Marx was also what we would classify today as a "futurist." His deterministic predictions about the technology and change, based on what he claimed was the "scientific" doctrine of historical materialism, lead to his now familiar assessment of the inevitability of a workers revolt as part of the evolution of modern states.

For him, the great driving force behind social change resided in the ownership and control of production. For him the key mental equation that could never be overlooked was that labor was unjustly treated as yet another commodity, just another form of capital. The abuse of labor by those holding vast amounts of capital was bound to unify the exploited proletariat. He tried to see his idealistic determinism as a historical inevitability. The exploited, he thought, would rise up by producing a humane state-sponsored socialism, and later: a refined "dictatorship of the proletariat." "History," he pessimistically concluded, "is nothing but the succession of the separate generations, each of which exploits the materials, the forms of capital, the productive forces of capital handed down to it."[40]

If Marx greatly overestimated the degree to which "workers" would see their own "exploitation" (and there is ample evidence to suggest that workers in many societies see themselves as *among* not apart from the holders of vast amounts of capital), his concerns for explaining the maintenance of unjust economic orders provided a wealth of productive sociological insights. Following the lead of Burke,[41] numerous contemporary scholars have pointed out the rich applications of Marx's sociology in describing the relationships between social stratification and political legitimization. In the milieu of prewar Europe Marx acquired a keen sensitivity to the economic and symbolic aspects of class. In the Soviet Union and its clients Marx's insights have been reduced to the stalest of all forms of rhetoric: rigid official dogma. But the impact of his intermediate sociological assumptions are still very much with us, particularly his sensitivity to the ways in which private interests can be represented in a rhetoric of the public good.

Two important concepts are especially relevant to the discussion of political communication intended to "argue" and justify existing regimes or existing policies. One is the encompassing notion of "ideology," or what Karl Mannheim has called the "collective unconsciousness" of shared and unchallenged cultural assumptions. The second is the description of a theory of social mystification: a multiform process of rhetorical placation directed to audiences denied political power by those who actually have it. As we shall see, both concepts are related. And although the discussion of both has drifted well beyond the original observations of Marx, they remain as significant conceptual tools for describing the ways in which the *acceptance* of administrative dicta can be coaxed out of political audiences.

Ideology and the Notion of Ruling Ideas

Any discussion of "ideology" is necessarily filled with many intellectual obstacles that are interesting, but have been adequately elaborated elsewhere.[42] The concept itself, as Burke has shown, is open to a wide range of interpretations.[43] Decades of debate have not resolved the question of whether the political and economic ideologies defined by Marxist and non-Marxist alike still govern the content of major forms of political discourse. For their part, most North American analysts (in contrast to many of their counterparts in Europe) today treat the subject of "class" less from the hard realities of nineteenth-century economics, and more from the individual's sense of status and self-worth. Where the workers cited by Marx were the victims of shameful economic exploitation, the workers studied by many contemporary social theorists are "individualists, concerned with their right to be exempted *personally* from shaming and indignity."[44]

At its simplest, an *ideology* is a set of widely held core beliefs about the ongoing relationships between the state and man. It is not a set of random ideas, but a cluster of basic assertions that represent a complete and orderly perspective about the proper goals of the state, or the inevitable consequences of certain kinds of political action. The conventional tenets evoked in the word "democracy" compose an ideology in much the same way that political Marxists assert a set of invariant conclusions and predictions. Ideologies give order and meaning to otherwise discrete events. As "familiar ways of thinking," they emerge as primary schemata for organizing our perceptions of the world, our consciousness. They give clarity to the confusing array of events that implicitly ask for our understanding.

To cite a few obvious examples, the political process in America is—at an ideological level—about "voting and choosing," "having a say" about who will govern, making decisions about ours and the nation's future. We know our ideological beliefs from the familiar and reassuring words that can be used to bring a sense of continuity to something that—left unexplained—might seem totally discontinuous and unwelcome. In political terms, our ideologies tend to be populist ("wisdom resides with the common person"), democratic ("everyone should be equal under the law"), religious ("One nation, under God"), cautiously activist ("the state has an obligation to provide what people who, through no fault of their own, cannot provide for themselves"), libertarian ("I'll defend your right to disagree"), and conservative ("America is a land that preserves individual initiative"). For these and other ideological forms one can specify clusters of beliefs that add a point of view to the vagaries of civil life. For the French, the Soviets, the Haitians, or any of hundreds of other cultures differences and similarities could be noted.

Although modern usage of the term tends to emphasize "radical" ideologies, Marx pointed out that the most pervasive function of ideological rhetoric is in the service of the status quo. He felt that the dominant groups in a society will naturally use language in a way that favorably extends and justifies their power. In doing so, elites tend to give favorable and benevolent accounts of themselves which—over time—may become seen as objective justifications of the existing social order. Without doubt his view was too deterministic; giving a diverse collection of people (a class) a unitary objective defies the fact that there is a natural pluralism in any group. But the underlying principle of using familiar and "comfortable" ideological views to ground administrative action is still an important principle in understanding administrative rhetoric:

The ideas of the ruling class are in every epoch the ruling ideas: i.e., the class, which is the ruling material force of society, is at the same time its ruling intellectual force. The class which has the means of material production at its disposal, has control at the same time over the means of mental production, so that thereby, generally speaking, the ideas of those who lack the means of mental production are subject to it. The ruling ideas are nothing more than the ideal expression of the dominant material relationships, the dominant material relationships grasped as ideas; hence of the relationships that make the one class the ruling one. . . . [45]

Marx believed that "the State is the form in which the individuals of a ruling class assert their common interests."[46] And, of course, he went on to assert that the largest holders of capital were the "oppressors" of the very people who provided them with their wealth. For him this exploitation was frequently based on planned and calculated deceptions. Elites were clearly discernable centers of power within the society. Starting from the fixed view of a "class struggle," it was inevitable to study political life (especially in Germany and England) as the product of economic interests. Today the world seems far more complex. While "elite theory" is still a matter of debate and refinement, it seems that we can be less certain that such a simple label fits easily in more diffuse and pluralistic societies.

Later usage of concepts that were first developed by Marx and Engels frequently separated their political doctrine from their sociological insights. Karl Mannheim, for example, looks at communication dominance from elites with a less suspicious eye, but with Marx's key thesis intact:

The concept "ideology" reflects the one discovery which emerged from political conflict, namely, that ruling groups can in their thinking become so intensively interest-bound to a situation that they are simply no longer able to see certain facts which would undermine their sense of domination. There is implicit in the word "ideology" the insight that in certain situations the collective unconscious of certain groups obscures the real condition of society both to itself and to others and thereby stabilizes it.[47]

In Mannheim's analysis the defense of political acts can be expected to routinely proceed with the universal idea that obscures a more divisive reality. Criticism is diluted if a point of identification is established. The widely accepted ideological maxim can divert attention from a partisan or controversial point, saving both administrator and audience from what may be painful evidence of an irrevocable split between the two. Familiar commonplaces of ideologies provide an ever-present reservoir of bases from which to justify potentially unpopular or threatening decisions. Consent is engineered by a political rhetorician capable of giving self-serving decisions a more acceptable and benign rationale.

An inverted order thus develops. Political discourse that could focus on the hard choices facing the administration of a government with limited means and resources instead becomes a vehicle of placation. The task becomes not to sharpen distinctions, but to deny them by moving to a higher and nondebatable level of ideological universals. Thus, in fighting to maintain administrative control of the Vietnam War in the face of growing congressional hostility, both Lyndon Johnson and Richard Nixon defined the stakes in general ideological terms. Both men were forced by will and circumstance to consider tactical military solutions: whether to bomb North Vietnam and Cambodia, whether to defoliate wide areas of the North, and so on. But their public justifications at home were both political and ideological, and therefore carried a far more appealing level of explanations. The United States was there to "stop the spread" of a presumably universal form of communism, and honoring necessary treaty commitments. In 1970 the bombing of North Vietnamese supply routes in neutral Cambodia became a way of "winning the just peace we all desire" and producing a "world of peace freedom and justice."[48] Ideas discussed initially as principles for the determination of a public philosophy were reduced to elements intended to appease an increasingly skeptical and unbelieving public.

In the short run such rhetoric worked.[49] But no extended debate could sustain the view that the outcome of a Vietnamese civil war could affect our own freedom and justice, nor that of the beleaguered South Vietnamese. Indeed, given the internal and international unpopularity of our participation in the war after 1967, it was at least as plausible to argue that continued fighting in Vietnam jeopardized both cherished principles. As for the eventual fall of South Vietnam, it produced little change in the political maps of neighboring states, and served to point up tensions within the region that decades of rhetoric about monolithic communism had caused us to overlook.

Mystery and the Rhetoric of Control

"Mysteries," notes Kenneth Burke, "are a good ground for obedience. . . . [I]f a man in accepting a 'mystery,' accepts someone else's judgment in place of his own, by that same token he becomes subject willingly."[50] In various ways most students of politics have had to come to terms with communication forms that induce greater acceptance than understanding. Ideological rhetoric is one such form, but not the only one. There are a special class of rhetorical appeals that play on the credulity of an audience, with the goal of producing greater reassurance than knowledge. It is a rhetoric that asks for acceptance, or at least tacit approval. But it does so in a way that avoids the need for detailed and thorough argumentation. Political discourse is especially prone to communication that *signals* more than it really says—a rhetoric of appearances rather than of explanation. Such rhetoric depends to a large extent on the use of communication within a context of "official" situations and formal authority. Respect is produced because the persuaded are ignorant, gullible, or trusting.[51]

In response to a rhetoric of mystification a listener adapts to the prevailing definition of the social order by trading status for security. Political language provides verbal evidence that legitimate authority is being exercised. The penniless may be told that their condition is "natural" ("The poor shall always be with us"), and that a better life remains after death ("The meek shall inherit the earth"). At the same time the powerful—in control of the symbols of authority and beneficiaries of the "ruling ideas"—cultivate symbols designed to impress, knowing in some cases that they will provide a basis for continuing the illusion that those at the top of the political hierarchy are there for natural rather than contrived reasons. Agency reports, presidential commissions, white papers, hearings testimony, policy addresses, press conferences, self-study surveys, all provide an aura of competence and governmental activism that extends well beyond what any of these forms can specifically yield in terms of individual comprehension. Like the visitor confronted with the bewildering new technology of a data processing center, one may be unable to assess the competence of those involved, but there is reassurance in the apparent knowledge and order that the computer paraphernalia confers on those who work there. The visit affirms the expertise of others, and just as importantly suggests our own need to defer.

Burke has pointed out the importance of mystery to religion.[52] But virtually every complex institution or body of knowledge has a built-in rhetoric of mystification. Such language is sometimes the last or only link that exists between the "outsider" and a complex governmental entity. Thurmond Arnold's now classic assessment of the impossibly opaque elements of the law points to how the symbols of authority can wear down potential hostility or disrespect. He notes that "the literature of jurisprudence performs its social task most effectively for those who encourage it, praise it, but do not read it. For those who study it today it is nothing but a troubling mass of conflicting ideas."[53] Arnold's point was that the very impenetrability of the language *communicates* a kind of permanence that conceals its fallibility.

One of the most productive analysts of verbal mystifications has been Murray Edelman at the University of Wisconsin. In a number of studies he has systematically explored the inexact but vital linkages between administrative rationales, and public opinion. Drawing on linguistic theory, Marx, Burke, and modern survey research, Edelman has constructed a valuable picture of a complex society that has taken refuge from the uncertainties of policy in the more reassuring symbols that accompany policy enforcement. He notes that the prime dimensions of public opinion reside in the emotional reactions that the symbols of government produce. If specific proposals and actions are only vaguely understood, there is a clearer sense of threat or reassurance that can be discerned on many issues. "Politics is for most of us a passing parade of abstract symbols, yet a parade which our experience teaches us to be a benevolent or malevolent force. . . . [I]ts processes become easy objects upon which to displace private emotions, especially strong anxieties and hopes."[54] Primed for the necessity to ease concerns about taxes, war, economic exploitation by corporations, restrictive laws, and powerful interest groups, most political establishments seek to defend actions in terms of reassurance. Hard choices are concealed or not seriously considered. Communicated effectively, especially on television, political rituals frequently replace open vigorous debate. For example,

Human interest stories are political events because they reinforce the view that individual action is crucial: that biography is the paramount component of historical accounts. A focus upon the "private" lives of celebrities underlines their significance as public figures. Stories about the heroic actions of ordinary people and the disasters from which they suffer similarly erase structural conditions from notice, even while they divert attention from the rest of the political spectacle. Heroic, pathetic, and prurient stories sell papers, build Nielsen ratings, and help prevent more revealing news from disturbing ideologies.[55]

As we note in the last chapter, mystifications represent a major form of political deceit.

ADMINISTERING POLICY: COMMUNICATION STRATEGIES AND TACTICS

Consider the following administrative dilemmas—all based on actual situations—and the appropriate strategic responses that they require:

• Published reports by former aides suggest that the President—beset by confusion and low morale—has lost interest in his work and regularly seeks escape by spending long hours watching old television movies.

- On the recommendation of his Education Commissioner, the governor of a state has established several specially funded "Governor's schools" for high school students with outstanding abilities in various fields. Only one in one hundred applicants will be admitted to the various programs, thus leaving thousands of students and their families angry at the governor for promoting an "elitist" program with taxpayer money.

- An outspoken member of the President's administration who has raised thousands of dollars for his party—and is strongly liked by party activists—has made comments at a public gathering that suggest a not-so-veiled racism. He has never broken himself of the habit of saying in public what others would confine to private conversation. The cabinet member has become a clear political liability in an election year, but the activists in the party have in support of the errant official a measure of the President's political mettle.

- The Vice-President, who has covered the nation making addresses favoring tougher enforcement of local and national criminal statutes, suddenly pleads "no contest" to a charge of accepting cash from contractors while a state governor, and resigns in disgrace. The much-promoted "law-and-order" campaign of the administration takes a drubbing in the press and loses its credibility.

- The Federal Aviation Administration has failed to act on what now appears to be clear evidence that the air worthiness of a large commercial aircraft is uncertain. A recent crash with heavy loss of life focuses attention on what is widely perceived as regulatory carelessness and bureaucratic lethargy.

- The presidential nominee for the sensitive position of Director of the CIA is given highly visible support from the administration. But in congressional hearings the nominee is charged with improperly using CIA data as a member of a previous administration. The President is left with a personal declaration of full support, and a nominee who is not inclined to fight for the appointment.

- A new press secretary has resigned just days after taking office, claiming that he cannot defend or explain a major presidential decision "in good conscience." In a public letter of resignation the secretary also indicates that a presidential decision violates a personal commitment that the President has made privately to the press secretary.

- An election campaign was based on promises to reduce government spending and to lower a dangerously high federal deficit. Neither action has occurred, and a second campaign is about to begin.

- In a nationally televised debate, the incumbent President has declared that some of the Eastern bloc nations, such as Poland, are not dominated by the Soviet Union. The press asks if the President "mis-spoke," and he says that he meant what he said. Every public appearance after that includes insistent questions asking if the President really believes that the Polish people have the right of self-determination.

- A big city mayor—once a policeman—expresses faith in the use of so-called "lie detectors": "If they say a man lied, then he lied." To demonstrate his confidence, he takes a widely publicized lie detector test. He fails it.

Each of these situations carries a common imperative: they require a response, an explanation. In each instance the credibility and accountability of an administrator is at stake. This section focuses on some of the practical options available to the administrators faced with the need to shape the public discussion of the actions taken during their tenure. Although our discussion can only be suggestive rather than definitive, its inclusion brings our study full circle. We started with a survey of several broad objectives contained in the administrative response. And we end with a look at the specific tactical options employed by political leaders and their staffs.

Controlling and Using the Bureaucracy

The chief problem that an executive faces is how to maintain a semblance of control over the agencies and offices that fall under his jurisdiction. The 1989 federal budget was nearly 1.2 trillion dollars spread over 1100 different domestic programs. The size of the federal bureaucracy is of legendary proportions, with over 400 separate agencies employing over 3 million civilians. One broad estimate is that ten times that number are indirectly supported by government contracts.[56]

At the local level the numbers can be equally impressive, with some 80,000 local governments and municipalities dispersed throughout the United States.[57] In the state of New Jersey, which is but a fraction of the physical size of most states, there are some 19 executive departments with over 80,000 employees, and a budget of nearly 6.5 billion dollars.[58]

When looking at the diffuse nature of most executive branches—local, state, or federal—one marvels not so much at the power of American chief executives, but at the ability of a transient leader to achieve a sustained and consistent policy over time. As some governmental insiders have noted, "the reins of command" seized by even the President are "more a skein of tangled threads that he must somehow weave into a coherent pattern." For all of his supposed power, "he must struggle mightily even to influence the course of events within his administration."[59]

The difficulty leaders face is how to get "the system" they are ostensibly in charge of to respond in a way that meets the high expectations that the promise of executive power produces in the popular mind. In contrast to the image of executive might, for example, a president must be concerned about how deputy officials with access to secret departmental data in various agencies can be made sufficiently loyal to avoid "leaking" to the press information that is at odds with official statements. A governor must be concerned with creating a chain of command that will make certain that the enforcement of an environmental policy (i.e., on strip mining) "fits" with previous statements, budgetary requests, and the interests of political allies. From an executive's point of view the possibilities for miscommunication and inconsistent action are nearly endless. His protection is partially based on having a staff that can serve as the political equivalent of a rearview mirror—checking for the consequences that will trail behind a sensitive political maneuver.

Using Surrogates

The safest approach to the introduction or implementation of controversial policies is also perhaps the most widespread. Politically elected administrators must be willing to use surrogates to carry most of the explanation and defense of policy. A public statement of any kind is a legacy that can come back to haunt the speaker. The rhetoric of the surrogate—Cabinet official, executive assistant, White House counselor, press aide—has the prime virtue of "Deniability." Some space or distance can always be placed between the statements of one official, and the views of the executive, if such a statement becomes a liability to an administration. The statement of an intermediary shields the executive. It can be disowned, downplayed, ignored, "explained" in the proper context, and—on occasion—repudiated. The press will generally be forgiving, knowing what the executive knows: that it would be unreasonable to expect that every official statement carried the authorization of the chief executive. If an announced decision is met with widespread approval the reverse is also possible. If it goes over well, it can be embraced as something that "reflects the thinking of the President" (or governor, or mayor).

Several specific tactics result from this objective of *shielding* the top political leader from the fates produced by even the most distant regions of the bureaucracy. One convention of bureaucratic life is the standard procedure of requiring agencies to announce their own bad news, leaving the prerogative of bearing good news to the leader in the State House or the Oval Office. For example, there was no surprise in the fact that the Johnson and Nixon administrations reserved statements of Vietnam troop pull-outs to themselves, and announcements of U.S. casualties to low-level military briefers in Saigon and Washington. The goal was obviously to put as much distance as possible between unhappy information and the politically sensitive White House. A president could not really deny the casualty figures, but he could at least put the burden of explaining their significance to reporters brave enough to query him on them. The effect of assigning negative reports to the bureaucratic "backwaters" of officialdom serves to subtly deny their importance, and to remove them from direct association with the executive.

Another variation of this pattern occurs when highly controversial proposals are announced by executive agency staffers who are particularly good at taking the heat that is certain to result. Every administration has the rhetorical equivalent of a lightning rod—the Cabinet official, commissioner, or aide who will divert potential criticism away from the executive. The individual that is going to draw the fire must necessarily be thick skinned. Some have actually relished this role, particularly if they have decided not to seek elective office on their own. Vice-President Spiro Agnew took the strongest antimedia speeches written by presidential speech writer Patrick Buchanan and delivered them with a zeal that increased their impact. President Nixon, who wished to maintain a more statesman-like image, denied that they reflected administration policy.

But he approved the texts, and allowed the first speech to be followed up by a second attack with equal vituperation.[60] Joseph Califano, former Secretary of Health, Education, and Welfare under President Carter, gladly voiced his long-held opposition to federally funded abortions, diverting attention from a President who had generally held the same highly controversial view.[61] William Bennett and James Watt served the same general purposes for President Reagan as heads of the Departments of Education and Interior. Bennett attacked "excessive" and liberal higher education practices that Reagan had opposed as Governor of California. Watt similarly baited the environmental movement with strong doses of the free-enterprise ethic applied to the unlikely topic of land management policy.

A slightly less flamboyant but related approach to the introduction of policy with indeterminate public support is the "trial balloon." On a "backgrounder" (not for attribution) basis, members of the press are appraised of "the administration's thinking" on a problem that will be the subject of an initiative. The official giving the briefing is occasionally the executive, but more likely some other high-placed source. The goal is to get the proposed action into general circulation to test public reaction. It is done, however, in a way that preserves the "deniability" of the administration. If reaction from the press, special interests, party leaders, congressional leaders and the like is negative, or if consequences are raised that an executive overlooked, the proposal can be abandoned before it carries an official endorsement. If reaction is favorable, a formal announcement "confirming" the administration-induced speculation may go ahead as planned. F.D.R. is known to have used his "backgrounder" press conferences for just these purposes, planting an idea in the press well in advance of a final decision, in order to prevent a significant failure in reading public opinion.[62]

Speaking with One Voice

Nothing eats away at the fabric of goodwill between an executive and the bureaucracy as quickly as executive's feeling that his stature is being weakened by dissent that is coming into public view. Executives new to their jobs can be counted on to resent the "leaks" that result when "unauthorized" information reaches the press and public. Almost every president, governor, and mayor talks about conducting an "open" administration at the start of their winter terms. But usually before the leaves are off the trees by the next autumn efforts are well under way to tighten up public access to staffers and subordinates. This pattern was especially obvious in the second term of the Reagan administration: a period plagued by a steady flow of internal dissent, conspicuous resignations, and unflattering "kiss and tell" memoirs written by former aides. Collectively, the memoirs documented an executive branch that was not only riddled with pockets of revolt, but was also preoccupied by concerns about the President's capacities to govern.[63]

In the jargon of organizational politics, what presidents and executives want from members of their closest appointees are people who are willing to "front" for the official policy line. They seek staffers who can resist the urge to "go native," that is, to place special or private interests above those of the "team" and the administration. This need for absolute loyalty is especially vital in an individual who serves in the capacity of press officer or press secretary. Such people must be willing to represent the President's views or the views of a cabinet official or agency they serve with a high degree of accuracy and considerable conviction. The task can be a difficult one, since it is impossible at times to determine what the "official" view is. That can be a problem in addition to the obvious one of occasionally being asked to defend the indefensible. But they must be prepared to face hard questioning on the potential inconsistencies, vagaries, and general criticisms that may come with the defense of "official" thinking. "Fronting" is not a job that is suited to people that place a high value on the rightness of their own individual thoughts. Political columnists who switch to the other side of the adversary relationship, for example, are not likely to make the adjustment easily from "opinion-giver" to "spokesperson." Straight reporters—such as the Ford administration's Ron Nessen and the Eisenhower regime's James Hagerty—have succeeded more ably.

On the Carter administration's position on abortion, for example, HEW spokesperson Eileen Shanahan made it clear to Secretary Califano before she took the job that she could not defend his view. Califano recalls her saying "What you have to know about me is that abortion is one subject I cannot front for you on. I cannot be your public affairs spokesperson on abortion."[64] But he notes that the *New York Times* reporter turned out to be an excellent department representative, largely because "her loyalty once a decision was made was as fierce as her arguments for her views in the course of making the decision."[65]

The scope of this problem cannot be over emphasized. Every capital city is infused not only with the traditional constituent-based politics, but with the organizational politics that come with the built-in insecurities of electoral life. Cabinet figures, major commissioners, key agency executives all have egos and ambitions almost as large as the executives who appointed them. Their careers depend on their outward loyalty to the administration under which they are serving. But because of the tenuous nature of their positions—in with one administration, but usually out with the next—most also cultivate independent ties to the outside institutions that they work with: businesses, the press, unions, lobbies, foundations, and universities. Organizational loyalty may be total and undivided, as in the devoted service of Harry Hopkins to F.D.R., or James Hagerty to Dwight Eisenhower. Or it may be as tentative and fragile as Press Secretary Gerald TerHorst's was to President Ford,[66] or David Stockman's to Ronald Reagan.

Every presidential or cabinet-level assistant can count on being courted by the press, as well as congressional and private groups in some ways at odds with the executive. Lyndon Johnson wanted his aides to have a "passion for anonymity." Among the best, such as Harry McPherson, there is always an awareness that political jobs require professional loyalty. Given the newly created White House job of special assistant for National Security Affairs, McPherson saw the sensitive structural problems built in to his duties. As an aide who had to deal with ambiguous lines of command, he had to assess his unique place in the hierarchy:

The debatable questions (1) to what extent the special assistant should press his independent judgments; (2) whether he should develop private relationships with foreign ambassadors and ministers; (3) whether he should impose his own intelligence and policy requirements on the departments; (4) to what extent he spoke for the President in interdepartmental meetings. . . . [67]

The word most frequently used to describe the process of approving an official administration view is "clearance." In most organizations there are clusters of individuals and separate departments through which press releases, proposals, and statements must be "cleared."[68] A statement on a budget request, for example, may need a president's or governor's approval before interested parties are notified, and the press is given a release. The purpose of such a procedure is obviously to unify the outlook and ideas that carry the "official" administration line. In most cases clearance channels evolve in piecemeal fashion, or end up being delegated somewhat unevenly to various agencies, departments, and executive staff assistants. These are the formal channels through which a speech, press release, "clarification," or proposal must pass. In theory at least, the agency or individual with special expertise on a question is involved in the clearance process. In practice, it is a fact of organizational life that access to an executive may become as jealously protected as a football on the two-yard line. No agency or major official wants to be bypassed on a proposal that is even remotely related to their jurisdiction. All want to have a chance at influencing the outcome of the political process. The author of a speech prepared for a president, to cite one kind of clearance discussed more fully in Chapter 8, may deliberately delay its preparation and "staffing out" through appropriate departments in order to preserve the cherished prerogative of writing the words of so prominent a figure.[69] The life history of a specific proposal or major speech is thus frequently a study in inter-governmental intrigue. The spoils go to the aide or high-ranking official who is able to establish open lines of communication that permit direct access to the decision maker.

Disinformation

There are times when high federal officials have convinced themselves that the national security will be enhanced by the distribution of deliberately "doctored" or incorrect information. A disinformation campaign is an organized effort to put out a string of stories that will confuse and mislead opponents. During wartime attempts at disinformation have been widely used, ranging from the crude to the complex. "Axis Sally" and "Tokyo Rose" were among several announcers who attempted to broadcast incorrect and morale-shaking information to American GI's in World War II. More sophisticated attempts have frequently involved the use of double agents to pass on misleading but ostensibly credible information to an enemy.[70]

The most troubling attempts at deception have involved civilian members of agencies who have passed on bogus information to Congress, the press, and the American public. Many of these attempts have involved deceptions about covert military activities in Third World regions.[71] Among the most consistent of recent disinformation specialists have been former CIA Director William Casey and National Security Adviser John Poindexter. Both worked in the atmosphere of extreme distrust of the press that dominated the Reagan administration. For example, during the "arms for hostages" Iran-Contra scandal in Reagan's second term, Casey mislead Congress about the extent and type of U.S. involvement in Nicaragua. Using a cover story that the CIA was only interdicting arms being sent to the Sandinistas from other countries, Casey deliberately avoided telling any members of Congress—including the Senate Intelligence Committee—that he had ordered the mining of Nicaragua's harbors. Grumbled Arizona's conservative Barry Goldwater, "Casey wouldn't tell you if your coat was on fire."[72] In the end, the CIA and the State Department lost much of their credibility with Congress.

The most revealing instance of a modern disinformation campaign came to light in October, 1986, when evidence accumulated indicating that the State Department leaked false information to *The Wall Street Journal* and other papers about phoney administration plans to attack Libya. The bogus stories were planted by John Poindexter and others as part of an organized effort to use the American press to scare Libya's Colonel Muammar al-Qaddafi. As Secretary of State, George Schultz noted in defense of the plan, "Frankly, I don't have any problems with a little psychological warfare against Qaddafi."[73]

Members of the American press were stunned to find that they were unwilling participants in the disinformation campaign. Was the outside chance of confusing one dictator worth the deliberate deception of the American public? ABC's Roone Arledge, charged that it was "despicable to tinker with the credibility of one of our most sacred institutions, the press."[74] But *Time* Magazine's Henry Muller voiced what most political journalists probably still believe:

It didn't strike me as something terribly new that the Government would attempt to mislead the press about something. The government very often tries to lead the press in one way or another, and it's the press's job to figure out what's going on.[75]

Even so, there is a difference between putting the best "spin" on a story that members of an agency want reported, and the quite different matter of designing a campaign of lies or half-truths. Arguably, no form of political communication creates greater cynicism and public distrust than the exposure of plans to deliberately falsify information. It can be little comfort to the press to know that a successful effort at disinformation will pass through the political process un-noticed and unquestioned.

Backchannels and Leaks

From an organizational perspective, public communication is channeled through a series of gatekeepers who scrutinize it for its overall appropriateness. But organizations are also riddled with what are sometimes known as more illicit backchannels, which serve as convenient but hidden byways around the normal bureaucratic chain. Some backchannels lead to other bureaucrats; others lead to interested parties outside, particularly regulated businesses or members of the press. Every bureau or agency chief also seeks to develop at least some back-channels to the top of the hierarchy that he hopes to influence. The goal is to bypass most intermediaries who might obstruct a cherished objective. These channels usually lead to a willing assistant who will convey the information around a bottleneck and to the very top. For example, a department head who is facing a major budget cut from an executive's own budget office may seek the personal intervention of a staffer who regularly has the executive's ear.

The use of "backchannels" has taken on some surprising forms in the recent history of the Presidency. In recent years the more savvy of White House staffers concluded that Nancy Reagan was—if you had her support—a reliable back-channel to her husband. Similarly, F.D.R. enlisted Eleanor Roosevelt as his "eyes and ears" to assess the concrete effects certain New Deal programs were having on the portions of the country. Roosevelt's paralysis obviously made all but the most essential travel difficult. But beyond that he sought to get information through ways other than the inflated optimistic reports submitted by the heads of his "alphabet agencies." Mrs. Roosevelt, in turn, became a backchannel for priorities and views that were slightly different than those of the staff surrounding the President.[76] Seeking the same kind of unfiltered assessment that he realized he was not getting from the Joint Chiefs of Staff, Lyndon Johnson belatedly sent some of his own independent-thinking staffers to Vietnam to assess the course of the war.[77]

Perhaps the most notorious backchannel in American political history was "Deep Throat," the name given to a secret administration source—still un-known—who allegedly passed on incriminating clues to the *Washington Post* during the unraveling of the Watergate Caper in 1973. But perhaps the most unusual backchannel developed during the tense days in October, 1962, during the Cuban missile crisis. America and the Soviet Union were perhaps never closer to open military conflict. Russia's new offensive missiles on Cuba forced the Kennedy administration into a dangerous blockade of that island that could have entailed the sinking of Soviet vessels thought to be carrying more arms. One of the first breaks to end the 13-day crisis began with an unlikely restaurant meeting between a high Soviet embassy official and ABC News correspondent John Scali. Scali was surprised to learn that his lunch companion was giving him what appeared to be an official proposal from Moscow for a face-saving compromise: the Russians wanted guarantees that the United States would not invade Cuba. He was urged to pass it on. For reasons that are still unclear, he became a participant as well as an observer. The information that he carried helped pave the way for an end to the conflict.[78]

"Leaks" of bureaucratic intelligence represent both a widely used and heavily condemned form of communication. As the term implies, a *leak* supposedly represents the unauthorized and unexpected release of information from within an official agency or government office. But political reporters today frequently note that the leak has been institutionalized. It now serves a number of functions: as a way for one agency to embarrass another, as a means for pushing a reluctant agency into action, and as a way for an internal dissenter to circumvent an organizational gag rule.[79] When done with official approval, its purpose is usually to conceal motives: to make information available to the press without having to face questioning on why it came from official sources. In the tradition of the political novel, for example, an incumbent might leak compromising information about his opponent's previous three marriages. As described by National Public Radio's Daniel Schorr, who was on the receiving end of many unofficial statements, the leak became

something consciously done to enhance an official, float a trial balloon, promote a viewpoint or torpedo a contrary viewpoint. The Air Force "leaked" classified information about what was wrong with the Army's missiles; at appropriations time the whole Pentagon leaked classified studies of Soviet armed might; a "senior official" traveling on Secretary Kissinger's shuttle diplomacy plane developed leaking into an art form.[80]

In its most interesting incarnation, however, the leak serves a "safety valve" function. Unauthorized information from an insider makes "secret" information available that serves at least the short-term interests of the press and the interests of the leaker. The reporter ostensibly gets an exclusive story (though most are wary of this bait), and the leaker frequently gets revenge. Such a person may have personal or organizational motives—the information may point out a blatant contradiction between public statements and private intentions, or may provide information of use to an agency but at odds with administration policy. At times a leak may compromise security, although the veil of "national security" can be a convenient mystification for a botched policy.[81]

Schorr himself tried his hand at this "art form," eventually losing his job at CBS because of the tangle he helped create. As the recipient of a damaging House study of covert and often illegal CIA activities known as the "Pike Report," he sought a place to publish it. His network paraphrased from the report, but not as extensively as Schorr felt was warranted. With the House voting to make the report secret, Schorr went ahead with his plans to find another outlet. Eventually he sold the document to the *Village Voice*, but only after an embarrassing episode in which he remained silent while colleagues at CBS were wrongly accused of having been involved.[82] Like the ''secret'' Pentagon-prepared history of the Vietnam War that was leaked to the *New York Times* by Pentagon analyst Daniel Ellsberg, the Pike Report became a major news story. Both also served to remind a decade of presidents that the Congress and most of the federal bureaucracy are, at best, fickle allies.

CONCLUSION

This chapter has only touched on a few of the possible approaches that could be examined for insights on the tactics and effects of administrative communication. Our plan here has been eclectic—mixing prescriptive and descriptive theory, discussing administrative tactics as well as much broader philosophical questions, and mentioning classical as well as contemporary thought. This topic admits to no one method or point of view. Countless other derivative theorists and analyses could be mentioned as outgrowths of the speculative insights of Machiavelli, Marx, Burke, and Edelman. As we have noted here, their analyses of the motivations of administrative elites have become benchmarks. The common theme that runs through most prescriptive studies of administrative leadership involves assessing human capacities. Can political leaders be motivated to act as public trustees rather than agents of limited interest constituencies? And can ordinary people exercise the judgment to know what is best for the polity? Descriptively, two general issues seem to dominate assessments of administrative leadership. The first involves the ongoing tensions that exist between elected leaders and their careerist subordinates spread over vast executive bureaucracies. The second raises the troubling question of whether communication in modern democracies has substituted benign but relatively meaningless symbols of accountability in place of genuine political dialogue. The key terms of this chapter— *public interest, ideologies, ruling ideas*, and *interest groups*—are themselves a reminder that the price for securing the political legitimacy of a regime can be very high if the effect is to numb rather than enlighten.

There can be no doubt about the need to continue the search for conceptual tools that help us explain the complex psychological and social processes that occur as political institutions continue to exercise their powers over public opinion. A huge spectrum of disciplines—some of which we have sampled here— have useful concepts and information to contribute: ranging from those doing traditional criticism, to those engaged in survey research on political attitudes; from ''neo-Marxist'' social scientists who explore the dynamics of concealed ''investments,'' to memoirists who remind us of the tactical options from which political leaders faced with the task of husbanding public support must choose.

NOTES

1. ''U.S. Explodes Turkeys as Fireworks Warning,'' *The New York Times*, June 23, 1988, p. C11.

1021

2. Harry Truman quoted in Arthur Bernon Tourtellot, *The Presidents on the Presidency* (New York: Doubleday, 1964), p. 129.

3. Franklin Roosevelt quoted in Emmet John Hughes, *The Living Presidency* (New York: Coward, McCann and Geoghegan, 1972), p. 184.

4. Godfrey Hodgson, *All Things to All Men* (New York: Simon and Schuster, 1980), p. 86.

5. See, for examples, Douglass Cater, *Power in Washington* (New York: Vintage, 1964); Charles Peters, *How Washington Really Works* (Reading, MA: Addison-Wesley, 1980); Kim McQuaid, *Big Business and Presidential Power* (New York: William Morrow, 1982); and Benjamin Ginsberg, *The Captive Public: How Mass Opinion Promotes State Power* (New York: Basic, 1986).

6. Smith Simpson, *Anatomy of the State Department* (Boston: Beacon Press, 1967), p. 132.

7. Morton H. Halperin, "The Presidency and Its Interaction with the Culture of Bureaucracy," in *The System: The Five Branches of American Government* ed. Charles Peters and James Fallows (New York: Praeger, 1967), p. 8.

8. Joseph A. Califano, Jr., *Governing America: An Insider's Report from the White House and the Cabinet* (New York: Simon and Schuster, 1981), pp. 184–87.

9. "A Mayor for All Seasons," *Time*, June 15, 1981, p. 23.

10. McQuaid, pp. 293–95.

11. Nick Kotz, "The Cheasapeake Bay Goose Hunt . . . " *Washington Monthly*, February, 1988, pp. 29–30.

12. Murray Edelman, *The Symbolic Uses of Politics* (Urbana, IL: University of Illinois, 1967), p. 56.

13. Daniel J. Boorstin, *The Americans: The Democratic Experience* (New York: Vintage, 1974), pp. 557–58.

14. Richard M. Nixon, "State of the Union Address," January 22, 1971 in *Presidential Rhetoric*, 2d Ed. Theodore Windt (Dubuque, IA: Kendall-Hunt, 1980), p. 155.

15. The inability of the American public to "stay the course" was one of Lyndon Johnson's most urgent complaints about his attempts to seek a victory in Vietnam. For his assessment see the chapter, "The Making of a Decision," in his *The Vantage Point: Perspectives on the Presidency* (New York: Holt, Reinhart, and Winston, 1971), pp. 365–424.

16. Jim F. Heath, *Decade of Disillusionment: The Kennedy-Johnson Years* (Bloomington: Indiana University, 1975), pp. 69–73.

17. The term, "imperial," is Arthur M. Schlesinger Jr.'s. For studies of the "powerful" Presidency see Schlesinger's *The Imperial Presidency* (Boston, MA: Houghton-Mifflin, 1973) and George Reedy's, *The Twilight of the Presidency* (New York: World, 1970).

18. A book that takes this general approach is Thomas A. Bailey's *Presidential Greatness* (New York: Appleton-Century, 1966).

19. See especially papers 67–75 of *The Federalist Papers* written by Hamilton, Madison, and Jay. Hamilton especially makes a defense for a strong executive. (New York: Mentor, 1961).

20. Kennedy quoted in *The American President* ed. Sidney Warren (Englewood Cliffs, NJ: Prentice-Hall, 1967), p. 54.

21. Robert F. Kennedy, *Thirteen Days: A Memoir of the Cuban Missile Crisis* (New York: Signet, 1968), p. 94.

22. In their fictional account, James Hacker is the former magazine editor who is defeated in every effort to institute change as Minister of Internal Affairs. See Jonathan Lynn and Antony Jay, *The Complete Yes Minister* (Topsfield, MA: Salem House, 1984).

23. Hugh Dalziel Duncan, *Communication and Social Order* (New York: Oxford, 1970), p. 196.

24. *Great Dialogues of Plato* trans. W.H.D. Rouse (New York: Mentor, 1956).

25. *Phaedrus*, translated by J. Wright, in *Five Dialogues of Plato* (New York: E.P. Dutton, 1947), pp. 215–87.

26. This is one of the views expressed by Karl Popper in *The Open Society and Its Enemies* (London: Routledge and Kegan Paul, 1947).

27. *The Republic*, Bk. vii, p. 340.

28. Stephen Toulmin, *The Uses of Argument* (Cambridge, England: Cambridge University, 1964), ch. 4.

29. A classic statement of this view is found in David Riesman's *The Lonely Crowd*, Abridged Edition (New Haven, CT: Yale University, 1961), especially Part II.

30. W.K.C. Guthrie, *The Sophists* (Cambridge, England: Cambridge University, 1971), pp. 3–13.

31. A selective but interesting representation of the dispute between the Sophists and Plato can be found in the best-selling "novel" by Robert M. Persig, *Zen and the Art of Motorcycle Maintenance* (New York: William Morrow, 1974).

32. Guthrie, pp. 170–71.

33. Guthrie, p. 187.

34. Niccolo Machiavelli, *The Prince*, trans. Luigi Ricci (New York: Mentor, 1952).

35. Kenneth Burke, *A Rhetoric of Motives* (New York: Prentice-Hall, 1953), p. 158.

36. Duncan, p. 216.

37. Machiavelli, pp. 93–94.

38. Machiavelli, p. 94.

39. For a brief biography and a partial bibliography on Marx see Neil McInnes, "Karl Marx" in *The Encyclopedia of Philosophy*, Volume Five, ed. Paul Edwards (New York: Macmillan and the Free Press, 1967), pp. 171–73. For a broad application of Marxist concepts to political communication see Claus Mueller, *The Politics of Communication* (New York: Oxford University, 1973).

40. Karl Marx and Friedrich Engels, *The German Ideology*, Parts I and III, ed. R. Pascal (New York: International Publishers, 1946), p. 38.

41. Burke's *A Rhetoric of Motives*, pp. 101–14, and various sections of *Attitudes Toward History* (Boston: Beacon, 1957) are two influential studies. The importance of Burke as an eclectic user of Marx and other innovators is well documented in the tribute, *Critical Responses to Kenneth Burke*, ed. William Rueckert (Minneapolis: University of Minnesota, 1969).

42. See *The End of Ideology Debate*, ed. by Chaim I. Waxman (New York: Funk and Wagnalls, 1968) and Daniel Bell, *The End of Ideology* (New York: The Free Press, 1960).

43. Burke, *Rhetoric of Motives*, p. 104.

44. Richard Sennett and Jonathan Cobb, *The Hidden Injuries of Class* (New York: Knopf, 1973), p. 150.

45. Marx and Engels, p. 39.

46. Marx and Engels, p. 60.

47. Karl Mannheim, *Ideology and Utopia*, trans. Louis Worth and Edward Shils (New York: Harvest, 1936), p. 40.

48. Richard Nixon, "Televised Address to the Nation," April 30, 1970, in Windt, pp. 139, 141.

49. The continuance of the Vietnam War produced angry clashes on college campuses, and four deaths at Kent State University in Ohio in a protest involving poorly trained National Guardsmen. But the president was always able to reclaim some credibility for the war after each speech. See Richard B. Gregg and Gerald A. Houser, "Richard Nixon's April 30, 1970 Address on Cambodia: The Ceremony of Confrontation." *Speech Monographs*, August, 1973, pp. 167–81.

50. Kenneth Burke, *The Rhetoric of Religion: Studies in Logology* (Berkeley, CA: University of California, 1970), p. 307.

51. Duncan, pp. 190–245, and Burke, *Rhetoric of Motives*, pp. 101–10.

52. Burke, *Rhetoric of Religion*, pp. 307–09.

53. Thurman W. Arnold, *The Symbols of Government* (New York: Harcourt, Brace and World, 1962), p. 70.

54. Edelman, *Symbolic Uses of Politics*, p. 5.

55. Murray Edelman, *Constructing the Political Spectacle* (Chicago, IL: University of Chicago, 1988), p. 99.

56. Peters, *How Washington Really Works*, p. 35.

57. George E. Berley and Douglas M. Fox, *80,000 Governments: The Politics of Sub-National America* (Boston, MA: Allyn and Bacon, 1978).

58. These are 1987 figures from *Information Please Almanac: 1987* (Boston, MA: Houghton Mifflin, 1987), p. 745.

59. Ben W. Heineman, Jr. and Curtis A. Hessler, *Memorandum for the President: A Strategic Approach to Domestic Affairs in the 1980s* (New York: Random House, 1980), p. xiii.

60. William Safire, *Before the Fall* (New York: Doubleday, 1975), pp. 352–53.

61. Califano, pp. 49–62.

62. Samuel and Dorothy Rosenman, *Presidential Style: Some Giants and a Pygmy in the White House* (New York: Harper & Row, 1976), p. 331.

63. The most revealing memoirs include David Stockman's *The Triumph of Politics* (New York: Harper & Row, 1986), and Donald Regan's *For the Record: From Wall Street to Washington* (New York: Harcourt, Brace, Jovanovich, 1988).

64. Califano, p. 36.

65. Califano, p. 36.

66. Shortly after his appointment, Press Secretary Gerald TerHorst resigned from the Ford administration in protest over the pardon of Richard Nixon. See Robert T. Hartmann, *Palace Politics: An Inside Account of the Ford Years* (New York: McGraw Hill, 1980), pp. 240–46, 265–67.

67. Harry McPherson, *A Political Education* (Boston: Little, Brown, 1972), p. 256.

68. For a discussion of clearance in the presidency see Richard E. Neustadt, "Presidency and Legislation: The Growth of Central Clearance," in *The Presidency*, ed. Aaron Wildavsky (Boston, MA: Little, Brown, 1969), pp. 601–32.

69. Transcript, Robert Hardesty Oral History Interview, August 2, 1971 by Joe B. Frantz, p. 11, LBJ Library, Austin, Texas. See also, Harold L. Wilensky, *Organizational Intelligence* (New York: Basic Books, 1967), pp. 48–57.

70. See, for example, J. C. Masterman, *The Double-Cross System: In the War of 1939 to 1945* (New Haven, CT: Yale University, 1972).

71. Donna A. Demac, *Keeping America Un-Informed* (New York: Pilgrim Press, 1984), pp. 28–29.

72. Hedrick Smith *The Power Game* (New York: Random House, 1988), p. 48.

73. Bernard Gwertzman, "Shultz Calls Use of Press to Scare Libya Justified," *The New York Times*, October 3, 1986, p. A1.

74. Robert McFadden, "News Executives Express Outrage," *The New York Times*, October 3, 1986, p. A7.

75. McFadden, p. A7.

76. James MacGregor Burns, *Roosevelt: The Lion and the Fox, 1882–1940* (New York: Harcourt Brace Javanovich, 1956), pp. 173–74.

77. Townsend Hoopes, *The Limits of Intervention* (New York: David McKay, 1969), pp. 159–85.

78. Robert Kennedy, *Thirteen Days*, p. 91.

79. See, for example, Leslie Gelb, "All About Leaks," *The New York Times*, May 22, 1986, p. B10; Richard Halloran, "A Primer on the Fine Art of Leaking Information," *The New York Times*, January 14, 1983, p. A16; and Tom Wicker, *On Press* (New York: Viking, 1978), p. 101.

80. Daniel Schorr, *Clearing the Air* (New York: Berkeley, 1978), p. 182.

81. Wicker, pp. 201–02.

82. For his own account, see Schorr, pp. 187–225.

Chapter Six

Mass Media and Politics

As the founders of the American republic very well understood, a successful regime caters more to the interests of its elites and more to the emotions of its masses.[1]

One of the basic troubles with radio and television news is that both instruments have grown up as an incompatible combination of show business, advertising, and news. Each of the three is a rather bizarre and demanding profession. And when you get all three under one roof, the dust never settles.[2]

In 1952 a small footnote to history became a milestone in the evolution of American political campaigns. That year saw a presidential race between Democrat Adlai Stevenson and the venerable Dwight Eisenhower. Eisenhower's running mate was a brash young senator from California named Richard Nixon. Like most vice-presidential contenders of his era, Nixon would have normally passed in and out of public attention with a minimum of public interest. That might have happened. But it did not. It was to be the year that Nixon single-handedly salvaged his political career on the tenuous thread of one 30-minute nationwide television speech.

The speech was a master political move brought on by a challenge to which a less adroit politician might have succumbed. The episode began with the charge that Nixon had used campaign funds to establish a private "slush" fund of $16,000. It was severely aggravated by the fact that the popular Eisenhower was slow to come to Nixon's defense, giving weight to press speculation that the scrappy California senator was in deep political trouble. Hours and days passed until it became evident to Nixon that he would have to engineer his own political salvation. Speaking to the nation from an empty theatre in Hollywood, he explained the necessity to seek outside financial support to run for the Senate.

The speech was both a masterful and tawdry apologia, dramatically recounting his own modest finances to an audience of perhaps 60 million.[3] Everything was seemingly mentioned to vindicate the charge that he was making a fortune in politics: the paid-off loan on his old car, his mortgage on a modest home, the necessity of buying only a "cloth coat" for "Pat," and—finally—his steadfast refusal to return the gift of a dog named Checkers. Nixon invoked a rhetoric of honor, but it was also a calculated attack on the press and the Democrats. With his roots in the hardworking middle class firmly established, he went on to challenge Stevenson to explain his own finances, and to urge voters to repudiate a campaign of "smears" and innuendos. Viewers were asked to decide his fate: "Wire and write the Republican National Committee whether you think I should stay on [the ticket] or whether I should get off. And whatever their decision is, I will abide by it."[4] The $75,000 telecast yielded thousands of supporting telegrams and letters. It ignited the campaign, and Eisenhower belatedly embraced his running mate.

Even today the impact of the Checkers speech is impressive. It saved the career of a leader who would go on to the Presidency, and on to a further attempt at rhetorical salvation against charges of covering up evidence. Arguably, 30 minutes of political rhetoric has never had a greater effect on the course of American history.

Was this an omen of the "new politics?" Did Nixon's decision to bypass the news media in favor of using paid time on an entertainment medium signal a basic change in the conduct of national campaigns? Did the fact that so much support was mobilized in a short period of time represent a dramatic departure in the uses of political leadership? It is easy to answer in the affirmative to these questions, but they only begin to hint at the realities of maintaining political power in the video age. What they suggest is the need to assess the alignment of American national politics with communications industries dominated by the imperative to attract and entertain audiences. This chapter explores a number of features of this marriage, beginning with three basic clarifications based on what we believe are several common misconceptions.

THREE CAVEATS

The Uncertain Epistemology of the Mass Media

By their very nature, the components of political culture are rarely witnessed in their raw forms. Instead, they are represented to us by intermediaries. Most of life's larger events are "out there" beyond the realm of the individual's capacity to experience them first hand. Like any arena where the discussion of human intentions and motives weighs significantly, politics invites layers of bureaucracies, writers, and journalists to construct versions of political reality. To those uninitiated in its folkways, debates in a state assembly, hearings on Capitol Hill, or thick reports issued by an executive agency research staff will often seem frustratingly inconclusive. It often takes a press report appearing in a morning paper to make sense of the unintelligible events that are too complex in their "raw" forms. As Walter Lippmann noted, "The world that we have to deal with politically is out of reach, out of sight, out of mind. It has to be explored, reported, and imagined." Through the mass media, man learns "to see with his mind vast portions of the world that he could never see, touch, smell, hear, or remember. Gradually he makes for himself a trustworthy picture inside his head of the world beyond his reach."[5] The political world is not experienced first hand. Instead, it is more the product of impressions that we gather from the vast information sources that incessantly sell, entertain, and inform.

Grounded in an inexact and illusory reality, political communication deals in firm and vivid ways with topics that have a far from certain epistemology. What we "know" to be the case—that government is taking care of the poor, that there is mismanagement and corruption in a federal agency, that a Latin American government is "democratic"—may be far less certain than the news summaries that give political realities a consumable form. Indeed, "full and accurate" news stories that actually matched the intricate contours of real events might well be considered "unreadable." Part of the news function is to give organization to what is inherently disorganized; we must mediate between the world we think we see, and the world inside that we know.

By the *mass media* we mean the news and entertainment organizations—large and small—who sell their wares to the general public on a routine basis. We include newspapers, films, magazines, radio and television programs, publishers, and even the music industry. Combined, they represent an enormous and sometimes diverse range of individual outlets: over 10,000 television and radio stations, about 1700 daily newspapers, perhaps 40 major "opinion" journals, and scores of large and small companies supplying programs and stories to individual outlets.

Media and Pluralism

It is important to remember that the term, *media*, is and should be considered a *plural* concept. In a trivial sense this is just a grammatical point. But the "singularizing" of media that is common in much writing (i.e., "the media ruined his chances for reelection.") implies much more. Properly used, references to the media refer to a number of information sources with a wide degree of diversity. A big city newspaper, for example, and a small town radio station are both part of the media. But their differences are as evident as their similarities. Each will have starkly different objectives and audiences, naturally different means of constructing messages, different types of owners, and so on. While they may share some key similarities—for example, each may use the same wire service or network news sources—the gulf that separates them is too wide to be glossed over with generalizations that attempt to unify them.

This inherent diversity poses a profound and often ignored conceptual muddle. The tendency to presuppose that the mass media represent identifiable sets of shared characteristics plagues much of the analysis of political communication. The problem is one of abstraction. Individual outlets surely do carry recognizable forms of political intelligence. We can describe and study, to cite several instances, editorials about George Bush in the *Christian Science Monitor*, CBS News' coverage of the Iran-Contra affair, or *Time's* editorial policy on Vietnam War coverage in the late 1960s. We may even be able to trace patterns evident in the coverage of a presidential election by the "national press," for example, in the wire services, the networks, and the *Washington Post*. But the limits of description are distorted by conclusions that attempt to bridge the enormous range of sources of information available to Americans. It makes no sense, for example, to talk about "media politics" or "media candidates." Virtually all but the very smallest of political offices depend upon various forms of mediated public communication. That reality has been with us since the first political tracts accompanied European settlers to North America in the first half of the seventeenth century. The historical counterpart to these abstractions might be the sixteenth century admonition of a religious fanatic against the influence of books—all books—on the lives of their readers.

Part of our difficulty is that we have equated the rapid development of radio and television in the interwar years with nothing less than a communications revolution. An obvious assumption behind this conclusion is that preelectric communication affected readers and subjects alike in far different ways. But in actual fact the vigorous print press of prewar America represented a kind of media that differed from its modern electronic counterparts more in degree than in kind. Even in the life of George Washington one finds public relations problems thought to have been invented with radio and television: press fascination with his personality, a chain of publicity-based "pseudo-events" leading up to his appointment as President, "news management" in the publication of his "farewell address," and the kind of elevation to celebrity status that would have made *People* magazine proud.[6]

All of these traps are ones that we have ourselves stumbled into. To clarify that scope of our own discussion here we will generally deal only with those national print and electronic mass media that service smaller outlets with programs and stories. These companies include the three networks and their growing cable competitors, their radio counterparts, the major wire services such as UPI and AP, the commercial film industry, and the major newsweeklies. Together these industry giants account for a huge portion of the political information delivered to Americans. Most local newspapers, television or radio stations receive a significant portion of their content from one or more of these national sources. In addition, these important giants tend to establish the patterns of reporting that are followed by other organizations.

Media and Determinism

For several decades now researchers and analysts have been exploring the intensely complex relationships that exist between news sources and public at-

titudes. Their conclusions invariably point to the difficulties involved in attrib-
uting the flow of public opinion to specific mass media sources. The questions
that media researchers ask are intriguing because they imply effects that touch
nearly everyone. Even so, attributions of causation assigned to various forms of
the media are notoriously difficult to establish. Extensive research over the last
50 years has still failed to resolve a number of questions. Are correlations between
public attitudes and intense public communication causally related, or simply
two artificially frozen points in a process that involves less apparent forces? How
accurate are recall surveys? How accurate are media usage studies? Are the mass
media collectively so powerful that they function like "magic bullets," piercing
the consciousness of everyone in their path? Or are they so diffuse that they are
analytically unpenetrable?[7] The more the research accumulates, the more the
last question seems to characterize the difficulties of coming to grips with mass
media research. The impression conveyed by the layman or the journalist is
often of all-powerful mass media that relentlessly control the flow of political
information, and thus influence public attitudes.[8]

A wide variety of specific studies—some of which are cited in this chapter—
often reveal the complexities that temper such determinism. The collective weight
of both critical and empirical studies on the effects of broadcast and print messages leaves a number of important qualifiers in force. From the early work of
Lang and Lang examining political television in the 1950s,[9] to the more recent
work of Michael Robinson, Sidney Krause, Thomas Patterson, Doris Graber,
and countless others,[10] a number of important antideterministic conclusions re-
appear, among them:

- No single mass media source commands total loyalty and certain credibility. There is
  little reflexive acceptance of persuasive or informative messages, including those of the
  most important mass media.

- People are generally selective about what they hear, making the actual effects of any
  political communication unpredictable. Conclusions other than those intended by the
  sender are sometimes reached. Messages may be considered, momentarily accepted,
  and then later rejected.

- Messages such as political commercials may produce the reverse of their intended
  effect: creating greater hostility rather than increasing support.

- There is a great deal of elasticity in the attitudes of individuals. Attitudes may be
  stretched and momentarily altered by the appeals contained in a news story, editorial,
  or political broadcast. But the individual psyche is likely to retain its original beliefs.

- And, finally, because opinions and attitudes are the products of aggregate experiences,
  the messages of the mass media must be treated as only one of many causes. To imply
  that the media alone are prime causes in attitude formation is to overlook both other
  sources of attitudes, especially those gained from interpersonal contact. Attitudes are
  produced interactively rather than unilaterally.

THREE EFFECTS OF MEDIATED COMMUNICATION

There are three dominant processes that routinely intrude on messages as they make their way through the labyrinths of mass media channels. First, outlets that distribute information and entertainment serve collectively to establish a public consciousness on a limited range of community and national concerns. Secondly, popular forms of media that provide news and entertainment cannot help but give substance to the raw and nearly inexhaustible world of events with potential political significance. And, thirdly, the electronic media naturally tend to reduce abstract and ideological principles to their human or personal components. All three processes are basic and important. The first involves what is often described as the agenda setting function; the second, the construction of specific political realities, and the third, the personalization of ideas.

Agenda Setting

There can be little doubt that even in our pluralistic environment the mass media collectively exert a considerable influence in determining the agenda of topics that will be given prominence. "The press," Walter Lippmann has noted, "is like the beam of a searchlight that moves restlessly about, bringing one episode and then another out of darkness into vision."[11] As a number of pioneering studies by Maxwell McCombs, E. F. Shaw, and others have suggested, what we conclude about what we see may still be up to us. Even so, the direction to which we are "primed" to look seems largely out of our hands.[12]

The potential number of political events that could be reported by any outlet in a given day will obviously always outstrip its time or space limitations. At the local level, the newspaper must decide how to divide up the available "news hole", leaving space for a limited number of stories that meet the formulaic and journalistic requirements of the paper. Should a story on the mayor be included? How much effort should be given to state legislative business?, to political party news?, to insurance reform proposals? Should space be used to report on the governor's reelection campaign, or to a third-party presidential candidate touring the city? How much, if any, space should be used to describe the pending divorce of a member of Congress? The range of choices is nearly limitless, and is governed to some extent by the sequence in which items become available for use. It would be incorrect to conclude that news readers and viewers are unaware of how much their concerns are shaped by press reports.[13] But there can be little doubt that the saliency of an event or issue is closely tied to its place on the news agenda.

The bases for story selection—and for the emergence of a leader or issue into public awareness—are diverse and represent some of the most interesting areas of exploration into the business of news. Some analysts, such as Herbert Gans, have emphasized the traditional journalistic rules for story suitability. Something has news value if it involves public officials, affects the nation, has an impact on large numbers of people, or says something about where we are going.[14] An event may be deemed worthy of coverage if it contains a degree of novelty, an element of action, actual or potential conflict, and so on.[15] These are familiar journalistic standards—based in part on pleasing the largest possible audience, and in part on a traditional journalistic criteria for assessing what is important for news consumers to know.

Others have approached the study of news and information content by exploring topic and story selection from a consensual perspective. In this view "news" is what our priorities, fantasies, and national history tell us it is. It is a group product: a matter of agreement based on shared attitudes and routines. For example, Timothy Crouse's widely admired book about reporters covering the 1972 presidential campaign firmly planted the concept of "pack journalism" in the lexicon of public communication studies. Crouse provided evidence that reporters traveling with a presidential candidate frequently let the work of their colleagues govern their own perspectives toward specific campaign events. Living and traveling together for days at a time, some members of the press became collaborators in developing their stories. By definition, "pack journalists" are governed by the rules of consensus building. For example,

The [New York] *Times* team filed a lead saying that [Hubert] Humphrey had apologized for having called [George] McGovern a "fool" earlier in the campaign. Soon after they filed the story, an editor phoned from New York. The AP had gone with a [George] Wallace lead, he said. Why hadn't they?

Marty Nolan eventually decided against the Wallace lead, but NBC and CBS went with it on their news shows. So did many of the men in the room. They wanted to avoid "callbacks"—phone calls from their editors asking them why they had deviated from the AP or UPI. If the editors were going to run a story that differed from the story in the nation's 1,700 other newspapers, they wanted a good reason for it. Most reporters dreaded callbacks. Thus the pack followed the wire service men whenever possible. Nobody made a secret of running with the wires: it was accepted practice.[16]

Conformity in reporting "protects" individual reporters as well as entire organizations by extending the illusion of "news" as something that selects itself. If a lead story or certain issues are standard across a wide range of media, the public has little reason to question the competence or credibility of any one source.

A variation on the idea of a news consensus notion was put forth in interesting detail in 1974 by Edward Epstein.[17] In his influential *News from Nowhere* Epstein argued that agenda setting in the television age is covertly affected by the organizational and structural constraints imposed by the business of the mass media. He was given unprecedented access to executives and the daily decision-making process at NBC News, finding that story selection was heavily influenced by political and organizational ground rules that sometimes had little to do with the intrinsic newsworthiness of an event. Does a story have accompanying pictures?

Will it interest a large group of television viewers? Are the images of the story readily identifiable? (Criminals should look like criminals; the poor should look poor; victims should look victimized.) These were real concerns, and largely independant of substantive considerations. As Epstein has summarized,

> To maintain themselves in a competitive world, the newtorks impose a set of prior restraints, rules and conditions on the operations of their news divisions. Budgets are set for the production of news, time is scheduled for its presentation, and general policies are laid down concerning its content. To satisfy these requirements—and keep their jobs— news executives and producers formulate procedures, systems and policies intended to reduce the uncertainties of news to manageable proportions. The timing, length, content and cost of news thereby becomes predictable. Since all of the networks are in essentially the same business and compete for the same or similar advertisers, affiliates and audiences, under a single set of ground rules laid down by the government, the news product at each network is shaped by similar requisites. The basic contours of network news can thus be at least partly explained in terms of the demands which the news organizations must meet in order to continue operating without crises or intervention from network executives.[18]

Yet another source of influence on the information agenda—an ideological requirement—has been proposed by a wide range of observers on both the political right and left. Some have claimed that the national press in particular has a left-wing, antibusiness, anti-Republican slant. The most systematic attempt to chronicle this bias was perhaps Edith Efron's *The News Twisters*.[19] Although many national political reporters may be nominal supporters of Democratic candidates—as Gans asserts[20]—few studies support Efron's questionable claims about liberal dominance.[21]

A more sweeping critique of the managment of public opinion, however, comes from the academic left. Where the right tends to criticize "latent" attitudes that surface in the reporting of specific stories, the left tends to focus on fundamental values that shape the general choice of news and informational topics. Their primary criticism—developed more fully at the end of this chapter—is that the news agenda encourages acceptance of the economic and political status quo. News story selection, such critics argue, at best reveals a bias for incremental change as a standard for dealing with serious social problems. From this viewpoint the great organs of mass communication appear to have deep investments in the society *as it is*, not as it could be. With primary interests in secure and undisrupted markets, their interests lie in protecting a delicate balance. On one hand they must go through the motions of reporting objectively on the urgent, unusual, and problematic. But they must do so in a way that will not jeopardize their advertisers' interests in a stable and acquiescent society. For authors such as Todd Gitlin, Lance Bennett, and Benjamin Ginsberg,[22] the steady diet of news and fantasy in the American mass media has served to "delegitimate" the possibilities for significant change. The ideological core of American television, Gitlin argues, is one of static acceptance—of consideration of social dislocations in terms other than weaknesses that may be inherent in American capitalism. The status quo is given all kinds of advantages. To name just two, establishment sources may often get "the last word" in a story, or more deference may be shown to the "official" than to the outcast. The net result is the maintenance of an informational and entertainment agenda that has generally been depoliticized. Problems such as poverty, substandard health care, and unemployment may be described in terms of their personal consequences rather than their deeper economic roots. Because it is usually easier to portray the physical dimensions of a problem than its historical or ideological roots, public understanding is limited to a superficial awareness of a problem's most visible elements.

The disorganized antiwar movement in the 1960s is a case in point. Those opposing the war failed to produce, at an ideological plane, what the grim carnage on the nightly news produced at a more visceral level. The news, Gitlin and others have asserted, rarely gave segments of the movement the kind of legitimacy it needed to make its arguments against the war credible. Our eventual withdrawal from the Vietnam struggle was not because there was a groundswell of feeling that we were intruders in a South Vietnamese civil war, but that we were in a militarily unwinable war. The national debate that slowly built on the war was for some years muted, at least in comparison to the more vivid scenes of anger and grief in what Michael Arlin aptly called the first "living room war."[23] The television networks, for example, agonized over every minute of Senate Hearings they carried that debated the assumptions and principles justifying our involvement.[24] But no such similar agony was evident in the decisions to present the vivid and riveting war footage night after night.

The Construction of Political Realities

In his well known study of staged news events, Daniel Boorstin recalls that "We used to believe there were only so many 'events' in the world. If there were not many intriguing or startling occurrences, it was no fault of the reporter. He could not be expected to report what did not exist."[25] If such a time ever existed, it has long since passed. In Chapter 2 we argued that political events and attitudes are quintessentially symbolic. What we know about the exercise of power is largely derived from verbal and symbolic constructions that give an immediate presence to policies, intentions, and attitudes.

No one can deny the existence of "spot" news that essentially demands coverage. The bizarre 1987 press conference of Pennsylvania's State Treasurer, R. Budd Dwyer, was such an event. After defending himself against charges of corruption, he urged local television crews to keep their cameras running while he pulled a gun from a large envelope, then put the barrel in his mouth and pulled the trigger. One of the most ordinary of political rituals had suddenly turned into a human tragedy, securing for Dwyer a prominent place in the evening news that no routine press conference could have guaranteed.[26]

Press conferences, speeches, bill signings, proclamations, heated exchanges in debates, are rhetorical constructions: designed to secure the attention and support of an audience, and timed to have the greatest impact. But Boorstin was perhaps only half right in calling them "pseudo-events." The term carries the connotation that they are somehow less real or less important than "startling" occurrences that seem to be more authentic. But their effects can be just as impressive. In the 1988 presidential campaign, for example, both Michael Dukakis and George Bush usually limited their appearances to friendly audiences in carefully staged events. But Bush's running mate, Dan Quayle, was under an even stricter curfew, having been limited even to appearances before carefully selected crowds mostly in small midwestern cities. The goal of the Bush campaign was to minimize opportunities for misstatements, and to reduce the campaign to a carefully orchestrated number of events focused narrowly on positive values and attacks on Michael Dukakis. A visit to a New Jersey flag factory was representative of the most vacuous of these issues and staged events, but their cynical use no doubt carried out the objectives of the campaign. Members of the press were usually gentle in their criticism of Bush for his refusals to meet the press. The complaints of more thorough reporters such as Elizabeth Drew— who called Bush's "distorting and demogoguing of Dukakis's record" a "debasement" of the campaign—went largely unnoticed.[27]

Political life has always involved the rhetorical arts—the construction and expression of states of anger, concern, threat, and reassurance. Just as religion is, in a rhetorical sense, "words about God,"[28] so is politics essentially words about pending and past decisions affecting the community. The events discussed are only partly "out there." In basic ways political occurrences start and are reported when individuals feel motivated to make such events happen. They may indeed be complete fabrications: "psuedo-events" turned into "managed" and manufactured news. Their acceptance, however, makes their occurrence no less real than the spot news of an assassination attempt or a declaration of war. What makes them "real" or urgent is their surfacing in the public consciousness. "Events are not events until they get themselves communicated."[29]

Much of this goes without saying, but Americans often seem reluctant to take the implications of this perspective to its full conclusion. Without difficulty, we accept the political speech as a "manufactured" event, yet we assume the *reporting* of it is somehow more objective and less creative. Public officials are expected to orchestrate events to serve their own political ends, but we frequently cling to the view that the news media stand apart, reflecting rather than transposing the manufactured occurrence. Politicians are easily cast into the role of the rhetorician. They are seen as *constructors* of selected visions. But journalists are not. The former are thought to engage in artful rhetorical deceits in order to please audiences. The latter are widely seen as observers rather than participants.

A more accurate picture of the rhetorical dimensions of reporting requires some revisions of these falsely dichotomized roles. Michael Novak has correctly noted what most good journalists will concede: "All reporting is angular, perspectival, selective."[30] It must be, because both the reporter and the politician are working at the same enterprise. Both must attribute motives. Both must explain the nontangible principles that form the honorable rationales for political action. And both must please audiences with reconstructions of attitudes and events which are inexact and diffuse. If the politician chooses to talk about the plight of "the poor in America," the reporter assigned to cover him must exercise similar rhetorical options to relay the tone and nature of the event to the reader or listener. As Novak notes, the pressures for pleasing a constituency are usually every bit as strong in the journalist as they are in the politician, and equally corrupting:

The tradition of American journalism demands "news." An "angle." Something "different." Something "fresh." . . . The world isn't made that way—"There's nothing new under the sun," men believed for thousands of years—and good politics is seldom a matter of novelty. But journalism has a voracious appetite for novelty. . . .

Commentators, I think, fail to see how *corrupting* the practices of journalism truly are: the cult of celebrity, the cult of "news," the manipulative skills of "riding the wire," supplying two new daily "leads," "grabbing headlines," manufacturing "events" and "statements." Journalists speak as if *money* were the great corrupter of our times; but the corruption of intelligence and imagination by the demand for "news" is deadly.[31]

The best studies of news-gathering organizations tend to bypass the epistemologically futile exercise of verifying the accuracy of stories against actual events. All seem to note the tendency to reduce the complex to its simplest elements.[32] The most insightful also focus on the conventions and news-framing routines that serve to "normalize" discrete events. Gans, Epstein, Robinson, MacNeil, Bennett, Nimmo, and Combs have all discussed the formulaic elements of news gathering, usually in terms of the stylistic and thematic dimensions that make popular news an accessible and entertaining commodity.[33]

It is impossible here to recount the various schemes that have been proposed. But it is worthwhile to offer a brief sketch of several of the more problematic routines that have been asserted.

1. *Ritual objectivity is given priority over synthesis and analysis: "Facts" add up to something less than "understanding."* Nearly every news organization gives priority to some form of fairness or objectivity. Aside from the ostensible goals of letting "the reader or viewer decide," an emphasis on fact gathering removes journalism from the risks that come with sharply critical or analytical rhetoric: the alientation of subscribers, readers, advertisers, and news subjects. The code of objectivity renders journalism motive-free. The obligation to "report" or "observe" is separated from the political persuader's more obvious suasory intentions. This has the effect of conserving journalism's credibility and commercial saliency.

2. *"Official" voices are the prime beneficiaries of the mass media.* Objectivity also serves the interests of political advocates with official positions. Routine

versions of news usually give an enormous amount of credibility to "official" sources, more or less by default. Few critics of a governor, party leader, legislator, or president will be able to make refutations that contain the force that comes with such officials. The reason is obvious. A "fact"-based system of reporting frequently gives officials two sources of legitimation: one based on their ongoing role as public officeholder, the other as a compulsory respondent to nearly any story affecting their work. The presidential press conference dramatically illustrates this power. The President is uniquely able to make claims that—by simple journalistic standards—must be reported. He is also invited to comment on other topics of the day. No other source—not the "objective" journalists present, his critics, or opposing leaders in the other party—are able to match his ability to use legal authority to communicate his attitudes and feelings. As Lance Bennett has noted, "most news stories reserve for official sources the first, the last, and many of the words in between."[34]

The irony in this "bias toward the official" is that the news media organizes its work around the perception that it has an adversarial relationship with government officials.[35] The reality is that access comes much easier, and with less critical scrutiny, to holders of official positions in government and business than to their noninstitutionalized critics. Gitlin makes the point in an extended study of the messages of the radical Students for a Democratic Society in 1965.[36] Their arguments against the Vietnam escalation—more reasonable now than they appeared in the 1960s—were largely reported as the work of destructive and rebellious youth. The pattern was repeated in press reporting of the Watergate break-in and coverup. David Paletz and Robert Entman similarly conclude that most of the coverage was at least initially always careful not to undermine the legitimacy of official White House explanations. For a very long time President Nixon's participation in the coverup was neglected in favor of reports about the possible involvement of other officials.[37] Based on Watergate and a number of cases they conclude that the "powerful should be grateful." The mass media help "prevent [the] erosion of legitimacy"[38] even as they are lauded as watchdogs of the powerful.

There is no unanimity among press critics and observers on how much support the media give the political mainstream.[39] Even so, the long-term effect of news that derives from official sources is enormous. If access to a medium itself is not power, it is at least a requisite condition to political control. And access frequently goes to governmental sources who have the most to gain by maintaining a steady stream of positive publicity about their work. Ronald Reagan successfully mastered presidential leadership by careful use of network television news.[40] Publicity via news is made all the more potent when it comes to the receiver in the guise of journalistic neutrality. A general effect of much straight news reporting is thus to make significant social change difficult, and outspoken advocates of reform seemingly disrespectful of legitimate authority.

3. *Political action is framed within the conventions of melodrama.* No frame of reference has proved more durable in studies of political behavior than the

superstructure of terms and concepts associated with drama. Political reporting rarely ignores the elements of theatre. Roles, scenes, acts, and audiences are endemic to descriptions of political events.[41] Characterizations of melodramatic images of foolishness, villainy, and heroes are common. And themes used to outline many stories are very familiar: the triumph of the individual over adversity, justice winning over evil, redemption of the individual through reform, and the rewarding of valor or heroism. We say "melodrama," because unlike the treatment of political figures in classical drama—in *Hamlet, Coriolanus,* or *King Lear*, for example—the characteristic popular reporting of today emphasizes optimism rather than tragedy; a sense of upbeat predictability rather than of haunting human imperfections. The plot lines of political reporting are modulated to conform to the need for familiar themes and unambiguous personas. Stories may not always have happy endings. But the reader or viewer is usually left with the impression of what the ending should be. Along with others, Nimmo and Combs have noted that contemporary news reporting is "a literary act, a continuous search for story lines."

Such story lines may incorporate the metaphors and plots of novels, folk traditions, and myths. . . . The same melodramatic formats available to entertainment programmers are options for producers of TV news: adventure, mystery, romance, pathos, nightmare, comedy. . . . When faced with an event that requires prolonged storytelling—say a presidential campaign, the seizure of hostages in a foreign country, a threat of war, and so on—a variety of melodramatic formats may be adapted to news coverage, thus imposing a thematic unity (a story) on what might otherwise seem unrelated events.[42]

Reflecting the logic that has long dominated the writing style of the newsweeklies such as *Time* and *Newsweek*,[43] former NBC News Chief Reuven Frank vividly made the same dramatistic point. In what is now a widely reprinted memo to his staff, the executive wrote:

Every news story should, without any sacrifice of probity or responsibility, display the attributes of fiction, of drama. It should have structure and conflict, problem and denouement, rising action and falling action, a beginning, a middle and an end. These are not only the essentials of drama; they are the essentials of narrative.[44]

Television news in particular, notes Paul Weaver, "is not governed by a political bias, but by a melodramatic one." It is characterized by intensified peril, simplified values, and exaggerated intensity.[45]

4. *Political reporting has drifted toward an emphasis on "strategy" rather than ideology.* Perhaps reflecting the pace of television, or the natural interest it places on human motives, political reporting is somewhat different from what it was several generations ago. The reader of a newspaper earlier this century was more likely to find news reports of political activity dominated by long excepts of speeches and remarks. For a number of years in the 1920s and 30s

even radio was content to carry political addresses with a minimum of commentary. This "journalism" was not necessarily better. But it was different. By contrast, the central objective of much contemporary political reporting focuses on political strategies and tactics. Faced with the choice of recounting to readers or viewers what a particular figure said, or analyzing the motives behind remarks addressed to a specific audience, more and more political journalism seems to emmphasize the latter.

This pattern is represented by the now familiar sight of a network correspondent delivering a "stand up" summary against the backdrop of a politician voicelessly explaining himself to an unknown audience. The option to let the politician's words speak for themselves is less often exercised. The reporter feels the need to act as narrator: not simply telling the viewer what has just been said, but assessing the motivations underlying the political scene. By serving as a constant presence (or intruder) in a report, the journalist is able to assign unseen motives, and to provide the pacing that is sought for a medium whose content is governed by the adage that time is money.

A sequence of three reports on a more or less typical 1980 CBS newscast illustrates how motive becomes more dominant than idea. The theme of political courtship is carried in campaign stories by correspondents Lesley Stahl, Jerry Bowen, and Bernard Goldberg. They were woven together in this instance by acting anchor Charles Kuralt.

Kuralt: Campaigns in this country traditionally start on Labor day. So President Carter went home to the South today. John Anderson went home to Illinois, and Ronald Reagan went to a place where he could make a speech with the Statue of Liberty over his shoulder—each of them trying to appeal to a constituency he will need to win the presidency.

Stahl: President Carter chose the heart of George Wallace country for today's traditional campaign kickoff; he chose Alabama because he was concerned that the Wallace vote among Southerners and blue collar workers may be slipping to Ronald Reagan.

Kuralt: To win Ronald Reagan will have to make inroads in the big industrial states. So he started out today in a tough one—New Jersey. Jerry Bowen has that story.

Bowen: Ronald Reagan seems to have pulled out all of the stops as he brought his campaign to heavily Democratic New Jersey for a rally set against the New York skyline and the Statue of Liberty. . . .

Kuralt: Independent John Anderson also bore down heavily on economic issues as he campaigned in Illinois. Bernard Goldberg has our report.

Goldberg: It almost rained on John Anderson's parade today, but after a few minutes under the umbrella the sun came out and Anderson began walking the suburbs of Chicago, trying to win some support in Calumet City, were workers wear blue collars and normally vote Democratic.[46]

This pattern of focusing on the *logistics* of politics occurs in all forms of political reporting. David Riesman tracked its rise in his seminal study, *The*

Lonely Crowd. Politics, he said, encouraged a game-player's enthusiasm for technique, and the sharing of the "insider's" superior understanding of how to play the game of politics well. "Inside dopester's" discount for the higher ostensible goals of political discourse, focusing instead on the status that is assured with access to inside knowledge:

There are political newsmen and broadcasters who, after long training, have succeeded in eliminating all emotional response to politics and who pride themselves on achieving the inside-dopester's goal: never to be taken in by any person, cause, or event.[47]

   5. *Polls have gained unwarrented importance*. A further deflection of attention away from the substance of a political campaign is the widespread attention given to public opinion polls. As we have noted earlier, political polls are now an important part of the campaign. Their use in news reports, however, can be intrusive when they create news that must compete with more substantive parts of the campaign. "It's almost gotten to the point," notes former NBC reporter Marvin Kalb, "where polls have become a substitute for old-fashioned leg work."[48]

Many public polls are now commissioned by news organizations, providing a private news angle that is at least initially denied to competing news outlets. For example, here is the way Tom Brokaw began the political coverage of the NBC Nightly News just 12 days before the 1988 presidential election:

Brokaw: Good Evening, Michael Dukakis today was promising a Harry Truman come-from-behind victory, and Vice President Bush was accusing his Democratic opponent of trying to scare the American voters as a cheap way of winning votes. All of this as the latest NBC News/ *Wall Street Journal* Poll indicates a nine point lead for the Vice President, still substantial, but down considerably from our last sampling. Almost 1300 likely voters were questioned this week. The Bush-Quayle ticket leads Dukakis-Bentsen 51 to 42 percent. In our last poll that lead was 17 points, 55 to 38. The candidates, of course, had just come off their final debate, with Bush widely perceived as the winner. Since then, several key voting groups have moved toward Dukakis, including Democrats who supported Reagan. They now support the Dukakis ticket by a wide margin: 56 to 37 percent. And just blue-collar voters? Well, they're now divided between the candidates. In our last poll they supported Bush two to one. A couple of other encouraging trends for Dukakis: 43 percent of those questioned believed that he has new ideas for solving the nation's problems. Only 23 percent credit Bush with new ideas.

Nearly everything in NBC's subsequent reporting on this night was then tied to the subject of political polling. Brokaw's report of the commissioned NBC poll was used as a reference point for the network's reports from the field:

Brokaw: NBC's Chris Wallace is with Dukakis tonight.
Wallace: Dukakis talked a lot about polls today, because his biggest concern now is to persuade voters the election is not over. At one stop he tried to create a backlash.

Dukakis: . . . as a matter of fact I think the American people are getting a little tired of being told in advance how they are going to vote, don't you?

Wallace: At another, he did an impression of a radio newsman, writing of Harry Truman in 1948.

Dukakis: (impersonating a radio announcer) There is no doubt that, when the final results are in, Mr. Dewey will be elected the next President of the United States.

In this report only brief mention was made about what candidate Dukakis said in the course of the day's campaigning. NBC's choice of subsequent items seemed to be chosen to give more weight to their in-house generated story—namely, the use of a poll as a vehicle for handicapping the presidential contest. Chris Wallace's closing was revealing:

Wallace: While polls show most voters have now made up their minds, Dukakis aides maintain opinion is soft, and can still be moved. What they don't explain is why a Bush lead that's held up for weeks will suddenly disappear between now and the election.[49]

The use of polls and insider information tends to produce reporters who talk in the same strategic terms and with the same tactical thinking of a press secretary or campaign consultant. To simply report a public figure's words may seem uncomfortably close to functioning as a "flack" for a certain point of view. The way to demonstrate insights about the *realpolitik* of American life is to report on its competitiveness and its theatre-like manipulations. The credibility of the reporter is presumably enhanced because he or she demonstrates the ability to see through the veneer of public rhetoric to supposedly different political realities underneath.

The Personalization of Politics

The final broad form of mediation that seems evident in many forms of political reporting is the linkage of policy discussion to the circumstances and charac-teristics of particular *individuals*. This is not simply to say that we focus more today on "personalities" than on "issues." The components of this pattern are more complex than this simple dualism. Fundamentally it means that political information is frequently made comprehensible to vast numbers when it centers on the actors involved: the agents for change, the victims of inaction or social neglect, and the villains responsible for creating social unrest. Public policy today is described largely in terms of the personalities of proponents, opponents, and affected citizens.

To be sure, it has always been the case that the character of the public figure has been a subject of public interest. The politics of ancient Greece enshrined the role of *ethos* and its central idea that personal qualities are important to strong leadership.[50] The plays of Shakespeare and didactic theatre in general, have encouraged the exploration of the linkages that connect specific personal qualities to the advocacy of doctrines of the public good. Freud, psychoanalysis, the popularity of literary and celebrity biographies, and television's thirst for the personal are but some of the influences that have fueled interest in the public personage. Every age has contained its share of mass literature identifying progress and change with the personal strengths and weaknesses of its leaders. As with the Checker's speech, the political agent's vivid personal response is always the more concrete part of the political equation. Motives, values, attitudes, decisions—all of the intangibles affecting work in the public domain—are made evident when reduced to the visible actions of individuals. As Machiavelli warned the casual observer, the apparent character of a public figure is a convenient if highly misleading window on the politics he seems to endorse.[51]

The intensification of this trend is to be seen everywhere. In news magazines ideas are not discussed apart from their advocates; they are portrayed as being *enacted by them*. In television both fictional and news forms of programming give preference to the agent over unseen conditions as the root causes of behavior. Television almost always illuminates policy through the eyes and actions of specific characters and stereotypes. Social problems are not discussed in general terms, but when the specific effects of the problems are shown at work on specific people. Countless network television films not only treat a range of social problems that imply political solutions—child custody laws, unemployment, police corruption, and many more—they also include "docudramas" on the final days of the Nixon administration, the Jim Jones People's Temple, or the "Baby M" case involving surrogate mothers. Supermarket tabloids and their television counterparts explore the personal tastes and attitudes of political celebrities. Hundreds of biographies of presidents, senators, flamboyant governors, and mayors offer glimpses of the human side of major political figures, often with more interest in their personal lives than their political accomplishments. These leaders are well-advised to heed this dramatic imperative. They know that they must pause for the inevitable sidetrack through the vital media/celebrity circuits: TV talk shows, "life-style" interviews, and the like.

Richard Sennett has written brilliantly on what he sees as a steady increase in the value we assign to the personal attributes of political figures. In *The Fall of Public Man* he notes that

A political leader running for office is spoken of as "credible" or "legitimate" in terms of what kind of man he is, rather than in terms of the actions or programs he espouses. The obsession with persons at the expense of more impersonal social relations is like a filter which discolors our rational understanding of society; it obscures the continuing importance of class in advanced industrial society; it leads us to believe community is an act of mutual self-disclosure and to undervalue the community relations of strangers.[52]

Sennett claims that we have forgotten the arts of formal public communication, where roles are clearly defined, and the decision to enter into public discourse

carries the responsibility to put the needs of institutions before private considerations. He argues that the devoted but largely anonymous public servant has
been partially replaced by the publicity hound, the agent who strives for a
fabricated sense of intimacy to win over skeptical audiences.

Such personalization may help explain why President Kennedy was widely
thought to be more progressive than he was. The Kennedy style which received
so much press attention contrasted with the "square" and old-fashioned style
of the previous Eisenhower-Nixon years. In the 1960 campaign stylistic differences between the two men were enormous: Kennedy was the paragon of grace,
self-assurance, and wit; Nixon was awkward, less handsome, and publicly defensive. But most of Kennedy's initiatives—in civil rights, European affairs, in
Asia, and in military spending—could have been (and usually were) accom-
modated by Nixon.

The same general trend was clearly evident in the Reagan era. Ronald Reagan
and his advisers increasingly miminized the use of speeches and public appearances as occasions for the public discussion of issues. In place of press conferences, for example, Reagan allowed himself to be deployed as a highly prized
piece of political furniture, to be used largely to decorate ceremonial events.[53]
Especially in the last few years of his administration, appearances were confined
to brief East Room or Rose Garden welcoming addresses, and set speeches
before uncritical supporters. By the time Reagan left office, he was averaging
far less than one press meeting every three months. Photo opportunities had
almost completely replaced the routine exchange of information that have characterized all modern presidencies except Richard Nixon's.[54]

The personalizing of twentieth-century politics is frequently laid at the feet
of the "compulsively personalistic" medium of television.[55] Broadcasting encourages the communicator to trade in a particularly superficial kind of imagery,
and on the details of presentation and style rather than the sustained discussion
of ideas. A print story more naturally focuses attention on a message—what was
said rather than the way it was presented. But political television is different.
As presidential specialist Rod Hart has noted, the assessment of a politician's
rhetorical skills has come to dominate how he or she is assessed by the general
public; in a sense, all Americans are now Hollywood talent scouts:

While the personal attractiveness of a candidate has always been part of the electoral
scene, voters now match up prospective leaders to standards suspiciously resembling
those employed by media talent scouts. There is a certain strategic logic to such an
approach, but it is nevertheless unnerving when one hears these criteria being applied
not by political insiders but by ordinary citizens.[56]

Placing the advocate immediately before us makes television an instrument
that invites the careful measurement of intention and motive. What we hear is
tempered and often eclipsed by the complementary (or occasionally dissonant)
image of what we see. A prime form of such imagery is a kind of artificial

interpersonal milieu that has the effect of presenting the performer as a close acquaintance of the viewer, a figure worthy of trust. The inanimate world of ideas that is intrinsic to political discussion is increasingly forced into an animate mold.[57] We frequently cannot conceive of the principles governing foreign policy until we see graphic portrayals of the residents who would be affected. We cannot tolerate extensive discussion of tax law revisions without seeing depictions of affluence or poverty. Television frequently reduces policy debates to their material and personal dimensions. The intimacy of television, notes Sennett,

connotes warmth, trust, and open expression of feeling. But precisely because we have come to expect these psychological benefits through the range of our experience, and precisely because so much social life which does have meaning cannot yield these psychological rewards, the world outside, the impersonal world, seems to fail us, seems to be stale and empty.[58]

The personalizing nature of the popular mass media has also lessened our interest and attention in the old supporting structures of American political life, most notably the party organizations and smaller political jurisdictions. That the parties have suffered has been chronicled by many observers.[59] They still wield a good deal of influence in the politics of particular states, especially in the Northeast and the South. But their national influence has waned as the television-intensive presidential primaries have taken over the presidential selection process. The quadrennial summer conventions now merely tend to affirm a selection process that is essentially over by mid-spring. Candidates at various levels of government have learned that skillful use of television can replace the party machinery that used to have control over the selection of candidates.[60]

Local politicians, such as state assembly members and mayors, still cultivate networks of support within local party organizations, particularly where news coverage is scarce. But national politicians have grown accustomed to building their own media-based bridges to constituencies. The public official with a broad constituency has learned that party support is capricious. At many levels of office the party means much less on election day than the availability of mass media exposure. The transition from organizational to "personal" politics came in full force in the 1970s. By then, traditional party loyalists—the Richard J. Daleys, Lyndon Johnsons, and Sam Rayburns—had faced challenges from "the pretty boys" who were using the "new politics" of the direct mass media appeal. The leaders of the old political machines lost ground to well-financed media candidates appealing to large segments of voters, often with only the thinnest veneer of party loyalty. In style and demeanor these new candidates often matched the finesse and rhetorical sophistication of the professional communicators and interviewers they are keeping company with on television—the news anchors, actors, and interviewers that dominate modern television. David Halberstam cites Lyndon Johnson's bitter response to the passing of this old order:

All you guys in the media. All of politics has changed because of you. You've broken all the [party] machines and the ties between us in Congress and the city machines. You've given us a new kind of people. . . . Teddy [Kennedy]. [John] Tunney. They're your creations, your puppets. No machine could ever create a Teddy Kennedy. Only you guys. They're all yours. Your product.[61]

THE STRUCTURE OF THE MASS MEDIA

The routine channels of political communication in the United States are well known. Aside from the vital roles played by television and print journalism, significant use is made of direct mail, radio and television advertising, and special-interest publications. In this section we will briefly examine some of the guidelines that govern the use of these forms, as well as some representative attempts to measure their efficiency in reaching citizens.

Media Usage and Credibility

Among the most common questions asked about political media is whether some forms are more persuasive than others. The simple answer to this question must be a qualified "yes." As we have seen, television news and advertising probably present the greatest potential for affecting citizen attitudes. But the details of available research also point out many exceptions and qualifications.

Perhaps the most widely followed work on mass media credibility has been conducted by the Roper Organization. Since 1959 it has asked a cross section of the American public a number of questions about media usage and attitudes toward various media forms. Their polling has generally been synoptic: asking respondents to record attitudes and estimate time spent with "television," "newspapers," "radio," and so on. The numbers generated are exact, but the categories naturally deal with media that have wide variations within them.

The key trends are worth noting.[62] Since 1959 the number of respondents getting "most" of their news "about what's going on in the world today" has gone up for television and down for newspapers. In 1986, 66 percent mentioned television and 36 percent mentioned newspapers. Radio trailed behind with 14 percent (see Table 6.1).

Since the early 1960s television has been seen as the "most believable" news source. In 1986, 55 percent rated it the most believable medium, followed by 21 percent for newspapers, and 6 and 7 percent each for radio and magazines (see Table 6.2). When asked to rank the overall quality of television news, most respondents (between 80 and 90 percent) thought it was "excellent" or "good."

Given the well documented evidence of how central a fixture television in the home has become, these results can hardly be surprising. In 50 short years television has grown from its status as a novelty to a household necessity. It has become a major source of information for the vast numbers of Americans who want to experience the sensation of news without the troubling and complex

Table 6.1
General Information Sources

"I'd like to ask you where you usually get most of your news about what's going on in the world today--from the newspapers or radio or television or magazines or talking to people or where?"

Source of most news (%)	12/59	11/63	1/67	1/71	11/74	12/78	12/82	12/86
Television	51	55	64	60	65	67	65	66
Newspapers	57	53	55	48	47	49	44	36
Radio	34	29	28	23	21	20	18	14
Magazines	8	6	7	5	4	5	6	4
People	4	4	4	4	4	5	4	4

Source: Television Information Office, 1983, p. 5, and 1987, p. 18.

Table 6.2
Relative Credibility of Sources

"If you got conflicting or different reports of the same news story from radio, television, the magazines, and the newspapers, which of the four versions would you be most inclined to believe--the one on radio, or television or magazines or newspapers?"

Most believable (%)	12/59	11/63	1/67	1/71	11/74	12/78	12/82	12/86
Television	29	36	41	49	51	47	53	55
Newspapers	32	24	24	20	20	23	22	21
Radio	12	12	7	10	8	9	6	6
Magazines	10	10	8	9	8	9	8	7
Don't know/ No answer	17	18	20	12	13	12	11	12

Source: Television Information Office, 1983, p. 6 and 1987, p. 18.

details. Even so, the Roper results, and the widely held views about television dominance among academics and journalists that they reinforce, need additional clarification and comment.

These surveys might lead one to conclude that these media are competitors, and that television is by far the clear victor. But increasingly detailed analyses

Table 6.3

Exposure to Network Evening Newscasts and the Daily Paper's Political News Sections (percent)

Level of News Exposure	Erie		Los Angeles	
	Newspaper	Network News	Newspaper	Network News
Regularly	48	34	33	24
Somewhat often	21	30	15	27
Once in a while	11	23	10	30
Infrequently	7	12	15	16
Never	13	1	27	3
Total	100	100	100	100

Note: Table percentages are average of respondents' replies for the five interviews. That respondents were questioned as many as five times provides a control on measurement error. To be classified as a regular user, a respondent had to consistently indicate frequent exposure. Typical of the questions asked was the following: "Most people don't have the time or interest to read the entire newspaper. They normally read only certain parts such as the sports, the comics, the news, the business pages, the women's pages, and so on. How often did you read the *news pages* of your daily newspaper? Do you read the news pages regularly, somewhat often, only once in a while, or almost never (infrequently)?" People who did not receive a newspaper or did not have a television set were placed in the never category.

Source: Patterson, *Mass Media Elections*, p. 59.

of media usage patterns indicate that there is a far more complementary routine of citizen involvement than might first be evident. There are problems in concluding that television is the *primary* news medium. As Thomas Patterson has noted,

The problem stems from the evidence on which the judgment is based. To ask people where they get most of their news is to fail to regard distinctions in the amounts of news they receive. . . .

A more precise assessment of the political audience is obtained by asking people how often they see the news on television or in the newspaper. When this is done a much different picture emerges. It is actually the newspaper, not television, which has the larger regular news audience.[63]

As Table 6.3 shows, Patterson attempted to isolate frequency of media use in his own study of consumers in Erie Pennsylvania and Los Angeles. He noted that, at least from a consumer's viewpoint, journalists from different kinds of media are not necessarily competitors (though they do compete for advertising dollars). News readers are also likely to be news viewers. And viewers—all except the least politically interested—also read newspapers.[64]

The research of Michael Robinson and Margaret Sheehan adds a further dimension to these comparisons. They have indicated that the network half hour newscasts may offer as complete a picture of a political story as their print counterparts at the major wire services. But it is also a slightly different one. At least with regard to campaign news offered by CBS and by UPI, CBS tended to cover more information about the candidate's personal behavior. It also tended to be more analytic about the political motivations and processes, and more critical of politics and politicians in general.[65]

Though few would argue with the claim that television has expanded the audience for political information, it is still the case that the prestige print press exerts the greatest influence on story selection. For this reason it is dangerous to underestimate the importance of the print media—especially the *New York Times, Washington Post, Newsweek, The Wall Street Journal*, and the smaller national political journals. Because their readers often include other journalists, they can play a critical role in focusing attention on a particular story, or a new angle to an existing one. A story printed in the *New York Times*, for example, is likely to be picked up by other reporters and editors as worthy of coverage. Traditionally the print press has provided the lead on stories that involve investigation, long-term research, and trend setting.

Finally, a judgmental caveat: Although there have been dramatic increases in the sophistication and quality of television news reporting, its increasingly important role as a filter for all kinds of political information must be considered disturbing. A "half hour" network newscast is actually about 22 minutes long. The formula for dividing up that precious space leaves little room for any detailed look at a political candidate, a complex issue, or an explanation of an emerging social problem or trend. Many reporters have become masters at the construction of miniature documentaries that cram a remarkable amount of information and clarity into 90 seconds or two minutes. But a story is still only as information rich as the selection of words and images will permit. Television is still as much oral as it is visual: The burden of explaining most political stories is usually in the oral narration, not in the accompanying pictures. The capacity of television news is thus naturally limited by the leisurely pace of spoken delivery.[66] A broadcast report might make a story more vivid, but it rarely has the space to develop the depth that comes from an extended print story in a serious newspaper or newsmagazine. As Walter Cronkite once noted, there is an "inadvertent and perhaps inevitable distortion that results through the hyper-compression we all are forced to exert to fit one hundred pounds of news into the one-pound sack that we are given to fill each night."[67]

CONTROLLED AND UNCONTROLLED MEDIA

There is no greater threshold in the world of politics than that which separates messages which have been paid for, and those which reach the public via "free" channels. The former include advertisments and political tracts purchased by their proponents, like Richard Nixon's redemptive Checker's speech. The latter include the much more persuasive conduit of "news" or "information" that reaches the reader, viewer, or listener without direct payment.

The political campaign is the event that most sharply focuses on the distinctions between free and paid media. Campaigners running for major elective offices purchase stunningly expensive blocks of television time to present messages wholly controlled by them. They do it, as political consultant John Deardourff notes, because there is a "constant tension between our interests and the media's interest. . . . " The requirement to use paid media, he argues, is virtually "forced upon us."[68] Other types of advocates sometimes face the same threshold, but usually in less dramatic ways. The supporters of a key congressional bill or members of a single issue movement will always think in terms of these two routes for reaching the American public. They may decide to pay for newspaper space or broadcast time to present their message. And they will often hire direct mail advertising firms to design and send messages intended for families on carefully chosen mailing lists.

But they will also have to plan ways to exploit "free media," finding ways to court bona fide journalists who will give them publicity in the context of a news story. A kind of implicit exchange is undertaken, based on mutual reciprocity. In return for the coverage newsgatherers give to a press conference or speech, publicity seekers make attempts to have these events conform to standard definitions of news. The currency that is exchanged is not money, but control. Unlike the advertisement that is constructed and paid for by the advocate, a news story is in the hands of the medium rather than the political persuader. From the advocate's point of view, the event may produce the "good press" that results when a story leaves a generally favorable impression with the reading and viewing public. The reporter's goal is a story that also preserves at least the appearance of journalistic independence.

Much of our discussion so far has focused on news media that are beyond the direct control of political newsmakers. Our observations here will emphasize paid messages.

One of the ironies of American life is that so few groups with political objectives can afford to purchase access to major forms of mass media. The vast majority of political candidates, parties, and special interest groups lack the resources to purchase the time or space that is used so freely to sell everything from soft drinks to deodorants. With the exception of the smallest local outlets such as small weekly papers or radio stations, the price for a one-time message must be figured in the thousands of dollars. Thirty seconds of network television time or a full-page ad in a newsmagazine may be sold for more than $200,000. The space in a highly rated local newscast or in a daily newspaper often runs between $5000 and $10,000. And these figures are only the beginning. The chance to have any sustained impact will only increase if such time and space purchases are duplicated many times over.

Advertising is thus relegated largely to the commercial segments of society, not to those in the public sector who are interested in communicating views on matters of national or regional policy. As John Kenneth Galbraith has noted, "Every corner of the public psyche is canvassed by some of the nation's most talented citizens to see if the desire for some merchantable product can be cultivated. No similar process operates in behalf of the nonmerchantable services of the state."[69] When applied to political candidates, the only significant exceptions are those celebrity-politicians who are running for major offices. And even their chances at success are narrowed by the necessity to start out as plausible winners, because only well-known candidates can attract the necessary campaign contributions that are needed to underwrite advertising costs. They must have enormous potential constituencies—as a future president, senator from California, mayor of a major city—in order to justify the economies of scale that ultimately make the mass media efficient. It is worth remembering that most of the people who directly participate in the 80,000 governmental units in the United States fall somewhere outside of these broad parameters.

Advertising has been perhaps the most studied and most debated of all of the controlled media. "The effect on politics," notes broadcast historian Eric Barnouw, "has been devastating."[70] Case histories of national and regional campaigns are rife with examples of potential or real abuses of advertising. In his landmark study of the 1968 presidential campaign, Joe McGinniss claimed that staffers packaged the Nixon persona like a product.[71] Theodore White declared that broadcasting "is subject to manipulation by experts in a way the printed press is not."[72] Reflecting the prevailing view, Robert Spero has noted that political advertising has the "ability to reach from 30 million to 80 million people at once" with the "unprecedented power to change their minds. . . . "[73]

The marriage of politics and television also has its defenders. One of Kathleen Jamieson's conclusions in her exhaustive study of political advertising is that specific ads are usually just restatements of what candidates have said countless times in their public speeches.[74] Others, such as Gary Mauser, have defended the strategic benefits of treating a political campaign as a variation on the techniques used to market new products. Marketing theory, he argues, has a legitimate place in the electoral process:

This procedure enables a political candidate to measure his image, determine how his image compares with those of other candidates, examine alternative positions and postures, and position himself in the contest so as to take maximum advantage of his strengths or his opponent's weaknesses.[75]

The only difficulty with such an approach is that commercial marketing uses major forms of mass media that require budgets which are unthinkable for all but a few of the nation's political candidates.

Several important studies have pointed out that some long-held views about the superficiality of political advertising need to be rethought. Perhaps the most interesting work challenging old assumptions was done in 1976 by Thomas Patterson and Robert McClure. Using both content analyses and attitude formation studies, they concluded that television ads may in fact be *more* informative than the widely respected newscasts of the television networks. Their portrayal of advertising is less bleak and less cynical than the one that is usually painted by the print press. The authors reserve most of their fire for the campaign reporting to which advertising is usually unfavorably compared:

> The only noticeable effect of network campaign news is an increased tendency among voters to view politics in the same trivial terms that the newscast depicts it. Regular viewers of network news are likely to describe an election campaign as a lot of nonsense rather than a choice between fundamental issues. . . .
>
> Although commercials are surely full of their own nonsense, blatant exaggerations, and superficial symbolism, presidential candidates do make heavy use of hard issue information in their advertising appeals. In fact, during the short period of the general election campaign, presidential ads contain substantially more issue content than network newscasts. This information is particularly valuable to people who pay little attention to the newspaper. Advertising serves to make these poorly informed people substantially more knowledgeable.[76]

Patterson and McClure also tackled the common belief that advertising is a very powerful, if not irresistible, form of persuasion. Their contrasting judgment was that political commercials are not necessarily effective in changing voter attitudes or behaviors. "[T]he vast majority of Americans are immune to advertising's propaganda. . . . And the reason is simple: They know too much; their views on politics are too clearly defined."[77] It would be difficult to make such a statement stick in every case. And the authors themselves temper it elsewhere in their study, noting especially that people who rarely seek out news about a campaign may be influenced by ads. Their work generally corroborates the work of other researchers who have discovered that the effects of ads by themselves are probably minimal. Even so, television can play a critical role in a small number of voters. If a contest between two candidates is very close, the attitudes of perhaps 3 or 4 percent could be vital, and within the reach of a successful ad blitz pitched to increase the casual voter's recognition of the candidate's name and image. Most advertising professionals believe that a crucial number of undecided voters can be persuaded to "support" a candidate if they are reassured that they "have seen" the politician, and they "know" something about him.[78]

Ads also allow the candidate lucky enough to be able to afford them an opportunity to speak directly to the electorate. The ad gets the candidate's message through without subjecting it to the conflicting imperatives of news gathering described earlier. The journalistic urgency for creating drama in campaign stories, for allowing reporters to have equal billing with their subjects, and for working under tight time restrictions, all point to the inadequacies that make campaign advertising something of a necessity. Seasoned political journalists may criticize its "sterile" and "contrived" nature. But some of the evidence cited above suggests that many who cover a political beat are doing very little themselves to increase the public's competence to master the substance of important political issues.[79]

In her detailed study of the 1974 California gubernatorial campaign, Mary Ellen Leary amplifies this problem. Larger than some European countries, California is a notoriously difficult state in which to run for public office. The major population centers are spread out on a long north-to-south axis, and a vague antipathy separates the interests of those living in the arid south from the water-rich north. The race produced significant press attention. Within the state it is a given that campaigns must be planned around the needs of the mass media centers. And yet none of the six television stations Leary monitored allowed the candidates to speak routinely or in any sustained way to the public. The eventual winner, Jerry Brown, accumulated only 57 minutes of speaking time on all of the newscasts over the course of the entire campaign. "With such abbreviated news exposure," she concluded, "advertising time became the critical avenue for getting a message across to television viewers."[80] "Even if thoughtful reporting had been available across so large a state . . . candidates would still have needed some opportunity to state their views directly."[81]

Radio and direct mail also play important roles as political advertising vehicles. Radio spots are inexpensive to produce and easy to prepare. The most specialized music formats make it easy to target messages to a particular audience. Few stations reach the levels of penetration that are possible with other forms of local or national media. And it goes without saying that radio messages usually lack the impact and attention-getting appeal of television. But for many political candidates, the American system of decentralized radio (with over 9000 stations across the United States) remains the most accessible and affordable of media buys.

As agents for political advocacy, one of radio's biggest drawbacks—and one it shares with television—is that those who manage stations and networks are reluctant to carry advertising that does not deal with consumer products or bona fide political campaigns. What is sometimes called "editorial" or "issue advertising" is discouraged in both media.[82] The most visible form of such issue advertising today is confined to the op-ed pages of major newspapers. Corporate sponsors such as Mobil, Kaiser, and Rodale Press, for example, regularly pay for ads offering what amount to corporate-sponsored editorials on topics ranging from congressional timidity on reducing the national debt, to praise for a president's economic policies.[83] The major networks in particular have been reluctant to grant access to such paid issue-oriented advertising. The ostensible reason is because their "fairness" obligations require airing too many differing opinions. A more likely explanation, however, is rooted in the economics of the industry. Advertising that pushes ideas rather than products is controversial, upsetting the general desire of networks and stations to keep audiences as stable and quiescent as possible. Anything other than the apolitical pitching for products is thought to endanger audience loyalty.

Direct mail is also important. It ranks just behind newspapers, magazines, and television in total advertising revenues.[84] Adopting the techniques used by bulk mail marketing strategists, politicians and "public interest" groups now frequently use direct mail appeals distributed to thousands of preselected addresses. A number of firms specialize in the collection and sale of mailing lists thought to list individuals with certain desirable social or political traits. Organizations with policy interests utilize elaborate polling and demographic data to match particular types of messages with receptive readers. As noted in Chapter 10, members of Congress have long used their free mail prerogatives to send newsletters and questionaires to their constituents. Given the potential to use computer assisted ways to target messages, members can send "personal" letters to specific types of constituents who might be favorably influenced by what they read.[85]

One such targeting scheme described by Vincent Barabba is called the Precinct Index Priority System.[86] The objective of this data collection method is to give priority rankings to individual voting precincts in a district, thereby determining which should be targeted for particular direct mail messages and other appeals. The system involves the collection and tabulation of data on a precinct's voter registration status, previous voting patterns, and census data. Census information is especially useful in providing a sharp profile of a community—its relative prosperity, the average income and educational level of its members, and so on. In one campaign, Indiana Republicans collected information ranging from the percent of welfare recipients in a precinct to the percent of homes with daughters who were Brownies members. Playing on a number of political hunches, they produced rankings of precincts which could be targeted for direct mail messages. Rather than spreading resources hapazardly, this computer-assisted system and many others like it permit the targeting of audiences who might be especially responsive to direct appeals.

THE SALIENCY OF INDIVIDUAL MESSAGES AND CAMPAIGNS

It is strong testimony for the power of the mass media that in 1973 Georgia's Governor Jimmy Carter could appear on the television game show "What's My Line?" and *stump* the panelists. The object of the show was to question a guest to determine his or her line of work.[87] Little could the questioners know that the anonymous man whose identity they were trying to determine unblindfolded would conquer the Presidency just four years later. That Carter could go from obscurity to prominence in so short a period of time demonstrates the potency of mass media exposure.

Estimating Saliency: A Range of Problems

By far the most vexing problem facing political advocates is attempting to predict the impact that individual messages or entire campaigns will have on mass media audiences. Our predicament at the end of the twentieth century is still much like that of tobacco magnate George Washington Hill at the beginning. He believed that half of the money that his company spent on advertising was wasted. The unresolved problem, Hill said, was to find out which half.[88] We tend to remember the spectacular successes—the effective speech or series of commercials that dramatically transformed a troubled situation into a victorious one. Richard Nixon's Checker's address cited at the outset of this chapter, the 1960 presidential debates between John Kennedy and Richard Nixon, George Bush's effective 1988 campaign against Michael Dukakis ("No one in this century is better prepared . . . "), are but a few of the hundreds of catalytic events where attitudes changed in response to an effective marriage of media and message. Like television advertisers who can dramatically increase the market share that comes to a given product, every public figure with access to mass media audiences is conscious of its possible benefits.[89]

But our knowledge of what makes successful appeals remains incomplete. "Some kinds of communication on some kinds of issues, brought to the attention of some kinds of people under some kinds of conditions, have some kinds of effects."[90] That was Bernard Berelson's 1948 summation of the state of mass media research. And it still seems valid. It is extremely difficult accurately to link media exposure to attitude change.

Probably the most compelling evidence of rapid impact in campaigns has come from private tracking polls that are used to detect changes in the electorate as heavy doses of media are introduced to the American public. These small sample polls are taken frequently—often everyday—as the campaign moves into high gear. Shifts in public interest in an issue, in approval for one political approach over another, and in candidate responses to attacks are all closely monitored and frequently lead to adjustments in daily tactics. Pollsters point out that they discover a great deal in tracking polls about what is working and what is not.[91] But these are largely limited to the last weeks of presidential campaigns, when events have usually turned the contest into an intense but short-lived national drama.

Consider some of the broad obstacles that must be addressed in assessing media impact in less volatile periods. One of the certainties regarding human attitude formation, for example, is that attitudes are highly resistant to short-term appeals. Opinions, beliefs, and attitudes tend to be elastic when pressed against the hard surface of an opposing point of view. They may momentarily give some ground to a persuasive appeal. But they are likely to assume their old shape when the stimulus for change is withdrawn or forgotten.[92] Individual speeches, occasional exposure to advertisements, and similar short-term encounters are unlikely to have much effect on what we think, and are even less likely to produce durable changes in attitudes and behaviors. Unfortunately, it so happens that short-term exposure is precisely the kind of variable that is most controllable in the experimental setting. When we concede as we must that attitudes are shaped by *long-term* factors, we are also forced to recognize that "neat" experimental or survey research on attitude formation becomes extremely difficult. Experimental studies that isolate specific effects with particular media and messages are difficult to devise, given the pluralism of influences that exist in ordinary life. The problem is confounded by the existence of many intervening variables that are both hard to account for, and highly variable across the entire population. A corporation introducing a new product on the market may indeed be able to trace the effectiveness of advertising and other marketing strategies, because public knowledge of the new item will have started from a zero base. No similar information vacuum exists for most presidential candidates, national issues, or pending legislative questions. All usually have some public history that makes it difficult to attribute attitudes to isolated message-centered variables.

It is also important to note that political attitudes or related behaviors, such as voting, signing a petition, or speaking in behalf of a position are more likely to be intensified rather than changed. This is because the process of *changing* attitudes is much harder for the persuadee than the process of *forming* them. The first involves the discarding of an inconsistent or conflicting belief in favor of a new one, a process that is very slow and usually incremental. The latter is psychologically easier; something is simply added or intensified rather than replaced. This explains why most changes that occur in individuals subject to political appeals are defined in terms of the *activation* or *crystalization* of attitudes.[93] Political persuasion is usually not so much a matter of rethinking a well-defined view, but intensifying an already latent attitude.

A further complication rises from the fact that there is often an assumed relationship between how one "feels" and what one does: between attitudes and beliefs on one hand, and concrete behaviors on the other. But correlations between thought and action do not always hold. Individuals, for example, may hold racist attitudes, as measured by a paper and pencil survey, but act in a nonracist manner when placed in an integrated environment.[94] The reverse is also possible, and perhaps even more likely. The way individuals actually vote may be at variance with what they say they will do. Pressure from peers or the desire to please a questioner may well result in a vocalized response that conceals deeper feelings. The saliency of a political issue is thus always contingent and conditional. What we can attribute to one source is always subject to a range of exceptions. A message can never be completely understood in isolation.

Message Saliency: Four General Conclusions

Even though our understanding of how messages work is very inexact, there is a long tradition of effect-centered discussion on the saliency of political messages in American life. Researchers, theorists and journalists have endlessly documented how Americans respond to these messages, and how the mass media collectively function to impede or enhance their acceptance. We can only touch on some of the more provocative and important conclusions that seem justified by some of these varied efforts.

First, consumers of all forms of political discourse are selective rather than reflexive. Most are primarily attentive to messages that corroborate rather than challenge existing beliefs; they seek to confirm what they already know or believe. Others can even carry this process one step further; they are able to read support into information that contradicts their basic view. The mechanism of selective perception works to ensure the stability of the individual's mental landscape. Change of any kind represents risk, work, and the readjustment of related attitudes. It is to be expected, therefore, that in the context of a campaign the most attentive listeners to a candidate's advertising tend to be solid supporters. Statements recalled after exposure to a candidate's positions tend to be those that fit preexisting beliefs.[95]

Second, for most consumers there is an enormous gap between time spent with any mass medium and what one would normally expect in the way of effects. For all the rhetorical skills utilized by a side in a political conflict, recall and attitude change levels can be surprisingly low. As we have noted, attitudes are far more inert than most persuaders, critics, and analysts often assume. The consistent failure to find dramatic changes in the predispositions of audiences is one ironic effect of the information explosion that has engulfed nearly every corner of the Western world. As a form of protection against the constant buffetings created by new information, the typical consumer apparently shuts much of it out.

Studies confirming the generally low level of political awareness are common. One 1970 project found that less than a third of a national sample could identify major newsmakers at the time, such as Ralph Nader and Martha Mitchell.[96] Similarly, in 1978 an Eagleton Poll researcher in New Jersey found that only one in three residents could identify one of their senators, Clifford Case. At the time Case was hardly an obscure politician. He had been in office for 24 years, and had maintained a consistently high level of local visibility.[97] Such evidence serves as a constant reminder of what voting behavior studies have demonstrated over the last several decades—that the size of the attentive, interested audience for political information and dialogue is extremely small. On most issues and toward most political actors the dominant characteristic is apathy. It is a familiar lament that—except for the Presidency—too many Americans consider the political world to be ephemeral to their own daily lives.

One view that explains how interest and knowledge can be so low in a media-saturated environment comes from what has become known as the "uses and gratifications" perspective. This approach begins with the simple notion that citizen interest in politics exists when there is some psychological reward or payoff.[98] From this perspective "information seeking" may not be the prime reason attention is given to such disparate bits of the political process, such as televised debates or issue-oriented editorials. For example, if a television viewer tunes to C-SPAN, the cable channel devoted to Congress, he may watch a debate not because he wants to be informed, but because the debate is on TV, and TV watching (or the promise of witnessing a heated confrontation) is considered a pleasurable activity. As Dan Nimmo has noted,

It is possible . . . to argue that the political media have substantial effects on lesser involved citizens even though these citizens do not derive information from the media. The argument rests on the notion that, from the standpoint of an audience member, the function of the media is not to inform but to act as a source of subjective play.[99]

News stories about a national campaign may well have the kind of novelty and entertainment value built into the dramas that occupy prime-time television. The heavy viewer that is sedated by a steady diet of low-demand entertainment is perhaps predisposed to strip away the minimal policy–oriented substance of a report, leaving the dramatistic and emotional elements intact.[100]

Third, political communication needs to be envisioned as occurring in *tiers* of influence, with the mass media viewed as carriers as well as shapers of messages. The mental reduction that sometimes occurs with intense interest in mass persuasion mistakenly gives the media sole possession of the power to persuade. But such a simplification distorts what is a far more complex reality. In addition to being initiators of their own forms of influence, the mass media are acted on by many external forces. They exist in the middle of a hierarchy. Networks, stations, and publishers are subject to the influence of various elites, among them political, business, and educational opinion leaders.

Elite theory has its limits, but it still brings us part of the total picture. Benjamin Ginsberg's savvy aphorism quoted at the beginning of this chapter, that "a successful regime caters more to the *interests* of its elites and more to the *emotions* of its masses," is a fitting reminder that controlling public opinion and exercising political power are not always the same thing.[101] Any review of a handful of presidential speeches will uncover decisions taken in behalf of powerful interests but defended in terms of the broad public interest. Elites are the brokers of significant power in their own respective fields, for example, managers and leaders in business, the arts, and the national mass media. In practical terms they are represented on the guest lists of White House state dinners, or the lists of those invited to relax along the shores of the Russian River at Northern California's exclusive Bohemian Grove.[102]

David Paletz and Robert Entman have concisely summed up the implications of elite theory for the mass media:

Despite the complications and exceptions, the general impact of the mass media is to socialize people into accepting the legitimacy of their country's political system . . . ; lead them to acquiesce in America's prevailing social values . . . ; direct their opinions in ways which do not undermine and often support the domestic and foreign objectives of elites . . . ; and deter them from active, meaningful participation in politics—rendering them quiescent before the powerful.[103]

Others have pointed out the tendency of press reports to sanitize and justify the sometimes marginal performance of elites in government and business, making them appear more efficient and organized than they really are.[104] A recent look at how Seattle's daily newspapers have generally suspended traditional journalistic scrutiny and skepticism in their coverage of the city's largest employer, The Boeing Company, is typical.[105] Such criticism may not mean that there is an overt conspiracy to make sure that every printed word supports the powers that be. The tie-ins that develop are less structured and more informal. But they are also so common that any consideration of how political discourse is shaped must include the inevitable crossovers between governmental and mass media elites.

A specific case from the Presidency of Lyndon Johnson is especially revealing. Johnson was long aware of his inadequacies as a television spokesman for his own administration. Television captured all too well the turgid defensiveness of his increasingly unhappy presidency. At best, he was a slow and stiff public speaker, a style that concealed what others who knew the private Johnson recognized as a more animated and likable man. He sought help from Robert Kintner by making the former President of NBC Television his special assistant. Although Kintner's duties varied, and his tenure was comparatively short, he worked to improve the sagging Johnson image.

A member of the media establishment was now helping the premier member of the nation's political establishment. A sampling of some of the confidential memos Kintner sent to the President just before and after the 1967 State of the Union Address points to the broadcaster's ability to tap the support of former colleagues for political gain. They demonstrate the tendency common in all forms of politics to build bridges between what are supposedly separate power blocks. In this case, Kintner sought to put Johnson's speech in a favorable context by using key White House figures to brief important members of the press:

I had a meeting with [Johnson advisors] Harry McPherson, Doug Cater, Joe Califano and Walt Rostow, particularly in relation to the meaning of the Civil Rights portion of your State of the Union address, but also in relation to the principal points of the talk. We divided up various key [journalism] people in town to background including . . . [Max] Frankel, . . . [James] Kilpatrick, [Joseph] Kraft, [Tom] Wicker, . . . [Hedley] Donovan, . . . [Charles] Bartlett, Joe Alsop, etc. . . . In addition, I will try to do some work with the news chiefs of ABC, NBC and CBS.[106]

[In planning for the coverage of the speech] I would guess that they [the networks] would not try to put a one-half hour entertainment show [after the speech] and would run major news reaction programs.

At least that is what I would do if I were running the networks. I have a pretty good idea of NBC's plans. . . .[107]

In talking with Newsweek about the Civil Rights section of your speech [Columnist] Ken Crawford volunteered that he thought your TV appearance was the best that you had done in a speech, and that you seemed well prepared and at ease.[108]

Another part of the tier of influence is closer to the grass roots level, where media-endorsed views have the power to influence opinion leaders with their own constituencies. In this view media influence on the general public is not direct, but through leaders who essentially act as relays. Their power derives from their credibility, and from their ability to give a conclusion inherited from a mass media source a local voice. This configuration is called the "two-step" or "multi-step flow" model. In the typical case of the two-step flow, the effectiveness of a particular media outlet is compounded by its ability to enlist agents that will carry its point of view. An understanding of the importance of this principle has been basic to political campaigners for years: There is no satisfactory substitute for direct interpersonal contact as a way to elicit influence.[109] People vote or acquire opinions based on what sources they respect say. What matters in the end, given this sequence, is that a message relayed through a medium ends up transposed into vital face-to-face encounters.

This process is also evident in news-gathering organizations. A definite pecking order exists within the national news industry, and extends down to local outlets. As was noted earlier, major wire service "budgets," stories in the *New York Times* and *Washington Post* are known to affect at least some of the subsequent reporting of the major television networks.[110] And because of what the networks report, local television news organizations may set their own patterns of national coverage. As a result, even though an opinion-leading publication such as the *New York Times* has a circulation that falls far below that of the networks and some other dailies and weeklies, its influence is still a significant force in daily determinations of what national events and trends are newsworthy.

Fourth and last, in spite of the widespread diffusion of political information via television, the gap between the "information rich" and the "information poor" is probably widening. The "information rich" we define as people who have the means and motivation to use a variety of carefully selected resources to increase their economic, political, and social leverage. Their position is in sharp contrast to the large stratum of Americans who use the mass media— especially television and the tabloid press—more for escape than for information.[111] What many in this category seek is a series of media-made reprieves from lives dominated by boredom or purposelessness. Instead of gaining salient data that increases their involvement in many planes of activity, they seek media as an escape. There is an undeniably large gap between audience-specific media that require effort (and cash) but yield significant returns, and the mass-oriented entertainment media that offer painless escapism. The former builds on and extends the intellectual capacities of its consumers. The latter, because it is cheap and directed to the largest audience levels, hopes to hold audiences by exploiting their capacity to consume aimless diversion. Many Americans seem to consume a media diet that offers the modern counterpart to ancient Rome's promise to citizens of free bread and circuses. The endless distractions of prime-time television and its print counterparts have the effect of draining off the motivation (outrage, anger, and sense of involement) that is necessary to produce political change. To use the term suggested by Lazarfeld and Merton, heavy exposure to less comprehensive forms of mass media can have a "narcotizing" function, substituting what is at best secondary contact with political reality in the place of more direct social action.[112]

It is probably no coincidence that television is the dominant medium in America's poorer neighborhoods.[113] In more affluent parts of the nation the viewing of television remains heavy, but it is augmented by other kinds of media that offer a greater diversity of information.[114] The diffused nature of the "massest" of the mass media provide little direction and less incentive for intense political involvement. Aiming at the lowest common denominator as a standard for programming discourages the use of information for all but the most trivial forms of self-help. The most popular programs on the broadcast television schedule are typically filled with remedies for loneliness or weight loss, but usually not for building a lifelong career, or a deeper understanding of the interrelationships that drive our perceptions of American politics. The pattern of presentation for most of the popular media, Marshall McLuhan noted of television, is a "mosaic" of discrete bits—game shows, melodramas, thousands of news headlines, and endless commercials and announcements—all of which have the likely effect of weakening the individual's capacity to concentrate experience and insights in any one area. "Television dependents" are thus thrust into a double bind that is a potential threat to themselves and to the society they can change through the vote. The medium to which they are wed tells them more about less and less, making them vulnerable to persuasive appeals that hang on the thinnest of insights. As Cliff Zukin has speculated,

There is clearly a segmentation in the American public in terms of media reliance and learning from the media. The poorer educated rely more and more on a medium that gives them little in the way of a framework in which to understand politics. News stories confined to 60 or 90 seconds cannot provide a context conducive to comprehension. Television-dependents are less knowledgeable about public affairs and more susceptible to persuasive messages.[115]

The problem is not that people easily succumb to simple persuasive appeals. As we have noted, they often do not. Rather, it is that if an enormous segment of the society fails to seek out diverse media to help understand complex political realities, the information vacuum to which the disenfranchised are heir makes their world a more incomprehensible and threatening place.

POLITICAL CONTENT IN NONPOLITICAL FORMS

One of Ronald Reagan's biographers noted that the former film actor only played a villain once, in what was by his own admission a forgettable film called *The Killers*. He preferred to play heroes,[116] as he did in two of his favorites,

Kings Row, and *Knute Rockne, All American*. That the former President would have rather enacted such roles cannot come as a surprise. In his preference there is a lesson about the importance of entertainment as a shaper of political attitudes. More than most presidents, Reagan's rhetoric was always heavily laced with graphic images of personal courage and selfless sacrifice.[117] Depictions of heroism, on film or in speeches, dramatized an essential premise of Reagan's brand of political conservatism—that the individual is fundamentally responsible for his own circumstances.[118]

From the abstract to the representational, all of the arts cannot help but serve as vehicles of explicit or implicit political commentary. Virtually everything from the largest grand operas to the humblest television situation comedies convey attitudes about values, organizations, and social relations, ranging from Verdi's nineteenth-century operatic themes of political repression, to action films about violence and retribution. It is estimated that only three percent of commercial television time is devoted to national public issues.[119] But it would be a mistake to assume that the rest of the remaining space does not contribute to political perceptions in both planned and accidental ways. Consider some representative cases where political sensibilities have surfaced in the arts.

- In 1987 the United States Information Agency was forced to cancel a planned exhibition of American portraits in Beijing. The reason: Chinese officials objected to the inclusion of paintings of General Douglas MacArthur and former Israeli Prime Minister, Golda Meir. MacArthur's likeness offended the Chinese who recalled his involvement in the Korean War. They apparently also feared that a painting of Meir displayed in a Chinese exhibition hall would offend Arab allies.[120]
- In November of 1988 NBC aired a television movie recounting some of the events surrounding the 1983 downing of a Korean airliner over Soviet territory. "Shootdown" apparently started its life as a screenplay intended to emphasize speculation that agencies in the United States were aware of the plane's fatal course, and perhaps engineered it for intelligence purposes. Before the program was filmed, however, NBC required a reworking of the story line to weaken its argument about possible United States responsibility.[121]
- In his 1988 collection of articles devoted to television criticism, the influential Mark Crispen Miller took on the most powerful icon of commercial television, "The Cosby Show." The popular funnyman, Miller argued, was guilty of falsifying what is for an overwhelming majority of black families a far tougher world. By making a black version of a 1950s situation comedy, Cosby also unwittingly gave white Americans the undeserved reassurance that black families are playing out life's problems on a flat playing field largely devoid of racism.[122]
- Over 50 years have gone by since the Mexican artist Diego Rivera painted murals in the United States. In 1933 he was commissioned by the Rockefellers to paint a series of frescos in the RCA Building at the heart of the center bearing their name. The commission set off an unexpected furor. One of the figures he painted on the walls of this temple of American commerce was the likeness of V. I. Lenin. The Rockefellers had the mural destroyed, but not before the painter gained hundreds of advocates who

still honor his work today. Major retrospectives of his paintings inevitably note his devotion to the imagery of the toil by ordinary workers. Rivera proved conclusively what he believed, that "all art is propaganda; the only difference is the kind of propaganda."[123]

• In 1987 the noted media writer, Herbert Mitgang, published part of his research revealing that the Federal Bureau of Investigation and other agencies have long collected files on controversial American writers. Mitgang was able to gain access to dossiers on a number of major figures in American literature, including Ernest Hemingway, Pearl S. Buck, Sinclair Lewis, William Faulkner, W. H. Auden, Tennessee Williams, Thomas Wolfe, and Thorton Wilder.[124]

Manifest and Latent Political Themes in Storytelling

A mainstay of American culture has always been the uncomplicated portrayal of evocative values and themes in films, theater, and music. From the earliest days of film political messages have often been explicit. For example D. W. Griffith's spectacular silent epic, *Birth of a Nation*, has long engendered controversy over the eulogistic treatment given to the Ku Klux Klan.[125] In World War I, government use of film as a suasive tool was augmented by all forms of media, including hundreds of popular recordings glorifying American honor and bolstering troops whose courage might waver. These recordings and the Victrolas to play them on were routinely issued to troops in the field. By the time World War II began, propaganda techniques had been refined. German films such as *Triumph of the Will*, and American efforts such as Frank Capra's *Why We Fight* series were vivid attempts to meld entertainment and political advocacy. Ronald Reagan's own war service was confined to this kind of work. He was assigned to a Hollywood production unit responsible for instructional and propaganda films.[126] Years later, while he was President of the Screen Actor's Guild, he convinced himself that groups of communist sympathizers were on the verge of taking over the Hollywood studios.

In some ways drama is the perfect vehicle for mass-oriented political discussion. It comes to the receiver in an attractive context (as entertainment) and in a perfect persuasive environment (when the viewer's defenses against persuasion are reduced). Dramatists routinely function as messengers to the society about its successes and failures.[127] In Hugh Dalziel Duncan's apt phrase, theater is "the means by which we become objects to ourselves . . . "[128] Plays and novels have "historically something of the same importance as journalism has for our own day."[129] They allow us to see our counterparts respond to shifting situations, many of which are personal, but many that also describe the extensions of public policy into our worlds. Even seemingly innocuous fare can have direct political connotations, such as Gershwin's musical *Strike Up the Band*, and the children's story, *The Wizard of Oz*. The first was a subtle but thorough send-up of presidential corruption and military spending.[130] The second was originally written in book form as a populist diatribe against the presidential lethargy of William McKinley.[131]

Popular melodramas and comedies are suited to conveying the ironies and hypocrisies built into institutions. Some, like *Citizen Kane*, *Grapes of Wrath*, or *Wall Street*, unmask the venality of wealth in ways that have struck a responsive chord with audiences. Others have taken on legal and moral issues with the same populist fervor. Films such as *To Kill a Mockingbird*, *Kramer vs. Kramer*, *Whose Life Is It Anyway?*, *The Conversation*, and *Cry Freedom* have entertained, while at the same time raised challenges to well entrenched attitudes seriously at odds with civil rights ideals.

The reverse is also possible. A story, a play or a film may legitimize and vindicate the existing political and social hierarchy in ways far more attractive than would be possible in a straight and unadorned rhetorical defense. That the established institutions of nearly every age have been prime patrons of the arts—from church-sanctioned morality plays to F.B.I. assistance in filming domestic police epics—points to the value many institutions assign to dramatizations complementary to their objectives. The steady stream of films that have been made with the assistance of the military (e.g., *The Green Berets*, *An Officer and a Gentleman*, *Top Gun*) suggests that the armed forces believe that these efforts will produce sympathetic audiences.

Even forms of mass media with ostensibly nonpolitical objectives frequently contain at least an implicit political subtext. A film, a play, a television melodrama that may have the manifest goal of simple entertainment may also project latent messages about the ways power and authority have been distributed in the United States. For example, we probably underestimate the importance of "arguments by omission," or what *could be, but is not* represented in a specific plot line. The consistently omitted perspective or image can carry its own weight in shaping public perceptions. In any vigorous open society critics with widely varied backgrounds will be asking questions about the features of ordinary life that are sometimes missing in popular entertainment. Why are Americans of Asian ancestry nearly invisible in commercials and series? Why is auto safety so rarely the subject of network television news? In contrast to most of the rest of the Western world, why are America's television stations so reluctant to purchase programming or documentaries from foreign producers? Where are the well financed lobbyists (the National Rifle Association, the National Association of Broadcasters, the Tobacco Institute) in ostensibly authentic dramatizations of American political life? To various extents all of these questions suggest that public opinion can be affected for better or worse by what is omitted as well as what is explicit.

Three Patterns of Analysis of Popular Entertainment

Several more systematic lines of thought are evident in much of the analysis of the contemporary entertainment media. We turn now to three traditional frames of reference for assessing political meaning in the artifacts of popular culture. One is that a good deal of what is seen or heard is ahead of its audiences, "liberalizing" their experiences and increasing their tolerance. A second is that most commercial film and television production is firmly rooted in a defensive "legitimizing" posture, protecting dominant social values and major institutions. The third involving a theory of hegemony is more process-oriented, pointing out how serious social problems are robbed of their full political (and often revolutionary) implications.

The Theory of Liberalizing Influence

Part of the conventional wisdom that comes with the study of the pluralistic mass media in Western nations is that they create "a window on the world" that has unprecedented breadth and scope. Mass media within the reach of nearly everyone provide a wealth of new experiences that expand horizons and widen perspectives. When measured against the limited experiences of any one individual, the opportunities made possible by television alone represent a vast increase in a person's awareness of distant parts of his and other's worlds. Marshall McLuhan's pivotal notion that we now live in a "global village" carries the implication that distance is no longer an impediment in gaining access to a diversity of human actions, attitudes, and tragedies. We can now extend ourselves far beyond the experiences that were possible to those even two generations ago. The devastating 1988 earthquake in Soviet Armenia, for example, created an unprecedented degree of foreign assistance. The generous international response was due in part to Soviet openness about the extensive damage and loss of life, but also to the free access to the area given to the world press.

No one can deny that these experiences come to us secondhand, or that they are the products of a fine screen of bureaucratic and commercial control. But it is an enlarged world, nonetheless. The landmark 1960 CBS documentary, "Harvest of Shame," for example, showed millions of Americans the exploitation and racism common to American farm labor practices at the time. As with many documentaries on social problems centered in one region, some network affiliates, fearing the wrath of advertisers or angry viewers, refused to air the program.[132] Even so, documentaries have always provided widespread access to views and ideas that would otherwise go unvoiced because of local or provincial concerns—on unionism, racism, socialism, religious beliefs, and political corruption.

There is no shortage of analysts who have expressed frustration over "watered down" attempts by the popular media to treat significant social issues, such as various forms of racism.[133] But even commercial television's strongest critics have found examples of entertainment programming that discuss issues that might otherwise never surface on the consciousness of some. Writing originally in the *Socialist Review*, Douglas Kellner noted,

Miniseries like Roots, Holocaust, Captains and Kings, Second Avenue, The Money-changers, and Wheels have dealt with class conflict, racism and antisemitism, imperialism, and the oppression of the working class and blacks. They have often sympathetically portrayed the oppressed, poor, minorities, and workers, and presented capitalists and right-wingers as oppressors and exploiters. Docudramas like Tailgunner Joe, Fear on Trial, and King have criticized Joe McCarthy, J. Edgar Hoover, and the FBI, and vindicated Martin Luther King as well as victims of McCarthyism and FBI persecution in the entertainment industry.[134]

In the entertainment field the individual often credited with making political issues subjects for prime time is veteran producer Norman Lear. His company was responsible for programs that frequently treated social issues in shows such as "All in the Family," "Sanford and Son," "Maude," and "The Jeffersons." "The essential strategy" of the programs, according to broadcast historian Eric Barnouw, "was to seize on topics and relationships involving deep tensions, and introduce them in a comedy aura."[135] One of Lear's goals was to ridicule disruptive prejudices and traditions deeply woven into parts of the American fabric. He introduced an element of doubt into issues that have often been discussed with a sense of rigid moral certainty. "Interracial marriage, . . . an older woman's pregnancy and indecision about abortion, were suddenly topics of warm comedy."[136] Whether the innovative producer succeeded in dramatizing the continuing sources of social friction, such as the deeply imbedded racism portrayed in "All in the Family," is uncertain. At least one study of audience reactions to the character of Archie Bunker noted a surprising sympathy for the fictitious bigot.[137]

The Theory of Defense of the Establishment

Another important critical judgment is that television programming is especially supportive of the political status quo. The argument generally runs along the following lines: Since the industry depends on gaining its revenues from corporate America's advertising, it is forced to deal with the values of that clientele. Most segments of the entertainment industry are supported by advertising which requires the satisfaction of two separate audiences, one in the business community, and one encompassing the general public. They must attract large segments of the public with their programming. In addition, they must "sell" that mass audience to potential advertisers. The first audience may accept some political content in popular drama. But even the short history of television indicates that corporate America has little interest in social criticism as a vehicle for reaching audiences. To advertisers and broadcasters the ideal selling environment is benign and nonthreatening. It is better to sell cars, toothpaste, and beer to a viewer who has been entertained rather than provoked to anger, reassured rather than threatened. As an ABC vice-president put it,

Program makers are supposed to devise and produce shows that will attract mass audiences without unduly offending these audiences or too deeply moving them emotionally. Such ruffling, it is thought, will interfere with their ability to receive, recall, and respond to the commercial message.[138]

Since politics involves controversy, and controversy intensifies anxieties and hopes, the most stable television entertainment is ideally seen by the average viewer as apolitical. But "apolitical" does not mean nonpolitical. Most popular entertainment avoids controversial issues and unpopular ideas. But this decision itself has political implications. The world of prime time opts for what amounts to a subtle deference to most of the segments of the established economic and social order. With some exceptions, this results in depictions of a world where individuals know their place, where order triumphs over disruption and dispute, and "the system" and its subsystems such as the police, the courts, and the schools, generally work. Few police shows suggest that murders go unsolved. It would be unusual for a continuing series to trace the grinding effects of poverty on its victims, or the severe lifelong traumas of the victims of crashes in unsafe cars, or the unremitting discrimination experienced by an immigrant family living in a major city. Films and occasional television dramas may present such unpleasant images without the closure of a happy ending, but programs depending on a loyal audience week in and week out generally do not. They may well suggest that a community or a city has problems, or that unemployment among black males is very high. But the roots of such dislocations are rarely traced back to fundamental failures in the society or its institutions. In the words of David Paletz and Robert Entman,

Advertisments and entertainment programs lead viewers away from political awareness. When television characters do exhibit imperfections or experience problems, their misfortunes are linked to bad luck, laziness, ineptitude. The structure of power rarely obtrudes into their lives; economic justice, class, race, or age discrimination, illness caused by the workplace, injuries or industrial pollution—these dilemmas are absent. . . . The implicit lesson is that people are not constrained by the social order.[139]

Thus, the doctors in recent medical dramas such as "St. Elsewhere" are shown to have all of the human motivations and impulses of other kinds of workers. But they are practically never incompetent, and always deserve the adulation they get from their devoted patients. In medicine, "Trapper John" and "Marcus Welby" rarely failed to do less than their best. In law, "Owen Marshall," "Perry Mason," and most of the regulars on "L.A. Law" have been models of competence in a fair and nominally efficient criminal justice system. With the possible exception of business tycoons, most of the professional heroes that populate the prime time schedule are seen enacting highly eulogistic versions of their roles. While ordinary television entertainment presents various social institutions that may need some refinement, it usually serves as the bearer of positive messages about things as they are, not as they might be.

The Theory of Hegemony: Forcing Fantasized Remedies to Intransigent Political Problems

The theory of hegemony is an outgrowth of the above analysis, and is generally associated with the work of Todd Gitlin, Herbert Gans, and Gaye Tuchman.[140] They have argued that many popular forms of media reflect fundamental class differences and tensions, which come to be defined for all members of a society by the most affluent. Given many individual exceptions, elites exercise their control through the society not just through direct channels, but through indirect but powerful ideological controls as well. Gitlin notes that "those who rule the dominant institutions secure their power in large measure directly *and indirectly*, by impressing their definitions of situation upon those they rule. . . . "[141] The power to reinforce the existing social order shows up in the news-gathering routines of journalists, in the kinds of fantasies and values of entertainment programming, and in the range of subjects that are considered appropriate for a given medium.

Gitlin describes a world with circles of power that are sometimes visible and sometimes invisible. It is a world of ruling classes perpetuating the "ruling ideas" of their own self-serving ideologies. With regard to news coverage of the actions taken by the political left, he asserts that the establishment media divested the major antiwar groups of the integrity and credibility of their arguments. In much of the 1960s, opposition to the Vietnam War was defined by mainstream media as the work of cynical and naive students.[142] In entertainment programming, a similar predisposition to minimize challenges to the official optimism of governments and established institutions is similarly evident:

However grave the problems posed, however rich the imbroglio, the episodes regularly end with the click of a solution: an arrest, a defiant smile, an I-told-you-so click of an explanation. The characters we have been asked to care about are alive and well, ready for next week. Such a world is not so much fictional as fake. However deeply the problem is located within society, it will be solved among a few persons: the heroes must attain a solution that leaves the rest of society untouched. The self-enclosed world of the TV drama justifies itself, and its exclusions, by "wrapping it all up."[143]

A hegemonic message is one that falls short of advocating the solutions that a frank look at reality might dictate. The problems befalling many of television's victims, such as the homeless, are redeemed by personal heroism rather than social activism. A generous person rather than a social agency is more likely to be portrayed as the force behind the restoration of a broken life. The show or film displaying serious crime may glorify police solutions (tracking down the criminal) rather than confronting the deeper social causes of crime that might reflect basic cultural deficiencies. This point has been made by Tim Bevan, a British filmmaker who has been associated with hard-hitting dramas about economic hardship in Britain (*My Beautiful Laundrette*, and *For Queen and*

Country). He notes that Hollywood in the 1980s has been reluctant to do the same thing. "There's really no comparable movement in the United States. There's not been any vitriolic, anti-Reagan films made there. I just don't think there's the guts in Hollywood to make that kind of picture."[144]

Hegemonic theory is extremely useful, but leaves some unexplained gaps if defined only in socioeconomic terms. What it overlooks is the key role that every society assigns to its most cherished myths. Part of our refusal to deal with actual causes of social problems resides not just in commercial motives, but in the desire to preserve key fantasies that support national visions of altruism and constructive change. A national fantasy is a generalized mixture of our collective wishes and values. The fantasy drama—as in Frank Capra's *Mr Smith Goes to Washington* or in the latest installment of a *Rambo* or an Indiana Jones adventure—lets us idealize our national character by implanting values in at least semiplausible dramatic events. Jimmy Stewart as Jefferson Smith makes the jaded kingpins of the Senate face up to their idealized public responsibilities, just as the fearless young warriors in *Rambo* and *Star Wars* overcome incredible odds to defeat repressive proto-Soviet regimes.

One important feature of these national fantasies is that they usually focus on the individual as a free agent, rather than on institutional solutions to complex problems. In popular drama there is a continuous preference for manufacturing obstacles that can be overcome by force of character rather than political or bureaucratic means. This predisposition, in turn, has profound political consequences. The reason is based in the fact that the melodrama of popular culture treats solutions as psychologically rooted. Policies and well-intended social agencies can never compete with characters as dramatic instruments. It is far easier to demonstrate conflict at an interpersonal level rather than at a culture-wide or governmental level. The political or governmental solution to a personal trauma is not the stuff of great art. Audiences would indeed feel cheated if a victim of social injustice were saved by a slow-working agency carrying out the mandates of a new state law. Melodramatic fantasy calls for something more sweeping and catalytic, for a victim to be transformed into an agent for his own redemption, for a person of no special talent—a rape victim, Clark Kent, or the boy who discovers an extraterrestrial—to be transformed into an idealization of heroism.

Films as diverse as *Death Wish*, *The China Syndrome*, and *Wall Street* presented problems (violent crime, nuclear safety, and insider trading of stocks) for which institutional remedies are available. Yet the pivitol dramatic moments in each involved personal nonbureaucratic solutions: fantasized personal responses that cut through the ambiguity that comes with less cinematic institutional outcomes. In all three cases victims became heroes by creating their own personal solutions. Their messages had an implicit political imprint: that organizational solutions often don't work, and that coordinated group efforts are often undependable. Remedies to crime that involve investigation and research, or the need to assure nuclear plant safety through laborious oversight, are the only suitable long-term ways to treat such problems. But they are not the kind of solutions that engender excitement or interest. This is one reason why the politician is normally a stock villain in popular entertainment; he represents the kind of incrementalism and shared responsibility that ruin fantasies of individualism.

Even a very popular television show about life during the Great Depression, "The Waltons," minimized the political solutions inherent in the New Deal. For the members of this remarkable family rural southern poverty was bearable, even nurturing. The power to overcome the dislocations caused by the collapse of the financial house of cards built in the 1920s lay in the collective resources of the family, not in the responsibilities of the state.[145] Members of the clan were idealized. Their individual strong personalities spoke to the average viewer's desire to witness mastery over severe and disrupting circumstances. It would have been totally out of character for a prime time television series such as "The Waltons" to have taken an overt political stance. Had Grandpa Walton cursed F.D.R. for not doing enough to help, or had John Boy turned into a Socialist and picketed the local bank, the program would have been deemed unsuitable as a series. The hegemonic response is to keep problems manageable, or to make their eventual resolution the task of the individual. Collective guilt for social problems, and the collective redemption offered by political parties and ideological systems often represent an unwanted form of social criticism. Feature films may sometimes imply such imperfection (e.g., *Taxi Driver*, *Midnight Cowboy*, *Missing*, and *Mississippi Burning*), but usually for a much more limited audience.

A FINAL WORD

The relationships between the news media and various types of political blocks are often so subtle and variable that they cloud the crystal ball of even the most penetrating of analyses. Our goal in this chapter has been to touch on a few of those relationships, and some of the pressures that shape the strategies of each side. What we have seen is that these patterns are complex, and reveal that no single block holds a devisive edge in the pursuit of approval from the American public.

Perhaps this balance provides some room for optimism about the future of American politics in the age of mass communication, but it equally invites pessimism. The American public is generally apathetic, uninformed, difficult to influence, and prone to exclude the most comprehensive forms of political media. Many seem enraptured with the drama of politics. Others are skeptical or inattentive. Although Americans have the technical means to provide full and adequate discussion of political affairs, those means are frequently turned to more lucrative commercial goals. All of these circumstances result not so much in a quagmire as a kind of socially redemptive stalemate. We have inherited a system that performs at far less than what is the capacity of the public or the press. But we have at least preserved a balance that disperses control and discourages blind manipulation by any single source.

Within governmental systems, the diffusion of power may produce stalemate and inaction. But the relationship between the political world and the mass communication industries is more varied. In a word, the relationship is redeemed by its pluralism. None of the many contributors to mass political communication—press, advertising industry, campaign consultants, film industry, political celebrities, and power blocks—have a complete franchise on the political process. At various times all are able to influence the news agenda, but most also have their own dissidents and alternative voices.

All of this is faint praise for a system that could do a far better job of representing local and national politics. But we also realize that at its best the "system" is made up of semiautomomous components. Press, commercial, and political segments need each other, and frequently develop alliances of convenience that ignore the larger public good. But each also remains capable of sustaining goals at odds with the self-serving interests of even the most powerful of national blocks. The society as a whole benefits from such friction, though the heat that is produced is often mistakenly viewed as evidence of our disintegration. In some ways events like the Watergate scandal—with its conflicting White House, congressional, and national press objectives—demonstrated the vibrancy that is possible in a pluralistic state. We should be grateful rather than weary for such moments in our political history. The more routine ties between politics and the mass communication industries give less reason for satisfaction. We should expect much more from a society so well endowed with the means for creating a truly enlightened democracy.

NOTES

1. Benjamin Ginsberg, *The Captive Public: How Mass Opinion Promotes State Power* (New York: Basic Books, 1986), p. 47.

2. Edward R. Murrow quoted in Fred W. Friendly, *Due to Circumstances Beyond Our Control . . .* (London: McGibbon and Kee, 1967), p. 251.

3. Richard M. Nixon, *Six Crises* (New York: Pyramid, 1968), p. 126.

4. Nixon, p. 125.

5. Walter Lippmann, *Public Opinion* (New York: Macmillan, 1930), p. 29.

6. Forrest McDonald, *The Presidency of George Washington* (New York: W.W. Norton, 1974), pp. 24–26.

7. For an introductory review of several evolving assessments of mass media impact on public opinion see Melvin L. DeFleur and Everette E. Dennis, *Understanding Mass Communication*, 3d Ed. (Boston, MA: Houghton Mifflin, 1988), pp. 443–74.

8. See, for example, Joe McGinniss, *The Selling of the President, 1968* (New York: Trident Press, 1969); and Robert Cirino, *Don't Blame the People* (New York: Vintage, 1971).

9. Kurt Lang and Gladys Engel Lang, *Politics and Television* (Chicago: Quadrangle Books, 1968).

10. Michael J. Robinson and Margaret A. Sheehan, *Over the Wire and on TV: C.B.S. and U.P.I. in Campaign '80* (New York: Russell Sage, 1983); Michael J. Robinson,

"Television and American Politics: 1956–1976" in *Readings in Public Opinion and Mass Communication*, 3d Ed., ed. Morris Janowitz and Paul Hirsch (New York: Free Press, 1981), pp. 98–116; Sidney Kraus and Dennis Davis, *The Effects of Mass Communication on Political Behavior* (University Park, PA: The Pennsylvania State University, 1976); Thomas E. Patterson, *The Mass Media Election: How Americans Choose Their President* (New York: Praeger, 1980); and Thomas E. Patterson and Robert D. McClure, *The Unseeing Eye: The Myth of Television Power in National Politics* (New York: G.P. Putnam's, 1976).

11. Lippmann, p. 364.

12. See, for example, Maxwell McCombs, and D. L. Shaw, "The Agenda Setting Function of the Mass Media," *Public Opinion Quarterly* (Summer 1972): 176–87; Maxwell McCombs, "The Agenda Setting Approach" in *Handbook of Political Communication*, ed. Dan D. Nimmo and Keith R. Sanders (Beverly Hills, CA: Sage, 1981), pp. 121–40; and Shanto Iyengar and Donald R. Kinder, *News That Matters: Television and American Opinion* (Chicago, IL: University of Chicago, 1987).

13. Doris A. Graber, *Processing the News* (New York: Longman, 1984), pp. 111–13.

14. Herbert J. Gans, *Deciding What's News* (New York: Vintage, 1980), pp. 146–52.

15. Gans, pp. 167–71.

16. Timothy Crouse, *The Boys on the Bus* (New York: Ballantine, 1972), pp. 22–23.

17. Edward Jay Epstein, *News from Nowhere: Television and the News* (New York: Vintage, 1974), pp. 37–43.

18. Epstein, pp. 258–59.

19. Edith Efron, *The News Twisters* (New York: Manor Books, 1971).

20. Gans, p. 212.

21. See, for example, Robinson and Sheehan, pp. 66–138.

22. Todd Gitlin, *The Whole World Is Watching: Mass Media in the Making and Unmaking of the New Left* (Berkeley, CA: University of California, 1980), pp. 249–82; and W. Lance Bennett, *News: The Politics of Illusion*, 2d Ed. (New York: Longman, 1988).

23. Michael J. Arlen, *Living Room War* (New York: Viking, 1969), pp. 6–9.

24. Friendly, pp. 213–365.

25. Daniel J. Boorstin, *The Image, or What Happened to the American Dream* (New York: Atheneum, 1962), p. 8.

26. David Bianculli and Gail Shister, "How TV Covered the Dwyer Suicide," *The Philadelphia Inquirer*, January 23, 1987, pp. D1 and D8.

27. Elizabeth Drew, "Letter From Washington," *The New Yorker*, October 10, 1988, p. 96.

28. Kenneth Burke, *The Rhetoric of Religion: Studies in Logology* (Berkeley, CA: University of California, 1970), pp. v–vi.

29. Robinson and Sheehan, p. 284.

30. Michael Novak, "Notes on the Drama of Politics and the Drama of Journalism," in *The Politics of Broadcasting*, ed. Marvin Barrett (New York: Thomas Crowell, 1973), p. 176.

31. Novak, p. 174.

32. An example of the older "accuracy of reporting" approach can be seen in Lang and Lang, pp. 36–77.

33. For analyses of the conventions of newsgathering see Robert MacNeil, *The People Machine: The Influence of Television on American Politics* (New York: Harper & Row, 1968), pp. 18–55; Dan Nimmo and James E. Combs, *Mediated Political Realities* (New York: Longman, 1983), pp. 23–46; Gans, pp. 146–81; and Epstein, pp. 152–80.

34. Bennett, p. 52.

35. See our discussion of this relationship in Chapter 11.

36. Gitlin, pp. 21–77.

37. David L. Paletz and Robert M. Entman, *Media Power Politics* (New York: The Free Press, 1981), p. 158.

38. Paletz and Entman, p. 157.

39. For a view that differs sharply from that of Gans, Gitlin, and Bennett, see Robinson and Sheehan, pp. 296–98.

40. Martin Schram, *The Great American Video Game: Presidential Politics in the Television Age* (New York: William Morrow, 1987), pp. 23–33.

41. A good example of political analysis spun off from the terms of drama is James E. Combs, *Dimensions of Political Drama* (Santa Monica, CA: Goodyear, 1980), pp. 1–17.

42. Nimmo and Combs, p. 28.

43. Robert P. Newman, "The Weekly Fiction Magazines," *Central States Speech Journal*, May, 1966, pp. 118–24.

44. Quoted in Epstein, pp. 4–5.

45. Paul H. Weaver, "Captives of Melodrama," *New York Times Magazine*, August 29, 1976, p. 6.

46. Quoted in Robinson and Sheehan, pp. 214–15.

47. David Riesman with Nathan Glazer and Reuel Denney, *The Lonely Crowd*, Abridged Edition (New Haven, CT: Yale University, 1961), p. 182.

48. Marvin Kalb quoted in "Looking for Better Ways to Run Elections," *The New York Times*, November 13, 1988, p. 3.

49. NBC Nightly News, October 28, 1988.

50. Aristotle discusses character extensively in Book II of *The Rhetoric*, trans. W. Rhys Roberts (New York: The Modern Library, 1954).

51. Niccolo Machiavelli, *The Prince*, trans. Christian Gauss (New York: Mentor, 1972), pp. 93–94.

52. Richard Sennett, *The Fall of Public Man: On the Social Psychology of Capitalism* (New York: Vintage Books, 1978), p. 4.

53. Steven R. Weisman, "The President and the Press," *The New York Times Magazine*, October 14, 1984, pp. 34–37, 71–74, 80, 82–83.

54. "The President Under Glass," editorial in *The New York Times*, October 17, 1988, p. A20.

55. The wording is Sennett's, p. 284.

56. Roderick P. Hart, *The Sound of Leadership: Presidential Communication in the Modern Age* (Chicago, IL: University of Chicago: 1987), p. 202.

57. Paul E. Corcoran, *Political Language and Rhetoric* (Austin, TX: University of Texas, 1979), p. 161.

58. Sennett, p. 5.

59. See Robert Agronoff, "The New Style of Campaigning: The Decline of Party

and the Rise of Candidate-Centered Technology'' in *The New Style in Election Campaigns*, 2d Ed., ed. Robert Agronoff (Boston, MA: Holbrook, 1977), pp. 10–23.

60. For a case study describing this pattern see Mary Ellen Leary, *Phantom Politics: Campaigning in California* (Washington, DC: Public Affairs, 1977).

61. Quoted in David Halberstam, *The Powers That Be* (New York: Knopf, 1979), p. 6.

62. W. Roper Burns, *America's Watching: Public Attitudes Toward Television* (New York: Television Information Office, 1987). All data in Tables 6.1 and 6.2 are from Roper. Sums of percentages equal more that 100 because Roper has accepted multiple answers.

63. Patterson, *Mass Media Election*, p. 59.

64. Ibid., *Mass Media Election*, pp. 59–60.

65. Robinson and Sheehan, pp. 208–13.

66. For a discussion of the problems of the 30 minute format see MacNeil, pp. 18–55; and Av Westin, *Newswatch: How TV Decides the News* (New York: Simon and Schuster, 1982), pp. 53–95.

67. ''Remarks by Walter Cronkite at the RTNDA Conference, Miami Beach, Florida,'' in *Rich News, Poor News*, ed. Marvin Barrett (New York: Thomas Y. Crowell, 1978), p. 195.

68. Quoted in ''Television and Presidential Politics: Brainstorming the Possibilities,'' *Broadcasting*, February 8, 1982, p. 92.

69. John Kenneth Galbraith, *The Affluent Society*, 3d Ed. (Boston, MA: Houghton Mifflin, 1976), p. 198.

70. Erik Barnouw, *The Sponsor: Notes on a Modern Potentate*, (New York: Oxford, 1978), p. 96.

71. McGinniss, pp. 33–37.

72. Theodore H. White, *The Making of the President, 1972* (New York: Atheneum, 1973), p. 250.

73. Robert Spero, *The Duping of the American Voter* (New York: Lippincott and Crowell, 1980), p. 5.

74. Kathleen Hall Jamieson, *Packaging the Presidency: A History and Criticism of Presidential Campaign Advertising* (New York: Oxford, 1984), pp. 451–52.

75. Gary A. Mauser, *Political Marketing: An Approach to Campaign Strategy* (New York: Praeger, 1983), p. 19.

76. Patterson and McClure, pp. 22–23.

77. Ibid., p. 130.

78. See, for example, Joseph Napolitan, *The Election Game and How to Win It* (Garden City, NY: Doubleday, 1972), pp. 64–88.

79. Patterson and McClure, pp. 47–58.

80. Leary, p. 90.

81. Ibid., pp. 90–91.

82. Sydney W. Head and Christopher H. Sterling, *Broadcasting in America*, 4th Ed. (Boston, MA: Houghton Mifflin, 1982), pp. 481–84.

83. See, for example, Robert G. Meadow, ''The Political Dimensions of Nonproduct Advertising,'' *Journal of Communication* (Summer 1981): 69–82.

84. ''Current Statistics on Mass Media in the United States, 1982,'' in *Readings in Mass Communication*, 5th Ed., ed. Michael Emery and Ted Curtis Smythe (Dubuque, IA: Wm. C. Brown, 1983), p. 533.

85. Michael J. Robinson, "Three Faces of Congressional Media," in *The New Congress*, ed. Thomas E. Mann and Norman J. Ornstein (Washington, DC: American Enterprise Institute, 1981), pp. 60–61.

86. Vincent P. Barabba, "Basic Information Systems—P.I.P.S." in Agronoff, pp. 224–36.

87. Betty Glad, *Jimmy Carter: In Search of the Great White House* (New York: W.W. Norton, 1980), p. 216.

88. Andrew Hacker, "Poets of Packaging, Sculptors of Desire," *The New York Times Book Review* (June 24, 1984), p. 31.

89. For a dramatic example of an ad campaign that is credited with greatly increased sales see Scott Hume, "Wendy's Aims to Get Better with Its Best," *Advertising Age* (April 30, 1984), pp. 4, 64.

90. Quoted in Cliff Zukin, "Mass Communication and Public Opinion," in Nimmo and Sanders, p. 385.

91. Larry J. Sabato, *The Rise of Political Consultants* (New York: Basic, 1981), pp. 76–77.

92. This emphasis on the dominance of attitude reinforcement rather than change was argued most convincingly by Joseph T. Klapper in *The Effects of Mass Communication* (New York: Free Press, 1960). For applications of the minimal effects theory see Dan Nimmo, *The Political Persuaders* (Englewood Cliffs, NJ: Prentice-Hall, 1970) pp. 167–79, and Doris A. Graber, *Mass Media and American Politics* (Washington, DC: Congressional Quarterly, 1980), pp. 183–89.

93. A summary of categories of media-affected attitudes is offered by Nimmo in *Political Persuaders*, pp. 164–67.

94. For a general discussion on differences between behaviors and attitudes, and on basic attempts to deal with these differences, see Philip G. Zimbardo, Ebbe B. Ebbesen, and Christina Maslach, *Influencing Attitudes and Changing Behavior*, 2d Ed. (Boston, MA: Addison-Wesley, 1977), pp. 49–53, 153–168.

95. Kurt Lang and Gladys Engel Lang, "The Mass Media and Voting," in Janowitz and Hirsch, pp. 327–39.

96. John P. Robinson, "Mass Communication and Information Diffusion" in Janowitz and Hirsch, p. 349.

97. Zukin, p. 369.

98. See Jack M. McLeod and Lee B. Becker, "The Uses and Gratifications Approach," in Nimmo and Sanders, pp. 67–100.

99. Nimmo, *Political Persuaders*, pp. 183–84.

100. A general discussion of the inability of many citizens to internalize well-presented information is given by Raymond A. Bauer, "The Obstinate Audience: The Influence Process from the Point of View of Social Communication," in *The Process and Effects of Mass Communication*, Rev. Ed., ed. Wilbur Schramm and Donald F. Roberts (Chicago, IL: University of Chicago, 1971), pp. 326–46.

101. Ginsberg, p. 47.

102. One gathering of leaders at the Bohemian Grove in 1982 reportedly included presidential adviser Alexander Haig, FBI Director William Webster, David Packard, Chief of Naval Operations Thomas Hayward, Eastern Airlines President Frank Borman, Federal Reserve Bank chairman Paul Volcker, World Bank President Alden Clausen, Union Oil chairman Fred Hartley, Atlantic Richfield Chairman Robert Anderson, William Randolph Hearst, Jr., William F. Buckley, George Bush, the Bechtel Corporation's Steve

Bechtel, and many others. See Laton McCartney, *Friends in High Places: The Bechtel Story* (New York: Simon and Schuster, 1988), pp. 13–15.

103. Paletz and Entman, p. 149.

104. Graber, pp. 80–81; Ben H. Bagdikian, "Journalist Meets Propagandist" in *Media Power and Politics*, ed. Doris A. Graber (Washington, DC: Congressional Quarterly, 1984), pp. 331–37; and William Rivers, *The Adversaries: Politics and the Press* (Boston, MA: Beacon, 1970), pp. 68–133.

105. Doug Underwood, "The Boeing Story and the Hometown Press," *Columbia Journalism Review* (November/December 1988): 50–56.

106. Memo from Robert Kintner to the President, January 11, 1967, State of the Union Address File, WHCF (White House Central File), LBJ Library.

107. Memo from Robert Kintner to the President, January 9, 1967, State of the Union Address File, WHCF, LBJ Library.

108. Memo from Robert Kintner to the President, January 11, 1967, State of the Union Address File, WHCF, LBJ Library.

109. See, for example, Lynda Lee Kaid, "The Neglected Candidate: Interpersonal Communication in Political Campaigns," *Western Journal of Communication* (Fall 1977): 245–52.

110. Westin, p. 232; Epstein, p. 37.

111. See, for example, Jarol B. Manheim, "Can Democracy Survive Television?," *Journal of Communication* (Spring 1976): 84–90.

112. Paul F. Lazerfeld and Robert K. Merton, "Mass Communication, Popular Taste, and Organized Social Action," in Schramm and Roberts, p. 565.

113. Donald F. Roberts and Wilbur Schramm, "Children's Learning From the Mass Media," in ibid., pp. 598–99.

114. John P. Robinson, pp. 351–57.

115. Zukin, p. 377.

116. Helene Von Damm, ed., *Sincerely Ronald Reagan* (New York: Berkley Books, 1980), p. 18.

117. Gary Woodward, "Heroic Imagery in the Rhetoric of the Reagan Campaign," unpublished paper presented at the Eastern Communication Association Annual Meeting, Pittsburgh, Pennsylvania, April 26, 1981.

118. See, for example, Reagan's flattering comments to the director of the film, "Patton," in Von Damm, pp. 19–20.

119. Paul M. Hirsch, "The Role of Television and Popular Culture in Comtemporary Society," in *Television: The Critical View*, 3d Ed., ed. by Horace Newcomb (New York: Oxford, 1982), p. 289.

120. Irvin Molotsky, "U.S. Cancels Show in Beijing Over China's Demand to Cut it," *The New York Times*, July 16, 1987, p. C19.

121. Stephen Farber, "Why Sparks Flew in Retelling the Tale of Flight 007," *The New York Times*, November 27, 1988, pp. 35, 42.

122. Mark Crispin Miller, *Boxed In: The Culture of TV* (Evanston, IL: Northwestern, 1988), pp. 69–75.

123. David E. Pitt, "Retracing Diego Rivera's American Odyssey," *The New York Times*, August 28, 1988, pp. 29–30.

124. Herbert Mitgang, "Annals of Government: Investigating Writers," *The New Yorker*, October 5, 1987, pp. 47–90.

125. Robert Sklar, *Movie-Made America* (New York: Vintage, 1975), pp. 58–61.

126. Ronald Reagan and Richard G. Hubler, *Where's the Rest of Me?* (New York: Karz, 1981), pp. 113–25.

127. Hugh Dalziel Duncan, *Communication and Social Order* (New York: Oxford, 1968), pp. 373–416.

128. Ibid., p. 79.

129. Ibid., p. 80.

130. Deena Rosenberg, "A 'Lost' Musical by the Gershwins Makes a Comeback," *The New York Times*, June 24, 1984, pp. H4, 13.

131. Dan Nimmo and James E. Combs, *Subliminal Politics: Myths and Mythmakers in America* (Englewood Cliffs, NJ: Prentice-Hall, 1980), p. 146.

132. Friendly, pp. 163–88; Epstein, pp. 52–53.

133. See the criticisms of Cecil Brown, "Blues for Blacks in Hollywood," in Emery and Smythe, pp. 153–63.

134. Douglas Kellner, "TV, Ideology, and Emancipatory Popular Culture," in Newcomb, p. 412.

135. Erik Barnouw, *Tube of Plenty: The Evolution of American Television* (New York: Oxford, 1975), p. 434.

136. Ibid., *Tube of Plenty*, p. 434.

137. Neil Vidmar and Milton Rokeach, "Archie Bunker's Bigotry: A Study in Selective Perception," *Journal of Communication* (Winter 1974): 36–47.

138. Barnouw, p. 114.

139. Paletz and Entman, p. 182.

140. Gans, *Deciding What's News*; Gitlin, "Prime Time Ideology: The Hegemonic Process in Television Entertainment," in Newcomb, pp. 426–54; Gitlin, *Whole World Is Watching*; Gitlin, *Inside Prime Time* (New York: Pantheon, 1983), Chapter 6; and Gaye Tuchman, *Making News: A Study in the Construction of Reality* (New York: Free Press, 1978).

141. Gitlin, *Whole World Is Watching*, p. 10.

142. Ibid., *Whole World is Watching*, pp. 146–246.

143. Ibid., "Prime Time Ideology," p. 447.

144. Marybeth Kerrigan, "A Movie Targets London Slums," *The New York Times*, March 6, 1988, p. 19.

145. For the general perspective of our analysis we are indebted to Anne Roiphe's "Ma and Pa and John-Boy in Mythic America: The Waltons," reprinted in Newcomb, pp. 198–205.

PART II

THE CONTEXTS OF POLITICAL COMMUNICATION

Chapter Seven

Political Communication and Executive Leadership

Do leaders lead or do they follow?[1]

When Ronald Reagan left office in 1989, he did so with the highest approval rating of any president since Franklin Roosevelt.[2] His 63 percent approval rating is near Roosevelt's 66 percent and considerably ahead of Eisenhower's 59 percent and Kennedy's 58 percent. In addition, 59 percent of the public think Reagan will be viewed by history as an "outstanding" or "above average" president compared to only 14 percent for Jimmy Carter when he left office. There is no doubt that Reagan was well liked by the public, but was he a good leader?

For years, scholars have noticed the increasing difference between campaigning and governing. Today, scholars are noting a new form of leadership, one based on style and public popularity rather than performance and accomplishment. In this chapter we review the current trend toward symbolic executive leadership and focus on the role of communication in creating, defining, and sustaining our relationship with the institutional presidency.

EXECUTIVE LEADERSHIP

Although the president is the most visible figure in American politics, the rise of the media have given a great deal of influence and power to local and state politicians. Mayoralships and governorships have become an important source of presidential candidates. Jesse Jackson, in 1988, even ran a credible campaign for the democratic nomination in spite of the fact that he had never served in an elective office. It appears that executive leadership is not a matter of electoral experience or geography. In fact, Eric Herzik finds substantial overlap in the nature of executive functions of mayors, governors, and the presidency.[3] In reviewing the literature, he discovered four major categories of research: the formal institutional definitions of leadership, the process of decision making, the politician as operational/bureaucratic actor, and the study of personality traits, among others. Although the majority of writing focuses on the presidency, many of the trends and issues of political leadership are relevant to other offices of public service.

Leadership is a term that is often used in connection with politicians and specifically the presidency. The American people look for a strong leader, an image that benefited Ronald Reagan. Theodore Sorensen, an advisor to President Kennedy renewed the argument for a strong and powerful presidency in the mid-1980s. He believes that "Congress can legislate, appropriate, investigate, deliberate, terminate and educate—all essential functions. But it is not organized to initiate, negotiate or act with the kind of swift and informal discretion that our changing world so often requires. Leadership can come only from the presidency."[4] It is, however, much easier to call for strong leadership than define the concept.

Dan Nimmo argues that political leadership "actually refers to a particular relationship that exists between a leader and his followers in specific settings."[5] The focus of much modern leadership theory is upon the willingness of followers to follow. There are no specific lists of traits that constitute leadership although certain traits are helpful in any specific situation. It is more useful, according to Murray Edelman, to look for leadership dynamics "in mass responses, not in static characteristics of individuals."[6]

Americans have generally denied hero status to contemporary politicians, unlike that granted to sports figures and stars of Hollywood. Our revolutionary heritage and democratic institutions have perpetuated a general mistrust toward governmental and centralized authority. The difficulty for leaders, argues Bert Rockman, is the balancing of governability and legitimacy.[7] Leaders must have powers to confront and solve problems yet be accountable to various groups and constituencies. This is difficult because while we demand inspired leadership we also encourage a basic lack of trust and respect for autocratic decision making and formal institutions. Many politicians traditionally run against government. This has contributed to a shift of focus from issues and policies to candidates and officeholders.

Several scholars have noted this trend. Theodore Lowi calls today's presidential government a new regime of the "second republic of the United States."[8] He characterizes the regime as a "plebiscite," a government based on "popular adoration." Inability to meet expectations of performance was masked by shows of personal popularity. Lowi suggests that Reagan was so good at creating the appearance of success that he earned the title of "Teflon presidency."

Dennis Simon and Charles Ostrom argue that "maintaining public support has become a key instrumental goal of the modern president" and the officeholder must actively engage in the "politics of prestige."[9] They conclude that "the value of public support reveals that presidents have an incentive to manage, manipulate, or otherwise control how they are evaluated."[10]

George Edwards recognizes that the "greatest source of influence for the president is public approval"[11] and Raymond Moore predicts that "the leadership style most likely to win in the future will be 'political presidents' who exhibit a high degree of salesmanship but low managerial skills."[12] Barbara Kellerman describes today's "presidential politicking" as a process of "transactional leadership" based upon private bargaining and public interaction.[13] The result is a personalized presidency that requires an engaging personality, an endless campaign, the maintenance of public relations activities and public approval.

Rockman speculates that the reasons we lean toward the personalization of the presidency are the slack between the social system (the public dimension) and the political system (the operational, organizational dimensions), the American culture of individualism, the structure of institutions that stress individual autonomy, and the contemporary role of political polls and public opinion.[14] There is a cost, however, in personalizing the presidency. Presidencies based solely on public approval and popularity will have a positive impact upon the legitimacy and prestige of the office but will have little influence on party cohesion or legislative programs. This rationale may account for the lack of "coattails" of the Reagan presidency in 1988 and the general lack of legislation in his second term. In contrast, a president who is elected based upon political reputation and bargaining skills has a better chance of impacting society through legislative enactments very much like Lyndon Johnson.

For Ryan Barilleaux, the trend toward the personalization of the presidency and Reagan's success of maintaining personal popularity have established a new era of presidential leadership and government. He argues that "the office occupied by Ronald Reagan and his successors is not merely an extension of the modern presidency created by Franklin Roosevelt, but is sufficiently different to warrant a new label."[15] He calls it the "post-modern" presidency. Although Reagan did not create the post-modern presidency, he consolidated and maximized efforts and activities that have revised the institution and its occupant forever. There are several key characteristics of the post-modern presidency: revival of presidential prerogative power, governing through public politics, a large, specialized and centralized staff, policymaking through public support and staff appointments in the courts and various regulatory agencies, the President serving as chief whip in Congress, and the Vice-President serving as a key adviser, envoy, and surrogate. Barilleaux poses a relevant question: "How do post-modern presidents govern in this environment? The answer is that they do not. The post-modern presidency does not govern, but is the premier part of a governing system."[16]

What these various scholars are acknowledging is that today, presidential communication activities are a source of tremendous power: power to define, justify, legitimize, persuade, and inspire. Everything a president does or says has implications and communicates "something." A president surrounds himself with communication specialists. Every act, word, or phrase becomes calculated and measured for a response. Every occasion proclaims a need for utterance.

James Ceaser, with several other colleagues, argues that three factors have attributed to the rise of the "rhetorical presidency."[17] The first factor is the modern doctrine of presidential leadership. The public expects a president to set goals and provide solutions to national problems. To be a leader is a cherished concept and a political expectation and, hence, necessity for our presidents. The second factor giving use to the rhetorical presidency is the development of the mass media. The mass media have increased the size of the audience, provided immediate access to the public, and changed the mode of communicating with the public from primarily the written word to the spoken word delivered in dramatic form. The final factor contributing to the supremacy of the rhetorical presidency is the modern electoral campaign. Contemporary presidential campaigns require national travel, public performances, image creation, issue definition, and the articulation of problem solutions. A "common man" can become known and win an election. Competition for communication opportunities is great.

Thus, the rhetorical presidency refers to more than a collection of speeches delivered by any one president. It refers to the communicative attributes of both the institution and its occupants. The Presidency is an office, a role, a persona, constructing a position of power, myth, legend, and persuasion. Although the Presidency is indeed a real office with an elected official, space, desks, and staff, it remains elusive and undefined. When consulting the ultimate authority—Article II of the Constitution which delineates the functions and duties of the President— one notices how short, sketchy, vague, and almost trivial the description of the office appears. In reality, as Grant McConnell argues, "the presidency is the work of the presidents."[18] Yet, virtually every American, from seven to 70 has a list of criteria of what makes a good president. Expectations are created through presidents' rhetoric, use of symbols, rituals, and sense of history. At home and in schools we are taught that America is the home of freedom, equality, opportunity, and democracy. Within such an environment, as Rossiter notes, the President becomes "the one-man distillation of the American people" reflecting their perceived dignity and majesty.[19] Consequently, elaborate criteria are envisioned for the person who desires the sacred office.

In terms of the Presidency, one should recognize the importance of what Orin Klapp calls "symbolic leadership."[20] The real appeal of public officials is what they symbolize rather than what they have done. Klapp argues that certain persons have enormous effect, not because of achievement or vocation but because they stand for certain things; they play dramatic roles highly satisfying to their audiences; they are used psychologically and stir up followings. Symbolic leadership is an emergent phenomenon resulting from the interaction of the public and the politician. As political drama begins, according to Klapp, roles are identified, interpreted, and projected upon the politician and no distinction is made between what a thing "is" and what the audience sees that it is. The key, therefore, in becoming a symbolic leader is to take advantage of the dramatic elements in any setting. Settings become drama when "things happen to audiences because of parts played by actors; the function of the actor is to transport an audience vicariously out of everyday roles into a new kind of 'reality' that has laws and patterns different from the routines of the ordinary social structure."[21]

The sources of images or preconceptions people have of the qualities of leadership are vast. There are, however, a couple of major influences upon such leadership construction. First, history rather carefully characterizes past national leaders. Washington was a man of integrity (the cherry tree episode), determination (Valley Forge), and was democratic (refusal to be king). Lincoln was a man of patience ("to preserve the union"), forgiveness ("with malice toward none"), and a lover of freedom (The Emancipation Proclamation). Second, television greatly contributes to the creation of leadership ideals. The open forums give the impression of being able to assess candidate qualities. In addition, the media allows the dramatic creation and presentation of heroic figures through media events, advertising, and crisis international events.

Thus, the greatest American mythic endeavor is to find a great person as leader. As a people, Americans find pleasure and comfort in searching as well as in finding heroes. "Two centuries ago," Daniel Boorstin argues, "when a great man appeared, people looked for God's purpose in him; today we look for his press agent."[22] Yet, ironically, hero worship counters democratic dogma. The heart of hero worship, however, is not reverence for divine qualities but appreciation for popular virtues. Heroes are admired "not because they reveal and elevate ourselves."[23] In addition, Walter Fisher argues, presidential heroes as romantic figures express certain American ideals, such as individualism, achievement, and success.[24] A true American hero will be visionary, mythic, and a subject for folklore and legend.[25]

In short, the Presidency is a national political symbol. And political symbols are the direct link between individuals and the social order as argued in Chapter 2. As elements of a political culture, political symbols function as a stimulus for behavior. They can provide insight into macro- and micro-level behavior. The use of appropriate symbols results in getting people to accept certain policies that may or may not provide tangible rewards, arouse support for various causes, and obedience to governmental authority. Political symbols are actually means to material and social ends rather than ends in themselves.

There is, however, a long process from symbol creation, definition, acceptance, and subsequent behavior. For implicit in the argument thus far is the notion that successful leadership and control is dependent upon the successful manipulation of political symbols. There is a constant competition and struggle for national symbols. At one level, a president attempts to manipulate symbols in order to mobilize support, deactivate opposition, and insulate from criticism. On a broader level, national symbols are perpetuated in order to preserve the prevailing culture, beliefs, and values. Thus, the ongoing manipulation of political symbols takes place in the context of an existing set of symbols grounded in the political culture.

In the remainder of this chapter, we will investigate the symbolic nature of the American Presidency by considering the symbolic aspects of the institution as well as individual occupants' attempts to reinforce the symbolic expectations associated with the office.

INSTITUTIONAL ASPECTS OF THE SYMBOLIC DIMENSIONS OF THE PRESIDENCY

Presidential Functions

Of all the major clauses in the Constitution, the one governing the Presidency is the shortest. The members of the Constitutional Convention simply did not delineate in great detail the powers and responsibilities of the Presidency. According to Rossiter, eight key decisions were made at the convention which really created the form and structure of the American Presidency.[26]

1. A separate executive office should be established apart from the legislature.
2. The executive office should consist of one man to be called president of the United States.
3. The president should be elected apart from the legislature.
4. The executive office should have a fixed term subject to termination by conviction of impeachment for high crimes or misdemeanors.
5. The president should be eligible for reelection with no limit as to the number of terms.
6. The president should derive power from the Constitution and not simply from Congress.
7. The president should not be encumbered with a specified body to seek approval for nominations, vetos, or other acts.
8. As president, one may not be a member of either house of Congress.

These key decisions created the office, but they contain little information as to what the office entails. Nearly half of Article II simply deals with tenure, qualifications, and election of the President. Section 2 of Article II states that the President "shall be Commander in Chief," "shall have power to grant reprieves and pardons," "make treaties, provided two-thirds of the Senators present concur," "appoint Ambassadors, other public Ministers and Consuls, judges of the Supreme Court, and all other officers of the United States . . . by and with the advice and consent of the Senate" and "shall have power to fill all vacancies that may happen during the recess of the Senate." Section 3 adds that the President "shall from time to time give to the Congress information of the State of the Union," "convene both Houses . . . on extraordinary occasions," "shall receive Ambassadors and other public Ministers," and "shall take care that the laws be faithfully executed."[27] These, then, are the duties as specified in the Constitution. On the surface, they appear rather simple and straightforward. It is the fulfilling of these functions that complicates the office.

Contemporary scholars, when addressing presidential functions, seldom delineate constitutional provisions. Rather, they group presidential tasks into broad, general categories. These categories, of course, differ in number. For Thomas Cronin, the job description of the president involves six major functions.[28]

1. Symbolic leadership which must generate hope, confidence, national purpose;

2. setting national priorities and designing programs which will receive public attention and a legislative hearing;

3. crisis management which has become increasingly important since 1940;

4. constant legislative and political coalition building;

5. program implementation and evaluation which has also become increasingly difficult in modern times; and

6. general oversight of government routines which forces the president to be responsible for governmental performance at all levels.

Somewhat related to Cronin, Bruce Buchanan identifies four "generic" functions of the Presidency: national symbol, policy advocate, mediator among national interests, and crisis manager.[29] Reedy believes, however, that what a president must do can be boiled down to two simple fundamentals: "He must resolve the policy questions that will not yield to quantitative, empirical analysis; and he must persuade enough of his countrymen of the rightness of his decisions so that he can carry them out without destroying the fabric of society."[30]

From this brief discussion of presidential functions, the Constitution as a job description is vague and general. A president clearly does more than what is outlined in the Constitution. Even as commander-in-chief, the President may undertake crisis management, legislative and political coalition building, and so on. It is how one meets or carries out the functions that provide insight into how the institution influences behavior.

Edward Corwin was the first to mention presidential roles as sources of power.[31] A president's power is based upon five constitutional roles: chief of state, chief executive, chief diplomat, commander-in-chief, and chief legislator. These roles are roughly analogous to the various areas of responsibilities outlined in the Constitution. A president who creates additional roles and hence additional power approaches a dangerous "personalization of the office."

As chief of state, the President functions as the ceremonial head of government not unlike the monarch of England. Some would argue that the majority of presidential activity is ceremonial. Projected upon the President is the symbol of sovereignty, continuity, and grandeur. As chief executive, the President is manager of one of the largest "corporations" in the world. Whether the President likes it or not, he is held responsible for the quality of governmental performance ranging from a simple letter of complaint to military preparedness. In event of war, the President as commander-in-chief must ensure strategic execution and victory. Within modern history, the field of foreign relations has become extremely important. The formulation of foreign policy and the conduct of foreign affairs force the president to serve as the nation's chief diplomat. Finally, by providing domestic leadership, the President must guide Congress by identifying national priorities for legislation. These legitimate, constitutional roles are obviously interrelated. Yet, the various hats require rather distinct approaches, strategies, and temperament. Even these, however, may be situationally bound.

Clinton Rossiter, building on Corwin's analyses argues that five extra-constitutional roles must be recognized: chief of party, protector of the peace, manager of prosperity, world leader, and voice of the people.[32] Rossiter, as Corwin, believes that the source of presidential power lies in the combination of the various roles. Rossiter, at least, recognizes the expanding nature of the Presidency. These extra roles resulted from the growing activities of a president plus the growing expectations of the public. As Myron Hale has succinctly stated, "roles became obligations and duties, as each role became a Presidential responsibility."[33] When speaking of presidential roles, most scholars cite Rossiter's classic *The American Presidency*. Hence, the list of roles is fairly stationary. Yet, as the functions or duties of the Presidency grow, so do the roles. As the various tasks become more complex, numerous roles may be required to carry out one function. One should also note that each role may require very different skills and techniques. Roles, then, are more numerous than functions. They are labels or characters that people see and each has a distinct mode usually congruent with public expectations which will be developed later. Finally, if a role set is good or successful, the set may become a model. The model may thus serve as an overall approach to the fulfillment of the functions. The role set, as a model, may be praised, condemned, imitated, or serve as a guide to performance.

Presidential Roles

Most all political scientists recognize that the Presidency is both an institution and a role. As such, the Presidency has a great deal of influence upon those who occupy the office as well as upon the general public.

Political roles are not concrete, static entities. Rather, they are ideas about what people expect to do in certain situations as well as what others expect them to do in certain situations. While the concept of role does deal with behavior, it is not the activity of behavior itself. The distinction between what individuals think they should do and what in fact they do should not be ignored. As Norton Long notes,

The actors in the world of politics are neither the rational calculators of economic man nor the uncultured savages of Hobbes' state of nature but are born into a political culture, albeit frequently an ambiguous one, and are socialized to a range of response patterns that may be invoked by diverse stimuli. With this equipment, they confront a reality that seems to each public, one-dimensional common sense but, in fact, through the differing glasses that it is viewed, presents widely differing perspectives.[34]

Political actors, therefore, possess a repertory of responses or roles. Upon any stimulus, the appropriate role behavior is a product of what the actor perceives the defined role to be which also fulfills the expectations of the public. "The existence of these patterned sets of roles is part of the technology of the political culture and permits the actors to function with the same ease as a ballplayer playing his position."[35]

Thus, roles (political or otherwise) are comprised of internal and external elements.[36] The former consist of the individual's own perception of what a task demands and how to fulfill it; the latter are the expectations and orientations of members of society. However, as Height and Johnston point out,

the division into roles can be deceptive . . . and one must never forget the fact that one man plays all the parts. The President can never separate his problems and divide them into preconceived categories for decision. Each decision will involve the President as a whole man, and he will need in some manner to accommodate several often conflicting roles in order to determine a course of action.[37]

Role Expectations

A "role set" is a set of "behavioral relationships that exist between positions."[38] Borden, Gregg, and Grove argue that there are two kinds of role sets: traditional role sets and unique role sets.[39] Traditional role sets refer to institutionalized relationships such as husband and wife, lawyer and client, and so on. These role sets provide general guidelines for behavior. Traditional role sets serve primarily task maintenance functions. Unique role sets refer primarily to person maintenance functions. Thus, traditional role sets provide already established interaction patterns and set up general expectations of the participants.

Certainly, the American presidency has established a rather clear traditional role set. The title of president implies more than simply a job description. To know that a person is president is to know in a very general way how the individual is likely to behave and how others will behave toward the individual. The title not only provides a means for anticipating a range of behaviors, but also confines the range of behaviors possible. Thus, behavioral expectations and restrictions are attached to all social positions. Richard Rose notes that "empirical investigation usually reveals that leaders are often constrained by the expectations of their followers and in some cases compelled to follow their followers or risk deposition as leader."[40] For example, when Reagan entered the White House in 1980, the public clearly expected him to reduce unemployment (72%), reduce inflation (66%), reduce cost of government (70%), increase government efficiency (89%), deal effectively with foreign policy (77%), and strengthen national defense (76%). For George Bush, the public was equally demanding expecting him to keep the nation at peace (77%), to keep the nation prosperous (74%), to increase respect abroad (74%), to improve education standards (74%), to raise environment quality (62%), and to help minorities (53%).[41]

Cronin recognizes the basic tendency of Americans to believe in great personages, "that someone, somewhere, can and will cope with the major crises of the present and future."[42] Within our society, the Presidency fulfills this need and becomes the symbol of our hopes. Presidents are much more likely, historically, to be placed on a pedestal rather than under a microscope. Although the tendency is acknowledged by political scientists, Cronin insists that political scientists have "usually not read in such meaning, or at least have not infused their view of the Presidency with connotations of a civil religion."[43] Consequently, to simply speak of presidential functions in no way adequately describes what the presidency really is.

Emmet Hughes, in *The Living Presidency*, states that a president faces two constituencies: "the living citizens and the future historians."[44] This certainly is not an easy task. Nearly all scholars agree that any American president inherits a vast, complex set of role expectations. "The fact that there are many roles involved in the most important political office gives a politician the discretion of deciding which to emphasize and which to ignore. He can, at the least, choose what he ignores."[45] But such a choice is not a one-way street. Roles create expectations but societal expectations can create political roles. Murray Edelman perceptively notes that

expectations also evoke a specific political role and self-conception for those individuals who accept the myth in question: the patriotic soldier whose role it is to sacrifice, fight, and die for his country; the policeman or National Guardsman whose role it is to save the social order from subhuman or radical borders.[46]

For Edelman, the degree of attachment to a political myth and the role it creates plus the fervor with which the role is acted out depend upon "the degree of anxiety the myth rationalizes, the intensity with which the particular expectation that forms the central premise of the myth is held."[47] When Alfred deGrazia speaks of "the myth of the President," he is referring to "a number of qualities [that] are given to every President that are either quite fictitious or large exaggerations of the real man."[48] He further notes that "the myth is not alone the property of the untutored mind, but of academicians, scientists, newspapermen, and even Congressmen."[49]

Thus, the office of the Presidency has grown because of interaction; interaction of the office with the public and the public with the office. As public expectations increase, so does the job. Concurrently, the job is forced to expand to meet public expectations.

As already mentioned, there appears to be a growth in public expectations of the Presidency. However, twentieth-century presidents, because of the use of mass media, have encouraged the public to identify with the candidate and potential of the office. Theodore White asserts that especially since 1960, our idea of government consists of promises—promises to take care of people, the cities, the sick, the old, the young. According to White, "by 1980 we had promised ourselves almost to the point of national bankruptcy.''[50] Consequently, the public has responded by holding the President accountable for meeting various demands. David Easton has identified two types of expectations that citizens have of political leadership.[51] One focuses on the office and the other focuses on the individual who holds the office. Thus, public expectations are vast and complex. Upon investigating the research on presidential and public expectations, Herzik and Dodson conclude that indeed ''a consensus does exist concerning public expectations of the President—a consensus focused around general traits of personality, leadership, and individual virtue.''[52]

Disappointment in presidential performance is not the only consequence of false expectations. False expectations also encourage presidents to attempt more than they can accomplish in any term of office. Thus, false expectations invite presidents to overpromise and overextend themselves. This, in turn, creates the need for image-making activities. Such activities, in some cases, become the major task or work function of an administration. Soon, the emphasis, out of necessity, becomes style over substance. ''The public-relations apparatus,'' as Cronin argues, ''not only has directly enlarged the Presidential work force but has expanded public-relations expectations about the Presidency at the same time. More disquieting is the fact that, by its very nature, this type of press-agency, feeds on itself, and the resulting distortions encourage an ever increasing subordination of substance to style.''[53]

Presidential Roles Created

Political roles, although undergoing constant modification, exist prior to any political event. Politicians, however, do not consciously decide each morning during what parts of the day they will act as a statesman, an administrator, or a partisan vote getter. Yet, as we already argued, public expectations of behavior and performance are rather clearly defined. Such expectations develop over time and consequently are slow in changing. Because political roles are fairly well defined, they are learned by politicians through the process of socialization. New legislators soon learn what roles are appropriate in various situations.

Role taking, as Edelman notes, is action.[54] It is both behavioral and observable. The process of role taking by politicians directly influences the behaviors of officeholders by revealing public expectations and hence expected behavior. Edelman succinctly explains the process as follows:

Through taking the roles of publics whose support they need, public officials achieve and maintain their positions of leadership. The official who correctly gauges the response of publics to his acts, speeches, and gestures makes those behaviors significant symbols, evoking common meanings for his audience and for himself so shaping his future actions as to reassure his public and in this sense ''represent'' them.[55]

This process of role socialization, argues Rose, is "emotionally intense and highly compressed in time; it is the chief means by which people fit and are fitted into place in established institutions."[56]

One of the major points made in discussing the paradoxical nature of the Presidency is that the expectations and functions of the office are often competing, conflicting, and contradictory. Role conflicts are an essential element in political life. Role conflict occurs "when contradictory types of behavior are expected from a person who holds different positions or when contradictory types of behavior are expected within one role."[57] A successful politician, therefore, is one who can handle role conflicts. Unfortunately, depending upon one's view, when a discrepancy develops between individual preferences and institutional role expectations, it is more often the individual who changes. For Richard Rose, the best measure of a politician's greatness is his or her ability to create new roles for an established office.[58] In fact, Rose views such an ability as one attribute of charismatic leadership.

Politics is a primarily symbolic activity that touches the lives of a significantly large number of people.[59] Such activity has a unique and often profound meaning because, in the words of Kenneth Burke, man is uniquely "the symbol-making, and symbol-misusing animal,"[60] Political reality, the implications and consequences of which are felt and observable, is conveyed through the creation of significant symbols. Images of politics are largely, therefore, symbolic. The degree to which images of politics are useful and gratifying, according to Nimmo, is related to three factors:

First, no matter how correct or incorrect, complete or incomplete may be one's knowledge about politics, it gives that person some way of understanding specific political events. . . . Second, the general likes and dislikes in a person's political images offer a basis for evaluating political objects. . . . Third, a person's self-image provides a way of relating one's self to others.[61]

Political images, then, are beneficial in an individual's evaluating and identifying with various political leaders, events, ideas, or causes.

Many attitudes about the presidency stem from messages received in childhood about the virtues of various presidents. Studies continually find that the president is ordinarily the first public official to come to the attention of young children.[62] Long before children are informed about the specific functions of the Presidency, they view individual presidents as exceptionally important and benign. David Easton and Robert Hess found that children stressed personal characteristics of the President which include: honest, wise, helpful, powerful, good, and benign.[63] Such attitudes probably result from parents not mentioning negative aspects of the political world in front of children plus the general tendency of children to selectively perceive more supportive characteristics of individuals in a wider environment. Generally, by the age of nine, virtually every American child has some detailed awareness of the Presidency and can identify the incumbent President. Such cognizance of the American President, according to Fred Greenstein, goes beyond national boundaries. He reports that surveys of children in Austria and Canada reveal that the name of the United States President is better known than the name of the prime ministers of their own country.[64] Even in 1973 at the height of the Watergate episode Greenstein found "numerous idealized references to the President."[65] Thus, esteem and respect for the office independent of the occupant is established at a rather early age.

Presidential Roles Permeated

Every year since World War II, seven or eight of the ten most admired men and women are involved in national politics. And the President, regardless of performance, is among them.[66] For example, Reagan was at the top of the list of Gallup's "Most Admired Men" for the eighth consecutive year in 1988. Five out of the top ten were politicians (Reagan, Gorbachev, Bush, Jesse Jackson, and Edward Kennedy).[67]

Doris Graber, in a study designed to analyze images of presidential candidates in the press during campaigns, found that citizens tend to selectively extract information about a president's personal image that is beyond the media content which ignores issue elements.[68] Therefore, apparently, citizens perceive and evaluate a president as a person rather than on their policies and skill in office. According to Greenstein, when people are asked to indicate what they like or dislike about a president, they usually cite aspects of personal image.[69]

Another result of childhood socialization is the heavy dependency for leadership on the presidency, especially in times of national crisis. Pious argues that in times of national emergency, we discard skepticism and return to childhood images of the Presidency.[70] As adults, we still desire to see the President as a combination of Washington and Lincoln, making wise decisions and working harder than the average citizen to preserve the quality of life.

A presidential campaign emphasizes the childhood visions and qualities of the office. Hence, campaigns themselves perpetuate the mythic and heroic role demands of the office. To mobilize a nation is indeed a somewhat mysterious process. For McConnell, it is the essential dimension of the presidency resulting from becoming a "national symbol" that in so doing, gives substance and purpose to the nation itself.[71] The process of selecting a president is important and vital. Campaigns may best be characterized as noisy, disorderly, contentious, and even absurd. "The gap between the indignity of the process and the grandeur of the end is enormous."[72] Yet, the process allows the opportunity to assess and project presidential qualities upon the candidates.

Media advisers must project appropriate images of the candidates that are always simplified depictions of reality. In a memo to Richard Nixon, Ray Price argued, "It's not what's there that counts, it's what is projected—and carrying it one step further, it's not what he projects but rather what the voter receives."[73] James Wooten, in addressing the 1976 Carter campaign, wrote that Carter

" . . . believed that the candidate who took clear positions on every issue was not long for the political world. There would be only one issue on which a successful candidate would be judged that year, the amorphous, ethereal concept of integrity, honesty, trustworthiness, credibility."[74] Patrick Caddell is quoted as warning Carter during the transition that "too many good people have been beaten because they tried to substitute substance for style."[75] Is this ethically, logically, or even morally right? Carter's pollster Gerald Rafshoon believed that there was nothing wrong with a candidate adjusting himself to an ideology or "rhetorical stance" judged to be acceptable by the voters. Rafshoon argued to Wooten, "He was always Jimmy Carter. . . . Hell, you wouldn't expect Sears Roebuck to step into a big multimillion dollar promotion without having the benefit of consumer research on what people are most interested in purchasing."[76] Consequently, the image projected by a candidate should meet the expectations and childhood visions of presidential behavior. The best image is one that is vague enough for voters to complete. In the simplest terms, this means that conservatives should be able to see the candidate as conservative and, likewise, liberals should be able to see the candidate as liberal. Above all, this should be done without seeming contradictory or insincere.

From this perspective an election is seen not simply as a reflection of the preference for one individual over another. Rather, it is a composite of all the individual desires, hopes, frustrations, and anger of citizens encompassing an infinite number of issues or concerns. However chaotic, the process has value. As McConnell notes,

Purists may well wish for more graceful campaigning, and more incisive and intellectually elevated debates. Quite possibly, however, achieving these desirable conditions might rob the process of much of its vitality and leave the ultimate winner with no accurate sense of the temper of the American people. A Presidential election is, above all, an articulation of the mood of the electorate.[77]

By inauguration day a candidate has emerged as President. A tremendous transformation, at least in the eyes of the public, has occurred. Americans want and even need to believe that the common man they elevated to the Presidency is a Lincolnesque bearer of infinite wisdom and benevolence. The perceived qualities are confirmed as soon as the candidate takes the oath of office.

The public's relationship with the Presidency is more than a search for the fulfillment of childhood notions of the office. For some time empirical and clinical evidence has shown that the office provides, for a large portion of the population, an outlet for expression of deep, often unconscious personality needs and conflicts. Harold Lasswell, as early as 1930 in his classic *Psychopathology and Politics*, argued that private needs become displaced onto public objects and rationalized in terms of general political principles.[78] Greenstein, a student of Lasswell, continually investigated these phenomena in relation to the Presidency.[79] He recognizes six major psychological uses of the Presidency for the population.

1. The office serves a cognitive aid by providing a vehicle for the public becoming aware of the functions, impact, and politics of government.

2. The presidency provides an outlet for affect, feelings, and emotions. The office serves as a focal point of pride, despair, hope, as well as frustration. It can easily be responsible, in the eyes of the public, for all that is bad or for all that is good.

3. The office serves as a means of vicarious participation. The president becomes an object of identification and consequently presidential efforts become citizen efforts resulting in a sharing of heightened feelings of potency.

4. Especially in times of crisis or uncertainty, the presidency functions as a symbol of national unity. When a president acts, it is the nation acting as one voice expressing one sentiment.

5. Likewise, the office serves as a symbol of stability and predictability. We assume that the president is knowledgeable and in control of events thus minimizing danger or surprise.

6. Finally, the presidency serves as a lightning rod or an object of displacement. The office is the ultimate receptacle for personal, which becomes national, feelings and attitudes. The president becomes either idealized or the ultimate scapegoat. Truman's cliché, "The Buck Stops Here," is true—at least in the minds of the public.

The Symbolic Nature of the Presidency

On each Inauguration Day history is being made and another chapter of American history is carefully recorded during the next four days. Every detail of presidential behavior is noted and significance is attached. The nation "joyfully" recalls that Millard Fillmore married his school teacher; that James Buchanan never married; that Grover Cleveland was the only President to be married in the White House; that William Taft was the largest President (six feet, three inches and 300 pounds); that John Tyler had 15 children; that John Adams was the first President to live in the White House; that Millard Fillmore had the first bathtub installed in the White House; that Andrew Jackson was the first President to ride a train; that Abraham Lincoln was the first to make a whistle-stop campaign tour; that Woodrow Wilson was the first to use radio to speak to the nation; that Franklin Roosevelt was the first to be on television; that Dwight Eisenhower was the first to travel by jet; and that there have been 24 lawyers, four military men, three teachers, three authors, three farmers, a tailor, a haberdasher, and an actor as presidents. Why are such trivia important to American citizens? Because these men are the leaders of the nation. They are chosen to lead and consequently they are a part of us. "America has provided the landscape and has given us the resources and the opportunity for this feat of national self-hypnosis." Daniel Boorstin concludes that "each of us individually provides the market and the demand for the illusions which flood our experience."[80] But such illusions make it difficult to distinguish between what is truly significant and what is merely a matter of curiosity. The overlay of myth and magic on the presidency makes assessment of the institution most difficult. "The fatal need

for personification of society, animation of ideals and worship of heroes introduces continuous disorder into the matter-of-fact problems of running a country."[81]

Of all the political myths of the nation, Theodore White argues that the supreme
myth is the ability of the citizens to choose the "best" person to lead the nation.[82]
From this belief followed the notion that the office would ennoble anyone who
holds the office. "The office would burn the dross from his character; his duties
would, by their very weight, make him a superior man, fit to sustain the burden
of the law, wise and enduring enough to resist the clash of all selfish interests."[83]
Thus, the presidency is a combination of symbol and reality. However, the
symbolic dimensions of the office are increasingly becoming more important as
the role of mass media has become both "maker and breaker" of presidents.
As Edelman notes, "the symbolic component is more crucial to the degree that
people lack meaningful social commitments that provide a benchmark for evaluation."[84] In fact, the manipulation of salient symbols clouds issues and blurs
situations resulting in emotionally charged but nebulously defined symbols.[85]

The Presidency as a symbol or image has six characteristics.[86] The Presidency
is synthetic, believable, passive, vivid, simplified, and ambiguous. As synthetic,
the impression of the office is carefully planned, manipulated, and created to
serve a specific purpose. Details of leadership become massive strategies. The
institution is believable in that it has prescribed meaning, significance, and
expectations attached to the symbol. The office is real and manifests criteria for
each occupant. Yet, the office is passive in the sense that the symbol is an ideal,
a mixture of hope, myth, and fantasy. In being believable, the office as a symbol
is vivid and concrete. As the ideal, whatever its composition, it becomes publicly
shared; the office is "real" in its significance and consequences. As is the case
with every symbol, however, it is more simple than the object it represents. The
intricacies and complexities of the job are reduced to a few broad, general
characteristics that are more readily identifiable. Symbols, as simplified, are also
ambiguous floating between imagination and reality awaiting people to fill in
the gaps and thus to attach personal significance to the symbol. Thus, the Presidency, as a symbol, aims at suggestion, comprehensiveness, the texture of
experience, and passional intelligence.[87]

Perhaps the forefathers were aware of the fact that the most practical method
of unifying people was to give them a symbol that all could identify. When the
symbol is manifested in a person, the efficacy and effectiveness are greatly
enhanced. Clearly the President of the United States is the focal point of the
political system. Every action by the President is symbolic because not only is
he merely an executive but also a carrier of meaning. What the individual
symbolizes to each person or group depends upon the system of interpretation
of the person or group. "Political symbols bring out in concentrated form those
particular meanings and emotions which the member of a group created and
reinforce in each other."[88] Consequently, according to Novak, "from the beginning to the end of his term in office, his every action is a means by which
citizens interpret life in the United States."[89]

Just what are the symbols through which the President communicates to the people? The answer: simply everything. To provide a laundry list of specific artifacts, phrases, or actions is not important. There is no way to gauge the intensity and saliency of every action. For some, whether the President wears a suit or not is important. Even the flag carries many levels of response in the nation. What is more important to understand is what makes various actions of the President symbolic is the cluster of memories and associations inherent in the actions while recognizing that responses differ for different audiences.[90] It is more beneficial, therefore, to speak of the Presidency as a highly symbolic office rather than identifying specific actions or isolated symbolic endeavors of a president.

Such a position, however, should not be viewed as attempting to avoid specifically describing the symbolic nature of the Presidency. The epitome of identifying the symbolic nature of the presidency is Taft's often quoted description of the President as ''the personal embodiment and representative of (the people's) dignity and majesty.''[91] Clinton Rossiter reflects Taft's statement in proclaiming that the President ''is the one-man distillation of the American people just as surely as the Queen is of the British people.''[92] The office is the symbol of justice, freedom, equality, continuity, and grandeur. The Presidency, more specifically, mirrors all that is best about America as perceived by each citizen. In accordance, Cronin notes: ''The Presidency is nearly always a mirror of the fundamental forces in society: the values, the myths, the quest for social control and stability, and the vast, inert, conservative forces that maintain the existing balance of interests.''[93]

It is a serious mistake, however, to view such a characterization of the Presidency as passive. The very potency of the Presidency as a symbol gives the office purpose and pragmatic nature. Americans expect presidents to prod, unite, as well as to provide direction and a sense of purpose. As such, the Presidency fulfills the parental functions of supreme leader, guide, and teacher. It is important to note, however, that symbolic power is the precondition of pragmatic power. Much legislation and many programs have failed because they were not symbolically acceptable. The key to success, of course, is presidential leadership. Not surprisingly, the most frequent complaint of the presidency since the Vietnam War is the lack of leadership. But leadership, from an interactionist perspective, is more than effective management and the ability to isolate and derive solutions to problems.

Recognizing the symbolic importance and dimensions of leadership is not to support the old notion that one is born a leader or that leadership is simply a matter of charisma. Rather, true leadership is granted by people comprised of their own unique perceptions, needs, and expectations. Klapp distinguishes three levels of leadership ranging from practical doers within social structures to those whose influence is entirely symbolic.[94]

The first level of leadership consists of those who do things without achieving popular images. This level includes such leaders as football coaches, ministers, or corporation presidents. The second level of leadership Klapp calls ''dramatic actor.'' At this level the leader escapes from the limitations within social structures. Impact on an audience is more important than outcomes or results. The final level of leadership Klapp identifies is the ''durable symbol'' where the leader is institutionalized. ''Finding such a niche means that an image has been consolidated and that a symbolic leader has hit upon a permanent function.''[95] Any systematic study of leadership reveals how society finds and serves its needs by choosing leaders who best symbolize something that others desire. They are leaders ''in the sense that they initiate feelings, orient multitudes, and are used psychologically so that audiences or followings can move to a state of mind, if not a course of action, that would not be possible without the leader's help.''[96]

It is in presidential elections, however, that symbolism is increasingly becoming the most powerful and planned component. A campaign attempts to legitimize the candidate's visions and to demonstrate leadership capabilities. During an election, the nation is not a classroom but a theater; not an event but a saga competing for the symbolic centers of America. Novak describes a presidential campaign as

a contest for the souls, imaginations of Americans as much as for the nation's levers of power. It is also a contest between national self-images. Not infrequently citizens will vote against their self-interest, coldly and economically defined, for the sake of symbols more important to them.[97]

The symbolic significance of campaigns is interwoven with their pragmatic quest for power.[98] One can recall when a single word or phrase may destroy a candidate's chances (Romney's ''brainwashed''), give a candidate serious trouble (Carter's ''ethnic purity''), or change a candidate's image (Bush's ''read my lips.''). An alarming show of personality may damage a campaign as, for example, Muskie's tears in New Hampshire, Nixon's rage in 1962, or George Bush's confrontation in the second candidate forum in 1980. Symbolic violations may inhibit electoral success as, for example, Stevenson's marital status and Teddy Kennedy's episode at Chappaquiddick. The rich do not always win (e.g., Lindsay, or Connally) and the underdog may triumph as did McCarthy in 1968, McGovern in 1972, Carter in 1976, and Dukakis in 1988. Simply stated, the intangibles are many and the realm of the symbolic is important. In electing a president, ''we elect the chief symbol maker of the land, and empower him in the kingdom of our imaginations as well as in the executive office where he supervises armies, budgets, and appointments.''[99]

Perhaps the most often used analog in describing the role of the Presidency in America is the link to royalty. As Barber argues, ''we elect a politician and insist that he also be a King.''[100] But kingly treatment of presidents is one source of trouble resulting in isolation of presidents from reality.[101] Yet, the continual respect, awe, and deference given presidents despite failures and disappointments are considerable. For Americans, the President both rules and reigns. To think of the Presidency as royalty brings unity and simplicity to the image of government. The role of television contributes greatly to the coronation. "Its cameras need a single actor, seek the symbolic event as the desert hart seeks water."[102]

For Novak, Americans not only elect a king, but also a high priest and prophet.[103] Together, the terms speak to the symbolic importance and influence of the office. For the President is king in the sense of being the symbolic and decisive focal point of national power and destiny. The President is prophet in the sense of being the chief interpreter of national self-understanding and defining future endeavors. He is priest in the sense of incarnating the nation's value, aspirations, and expressing these through his behavior.

Thus, to define the Presidency as principally a symbolic institution is not to lessen the significance and importance of the office. Rather, it emphasizes the subtle impact of the institution upon every citizen. To describe the President as priest, prophet, and king is to acknowledge the respect, expectations, hopes, and values of the American people. And the interactionist perspective best reveals the public's response to the institution and their effect upon its nature.

OCCUPANT ASPECTS OF THE SYMBOLIC DIMENSIONS OF THE PRESIDENCY

Generally, most presidential scholars, although using somewhat different terminology, believe that the American people expect three major aspects of presidential behavior. First, the President is expected to be a competent manager of the vast machinery of government. Second, the American people expect the President to take care of their needs by initiating programs, legislation, and safeguarding the economy. Finally, the people want a sense of legitimacy from the President. The office, while providing symbolic affirmation of the nation's values, should faithfully represent the opinions of the public as well.

What type of person should be President of the United States? What qualities should one have for the job? On the surface, these seem to be legitimate questions. Scholars and citizens alike have confronted the issue. Indeed, judgment is required at least every four years. Simple surveys easily produce a laundry list of desired presidential qualities, a very demanding list to be sure. It is much more difficult, however, to isolate the roots of such qualities. Are desired presidential qualities founded in history, myth, and merely perpetuated through the textbooks? The implications of the answer to such a question are important. For example, a poll conducted in 1979 found the following desired characteristics: intelligence, sound judgment in a crisis, job competence, high ethical standards, sense of humor, imagination; and personal charm.[104]

Rossiter, in his classic work, identified seven qualities "that a man must have or cultivate if he is to be an effective modern President."[105] First, a president must have bounce; "that extra elasticity, given to few men, which makes it possible for him to thrive on the toughest diet of work and responsibility of the world."[106] In addition, the Presidency demands affability, political skill, cunning, a sense of history, the newspaper habit ("must be on guard lest he be cut off from harsh reality''), and a sense of humor. Such qualities are indeed needed. However, they would also be an asset for anyone in a managerial position. And certainly presidents of major corporations should probably likewise be so characterized.

Hughes' *The Living Presidency*, also of a "White Knight" orientation, prefers to address the quality that "shapes and makes an effective Presidential style."[107] Such a style includes:

1. A sense of confidence; "with no harm to his leadership so grave as a show of hesitation."

2. A sense of proportion; "the avoidance of excess and extravagance."

3. A sense of drama; "a truly important presidency has never failed to raise the noise and dust of combat."

4. A sense of timing; "sure instinct for pace and rhythm."

5. A sense of constancy; "With no necessary loss of popular trust, he may vary his methods, but he must not appear to vary or to waver."

6. A sense of humanity; "humility and humor, and toward the people, with warmth and compassion."

7. A sense of perspective; "no saving quality that a president may lose more swiftly upon entering the White House. . . . "

8. And above all, a sense of history.

Such an approach is more profitable. It provides more of a guideline to presidential performance than a list of specific qualities.

Another way to ascertain the qualities a president should have is to confront those who have worked closely with presidents. They not only know the qualities of specific presidents but also know the demands of the job. Many of their assessments, however, are equally as vague and disappointing.

Sherman Adams, a key figure in the Eisenhower administration, believes that the two qualities vital to the success of any president are "intellectual receptivity and the instinct to recognize his own prejudice or bias."[108] Clark Clifford, counselor to Truman, Kennedy, and secretary of defense for Johnson, cites in order of importance the qualities of "character, intellect, decisiveness, political understanding, and awareness of the potential of the office."[109] Theodore Sorensen, a close aide to John Kennedy, believes that the personal qualities of judgment and leadership are the most important.[110] How does one measure the qualities? What are character and leadership? In terms of intellect, one is reminded of a quip by Holmes: "For a President can always hire brains. But there is no way for him to lease fortitude or borrow intuition."[111] Yet, how does one *develop* intuition? More importantly, how does one *measure* intuition during a campaign?

Perhaps a better approach in attempting to view the qualities a president should have is to view the characteristics of specific popular presidents and to view specific behaviors the public would oppose. A Gallup poll conducted in 1980 asked respondents, "Of all the Presidents we've ever had, who do you wish were President today?"[112] The results revealed in order of preference: John Kennedy, Franklin Roosevelt, Harry Truman, Dwight Eisenhower, Abraham Lincoln, Gerald Ford, Richard Nixon, Theodore Roosevelt, Jimmy Carter, and Lyndon Johnson. Even these results are suspect. Are Jimmy Carter and Gerald Ford really better presidents than Washington, Jefferson, or Jackson? Did Kennedy really provide more unity, leadership, and legislation than did Franklin Roosevelt or even Lyndon Johnson? Of course, the public's mind is somewhat fickle. By 1989, Carter, Nixon, and Ford were no longer of the chosen few. Not surprisingly, Reagan had entered the distinguished group of names. The fact is that myth, age, and situational elements greatly influence the public's determination of greatness. Patrick Kenney and Tom Rice found that a president can expect being highly regarded and even labeled "great" if "he is an elected president, wins a large majority of the popular vote, serves two terms, is assassinated, serves during a war, presides over a healthy economy, works smoothly with Congress, and avoids major scandals."[113]

Most characteristics or job specifications for the Presidency can be grouped in three major categories: "the body," "character and temperament," and "brains or intelligence."[114] First, a president must look like a president—mature, tall, healthy, and athletic. The public was often reminded of Ford's golfing and days of playing football; Carter's jogging and fishing; and Reagan's chopping wood and horseback riding. Second, presidents are judged on qualities of integrity, perseverance, compassion, dignity, courage, and mental stability. Finally, a president must display intelligence and common horse sense by providing a vision of the future, solutions to problems, knowledge of detailed facts of situations, and wisdom in judgments.

The general public is rather clear, however, on what they do not want a president to do. A national survey by Gallup found that:

70 percent oppose a president smoking marijuana;

43 percent object to a president telling racial or ethnic jokes;

38 percent object to a president not belonging to a church;

36 percent object to a president occasionally using tranquilizers;

33 percent object to a president using profanity;

30 percent object to a president having seen a psychiatrist;

21 percent object to a president wearing jeans in the oval office;

17 percent object to a president being divorced;

14 percent object to a president having a cocktail.[115]

Although some of the percentages appear to be rather low, scholars generally agree that if as few as 33 percent of the public object to any practice, a candidate's chances of election are very slim. The survey also revealed that 74 percent *would not* vote for an atheist. Interestingly, only 58 percent thought a divorced individual could be elected, 40 percent that a Jew could be elected, 37 percent that a black could be elected, and a mere 33 percent that a woman could be elected. Reagan's divorce never became an issue.

What can be surmised from such diverse lists of desired presidential qualities? First, they are largely useless. The qualities may be characterized as admirable, often contradictory, general, abstract, and even biblical. Many do not have a direct relationship to job or task performance. Second, as a result, the question becomes whether the public imposes these qualities on the President or do presidents create the impressions of meeting these qualities. Clearly, the answer is both. As a result of the interaction, when presidents appear to meet the desired qualities, then the qualities become embedded as part of the public's expectations. Finally, the desired qualities often reflect individual senses of goodness, morality, and ideas of right and wrong. Individuals may occasionally drink but be appalled at such behavior from their ministers. Consequently, it is not surprising that the public desires presidents "not to do as the citizens do, but what they say to do." There is no test that presidential candidates take to reveal true intelligence, integrity, a sense of history, and so on. They are simply forced to demonstrate through campaigning that they, in fact, are intelligent, honest, knowledgeable, and so on. Hence the qualities are in the mind and largely depend upon perception as to their reality.

The President as Priest, Prophet, and King

The importance of presidents meeting the expectations of the public cannot be overemphasized. Carter was very successful in rising from obscurity in 1976 to becoming President of the United States. As a presidential candidate, Carter was most successful in presenting himself as a common man and a man of the people. James Wooten noted that Carter "worked hard at establishing himself in the eyes of the public as a common man, just another American hired to do a particular job."[116] Carter also effectively articulated the traditional values of an average American citizen. Carter's campaign rhetoric reflected how Americans wanted to conceive of themselves and the myth they wanted to live by as evident in Carter's slogan of "a government as good as its people." A vote for Carter became a vote for us reaffirming our national values and virtues in the wake of Nixon's disgrace.

But an interesting paradox of the American Presidency is that once elected we demand uncommon leadership, great insight, and vast knowledge from our presidents. A president must appear presidential as defined by history, culture, and status of the position. Carter was often criticized for his lack of presidential behavior, dress, and demeanor. Carter wore a blue suit for his inaugural rather than a morning coat and top hat; took the oath of office as Jimmy Carter rather than as James Earl Carter; walked down Pennsylvania Avenue rather than rode in a limousine; prohibited the playing of "Hail to the Chief"; sold the presidential yacht *Sequoia*; sent Amy to a public school; carried his own luggage; and wore blue jeans at the White House.

In July 1977, Carter received a 64 percent positive rating on the question of restoring public confidence in government. Just one year later, however, Carter received a 63 percent negative response to the same question.[117] There is evidence to suggest that the public soon resented and rejected Carter's attempts to reduce the perceived stature and dignity of the Presidency. Carter, much too late, realized the fact. In his memoirs he writes:

However, in reducing the imperial Presidency, I overreacted at first. We began to receive many complaints that I had gone too far in cutting back the pomp and ceremony, so after a few months I authorized the band to play "Hail to the Chief" on special occasions. I found it to be impressive and enjoyed it.[118]

Simply stated, the Presidency is both our administrative office and our ceremonial office. Our president must meet and entertain other kings and rulers of nations. The office, and hence the individual embodies the hopes, desires, dignity, and wealth of our nation.

Ronald Reagan clearly understood the importance of this notion. Early in his Presidency, he significantly increased the parties, dinners, and receptions at the White House. After only three years in the White House, Reagan had personally entertained 222,758 guests and hosted 28 state dinners at a cost of more than $500,000 a year.[119]

Treating the Presidency as a royal office is a large task and an expensive one. When Reagan visited Jamaica in 1982, for example, for a few days of rest,

1. One hundred workers had to lay communication cable and install 50 phones for his use;

2. Three cargo planes took three armored limousines, four armored cars, four helicopters, two fire engines, and *all* the President's food—even his own water to drink;

3. One hundred fifty Air Force personnel attended to fix and guard vehicles and equipment, 50 Secret Service, two photographers, and Reagan's personal staff of 30—over 300 people at a cost of over $5 million.[120]

Just to visit his home in California for a few days' rest required over 200 people to accompany him.

Of course, personal indulgences are indeed part of the office. Everything and virtually anything the President wants is granted. For example, on the fourth space shuttle mission, the shuttle spent two extra hours circling earth so Reagan could sleep in to 9:15 A.M. rather than getting up at the scheduled 7:30 A.M. landing.[121]

The same expectation of treatment is also afforded ex-presidents. In 1958, Congress provided presidential pensions and other perks because of Truman's financial situation. Truman was not a millionaire. He refused to take any job after leaving the Presidency because he feared that the employer would trade upon his past contacts and position. Truman spent most of his time answering correspondence, speaking to public groups, and various other activities that were indeed a financial burden. In two weeks of being home he received over 70,000 letters and spent $30,000 from his private bank account to pay for postage and paper. It was clear that former presidents needed assistance.[122]

Today it costs over $12 million a year to pay for the upkeep of former presidents. Maintaining presidential libraries costs an additional $14 million a year. The life-style of former presidents is not much less than that of the current president. Note some of the bills we paid for recent former presidents: $2,826 for periodicals a year for Nixon; $500 to open Nixon's file cabinets after he lost the keys; $249,000 office expenses in 1983 for Ford; $34,549 phone bill in 1982 for Ford; $12,000 for an Oriental rug for Carter's office; and $292,800 office expenses in 1983 for Carter. Yet, few Americans complain of the cost to maintain the life-styles of former presidents; "Somehow it just wouldn't be right to treat former leaders of the most powerful nation in the world as common folks." To do so would violate the very majesty and dignity of our national self-pride.

CONCLUSION

The American Presidency is a center of ever-accumulating functions, roles, obligations, and expectations. It is a universe unto itself which is constantly growing and expanding. From a distance one only notices singular "planets." But closer observation reveals a strong interdependence of the planets. As an individual interacts with the constitutionality of the office, roles develop. These roles not only constrain individual behavior but also help create expectations of specified behavior. As expectations grow, so does the job. The public's perceptions of the office are institutionalized into models, myths, history, and textbooks. Unrealistic demands and expectations produce reliance upon style over substance; image over issues. A president must appear active, moral, fair, intelligent, common, and so on. But appearances are deceiving and paradoxical. For how can one be both active and passive, common and uncommon, impotent and powerful?

Such ambiguity attests to the symbolic nature of the Presidency. As an institution the Presidency is synthetic, believable, passive, vivid, simplified, and ambiguous. The office is our symbol of justice, freedom, equality, continuity, and national grandeur. The Presidency is itself a significant symbol, comprised of many levels and elements. The institution reflects the beliefs, attitudes, and values of the public already established through socialization. All occupants, therefore, must demonstrate that they possess the perceived qualities of the office. Presidential authority is largely a matter of impression management. Presidential elections, as were discussed in Chapter 4, are also largely a contest for symbolic legitimation.

NOTES

1. Donald Searing, "Models and Images of Man and Society in Leadership Theory," *Journal of Politics* 31 (1969): 10.

2. *The Gallup Report*, No. 280, January 1989, p. 12.

3. Eric Herzik, "The President, Governors and Mayors: A Framework for Comparative Analysis," *Presidential Studies Quarterly* 15, no. 2 (Spring 1985): 354.

4. Theodore Sorensen, *A Different Kind of Presidency* (New York: Harper & Row, 1984), p. 10.

5. Dan Nimmo, *The Political Persuaders* (Englewood Cliffs, NJ: Prentice-Hall, 1970), p. 8.

6. Murray Edelman, *Politics as Symbolic Action* (Chicago: Markham Publishing, 1971), p. 73.

7. Bert Rockman, *The Leadership Question* (New York: Praeger, 1984).

8. Theodore Lowi, *The Personal President* (Ithaca, NY: Cornell University Press, 1985), p. xi.

9. Dennis Simon and Charles Ostrom, "The Politics of Prestige: Popular Support and the Modern Presidency," *Presidential Studies Quarterly* 18, no. 4 (Fall 1988): 742–55.

10. Ibid., p. 755.

11. George Edwards, *The Public Presidency* (New York: St. Martin's Press, 1983), p. 1.

12. Raymond Moore, "The Constitution, the Presidency and 1988," *Presidential Studies Quarterly* 18, no. 1 (Winter 1988): 60.

13. Barbara Kellerman, *The Political Presidency* (New York: Oxford University Press, 1984), p. 44.

14. Rockman, *The Leadership Question*, pp. 177–78.

15. Ryan Barilleaux, *The Post-Modern Presidency* (New York: Praeger, 1988), p. 2.

16. Ibid., p. 77.

17. James Ceaser, et al., "The Rise of the Rhetorical Presidency," in *Essays in Presidential Rhetoric*, ed. Theodore Windt (Dubuque, IA: Kendall/Hunt, 1983), p. 7.

18. Grant McConnell, *The Modern Presidency* (New York: St. Martin's Press, 1976), p. 9.

19. Clinton Rossiter, *The American Presidency* (New York: Mentor Books, 1962), p. 16.

20. See Orrin Klapp, *Symbolic Leaders* (Chicago, IL: Aldine Publishing, 1964).

21. Ibid., p. 32.

22. Daniel Boorstin, *The Image* (New York: Atheneum, 1962), p. 45.

23. Ibid., p. 50.

24. Walter Fisher, "Romantic Democracy, Ronald Reagan, and Presidential Heroes," *The Western Journal of Speech Communication* 46 (Summer 1982): 301.

25. Ibid., pp. 299–310.

26. Rossiter, pp. 72–75. See also Charles C. Thack, *The Creation of the Presidency* (Baltimore, MD: The Johns Hopkins Press, 1969).

27. For a good discussion of the Constitution see Thomas J. Norton, *The Constitution of the United States: Its Sources and Its Application* (New York: Committee for Constitutional Government, 1965).

28. Thomas Cronin, *The State of the Presidency* (Boston, MA: Little, Brown, 1975), pp. 250–56.

29. Bruce Buchanan, *The Presidential Experience* (Englewood Cliffs, NJ: Prentice-Hall, 1978), p. 29.

30. George Reedy, *The Twilight of the Presidency* (New York: World, 1970), p. 29.

31. Edward S. Corwin, *The President: Office and Powers*, 3d ed. (New York: New York University Press, 1948), pp. 20–23.

32. Rossiter, *The American Presidency*, pp. 28–37.

33. Myron Hale, "Presidential Influence, Authority, and Power and Economic Policy," in *Toward A Humanistic Science of Politics*, ed. Dalmas Nelson and Richard Sklar (Lanham, MD.: University Press of America, 1983), p. 404.

34. Norton Long, "The Political Act as an Act of Will," in *The Political Vocation*, ed. Paul Tillett (New York: Basic Books, 1965), p. 179.

35. Ibid., p. 179.

36. For a good concise discussion of these two dimensions see Fred Greenstein, "What the President Means to Americans: Presidential 'Choice' Between Elections," in *Choosing the President*, ed. James D. Barber (Englewood Cliffs, NJ: Prentice-Hall, 1974), pp. 121–47.

37. David Haight and Larry Johnston, *The President: Roles and Powers* (Chicago: Rand McNally, 1965), p. 366.

38. Don Faules and Dennis Alexander, *Communication and Social Behavior: A Symbolic Interaction Perspective* (Reading, MA: Addison-Wesley, 1978), p. 67.

39. As stated in ibid., p. 67.

40. Richard Rose, *People in Politics: Observations Across the Atlantic* (New York: Basic Books, 1965), p. 110.

41. Edwards, *The Public Presidency*, p. 98 and *The Gallup Report*, No. 281, February, 1989, p. 13.

42. Cronin, *The State of the Presidency*, p. 34.

43. Ibid., p. 34.

44. Emmet J. Hughes, *The Living Presidency* (New York: Penguin Books, 1972), p. 26.

45. Rose, *People in Politics*, p. 111.

46. Murray Edelman, *Politics as Symbolic Action* (Chicago, IL: Markham, 1971), p. 55.

47. Ibid., p. 55.

48. Alfred deGrazia, "The Myth of the President," in *The Presidency*, ed. Aaron Wildavsky (Boston, MA: Little, Brown, 1969), p. 50.

49. Ibid., p. 50.

50. Alvin Sanoff, "A Conversation with Theodore H. White," *U.S. News and World Report*, July 5, 1982, p. 59.

51. David Easton, *A Systems Analysis of Political Life* (New York: Wiley, 1965), pp. 273–74.

52. Eric Herzik and Mary Dodson, "The President and Public Expectations: A Research Note," *Presidential Studies Quarterly* 12 (Spring 1982), pp. 172–73.

53. Thomas Cronin, "The Presidency Public Relations Script," in *The Presidency Reappraised*, ed. Rexford Tugwell and Thomas E. Cronin (New York: Praeger Publishers, 1974), p. 168.

54. For a good discussion of political roletaking see Murray Edelman, *The Symbolic Uses of Politics* (Urbana: University of Illinois Press, 1964), pp. 49–51, 188–94.

55. Ibid., p. 188.

56. Rose, *People in Politics*, p. 99.

57. Faules and Alexander, *Communication and Social Behavior*, p. 71.

58. Rose, *People in Politics*, p. 114.

59. For such an orientation to political behavior see Dan Nimmo, *Political Communication and Public Opinion in America* (Palo Alto, CA: Goodyear, 1978).

60. Kenneth Burke, *Language as Symbolic Action* (Berkeley: University of California Press, 1966), especially pp. 3–24.

61. Nimmo, *Political Communication*, pp. 227–28.

62. Fred Greenstein, "What the President Means to Americans," pp. 121–47 and Fred Greenstein, "Popular Images of the President," in *The Presidency*, ed. Aaron Wildavsky (Boston, MA: Little, Brown, 1969), pp. 287–95.

63. David Easton and Robert Hess, "The Child's Political World," *Midwest Journal of Political Science*, no. 3 (August 1962), pp. 241–42.

64. Greenstein, "What the President Means to Americans," p. 129.

65. Ibid., p. 134.

66. Bruce Campbell, *The American Electorate* (New York: Holt, Rinehart, and Winston, 1979), p. 78 or the yearly issues of *The Gallup Report*.

67. *The Gallup Report*, January 1989, p. 16.

68. Doris Graber, "Personal Qualities in Presidential Images: The Contribution of the Press," *Midwest Journal of Political Science* 16 (February 1972), p. 142.

69. Greenstein, "Popular Images of the President," p. 292.

70. Richard Pious, *The American Presidency* (New York: Basic Books, 1979), p. 6.

71. McConnell, *The Modern Presidency*, p. 19.

72. Ibid., p. 21.

73. As quoted in Pious, *The American Presidency*, p. 90.

74. James Wooten, *Dasher: The Roots and Rising of Jimmy Carter* (New York: Warner Books, 1978), p. 35.

75. As quoted in Pious, *The American Presidency*, p. 91.

76. Wooten, *Dasher*, p. 277.

77. McConnell, *The Modern Presidency*, p. 39.

78. Harold Lasswell, *Psychopathology and Politics* (Chicago, IL: University of Chicago Press, 1930).

79. His findings are usually contained in any book on the presidency. In addition, Greenstein has written many articles on the subject expressing six basic psychological uses of the presidency. For rather concise statements see: Greenstein, "Popular Images of the President" and "What the President Means to Americans."

80. Boorstin, *The Image*, p. 3.

81. Alfred deGrazia, "The Myth of the President" in *The Presidency*, ed. Aaron Wildavsky (Boston, MA: Little, Brown, 1969), p. 50.

82. Theodore H. White, *Breach of Faith* (New York: Atheneum, 1975), pp. 323–24.

83. Ibid., p. 324.

84. Murray Edelman, "The Politics of Persuasion," in *Choosing the President*, ed. James D. Barber (Englewood Cliffs, NJ: Prentice-Hall, 1974), p. 160.

85. Roger Cobb and Charles Elder, "Individual Orientations in the Study of Political Symbolism," *Social Science Quarterly* 53 (June 1972), p. 87.

86. These characteristics are provided by Boorstin in discussing an "image." The "presidency" as a symbol clearly has the same characteristics. See *The Image*, pp. 185–93.

87. For an outstanding discussion of the distinction between the functioning of signs and symbols in relation to the presidency, see Michael Novak, *Choosing Our King* (New York: Macmillan, 1974), especially pp. 7–10.

88. Edelman, *The Symbolic Uses of Politics*, p. 11.

89. Novak, *Choosing our King*, p. 8.

90. For a discussion of specific symbols through which a president communicates to the people see ibid., p. 8.

91. This quote by Taft appears in almost every major textbook on the presidency. See Rossiter, *The American Presidency*, p. 16.

92. Ibid., p. 16.

93. Cronin, *The State of the Presidency*, p. 239.

94. Klapp, *Symbolic Leaders*, pp. 52–58.

95. Ibid., p. 58.

96. Ibid., p. 51.

97. Novak, *Choosing Our King*, p. 46.

98. Novak is good at such analysis; see ibid., Part One, pp. 3–56.

99. Ibid., p. 28.

100. James D. Barber, "Man, Mood, and the Presidency," in *The Presidency Reappraised*, ed. Rexford Tugwell and Thomas Cronin (New York: Praeger, 1974), p. 205.

101. See George Reedy, *The Twilight of the Presidency* (New York: World, 1970).

102. Novak, *Choosing Our King*, p. 20.

103. Ibid., especially pp. 3, 50–52.

104. As reported in Edwards, *The Public Presidency*, p. 99.

105. Rossiter, *The American Presidency*, pp. 172–74.

106. Ibid., p. 172.

107. Hughes, *The Living Presidency*, pp. 107–34.

108. As quoted in ibid., p. 312.

109. Ibid., p. 315.

110. Ibid., p. 364.

111. Ibid., p. 278.

112. *Every Four Years: A Study of the Presidency*, Public Broadcasting Service, 1980, p. 5.

113. Patrick Kennedy and Tom Rice, "The Contextual Determinants of Presidential Greatness," *Presidential Studies Quarterly* 18, no. 1 (Winter 1988): 167.

114. This discussion is based upon Hedley Donovan, "Job Specs for the Oval Office," *Time*, December 13, 1982, pp. 20–29.

115. *Every Four Years*, p. 11.

116. Wooten, *Dasher*, p. 361.

117. As reported in Victor Lasky, *Jimmy Carter: The Man and The Myth* (New York: Richard Marek, 1979), p. 16.

118. Jimmy Carter, *Keeping Faith* (New York: Bantam Books, 1982), p. 27.

119. As reported in Patricia Avery, "Reagan White House Steps Up Social Pace," *U.S. News and World Report*, January 23, 1984, pp. 52–54.

120. As reported in "Trapped in the Imperial Presidency," *Time*, April 26, 1982, p. 20.

121. As reported in "Protecting Presidential ZZZZ's." *Chicago Tribune*, June 20, 1982, sec. 12, p. 2, col. 2.

122. "Being Ex-President is Lucrative Business," *Chicago Tribune*, April 10, 1983, sec. 16, p. 5.

Chapter Eight

Ghostwriters, the Presidency, and the Bureaucracy

It is a pity that modern Presidents have abandoned even the pretense of handcrafting their public utterances. Except for waiting to be hanged, nothing else so concentrates the mind on truly important matters.[1]

From politicians to business leaders, judges to sports figures, our public discourse is carried forward on the backs of a battalion of anonymous scribes.[2]

Throughout history ghostwriters have lived in the shadows of public awareness, at least since a Sicilian named Corax received payment to coach awkward orators over 2000 years ago. Academics such as Plato might later quarrel about the presumptuous ethics of teachers and writers who would help "the weaker look the stronger." But the existence of republican government has always required coaching in the arts of rhetoric. Like other arts, political persuasion must be learned. The propriety of using a collaborator is arguably as acceptable as the relationship between mentor and apprentice, legal counsel and client, or expert and layman.

But there is a threshold that is crossed at some risk. Most Americans know that a high proportion of the President's rhetoric originates in the minds of subordinates. Few journalists even bother to inquire about the writers who assisted in preparing a particular message. While this sharing of a political burden is an accepted folkway, public figures must not seem to relinquish control over what is issued in their name. Collaboration cannot be capitulation. With the presumption of authorship comes the burden of responsibility. When rumors were broadcast that John F. Kennedy's Pulitzer Prize–winning book, *Profiles in Courage*, was actually the handiwork of the senator's aide, that boundary had been crossed. Kennedy angrily denied the charge and started legal action against ABC Television for allowing columnist Drew Pearson to make it. He admitted that Theodore Sorensen provided extensive help in gathering part of the book's materials. Sorensen's collaboration was acceptable; his alleged total responsi-

bility was not.[3] Arguably more harmful was the 1988 admission by Press Secretary Larry Speakes that he had drafted presidential statements for release to the
press that were never actually made by Ronald Reagan. During a 1985 meeting in
Geneva with Soviet General Secretary Gorbachev, Speakes prepared upbeat ''remarks'' allegedly spoken by the President on the positive nature of the talks. His
motive, he noted, was to offset the favorable publicity the Soviet leader received
for his own candid comments. The revelation and public furor over these fabrications embarrassed the President, who was already seen as too disengaged from
his responsibilities.[4] In the first instance, what eventually appeared in the book
went out with the approval and knowledge of Kennedy; in the second, however, Reagan apparently had no such opportunity to approve the comments.

Among the peculiar characteristics of the Presidency is that one of its most
personal elements—what the executive says and professes— is to a significant
extent the work of others. Samuel Rosenman, Emmet Hughes, William Safire,
Robert Hartmann, David Gergen, and Peggy Noonan are not household names.
But all had significant power to shape a president's public statements.[5] As a
natural adaptation of their trade as writers, and spurred with perhaps a touch of
rebellious vanity, most of these aides have concluded their period of enforced
anonymity with articles and books about their roles as aides and writers. We
thus know a great deal about ghostwriters after they leave the White House.

This chapter has two purposes. Most obviously, it describes how presidential
ghostwriters do their work. Greatest attention is paid to three quite different
presidents: Lyndon Johnson, Gerald Ford, and Ronald Reagan. A second goal
is to outline some of the routine ground rules that affect the flow of information
between government units. To be sure, presidential ghostwriting is a very specialized and prized occupation. But perhaps the most valuable lesson its study
teaches us is that it is bound by the same kinds of organizational constraints that
affect most political institutions. What we note here about how responsibilities
and prerogatives are delegated in the White House ultimately says a good deal
about how intragovernmental communication works at all levels.

We begin with a reminder of just how critical the speech-writing apparatus
has become to the Presidency.

MANUFACTURED PROSE: THE SHIFT FROM ELOQUENT
TO EFFICIENT SPEECH

A romantic but not entirely inaccurate view of the Presidency is that it once
nurtured a grandiloquent rhetorical tradition. Washington's Inaugural, Jefferson's
First Inaugural, Jackson's popular challenges to Calhoun on the issue of nulli-
fication, and Lincoln's wartime and emancipation statements have all become
part of America's political literature. The sonorities and spaciousness of eight-
eenth- and nineteenth-century rhetoric vividly recalls the heyday of the orator,
but also what seems at first glance to be an old art in a state of advanced decay.
The conciseness and ordinary prose of today's political rhetoric often renders it

incapable of provoking the range of emotions that a Lincoln-Douglas debate could muster in the mid–1800s. Its metaphors and images are more mundane—taken from the broken rhythms and incomplete sentences of conversation rather than the fuller images of the printed word. Where Lincoln drew images from Shakespeare and the Bible, Presidents Reagan and Bush found models in Hollywood characterizations of Knute Rockne and Dirty Harry ("Make my day . . . ," "Read my lips . . . "). "Few species of composition seem so antiquated, so little available for any practical purpose today," Richard Weaver noted, "as the oratory in which the generation of our grandparents delighted."[6]

If the style of political discourse has changed, and if the less than monumental scope of contemporary address shows more pragmatism than vision, the immediate political consequences of many presidential statements remain important. Even the self-conscious prose of George Bush can surpass in immediate impact the profoundest efforts of presidents in power before the age of the microphone. Jefferson's Inaugural, for example, was uttered in barely audible voice before just several hundred members of Congress in the still uncompleted Capitol building.[7] Bush, in sharp contrast, easily reached over 30 million Americans in his own 1989 inaugural.[8]

The potential for rhetorically altering the nation's climate of opinion has never been greater. With the evolution in the 1920s of mass radio audiences for a single speech, presidential utterance was rendered cautious and tactical rather than spacious and all-encompassing. Franklin Roosevelt addressed the rough equivalent of all of Jefferson's presidential audiences in just one 15-minute "fireside chat." Changed most dramatically by radio, oratory that previously had to be suited to only the immediate audience on hand (and a secondary audience of newspaper readers) suddenly had to suit a nation of diverse constituents and accidental listeners held together by the invisible thread of the radio network. The temptation to use this medium and to widen the appeal of key speeches made the speechwriter an attractive addition to the White House staff. By allowing a writer to undertake what had been for Woodrow Wilson and Theodore Roosevelt an immensely time-consuming task of speech drafting or dictation, a president not only saved time, but gained the confidence of knowing that someone was available to flag an ill-conceived remark.

The broadcasting of presidential addresses and increased reporting of all public appearances naturally meant that political rhetoric had to be adapted to a wider audience than ever before. The risks of an unintended slur were increased, and meant that others would not intervene in what had been to most presidents the least delegatable of all their tasks. As a public document having the widest possible distribution, it was thought a speech could no longer risk the candor expected by a gathering of a limited size. Presidents after Theodore Roosevelt were largely unwilling to jeopardize their political power by depending on their own memories, or their skills at speaking "off the cuff." The broad dissemination of virtually every message now meant that too much was at stake.

GROWTH OF THE WHITE HOUSE STAFF

The steady growth of full-time presidential aides over the decades has been well documented. For instance, Abraham Lincoln employed two close aides, both young and extremely effective. John Hay not only worked for Lincoln, but would later befriend Theodore Roosevelt and serve for a time as his Secretary of State. John Nicolay became almost an alter ego to Lincoln through the long war years when the War Department telegraph office across the street from the White House was the scene of endless presidential vigils.[9] Over a hundred years later the presidential staff has grown to nearly 700 people, pigeonholed into a complex array of titles and responsibilities, and spilling into the Executive Office Building nearby.[10]

White House support staff generally fall into five more or less discrete areas of responsibility. Some coordinate White House activities with members of the Congress. Others serve as domestic aides, preparing and organizing legislative initiatives to be taken to Capitol Hill, and counterproposals to deal with the opposing party's own legislative agenda. Some are economists, particularly responsible for coordinating the Council of Economic Advisers and the powerful Office of Management and Budget. And still others are charged with formulating administrative positions on national security and foreign relations. Among the most influential are those who make decisions about who sees the President and how his time is scheduled. In the Nixon years these tasks were handled at various times by H. R. Haldeman and John Ehrlichman. John Sununu, a former governor of New Hampshire, was appointed in 1989 to carry out the same responsibilities for George Bush.

The remainder of what is the first line in the sprawling executive bureaucracy is the public relations staff, including press aides, writers, mail answerers, speechwriters, and others. Among the most admired and controversial of recent White House publicists has undoubtedly been Michael Deaver, who arranged most of President Reagan's scheduled highly publicized outings, including a touching 1984 visit to a beach in northern France, 40 years after the successful D-Day invasion of the Allies against Germany. He resigned in Reagan's second term, and was later convicted of perjury in 1987 after being charged with improperly lobbying White House aides as the head of his own public relations firm.[11] Deaver worked with a White House Office of Communications that was first established by Richard Nixon to coordinate press relations and to formulate timely responses to leaders in Congress. Reagan's own version of this office was initially headed by the highly regarded David Gergen, but became a source of greater controversy and criticism under the flamboyant leadership of arch-conservative Patrick Buchanan. Under President Bush, it still handles the usual duties of preparing press releases, proclamations, speeches, letters, and "White House messages" (statements written under the President's name, but presented in written rather than oral form).

As important as press relations are to the Presidency, the heart of presidential image-making remains centered on the skills of the speech staff. We have a very clear record of this group in the administration of Gerald Ford. It was divided into two crews: one for oral remarks, and the other for written messages and research. The writers of major messages were often Robert Hartmann, Robert Orben and Milton Friedman, with help also coming from major agency heads such as Secretary of State Henry Kissinger and Treasury Secretary William Simon. Messages of lesser import were drafted by what Hartmann described as "a new editorial team of fresh, enthusiastic, facile writers," including this representative cross section:

Pat Butler, a Georgia preacher's son, fluent, fast, ambitious, always eyeing the main chance; David Boorstin, our intellectual would-be play-write, son of the Librarian of Congress; George Denison, a calm, mellow *Reader's Digest* alumnus; John Mihalec, from a congressional staff, intense, intrigued by politics, and Craig Smith, a bearded University of Virginia speech professor who filled in during the summer trying to disprove that "those who can't, teach."[12]

There was also a separate staff for written messages and research, which rounded out the 41 spots allocated to all forms of message preparation.

The total size of the White House staff varies from year to year, because many assistants, including speechwriters, serve on temporary assignment from other federal agencies. Specific numbers also vary, depending on who is counting. This is because some large offices, such as the Office of Policy Development, are under nominal control of the White House, even though its workers are elsewhere in Washington. To take figures on the low side, in the middle of Ronald Reagan's Presidency, about 380 people worked full-time as part of the White House office staff, with another 61 serving part-time. About half were estimated to be secretarial and support staff, the other half were considered professionals.[13] In the recent past these numbers have been fairly constant. In the long term, they reflect a gradual increase, especially since the Eisenhower administration.

The growth in the number of special assistants and aides concerned with public relations and speech writing is what presidential scholar Thomas Cronin considers "one of the more disquieting aspects of the recent enlargement of the presidential establishment."[14] The first speechwriter hired to assist a president was Judson Welliver, who joined the Harding administration with that designated role in 1920.[15] By any standard Harding needed all the help he could get to defend what became an increasingly troubled and corrupt administration after the Teapot Dome and Justice Department scandals in the early 1920s. Even earlier, in the 1880s, Chester Arthur employed a friend named Daniel Rollins to help draft a number of presidential messages clandestinely from New York. Perhaps because ghostwriting would have been an unthinkable sharing of responsibilities at the end of the nineteenth century, Rollins went to great pains to keep his help to the ailing Arthur a total secret.[16]

To a large extent speechwriters were to remain a rarity until the administration of Calvin Coolidge in 1923. Prior to Coolidge, the White House worked at whatever pace its officeholder set. Theodore Roosevelt not only answered the phone on occasion, but relished the chance to write speeches on as broad a range of topics as a president has ever claimed to conquer. War, physical fitness, politics, conservation, human rights, corporate monopolies, and natural history were frequent topics heard from his "bully pulpit." For Woodrow Wilson, who followed William Howard Taft in 1912, speeches remained a high priority. Trained by a Scots Presbyterian minister who placed the highest value on his son's oratory, Wilson spent hours perfecting what still remains as some of the most thoughtful and coherent of all presidential rhetoric.

Calvin Coolidge managed to vastly increase the number of presidential speeches through the continued aid of Judson Welliver and others, thereby establishing both an important precedent and a harmful liability for the publicity-conscious executive branch. The precedent was that the enlarged staff became known to the public, and perceptions of the office changed accordingly. With the Coolidge administration, Americans began to think of a president in the contemporary sense: as a leader whose fate was determined by the quality of his staff as well as by his own efforts. The liability was that rarely again would an executive's words reflect the undiluted visions and attitudes of just one person. The impact of these changes did not go unnoticed for long. "It is a misfortune," wrote an observer of the Coolidge administration, "that as President he had permitted so many of his formal addresses to be written for him by members of his staff. These have made him seem prolix, jejune, and ordinary to a degree."[17]

"Silent Cal" had managed to double the number of addresses over his eloquent predecessor, but at a heavy cost. No longer would presidents be content to write their own speeches, offer them for review and comment to close friends and advisers, and then deliver them. The emerging pattern was to be a reversal of that process for all except the most important statements. Others would write early drafts, with varying degrees of guidance, while only the editing would be done by the president.

This basic pattern remains today. Though presidents occasionally write sections of important addresses such as convention acceptance speeches, inaugurals, and portions of state of the union addresses, they now more usually function as final editors of drafts written elsewhere. The highest praise that one usually hears from aides working with a president is not that he is a good cowriter, but a good editor. His ability to quickly rework an aide's manuscript so that it represents an authentic copy of his own prose "signature"—what is characteristic of him in terms of idiom, ideas, and style—is a major test of his editorial skill. The result is the synthetic duplication of a rhetorical style that only approximates what a president might produce, had he spent the necessary time.

As will become apparent, the demands placed on writers charged with shaping this rhetorical legacy create a number of opportunities and dangers.

HOW SPEECHES ARE ASSIGNED

A president looks to a writer not just for nice slogans. A ghostwritten speech must be faithful to the personal history, legislative record, and political philosophy of the speaker. An address must show deference to the speaker's carefully constructed public persona. John Kennedy might have been heard quoting Plato or Camus; but it would be an awkward violation of role-types to give the same quotes to Lyndon Johnson or Ronald Reagan. The response the ghostwriter seeks is the political leader's recognition of the tone and feeling of a message as his own. Robert Hartmann, for example, had been a member of Vice President Ford's staff long enough to recognize the genuine closeness of Ford to his wife and family. When the former congressman was thrust into the presidency by Richard Nixon's resignation, Hartmann was able to draft the first critical national address with an empathy that assured his place in the new administration. Ford recalled his reactions to Hartmann's words calling for a "healing" of the national wound of Watergate: "As I read his draft, tears came to my eyes. 'I am indebted to no man,' he had written, 'and only one woman, my dear wife.' Hartmann understood my feelings perfectly."[18]

Major Addresses

In the recent past, key writers of important speeches have usually had a comparatively long association with the president, often in many capacities other than as speechwriter. Hartmann was a one-time staff coordinator for Ford, but not a very successful one. As Ford tells it, disorder tended to follow Hartmann around.[19] Bill Moyers was a personal assistant, press secretary, and general sounding board to Lyndon Johnson. Theodore Sorensen was one of Senator John Kennedy's legislative assistants.

Ronald Reagan partially broke with this tradition of depending on long-term staffers for his rhetoric. Perhaps because Reagan for so long prospered as his own creative advocate—first as a spokesman for General Electric, and later as Governor of California—he employed a wide range of writers who had the relatively simple task of orchestrating what was already a well-worked litany of antigovernment, pro-self-initiative themes.[20] Most did not stay in the White House for the full two terms, and more than a few became victims to staff disputes about the extent to which Reagan should accommodate his ideas to fit the politically moderate Congress.[21]

When pondering a major speech, a president will typically seek out whoever has been a reliable writer among his closest aides. For Franklin Roosevelt it was Judge Samuel Rosenman, an old friend and former member of the New York Supreme Court. For Kennedy the call was inevitably to Sorensen, Arthur Schlesinger Jr., or Richard Goodwin. Dwight Eisenhower used Emmet Hughes and the politically astute Bryce Harlow; but Sherman Adams more regularly assigned first drafts to one of any number of subordinates. More recently, Aram Bakshian,

Jr., Anthony Dolan, and Patrick Buchanan served as principal writers of Ronald Reagan. All of these individuals initiated first drafts themselves, or served as final editors in what has become an elaborate process of bureaucratic review.

Under every president the White House functions differently, and no less can be said of the speech-writing staffs. Some administrations—such as those guided by Eisenhower, Nixon, and Carter—made a greater show of organizational and management technique. But in most administrations those actually responsible for contributing remarks have not fit neatly into organizations that characterize other related areas, such as the White House Press Office and the Congressional Relations staff. One reason for this anonymity is due in part to a certain amount of presidential ego. Lyndon Johnson reminded one new recruit who devoted nearly all of his time to speeches that "A speech writer is supposed to stay in the background. If somebody asks you about a speech, just say 'I don't know anything about that.' "[22] Johnson's personal vanity was notoriously large. A larger reason for the organizational limbo of a writer reflects the hazy division between speech writing and a number of other very different tasks, such as advising on domestic, foreign, or political affairs. Some senior aides are intended to be "floaters" who are available for a wide range of tasks of limited duration. They may negotiate on behalf of the President with members of Congress, or serve as political advisers, in addition to drafting speeches. Bill Moyers and Ted Sorensen clearly had such diverse responsibilities, and the ulcers to go with them.

Reflecting the inevitable tie between policy and the way it is articulated, a neat organizational chart outlining staff responsibilities also misses the fact that key policymakers regularly function to subvert or intercept major addresses. What better method is available to ensure that a good intention is translated into a firm commitment than to write the script of that commitment in behalf of the president? As a matter of routine, new policy initiatives in foreign and domestic affairs are in effect sponsored by a cabinet head or presidential staffer with a deep interest in their success. As the last section of this chapter explores in more detail, Secretaries Dean Rusk and Robert McNamara, along with aides Clark Clifford and Walt Rostow, regularly guarded their cherished access to Lyndon Johnson in order to shape his Vietnam War statements made on national television.[23] Under Eisenhower, Secretary of State Dulles often submitted entire drafts of speeches prepared at the State Department for presidential use. Dulles hoped he could keep the President's internationalist tendencies in check by providing virulent anti-Communist speeches. Similarly, Patrick Buchanan reportedly took a pay cut of $300,000 to return to the White House in Reagan's second term to prevent other writers from toning down the President's conservative rhetoric.[24]

Since Coolidge speech writing has rarely been the exclusive process of any one group or individual. The stakes are too large. A president may give as few as 15 major addresses in one year. To see a personal wish translated into a presidential utterance—with the reflected glory of a sound bite on the networks' evening news, or use of a passage in the New York Times' Quotation of the Day—is enough to make writing for the President a cherished competitive prerogative.[25]

Minor Remarks

Lesser speeches usually involve one or two subordinate speech writers serving nominally under a senior aide and writer. These second-line staffers may also work on press releases, important mail, and reports. An assignment will usually come with advice on who should be contacted for background information (although, in the Reagan White House many speeches were written by the President's political advisers with sometimes minimal contact with Cabinet heads and others in major agencies with substantive interests). If a minor message directly involves a shift or new development in policy, a first draft or an outline of "talking points" is usually requested from the agency responsible for the area. If the address is political, it may incorporate the suggestions of a supportive member of Congress, as in Figure 8.1.

Only on rare occasions will a president be involved before several drafts have been refined and edited by senior writers. Normally he is given a final draft from a few days to several weeks before it is delivered. It may be rejected, sending the staff into frantic high gear to produce something new in a short period of time. More commonly, it is edited by the President, sometimes with the order to clean up or alter one or two passages. Except for Gerald Ford, no contemporary have followed Franklin Roosevelt's occasional practice of permitting two teams of speech writers to come up with competing drafts for approval. That can be understandably trying on the morale of those laboring in front of the word processor. What is somewhat more common is a pattern whereby a formal speech is generated from within the normal White House channels, while at the same time unsolicited manuscripts or offers of ideas come from close aides or friends. John Kennedy, for example, received several unsolicited inaugural speech drafts from friends, newsmen, and complete strangers.[26] Most of the suggestions that the primary writers receive usually carry a different emphasis in one area which reflects the sender's attempts to neutralize certain suspected biases. In the Nixon White House each of the three top-level writers earned a more or less accurate caricature reflecting what key staff members perceived as their strengths and weaknesses. If a speech was to offer heavy doses of compassion, the liberal Ray Price was said to offer the most philosophical and least partisan prose. Patrick Buchanan, in contrast, could carve up liberals with a sabre of righteous right-wing indignation, as was clearly evident in the well publicized attacks on the press that he wrote for Vice President Spiro Agnew. William Safire was known for his ability to make almost any idea memorable and at least superficially eloquent.[27]

Surprisingly, however, there is little evidence to suggest that a writer chosen for a routine speech is selected because of his or her expertise on the topic. The mundane realities of office work, such as who has the time, may be important in determining an assignment than who will produce the best draft. What emerges from various memoirs and accounts is that anybody from as many as five or six writers might produce a first draft. There is also little support for what would seem to be the natural conclusion that a president at least oversees the assigning

Figure 8.1
Suggestions from a Senator to the President for Some "Helpful" Remarks during the 1962 Campaign

---

ABRAHAM RIBICOFF
FORTY MOTT AVENUE
NEW LONDON, CONNECTICUT

October 12, 1962

Dear Kenny:

If the President wants a few sentences that

would be helpful to me, here are some

brief suggestions.

I hope you are along when he comes to

Connecticut.

Best personal regards.

Sincerely,

Abe

The Honorable Kenneth O'Donnell
The White House
Washington, D. C.

Figure 8.1 (continued)

This year the medicare bill was defeated in the United States Senate.
One vote would have made the difference. Abe Ribicoff's vote can be that one
vote needed to pass this bill.

It is vitally important that Abe Ribicoff be in the Senate of the United
States when the medicare bill comes up next year. No man in this country
knows more about this great problem than he does. No man is in a better
position to supply leadership within the Congress. If we are to pass the medicare
bill next year, we will need Abe Ribicoff in the United States Senate to be in the
forefront of this fight.

* * * * * * * * * *

Abe Ribicoff was a source of great strength in my Cabinet. He served
with distinction as Secretary of Health, Education and Welfare. I was proud
to appoint him, and I would have been proud to appoint him to any position he
wanted. But Abe Ribicoff came to me some months ago and told me that he
wanted to relinquish his appointed position and seek election to the United States
Senate. He told me in the privacy of my office that the type of public service he
felt was most useful was elective office and that he wanted to serve in the Senate
as long as the people of this state would support him. I respected his decision,
and I respect and admire the man for making this decision.

Abe Ribicoff knows Washington. Abe Ribicoff knows Connecticut. His
experience as Congressman, Governor and Cabinet officer will make him an
outstanding senator for this state. And his sound judgment and independent
thinking will be a great asset to the people of Connecticut and the entire nation.

Note: Some of the suggestions were included in the President's prepared notes, but at the last
moment he ad-libbed his comments, and thus did not use the suggestions.

Source: John F. Kennedy Library, Boston.

and outline of a speech. The memoirs of most presidents contribute to this false impression. They frequently speak of "the need for a speech" to the National Association of Broadcasters, the V.F.W., the National Press Club, or thousands of other potential audiences. In fact the decision to appear before a group—and the secondary step of assigning a writer—may well fall to one of several of the President's chief political advisers. Eisenhower, Johnson, Carter, and Reagan all largely delegated these decisions to subordinates, obviously retaining the option to overrule them.

Most of the time these processes work well, as when Peggy Noonan was assigned the task of writing what became President Reagan's eloquent tribute to the crew killed in the Space Shuttle, "Challenger," in 1986. A classic case of how this process of delegation can go terribly wrong occurred in 1985, when Michael Deaver arranged for President Reagan to make a speech affirming the postwar unity of Germany and the United States. Reagan was to be in Bonn attending an economic summit. In preparing for the visit Deaver, at Chancellor Helmut Kohl's suggestion, decided to have the President make his case for German-American amity at a small military cemetery in Bitburg. It was soon discovered that among the deceased were 40 members of the "SS," Adolf Hitler's hated police had guarded many World War II concentration camps. An enormous outcry developed in the United States. Reagan was urged by scores of American groups to show his solidarity somewhere else besides that cemetery. But German feelings also ran high; Kohl was certain his nation would look foolish if the President of the United States decided to back away from a visit to their war dead. Reagan went ahead with his visit, largely because a change of location would have probably had the reverse effect of what his speech intended. But for Deaver and the administration the episode became a public relations nightmare.[28]

More routine decisions about where to speak rarely involve such controversy. Sherman Adams cites a more usual chain of events that led to a routine address by Dwight Eisenhower, in this case, to a meeting of the Future Farmers of America in Kansas City:

The invitation came to the White House through [Agriculture Secretary] Ezra Taft Benson, whose policies even in that first year of the Administration were already under fire. . . .

Leonard Hall, then the Republican national Chairman, came to ask me to help him. "Can't we get the President out there to make a speech?" I told Hall that I would see what I could do, and immediately summoned the indispensable [Gabriel] Hauge and a few experts from the Department of Agriculture to see if we could work out a plan for a speech. In this instance we agreed to steer clear of any partisan approach and work on a world peace theme stressing the contribution of the American farmer. A few days later we met again to study the first draft of the writing and decided that the slant was right but it needed better brushwork and stronger treatment. So it was agreed that I would call a farm expert in Des Moines and ask him to come and help.

In preparations like this, Eisenhower would not know about the plans in progress. Instead, until an acceptable working draft had been prepared and tentative plans drawn up by myself and the staff, he would not want to know. . . . The preparation usually meant days, sometimes weeks of staff work. . . . Then Hall and I, probably with [Jerry] Parson and Hauge, would tell Tom Stephens that we wanted fifteen uninterrupted minutes with the President.

A few days later, the President would call Hauge or myself into his office. The speech would be on his desk. "This moves along pretty well," he would say, handing back the draft, "but it seems to labor too much in trying to meet a lot of picayune criticism. . . . " That would mean more hours of brain-racking and writing by Hauge. Finally Eisenhower would sit down at his desk alone, marking up the revised draft himself.[29]

Eisenhower, like Ronald Reagan 20 years later, was willing to delegate nearly all of the writing chores to others. Lyndon Johnson, however, was somewhat different. Even though he was not especially good at it, he treated speech making as a solemn presidential ritual. In his long, successful congressional career the former Senate majority leader had been a nonstop ad-libber, a politician who genuinely enjoyed the euphonious "corn" so much a part of the first political speeches he heard on the steps of the Johnson City courthouse. He remembered trips with his father through Texas towns with their wide streets, where the long-winded "speak'n" would fill the air of late fall political rallies.[30] His ascendancy to the Presidency took some of the pleasure out of this part of his political life, perhaps because his audiences had grown too large and too diverse to be stroked by the hill country idiom that he loved to use. Ad-libs became more risky for the leader of the Western world. Speaking to an audience offered diminished rewards as the burden of defending the failing attempts to prop up South Vietnam increased.

In recalling a happier cause in his memoirs, Johnson briefly sketched the evolution of his perfectly timed March 1965 address to Congress on civil rights, which led the way for the Voting Rights Act four months later:

I assembled some of my key staff men to help prepare the message. A Presidential speech is rarely a private product. The pressures of the office do not afford the luxury of such personal handicraft. But this time, as much as humanly possible, I wanted to reach the American people in my own words.

I sat with my staff for several hours. I described the general outline of what I wanted to say. I wanted to use every ounce of moral persuasion the Presidency held. . . . And I wanted to talk from my own heart, from my own experiences. Between midnight and dawn these loose thoughts were translated into sentences for the first draft of the speech. I received that draft shortly after awakening. I penciled in changes and rewrote sections. The draft went back to the speechwriters. Several hours later a new draft came back. I made additional changes. And so it went, back and forth, right up to the final moments.[31]

In this instance the writers were subordinates to the will of a president sitting in on the crucial formative stages of a nationally televised address. The extent of the President's intervention was immediately evident to those who heard the personal allusions that no writer could "ghost" for someone else.

For lesser occasions Johnson depended on the first drafts coming from the "scribes," who faced a challenge to chart a path of ideas that virtually included a wilderness of other possible alternatives. "What he was doing, of course," recalls one of his writers, "was reposing great trust, great responsibility, and ultimately great confidence in the individuals he deputized to act as his alter ego in the middle stages of the speech process."[32]

Even less involvement is recalled by a writer for Gerald Ford in the middle of 1976. Ford, it seemed, had infinite faith in the ability of his staff to pull the right ideas together—without a great deal of initial direction—in a recognizable nine-step sequence.

1. The President and his advisor decided that he would speak on a given occasion. 2. One of the five speechwriters working under Presidential counselor Robert Hartmann was assigned the task of producing a draft. He was given background information, and an assessment by the "advance team." 3. The draft was examined for errors by an editor, Robert Orben, and the research staff. 4. The speech was "staffed." That is, appropriate members of the administration studied the draft to see whether it was consistent with White House policy. 5. The speech was then returned to the original writer for correction. 6. Next, a final draft was typed for the President on large cards in large script. 7. The President then rehearsed the speech, meeting with the writer to suggest changes. 8. The speech was delivered. 9. Finally, at an "evaluation session" press review of the speech, along with staff comments, were [sic] taken into consideration.[33]

One can only estimate the ease with which individual presidents could delegate authority for the construction of their most public moments: Kennedy, holding the prerogatives of the podium to himself by using his cool sense of style and ability to ad-lib to make immediate detours around carelessly written paragraphs; Johnson, alternately using and ignoring his large but disorganized corps of writers in a vain attempt to recapture the old persuasive clout he enjoyed in the Senate; and Reagan, confident that a trusted lieutenant would suitably clothe the details of policy in his familiar upbeat style.

The size of the group that may be involved in even the early stages of routine addresses can be sensed from Figure 8.2, a memo from Johnson's one-time speech coordinator and former president of NBC. The note from Kintner to aide Marvin Watson shows the initial assignments of four speeches for a 1968 trip to the Midwest. Each of the listed stops includes a location, a theme, the writers responsible for development of a draft, and the intended length of the speech. Figure 8.3 is a clearance form for such routine speeches. It is to this surprisingly complex process of "clearing a speech" through individuals and agencies that we next turn.

MULTIPLE DRAFTS AND THE PROBLEM OF CLEARANCE

In many ways the life of an American chief executive has been made more difficult since the advent of the Xerox machine. Twenty years ago the number

Figure 8.2

Memo Making Staff Assignments for Future Speeches for Lyndon Johnson, July, 1966

MEMORANDUM

THE WHITE HOUSE

WASHINGTON

July 19, 1966
10:55 a.m. Tuesday

PERSONAL AND CONFIDENTIAL

MEMORANDUM FOR MARVIN WATSON

SUBJECT: Possible Presidential Trip

I held a meeting this morning attended by Messrs. Rostow, Hardesty, Sparks, and Jim Moyers. I also talked with Bill Moyers and Harry McPherson. Perhaps you might like to indicate to the President the themes that are being developed (they will be ready in all cases but McPherson by noon Thursday) on the possible speeches:

1.   AMVETS - theme of how the U.S. military organization is meshed with civilian government to obtain Presidential objectives.

   Rostow-Hardesty-Sparks   6 minutes

2.   Fort Campbell - a continuation of the same thing, with stress on contributions of the units in Vietnam and around the world with special emphasis on the 101st Airborne.

   Rostow-Hardesty-Sparks   15 minutes

3.   Vincennes - This would be one of two talks on the responsibility of American citizens - this one in connection with civil rights, civil disorders, etc. which seem to be what Harry McPherson wants to write about.   20 minutes

4.   Indianapolis -   the theme of responsibility of citizens, business, and labor and the consumer would be continued - with discussion of the domestic economy, individual prosperity, necessities for restraint, and our objectives throughout the world.
   James Moyers   -
   Hardesty-Sparks - with background to be supplied by Fowler, Ackley, Califano without disclosure of the occasion.

                                   20 minutes

Both the Vincennes and Indianapolis speeches would tie in the Vietnam operation and foreign aid policy as part of the responsibility theme.

                    Robert E. Kintner

CC: Bill Moyers

Source: Lyndon Baines Johnson Library, Austin, Texas.

Figure 8.3
Standardized Clearance Form for Speeches Given by Lyndon Johnson

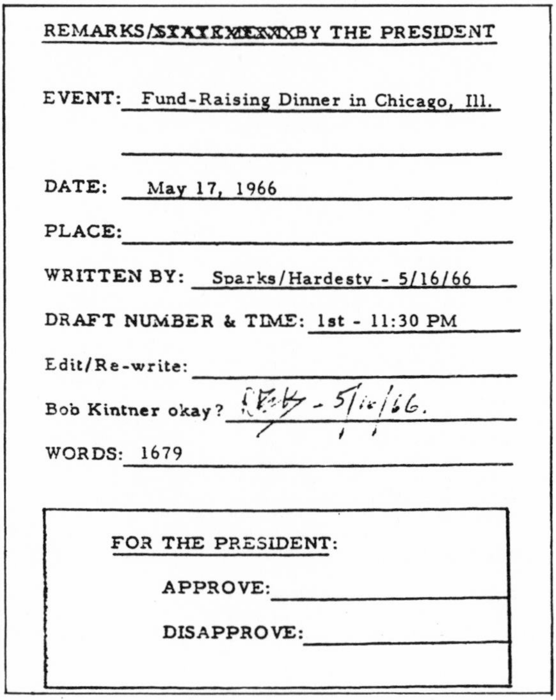

REMARKS/~~STATEMENT~~BY THE PRESIDENT

EVENT: Fund-Raising Dinner in Chicago, Ill.

DATE: May 17, 1966

PLACE:

WRITTEN BY: Sparks/Hardesty - 5/16/66

DRAFT NUMBER & TIME: 1st - 11:30 PM

Edit/Re-write:

Bob Kintner okay? *[signature]* - 5/16/66.

WORDS: 1679

FOR THE PRESIDENT:

APPROVE:

DISAPPROVE:

Source: Lyndon Baines Johnson Library, Austin, Texas.

of people who could get an advance look at a draft copy of a speech was limited by the good will of the secretary facing the tedious task of making multiple copies. As few as two copies of any presidential speech draft were produced in the Lincoln, Taft, or Roosevelt years. But today the copier makes it possible virtually to publish a draft copy of a speech by making hundreds of offspring. Circulating them to any or all of the mandarins of the White House staff can be achieved with the least amount of effort. In the past, when a president wrote his own drafts he was perhaps less compelled to permit the speech to circulate. But with delegated speech writing a fact of life, widespread circulation is a partial guarantee to a busy president that a foolish mistake will be caught.

Even so, the widespread editing of speeches is a mixed blessing. Mistakes are found, but an enormous amount of gatekeeping can dilute rather than enhance a message. State of the union messages have been especially prone to the advice of too many aides. Gerald Ford recalled, for example, that the delivery of his message in 1976 was preceded by the chaos of two teams—a total of ten people— working on two different messages. A key aide, Richard Cheney, had disliked a first draft prepared by Robert Hartmann and his staff. When a roundtable discussion among the participants predictably failed to produce a final compromise, Ford recalls a rare loss of temper: " 'Damn it,' I said, slamming down my hand on the table, 'we've got to stop bickering over these details. I want a final draft by tomorrow.' "[34] It was the second time in as any years that Ford faced a deadline for the annual message with two teams working independently.

Those working for Johnson also remember occasions when it seemed as if no one was in charge. Interviewed just after he had helped the President draft his 1969 State of the Union Message, aide Harry McPherson recalled that its preparation was a total fiasco:

Every state of the union speech has been a trauma for President Johnson. He gets into an incredible mood, horrible mood, and things start flying out. Other people get brought in, everybody but the cook gets brought in to make it more personal or human or whatever. I gave up in the last two days. I just couldn't bear it anymore. I fought some a little the last couple days, but not as much, as things were further added to it.[35]

Of the previous attempt in 1968 McPherson lamented that "it had been sent to God knows how many people."[36]

Under similar pressures, Hartmann mourned "the course of universal literacy" that led nearly every person in the White House to the conclusion that they were "Shakespeare, or at least a Bacon."[37] It is tempting to dismiss such complaints from disgruntled speechwriters. After all, it is a natural vanity to have a president use what one has agonizingly prepared, especially in a city that gives its highest prestige to those who can husband the prerogatives of power. Presidential speechwriters are the proudest when pointing out their contributions to the public record of an administration. It is not uncommon to find two or more writers claiming to have written the same remarks.

A further problem with speeches that have been widely circulated is that presidential commitments to new ideas often seem to become diluted. Presidents do not seem to be immune from the "group think" phenomenon described by Irving Janis and others.[38] Janis has noted that one common outcome of group attempts at problem solving is that solutions tend to evolve out of the middle ground of ideas accepted by the largest number. In the process of finding an acceptable solution to all the creative fringes tend to get ignored. As George Reedy documented with regard to the Johnson administration's Vietnam policy, the deviant edges of individual opinion on what to do were frequently abandoned as the risk of holding them became greater.[39] There was strong pressure to go along with the administration's ill-fated support for a military victory. Speeches are captive to this same kind of logic. The rhetorical equivalent to "group think" can be prose that offers offense to no one, and is easily forgotten.

This pattern was clearly evident at a pivotal point in the first presidential campaign of Dwight Eisenhower. One particular speech had been so clearly sanitized that eventually the calculated blandness itself became a news story.

Emmet Hughes had written a campaign address for a stop in Milwaukee which included a modest but courageous defense of Eisenhower's long-time friend, General George C. Marshall. Marshall had recently been attacked by Wisconsin's rabid anti-Communist Senator, Joseph McCarthy. One paragraph specifically rebuked McCarthy for his baseless charges of disloyalty against Marshall, an attack initially sanctioned by the candidate himself. Nonetheless, the remarks were deleted from the address at the last moment, though printed in press copies distributed in advance. According to Hughes, the culprit was aide Jerry Parsons who inserted himself between the speechwriter and the candidate in an effort to avoid what was seen as a needless political snub to the local Wisconsin audience.[40] The incident contributed to an emerging perception that Eisenhower lacked political courage.

The number of people or agencies that may be asked to clear a speech prior to its delivery is obviously subject to a number of variables. Theodore Roosevelt used to invite Oval Office visitors with completely unrelated business to read over a pending address, a habit sometimes practiced by his later namesake.[41] Lyndon Johnson, with much of his ambitious legislative program in the hands of what was then the Department of Health Education and Welfare, kept Secretary Anthony Celebrezze and domestic policy coordinator Joseph Califano well-posted on speech themes. Richard Nixon consulted with a relatively small group of trusted aides, and a few cabinet secretaries, particularly those running the Departments of Commerce, Treasury, and Agriculture. Jimmy Carter, in contrast, often worked with so many suggestions for speeches that the staff sometimes succumbed to the fatal expedience of putting incompatible elements together in one unwieldy whole. Efforts to overreach the natural limits of compromise were evident to both insiders and the press in an address to the Naval Academy in June 1979. It was an incompatible mixture of the anti-Soviet militance of national Security Adviser Zbigniew Brzezinski, and the more conciliatory ideas of Secretary of State Cyrus Vance.[42]

Perhaps Carter was tempted to use the speech-drafting process as a kind of soothing reminder to neglected staffers that their advice still mattered. The ploy of asking for suggestions is a common bureaucratic maneuver to buy peace from jealous members of an organization. But oral messages demand a singular point of view. There is simply no good mechanism available in oral address for the faceless anonymity that can exist in print. Written prose can be understood with or without personal pronouns. But a speech is a more personal medium. As Ronald Reagan understood so well, it always implies the existence of a specific personality and a unitary set of values and priorities. Unlike the faceless writer giving directions or information *en vacuo*, the speaker's public persona necessarily stands as an equal presence with his or her words. Speeches need the context of the advocate's background. It is not surprising that a speech that labors under the weight of 14 or so different contributors, and perhaps nine or ten drafts, ceases to be an extension of anyone.

The watchword of the so-called "hard core conservative wordsmiths" in the

Reagan administration to "let Reagan be Reagan" reflected this dilemma of clearance. Some aides and agency heads wanted to make his rhetoric less ideological and more inclusive; others wanted to maintain the well-known Reagan image that was so successful in both presidential campaigns. To allow "Reagan to be Reagan" meant writing less in the conciliatory style of a head of state, and more in the immediately familiar idiom of the committed partisan. Chief of Staff Donald Regan's tendency to circulate speeches to various agencies and administration officials angered the writers, who watched while their efforts to duplicate the famous Reagan fervor grew more timid as changes were made.[43]

In response to this need for a single voice behind a message, writers may go to elaborate lengths to protect their work from unwanted contributions other aides and assistants may be all too eager to offer. Robert Hardesty, for example, complained that while Johnson himself was a good editor of speeches, too many others (presumably Jack Valenti, Robert Kintner, Bill Moyers, and others) could supersede a second-level writer and substitute a portion of a draft with words of their own. "I don't know that anybody did it deliberately, but your tendency was to not turn them [the drafts] in until the last minute so that you could preserve what you thought ought to be preserved."[44]

MARCH 31, 1968: A CASE STUDY IN DELEGATION AND CLEARANCE

In what was perhaps the most dramatic and pivotal presidential address of the 1960s, Lyndon Johnson went on national television in the middle of the Vietnam-clouded 1968 political primaries to announce a partial bombing halt. The tired and relieved President also closed his address with a statement virtually no one expected—an announcement that he would not seek reelection for a second term. Not since Calvin Coolidge's decision to bow out in 1928 had a first-term incumbent made such a move.[45]

In retrospect, the events of 1968 seemed to require Lyndon Johnson's withdrawal from politics. His arch political enemy, Robert Kennedy, had been martyred by an assassin in the dingy back hallway of a California hotel. Senator Eugene McCarthy had emerged as the nominal leader of the antiwar movement, and made national headlines with a second-place primary finish against Johnson in New Hampshire. At the time, the news of the President's decision still came as a shock to the nation. It was an unmistakable confirmation of America's failure in Vietnam, and a reflection of a break in the nation's normally endemic spirit of optimism.[46]

The behind the scenes events leading up to the withdrawal provide a fascinating account of how writers and aides use speeches to forward their own views, and how they try to win the president's favor. In this case the suggestions of at least 17 top-level aides and cabinet secretaries were involved in shaping the rhetoric that tried to elicit face-saving concessions from North Vietnam's Ho Chi Minh. The speech itself went through 16 separate drafts as it evolved.

The decision to do the address began in mid-March when Johnson consulted with his informal Vietnam Advisory Group, a virtual Who's Who of Washington power brokers. They included Dean Acheson, former secretary of state under Truman, Douglas Dillon, ambassador to France under Eisenhower, as well as Cyrus Vance, Clark Clifford, McGeorge Bundy, General Omar Bradley, Walt Rostow, and others. Some "hawks" among the group, such as Omar Bradley and Walt Rostow, wanted to maintain or increase the current levels of bombing and military involvement in the war. Others were counseling the President to find a more conciliatory way to deal with the unwanted war. All were increasingly aware that reactions about Johnson's options on the domestic battlefield were becoming as hotly contested as the airstrips and villages near the Demilitarized Zone.[47] The idea of a televised speech to the nation was embraced by both "hawks" and "doves" in the administration, and quickly became the prize each faction wanted to own.

Initial work on the address actually began in February. Harry McPherson had gone through five drafts of a tentatively planned message to the nation asking for patience in the face of North Vietnamese successes during the Tet offensive. But a new series of drafts was begun when the speech date was moved back to the end of March. The first of a second round of attempts was written by McPherson in longhand on a simple tablet. It was typed and submitted to the President, and also to Bundy, Clifford, Rusk, Rostow, William Jordan, Juanita Kreps, and Arthur Okun.[48]

Johnson had many reasons for giving the speech. There was the continuing need to appear presidential at a time when urban riots in the nation's inner cities had created a sense of national unease. It was also the political season. Increasingly bitter attacks against the President reflexively led him to seek a forum where he could shore up support for an Asian policy that appeared to be coming apart at the seams. In Johnson's words:

I wanted to put the enemy's Tet offensive in proper perspective, and now that the offensive had been blunted and there was a chance that the enemy might respond favorably, I wanted to announce our new initiative for peace. If we were going to take the risk of a bombing pause, I felt I would make it clear that my decision has been made without political considerations . . . The most persuasive way to get this across, I believed, would be to couple my announcement of a bombing halt with the statement that I would not be a candidate for reelection.

I also hoped that the combined announcement would accomplish something else. The issue of Vietnam had created divisions and hostilities among Americans, as I had feared. I wanted to heal some of those wounds and restore unity to the nation. The speech might help do that.[49]

In fact, Johnson was also under extreme political pressure to back away from his bombing and troop commitments. Insiders close to him, most notably Clifford, Bundy, Dillon, and Vance had begun to challenge his assumptions about the war to each other and some members of the press.[50] He did not need his normally sophisticated political barometer to register the obvious discomfort that was building behind their outward expressions of support.

The speech went through six drafts between March 20 and 27. McPherson feverishly wrote and rewrote various sections as well as a new ending, submitting revisions to the President, Bundy, Rostow, and others. So many drafts came and went so quickly that on at least several occasions some of the President's own contributions were cut as they lost the identity of their author. At its earliest stages it had a cohesive theme to it, reflecting McPherson's original intention to develop a defensive rather than conciliatory stance on Vietnam. Later, reduced by 5000 to 4000 words, it would sound more eclectic as the compulsion to maintain a consistent policy was tempered by the desire to appear less war-like. The long and sometimes complex sentences of the original draft grew shorter as various editors corrected what were for them ambiguous and unclear references in consecutive revisions.

Working in secret during this time was another aide and writer, Horace Busby, who was preparing the final bombshell lines announcing the decision not to seek re-election in 1968. Shaping the terms that would announce the President's retirement was an important task. Johnson wanted to sound brave and unequivocal. He also wanted to leave with whatever tattered remnants of his image as a statesman that he could salvage.[51] Busby's words would mark a monumental transition for him and the nation. They had to strike a tone of courage rather than defeat.

March 27, just four days before its delivery, the speech took a major turn. Memos from this date reveal that the address itself became an instrument in the intense high-level policy struggle over the possibility of winning by military means. Factions were beginning to organize. A memo from Bundy to a White House aide noted that "Harry's present draft does just what was decided yesterday, but I think as it stands it will be profoundly discouraging to the American people."[52] Clifford also objected to the tone of the speech, noting that "What the President needs is not a war speech, but a peace speech."[53] As a result of their dissatisfaction, McPherson started a third round of drafts on March 28, emphasizing a limited bombing halt over most of North Vietnam. For the first time these alternate drafts showed elements of what would actually be delivered on March 31. Doodles in the margins of the manuscript indicate that the beleaguered McPherson had been reading Irwin Ross's book, *The Loneliest Campaign*, which prophetically documents the low popularity and uphill battle facing Harry Truman before the 1948 elections.[54]

Succeeding drafts were distributed, and among those observing the evolution of the speech was Mrs. Johnson, though her office returned copies that were read but unmarked. Clifford, in contrast, saw himself as one who was thrust into the middle of a great silent war over access to the delicate terrain of the President's agreement. The soft-spoken lawyer, a quintessential Washington insider, raised a number of points in attempts to soften the speech's hawkish tones. One particularly troublesome line was in reference to the dangers of pulling completely out of Vietnam. The speech contained the warning: "God help us if we do.'' Clifford objected. ''The speech still locks us into a war that is pictured as being essential to our security but is not proven as being essential to our security.''[55] In the give-and-take that followed, the drafting of the message *and* American policy had essentially collapsed into one process.

This was surely not the first nor the last time the writing of a speech was to become a vehicle for the formation of policy. A speech draft is often an instrument for the articulation and resolution of conflicts among high-level policymakers. Such was the case in the decision-making process that was underway during the national trauma of the Cuban Missile Crisis. After numerous deadlocks, Sorensen used speeches as ''a means of focusing on specifics'' and moving the discussions forward.[56]

On March 30, McPherson finished working on still another draft of what was clearly emerging now as a peace overture. He added new lines in the middle to assure Americans that the South Vietnamese would do more of the actual fighting, incorporating comments from Rusk and others. This new version—at this point labeled as ''alternate draft no. 4''—was actually the fifteenth attempt since February. In a memo to the President he indicated that he was working on another more conciliatory closing in order to avoid ''lighting up the sky with rockets.'' McPherson was anxious to have the President appear to be the guardian of peace. If the closing was too harsh, he noted, people will say, ''ah—now here comes the real Johnson, old blood and thunder. . . . ''[57]

After final revisions and editing by Johnson, the address was typed in large-sized letters on 8 1/2-by-11 inch sheets of paper. This was to be his backup delivery copy of the address, bound in a loose-leaf folder, marked for emphasis, and ready to use should the TelePrompTer fail. The networks had been notified several days earlier, and agreed to carry the speech without the complaints and suspicion which had accompanied some of their previous approvals for air time. Preparations were made for CBS to offer ''pool'' coverage with a single camera in the Oval Office, beginning at nine P.M. in the east. The networks hoped that it would be limited to a half-hour so that the remainder of their lucrative prime-time schedule would be intact. Johnson's address would put the impatient audiences for ''Bonanza'' and the ''Smothers Brothers Comedy Hour'' on temporary hold.

The day of the speech Johnson rehearsed before a small television camera and video recorder given to the White House by a Japanese electronics firm. The run-through was planned primarily to smooth out the TelePrompTer reading copy of the speech. TelePrompTers are now standard equipment for presidential candidates, presidents, and many governors. But Johnson still had difficulty reading the one-inch high words that were projected onto a transparent mirror located directly in front of the camera lens. At one point he stopped his rapid read-through of the remarks to correct an awkward phrase. ''Gosh, if that's not State Department language I never saw it,'' he remarked to no one in particular.[58] Perhaps reflecting his own unconscious attempt to transform the difficult political decisions of the last two weeks into a performance that would exude a style of confidence and resoluteness, he matter-of-factly now referred to the address as a ''script.''

The message given to the battle-weary nation on that Sunday evening was a reflection of those who helped shape it. From Acheson, Clifford, and others counseling peace came as much a concession as Johnson could tolerate: "Tonight, I renew the offer I made last August—to stop bombardment of North Vietnam. We ask that talks begin promptly, that they be serious talks on the substance of peace. . . . And we are doing so unilaterally, and at once."[59] But the voices of his military advisers were also to be heard. Johnson committed more U.S. troops to the struggle in order "to reequip the South Vietnamese forces, [and] to meet our responsibilities in Korea, as well as our responsibilities in Vietnam." In deference to the hard-liners unchanged by the deteriorating climate of opinion at home, the address also fell back on the harsh eloquence of lines spoken by John Kennedy in more idealistic times:

Of those to whom much is given much is asked. I cannot say and no man could say that no more will be asked of us. Yet I believe that now, no less than when the decade began, this generation of Americans is willing to pay any price, bear any burden, meet any hardship, support any friend, oppose any foe, to assure the survival and the success of liberty.

And then came the end. Knowing that the specter of defeat later in the fall elections was a very real possibility, Johnson consigned himself to a humiliating and premature political retirement. Horace Busby's clandestinely prepared words were to become the most widely reported of any in the speech:

With America's sons in the fields far away, with America's future under challenge right here at home, with our hopes and the world's hopes for peace in the balance every day, I do not believe that I should devote an hour or a day of my time to any personal partisan causes or to any duties other than the awesome duties of this office—the Presidency of your country. Accordingly, I shall not seek, and I will not accept, the nomination of my party for another term as your President.

Charged with the overtones of an unfolding political tragedy, the speech was a magnified example of the eclecticism of most presidential rhetoric. No one author except the President could claim ownership of it. Containing both ritual platitudes and specific statements of policy, it was, in miniature, an unintended guide to the era and its changing climate of opinion. The careful reader finds within its well-edited statements ample evidence that it was both a battle for the support of the President, and for the sympathy of his shrinking national constituency.

WHOSE MESSAGE IS IT? GHOSTWRITING AND ACCOUNTABILITY

The equating of who we *are* with what we *say* is a basic article of faith in human relations. Oral language is rightfully thought to be "a fingerprint of the man."[60] In ordinary life we can justifiably assume that cues to the inner person's dreams, values, and beliefs linger just under the transparent surface of speech.

Prejudiced persons, for example, will probably betray their views in their choice of language and patterns of thought that are not easy to conceal. But political language is not like everyday discourse. It is more carefully constructed. It carries the burden of speaking for many rather than one or a few. And it obviously shares many of the same mixed signals common to other messages that are also "ghosted" by professionals, including advertising, popular biography, corporate reports, and endless forms of similar public relations activities. Ironically, we remain suspicious of politicians who use professional writers to help craft their messages, but we show no similar concern for the fact that corporations and organizations hire advertising agencies and public relations firms to shape their own identities.

Even so, the essential dilemma of ghostwriting remains: Few Americans would quarrel with Ernest Bormann when he notes that if an audience is to truly "know" a speaker by what he says,

> then he must be honest with them and present himself as he really is. When he reads a speech that reveals to his audience a quiet humor, an urbane worldliness, subtle and incisive intellectual equipment, then he should be that kind of man. If his collaborators . . . are responsible for the "image" revealed in the speech, and if the speaker has different qualities and intellectual fiber, the speech is a deceit and it can be labeled as ghostwritten and condemned as unethical.[61]

Bormann raises the nub of the ghostwriting issue; there is little doubt that a person *can* conceal his or her identity behind a facade of rhetoric carefully constructed by someone else. This was the source of the accusations that were made when it was discovered that Senator Joseph Biden had plagiarized someone else's prose, a case we explored at the beginning of this book. Biden used imagery and ideas specific to the experiences of one British politician, and passed them off as his own.[62] But Bormann's determination of what is deceitful rarely looks so simple when specific cases like the previously discussed Johnson address are considered. Among many complications that arise, for example, is the realization that individuals may construct their *own* deceitful rhetoric without ever resorting to the help of ghostwriters. Novelists and psychologists have long demonstrated that we are all truly authors of many personal identities. Life requires a series of managed "performances" that grow out of our desire to construct personas we want others to accept. Harry Truman noted that "almost every presidential message is a complicated business."[63] But everyday communication is not necessarily simpler, especially when we take into account the resourceful techniques of "impression management" that are part of the survival skills of ordinary life.[64]

This view that ghostwriting is not so far removed from the routines of most forms of communication is not widely accepted. Resistance to it stems from two broad assumptions that we believe apply less and less to modern executives. One is that the President—like other public figures in politics, religion, and business—is engaged in a form of communication that aspires to a kind of visionary rhetoric, with the appropriate aesthetic components that are part of other forms of timeless utterance. In this view presidential rhetoric must not only communicate information and attitude; it is also expected to provide a visceral feeling of pleasure, stateliness, and grace. The problem, of course, is that a committee consisting of a group of writers cannot usually write monuments of English prose. The more pens on the paper, the less unified and elegant the style. The entire process of clearing or "staffing" a speech has the effect of breaking down its potential unity and style. Whatever their value as documents of state, today's remarks are usually pale imitations of better attempts written by great presidential orators such as Lincoln, Wilson, and Theodore Roosevelt. "Style may be the man," Bormann notes, "but when that style is five men, it ceases to be any style at all."[65]

This loss of visionary grace flows from the fact that, since the end of World War II, political rhetoric has been homogenized. John Kennedy and Ronald Reagan perhaps rediscovered what used to be called "the grand style" in their campaign and inaugural addresses, but arguably more in the fleeting drama of the moment than as sustained expressions of a personal rhetorical style. For example, the most lauded phrase in the Kennedy-Sorensen inaugural was the famous "Ask not what your country can do for you, ask what you can do for your country."[66] But even this seemingly eloquent balanced phrase was a deceit; it was actually at odds with the new administration's brand of activist federalism. Kennedy wanted his government to do more for individuals, not less.

Today, style is an after-the-fact consideration for what is often a rhetoric concerned primarily with the amplification of administrative policy. What was once a common form of ceremonial oratory is now used more and more to support specific political policy objectives. Where Lincoln could construct what was essentially a poem to the dead at Gettysburg—noting the anguish and human sacrifice necessary to preserve the Union—a modern president more regularly lives by his wits as a tactician defending specific policy goals. To be sure, the elements of celebration, eulogy, and effusive hyperbole have not disappeared from the Presidency. Indeed, they were revived by Ronald Reagan's fondness for homilies to America's virtue and "spiritual values." But in comparison to the Lincoln, Wilson, or Roosevelt eras, little of what is said today will become part of the nation's oral literature. The ideas of a single great statesman have gradually but consistently lost ground to the policy defenses of an *administration*. As such, this applied rhetoric invites the contributions and involvement of alliances and groups frequently represented by ghostwriters. A pluralism of viewpoints *in* means a pluralism of viewpoints *out*. A president today speaks not only for himself and his party, but for an enormous bureaucracy with diverse constituencies and obligations. The result is a rhetoric that is more corporate than individualistic, and one that seeks to cast a wider net in which to capture temporary allegiances.

This is not to say that presidential speeches are devoid of style. Rather, the style that remains is less a matter of the accidents of a president's biography and more the product of the calculations of professionals. Much like characters appearing week after week in a television series, presidents must now bring to their roles specific sets of traits and predispositions that cannot be abandoned by those who help script their performances. The rise of radio after 1920 especially required collaboration with professional writers in scripting a consistent political persona. In place of oratory intended for one audience in a large hall, the radio address was intended to reach listeners with a new in-the-room intimacy that required issues of state to be discussed as if in a conversation. Radio dictated that Americans would pay less attention to the hall-filling thunder of a William Jennings Bryan and more attention to the calculated ease of Will Rogers. Along with television some 20 years later, radio became a new form of theater that politicians would have to learn to share. Like actors moving from the stage to the studio, they too would have to master the illusions of spontaneity and intimacy, but within the bounds of what were essentially performances scripted by writers with an ear for dialogue.

Franklin Roosevelt was especially attuned to radio's potential. To the surprise of many of his listeners, he read his "fireside chats." Such was the illusion provided by his skills that these radio addresses presented a seamless cloth of exposition made from the individual threads of many. With the help of Grace Tully, Raymond Moley, and Samuel Rosenman, he introduced and nearly perfected a dialogue within a monologue, the scripted conversation as a means of political persuasion.[67]

A second assumption also leads to a suspicion about the influence and acceptability of ghostwriters. It is that if a president is not the author of his remarks, his commitment to them is indeterminant. In some ways it is easy to see why it might be believed that ghostwritten statements inherently carry less weight for a leader than those he utters under the power of his own creativity. Michael Medved, once a speechwriter for a senate candidate, recalled his own feeling of awe in writing words someone else would ultimately have to be responsible for:

I had been given the authority to issue statements in his name through our press office even if he had never seen the material before its release. It was an eerie feeling to read in the newspapers "the candidate said today . . . " and to know that all the press was really reporting were words that a totally obscure . . . aide had put into the candidate's mouth.[68]

How committed could any politician be under a similar situation, if asked to defend positions put forth by an inexperienced subordinate? Surely common sense tells us that ghostwritten remarks carry a broken and dangerously obscured line of responsibility.

But what would seem to be the case often is not. National politicians are in fact very loyal to both their staffs, and staff decisions taken in their name. None of the numerous memoirs cited in this chapter, for example, provide evidence that writers misdirected the intention of a president in any significant way. To the contrary, most presidents have been somewhat reluctant to give full credit to their writers, not only for the best of their efforts, but their worst rhetorical moments as well. Whatever doubts exist prior to a decision, once it is consummated by a public remark, presidents as least outwardly assume Harry Truman's dictum that "the buck stops here."

The key to this readiness to accept responsibility lies in the fact that ghost-writers are really subordinate collaborators, rather than independent authors. It is easy to overlook this middle ground and assume that presidents are essentially the captives of someone else's script. But there is no reason to believe that he is other than a free agent, fully able to decide what he will and will not say. The decision to choose to utter remarks prepared largely by someone else carries with it the full obligations of authorship. In various ways every president has signaled his adherence to this commitment. Eisenhower, for example, in a barely veiled attempt to say that every speech was at least partially his own, reminded the readers of his memoirs that "I have never been able to accept a draft of a suggested talk from anyone else and deliver it intact as my own."[69] Even if the imprint of the President was minor and largely cosmetic, the superficial changes essentially made the speech his. Truman was also sensitive to this burden, noting that, regardless of who wrote the drafts of a speech, "The final version . . . is the final word of the President himself, expressing his own convictions and his own policy. These he cannot delegate to any man if he would be President in his own right."[70]

Whether the result of a corporate psychology, or a desire to seem to be at the center of all White House activities, taking responsibility for speeches is a source of personal pride. A clearly weak speech will be rejected, an occurrence frequently known to writers for Kennedy, Johnson, and Nixon. Other presidents have protected themselves by becoming skillful at improvising from the podium. What is used, therefore, reflects what a president authentically endorses, even if the wording of the ideas strays from their own personal idiom. "When the President walks to the podium with that black ring-binder notebook," noted L.B.J. aide Ben Wattenberg, "it doesn't make a damn bit of difference who wrote what paragraph—it's his speech. The speechwriter is a creature of the President, not the other way around."[71]

Ghostwriting is thus a peculiar activity. Functioning as editors rather than true writers of their own prose, presidents have been forced to treat speeches as documents: more reflective of the joint decisions of an administration and less revealing of the inner person. But is is equally apparent that presidential rhetoric has not been rendered meaningless by the fact of ghostwriting. Writers are an adjunct to the executive, not a replacement for him. Anyone who has traveled so far and so successfully through the minefield of public life should rightly carry the presumption of full accountability. As Emmet Hughes has noted,

the only politically meaningful fact is not what the aide writes, but what the President says. The former may give important inflections to the latter. But the only decision of political moment belongs, wholly and unqualifiedly, to the President. Whatever he publicly declares is profoundly his.[72]

NOTES

1. Robert T. Hartmann, *Palace Politics* (New York: McGraw-Hill, 1980), p. 404.

2. Ari Posner, "The Culture of Plagiarism," *The New Republic*, April 18, 1988, p. 19.

3. Theodore Sorensen, *Kennedy* (New York: Harper & Row, 1965), pp. 68–70.

4. David Johnston, "Speakes Says He Told Reagan of Bogus Quotes, but later," *The New York Times*, April 19, 1988, p. A29.

5. This chapter, for example, draws upon the published recollectons of many speechwriters including: Robert Hartmann, *Palace Politics*; Raymond Price, *With Nixon* (New York: Viking, 1977); Emmet John Hughes, *The Ordeal of Power* (New York: Atheneum, 1963); William Safire, *Before the Fall: An Inside View of the Pre-Watergate White House* (New York: Doubleday, 1975); and Samuel I. Rosenman, *Working with Roosevelt* (New York: Harper, 1952).

6. Richard Weaver, *The Ethics of Rhetoric* (Chicago: Henry Regnery, 1953), p. 164. The author also discusses the style of "spacious" old rhetoric (pp. 164–85).

7. Page Smith, *Jefferson: A Revealing Biography* (New York: American Heritage, 1976), p. 258.

8. "From Pomp to Unforeseen Circumstance," *Broadcasting*, January 23, 1989, p. 67.

9. Michael Medved, *The Shadow Presidents* (New York: Times Books, 1979), pp. 15–28.

10. Ibid., p. 6.

11. Larry Speakes and Robert Pack, *Speaking Out: The Reagan Presidency from Inside the White House* (New York: Avon, 1989), pp. 87–89. For Deaver's own description of his role of media adviser in the White House see Michael K. Deaver and Mickey Herskowitz, *Behind the Scenes* (New York: William Morrow, 1987).

12. Hartmann, p. 387.

13. John Hart, *The Presidential Branch* (New York: Pergamon, 1987), pp. 104–6.

14. Thomas E. Cronin, *The State of the Presidency* (Boston, MA: Little, Brown, 1975), p. 137.

15. Elmer E. Cornwell Jr., *Presidential Leadership of Public Opinion* (Bloomington: Indiana University, 1965), p. 70.

16. Medved, p. 73.

17. Cornwell Jr., p. 95.

18. Gerald R. Ford, *A Time to Heal* (New York: Harper & Row/Reader's Digest, 1979), p. 26.

19. Ford, pp. 184–85.

20. Ronald Reagan is perhaps alone among modern presidents as the creator of a lifelong set of rhetorical themes that would be ceaselessly reworked into durable variations. Reagan's speeches given while he was a spokesman for General Electric in the 1960s are remarkably similar to major portions of remarks made during his two terms as president. For background on "the speech" and its evolution see Paul D. Erickson, *Reagan Speaks: The Making of an American Myth* (New York: New York University, 1985), pp. 12–30.

21. Gerald M. Boyd, "Hot and Angry Words from the Wordsmiths," *The New York*

Times, June 12, 1986, p. B6.; "Reagan Speechwriter Says He Was Dismissed in Dispute," *The New York Times*, June 10, 1986. p. A20.

22. Transcript, Robert Hardesty Oral History Interview, August 2, 1971, by Joe B. Frantz, p. 29, LBJ Library.

23. Townsend Hoopes, *The Limits of Intervention* (New York: David McKay, 1969), pp. 57–61, 119–34.

24. Boyd, p. B6.

25. Transcript, Charles M. Macquire Oral History Interview, July 29, 1969, by Dorthy Pierce McSweeny, p. 39, LBJ Library.

26. Sorensen, p. 240.

27. These are, in part, Henry Kissinger's characterizations from *The White House Years* (Boston, MA: Little, Brown, 1974), pp. 77–78.

28. Deaver, pp. 179–92.

29. Sherman Adams, *Firsthand Report, The Story of the Eisenhower Administration* (New York: Harper, 1961), pp. 81–82.

30. See Doris Kearns, *Lyndon Johnson and the American Dream* (New York: Signet Books, 1976), pp. 36–39, 72–73.

31. Lyndon B. Johnson, *The Vantage Point* (New York: Holt, Rinehart and Winston, 1971), p. 164.

32. Transcript, Charles Macquire Interview, p. 14.

33. Craig R. Smith, "Addendum to 'Contemporary Political Speech Writing,' " *Southern Speech Communication Journal* (Winter 1977): 191–92.

34. Ford, p. 350. For a different version of the same event see Hartmann, pp. 287–97. Hartmann suggests that the president had the habit of making unclear dual assignments.

35. Transcript, Harry McPherson Oral History Interview, tape 4, January 16, 1969, by T. H. Baker, pp. 10–11, LBJ Library.

36. McPherson Interview, p. 12.

37. Hartmann, pp. 382–83.

38. See, for example, Irving Janis, *Victims of Groupthink* (Boston, MA: Houghton Mifflin, 1972), and Soloman E. Asch, *Social Psychology* (Englewood Cliffs, NJ: Prentice-Hall, 1952), chap. 16.

39. George E. Reedy, *The Twilight of the Presidency* (New York: World, 1970), pp. 91–98.

40. Hughes, p. 43.

41. Richard Murphy, "Theodore Roosevelt," in *A History and Criticism of American Public Address, Vol. 3* ed. Marie Kathryn Hochmuth (New York: Russell and Russell, 1965), pp. 333–34.

42. James Fallows, "The Passionless Presidency," *The Atlantic Monthly*, August 1977, p. 43.

43. Boyd, p. B6.

44. Hardesty Interview, p. 11.

45. Lyndon B. Johnson, Address to the Nation Announcing Steps to Limit the War in Vietnam . . . and not to Seek Reelection, March 31, 1968, *Public Papers of the Presidents, Book 1, 1968* (Washington, DC: U.S. Government Printing Office, 1970), pp. 469–76.

46. For a review of the political and social problems that contributed to perhaps the worst year in the civil life of the nation since the Civil War, see Bruce Page, Lewis

Chester, and Godfrey Hodgson, *An American Melodrama: the Presidential Campaign of 1968* (New York: Viking, 1969), especially Chapters 1, 2, 7, and 10.

47. Hoopes, p. 224.

48. Much of the narrative that follows is based on a review of memoranda surrounding the preparation of the speech from the White House Central File (WHCF), Statements of Lyndon Johnson, March 20 to March 31, LBJ Library.

49. Johnson, *The Vantage Point*, p. 427.

50. Hoopes, p. 224.

51. Johnson, *The Vantage Point*, p. 427–30.

52. Memo, McGeorge Bundy to the President, March 21, 1968, Speech File, WHCF, LBJ Library.

53. Hoopes, p. 219.

54. Harry McPherson, "Alternate Draft," March 28, 1968, Statements of Lyndon Johnson, WHCF, LBJ Library.

55. Memo from Clifford to Harry McPherson, March 28, 1968, Alternate Draft No. 2, Statements of Lyndon Johnson, WHCF, LBJ Library.

56. Sorensen, p. 629.

57. Memo from Harry McPherson to the President, March 30, 1968, Alternate Draft No. 5, Statements of Lyndon Johnson, WHCF, LBJ Library.

58. Videotape of President Johnson's rehearsal of the March 31 speech, March 31, 1968, LBJ Library.

59. Johnson, Address to the Nation Announcing Steps to Limit War . . . pp. 469–76. All remaining quotes in this section are from this speech.

60. Weaver, p. 9.

61. Ernest G. Bormann, "Ethics of Ghostwritten Speeches," *Quarterly Journal of Speech*, October 1961, p. 267.

62. See the summary of this event in Chapter 1.

63. Harry S. Truman, *Memoirs: Years of Decisions* (Garden City, NY: Doubleday, 1955), p. 36.

64. Irving Goffman, *The Presentation of Self in Everyday Life* (New York: Doubleday, 1959).

65. Ernest G. Bormann, "Ghostwriting and the Rhetorical Critic," *Quarterly Journal of Speech*, October 1960, p. 288.

66. John F. Kennedy, Inaugural Address, January 20, 1961, *Public Papers of the Presidents, 1961* (Washington, DC: U.S. Government Printing Office, 1962), p. 3.

67. See Cornwell, pp. 253–69.

68. Medved, p. 4.

69. Dwight D. Eisenhower, *Mandate for Change, 1953–1956* (New York: Doubleday, 1963), p. 60.

70. Truman, p. 36.

71. Wattenberg quoted in L. Patrick Devlin, *Contemporary Political Speaking* (Belmont, CA: Wadsworth, 1971), p. 9.

72. Hughes, p. 25.

Chapter Nine

Political Communication and the Courts

The judicial organization of the United States is the hardest thing there for a foreigner to understand. He finds judicial authority invoked in almost every political context, and from that he naturally concludes that the judge is one of the most important political powers in the United States.[1]

... association for litigation may be the most effective form of political association.[2]

At first glance the various local, state, and federal courts of the United States would seem to be largely outside of the rest of the political system. It was clearly the intent of the writers of the Constitution to give the courts the status of impartial arbiters and fact finders insulated from the influences of individual factions. Federal judges and many of their counterparts in the states are appointed for life, immune from the more obvious pressures of public opinion. Such permanent tenure, Alexander Hamilton noted in *The Federalist Papers*, is an "excellent barrier to the encroachments and oppressions" of Congress, and the best way to assure "steady, upright, and impartial administration of laws."[3] More than any other high level governmental employees, judges—even those who are elected in some of the states—can usually count on holding their positions until they retire or resign.[4]

The idea of justice is synonymous with fairness and impartiality. In theory at least, the courts are not agents for any one faction, but guarantors of order and fairness for all parties involved. The obvious symbolism of the traditional courtroom communicates this judicial ideal. With its flags and state symbols placed near the judge's elevated dais, its architecture suggests that the power of the state has been vested in one figure. The judge is the beneficiary of what Jerome Frank has called "the cult of the robe." The special black uniform makes a symbolic plea to view the ordinary men and women of the judiciary as a "priestly tribe" removed from the rest of government.[5] All seating within the court gives the litigants equal distance and equal access to this arbiter. Juries are literally and figuratively held apart from the proceedings by a barrier that defines their status as close observers, but also suggests their separation from the maneuvers of defendants, prosecutors, and other agents of the court. To be sure, most judicial business occurs in conference rooms designed to bypass the rituals of the courtroom. Private bargaining for quicker resolution of cases is the norm rather than the exception in both civil and criminal sides of the law. Even so, the courtroom still reflects the ideals of the judiciary.

THE SPECIAL FUNCTIONS OF THE COURTS

As agencies of the state, courts perform three general functions. Most obviously, they exist in large measure to settle disputes, ranging from the simple conflicts that arise between individuals, to legal challenges that develop between corporations, municipalities and states. When cases involve single individuals, this spectrum can range from family and divorce courts, where the fallout of domestic crises are resolved in relative privacy, to much more complex cases where courts are asked to determine if certain contracts are enforceable. Nearly all disputes in the business community follow a relatively predictable routine; a settlement is either worked out prior to the start of a court trial, or a trial takes place that results in a decision about whether one of the parties has satisfied the conditions of a contract. Occasionally these business and domestic forms of conflict resolution will meet, as in the widely reported "Baby M" case involving the custody of a child as part of an adoption arrangement. After a pregnancy that began when Mary Beth Whitehead was artificially inseminated with sperm donated by William Stern, and after making a contract with the Sterns to give them the child, Ms. Whitehead decided to keep the baby. In 1986 and 1987 the nation read daily accounts of the New Jersey trial that would determine if a surrogate mother who underwent a change of heart could break a $10,000 contract with an adopting couple. The Sterns eventually won the right to raise the child, but not until after this court case created a good deal of national soul-searching.[6]

A second important function of the courts is to determine whether individuals or groups have violated norms that also carry the force of law. This is the familiar territory of the criminal trial, the kind of judicial action is for many Americans the essence of what the legal system is about. In both fictional and news forms, the details of crime and punishment provide a continuing and vital form of public theatre. The courtroom melodrama remains as much a staple of popular entertainment as it is an enduring form of basic journalism. Between 1963 and 1973, for example, at least 16 separate courtroom dramas ran on the three television networks in prime time.[7] If the reality is that the vast majority of criminal cases are plea-bargained and never come to trial, it is still true the news agenda on any given day is likely to contain sensational details of villainy and victimage culled from testimony or videotape of a criminal trial. Most major newspapers devote copious amounts of space to crime and criminal justice processes, leading many of their readers to overestimate the actual number of instances of crime in their communities.[8]

With its riveting details of character and conflict and its almost certain all-or-nothing resolution, the criminal trial plays out a range of class frictions and social fantasies that can be given satisfying closure in the form of a verdict. When Bernhard Goetz went on trial in 1987 for shooting four young men who demanded that he give them money, he was alternately seen by various Americans as a hero or a villain. The case gained its national notoriety in part because of its racial angle: Goetz was a white Manhattanite who claimed that he was threatened by the black youths on a subway. The youths, one of whom was permanently paralyzed by one of the bullets from Goetz's .38 revolver, claimed they were simply panhandling. The familiarity of the circumstances hit a raw nerve, turning into a story New York City's tabloids and the nation's television news programs would not allow to fade away. If the basic facts in the case were relatively clear, questions about Goetz's motives have been elusive.[9] Was he guilty of nothing more than standing up to another band of parasitic misfits, or of succumbing to the racism of a city where the destitute must sometimes resort to extraordinary means to survive? The trial of the "subway vigilante" provided a momentary catharsis for a nation that is fascinated and satiated by reports of serious crime.

The third function of the justice system in the United States is as much a consequence as a formal goal. A whole range of high state and federal courts increasingly share the function of policymaking with the legislative and executive branches. This rule-making process comes in sharp focus periodically when senate hearings are held to confirm federal judges. Conservatives routinely decry "activist" judges who "legislate" social policy without the accountability that goes with elective office. But in fact the making of guidelines for carrying out decisions has always been part of the business of settling disputes in high courts. The growth of federal and state agencies dealing with everything from forests to public housing has increasingly involved federal and state supreme courts. Many of these agencies have been under the leadership of executives hostile to the rulings of these courts, making judicial policymaking a source of constant friction within the three branches of government.

School integration cases in the 1970s presented such divided jurisdictions. In a significant number of instances federal judges ruled that individual districts needed to take specific steps—including busing—to racially integrate schools in their districts. Lower courts increasingly built on the Supreme Court's landmark 1954 ruling in *Brown* vs. *Board of Education* and other subsequent cases that have been used to prod school boards into equalizing the educational resources available to black and white families. In one 1970 case, the Court agonized over whether to uphold a U.S. district Court judge's decision to enforce a desegregation plan for a North Carolina school district. The plan called for the busing of 13,000 students to achieve a racial mix in each of the district's schools. Characteristically, the Court ended up endorsing the principle of mandating racial balance, but it gave no conclusive support to the busing plan worked out by the district court. It fell to that lower court to mandate and police another plan that would have to be executed by the reluctant school district.[10]

This pattern of creating a decision that has the effect of policy is a common occurrence. Federal judges routinely enforce actions that take on the features of policy. As Donald Horowitz has noted,

Federal courts have laid down elaborate standards for food handling, hospital operations, recreation facilities, inmate employment and education, sanitation, and laundry, painting, lighting, plumbing, and renovation in some prisons; they have ordered other prisons closed. Courts have established equally comprehensive programs of care and treatment for the mentally ill confined in hospitals. They have ordered the equalization of school expenditures on teachers' salaries, established hearing procedures for public school discipline cases, decided that bilingual education must be provided for Mexican-American children, and suspended the use by school boards of the National Teacher Examination and of comparable tests for school supervisors. . . . They have told the Farmers Home Administration to restore a disaster loan program, the Forest Service to stop the clearcutting of timber, and the Corps of Engineers to maintain the nation's non-navigable waterways. They have been, to put it mildly, very busy, laboring in unfamiliar territory.[11]

All of the examples cited as illustrations for the three functions of the courts serve as a reminder that the legal system travels down the same political tracks that have been well worn by leaders in the executive and legislative branches. Cases like those involving surrogate parenting or school desegregation are constant reminders that the courts must always deal with problems that have not been disposed of by legislative or administrative action. The remainder of this chapter focuses especially on the communication dimensions that exist when such cases emerge as part of the political dialogue on a controversial issue.

THE COURTS IN A POLITICAL WORLD

In some ways the diffuse American legal system provides ideal ground to nurture political debate. Because the trial process has the effect of personalizing the consequences of laws in ways that other political agencies might shun, courts provide a ready source of social details from which to construct popular narratives of social change and tension. Although it is a by-product rather than a purpose of its structure, the trial has the effect of eliciting for the public record the uniquely private features of personal and social conflict. Other institutions may reduce issues to generic principles and abstract "what ifs"; the courts—even top state and federal courts—deal in the personalistic details of conflict. The common law tradition is to build judgmental principles based on the particulars of individual cases. The insanity defense, for example, is almost always discussed in the popular media in the context of a specific trial rather than through the abstract discussions of psychiatrists and legal scholars who focus on the underlying principles. For example, most Americans heard and judged arguments about the insanity plea of John Hinckley, the loner who searched for a strange kind of fame by attempting to take the life of Ronald Reagan in 1981.[12] Fewer have probably ever encountered the bitter academic debate between legal and mental health professionals over the legitimacy of basic psychiatric categories routinely used in the construction of legal defenses.[13] In the public mind there may be a vague sense in which "The Law" exists as a body of abstract codes, but for most Americans the legal system exists at any one time as a handful of dramatic cases that have surfaced on the national news agenda.

In addition to becoming the arena of focused attention on a political controversy, the nation's courts are also overtly political in several other ways. Judicial selection procedures are an obvious case in point. Fourteen states still choose some or most of their judges in partisan elections. In New York, for example, party dominance is so strong in various regions that the power of local political bosses to choose a candidate for a judgeship is tantamount to the power to appoint. As New Yorker and former Secretary of State Cyrus Vance has noted, in many instances "judges are selected for their political service rather than their judicial ability. Far too often judges chosen by the bosses have been lazy, incompetent or, worse, corrupt."[14] The other common route for selection of judges is by executive appointment. All members of the federal judiciary are chosen in this way, but these appointments can also have their own problems. The principle of "senatorial courtesy" makes the candidate for any judgeship the subject of considerable political maneuvering between the President and the senators from the district of the vacancy. By tradition, senators expect to be invited to submit nominees before the nomination is made, especially if they have bargained for a positive working relationship with the White House. If a senator is not happy about a nominee, he may well indicate that the White House will lose an ally on future legislative action. If he wants to press the matter further, he can block Senate confirmation by declaring the candidate "personally obnoxious." A long-standing custom obliges other members to honor that objection by denying confirmation.[15] Neither election or selection processes guarantee good or weak judges, but they serve as a reminder that access to the third branch of government is frequently gained by winning the favor of leaders from the two elective branches.

Further evidence of the implicit link between the political world and the judiciary has steadily accumulated over the years in memoirs, speeches, articles, that have generally served to demystify court processes and members. What Thurman Arnold did to the "mysteries of jurisprudence" in a book written before he became Franklin Roosevelt's attorney general, countless others have done more recently in unmasking the banality of many court rulings and procedures. In *The Symbols of Government*, Arnold took a fresh look at legal processes and found a number of "fictions" and "myths" that better served the hierarchical needs of the law profession than the needs of comprehensible decision making. He understood well the ritualistic powers of the legal system. "Here is a subject," Arnold noted, "which not even lawyers read." To the extent legal philosophy is discussed in public, its purpose is largely symbolic and reassuring. "Without a science of jurisprudence, law might be considered a collection of man-made rules for practical situations. With it the Law becomes the cornerstone of government."[16]

This tendency to unmask the special status of the courts probably reached its high point in 1979 with the publication of *The Brethren* by Bob Woodward and Scott Armstrong. This hugely popular 450-page book gave the impression that a large number of former Supreme Court law clerks and perhaps several associate justices abandoned their pledges to secrecy about the inner workings of the nine-person tribunal. No book had ever attempted to describe the peculiar proclivities and working habits of members of the court. It provided a riveting account of the vote swapping, earthiness, and office politics behind the most revered of all federal institutions. Whole sections were devoted to descriptions of the bargaining and hard work that helped shape key court opinions. Members were variously portrayed as devoted, often diligent, sometimes lazy or confused, and usually careful to withhold opinions until others had committed themselves to an emerging view. Consider, for example, how the authors recount one instance of friction in 1974 between Associate Justice William Brennan and Chief Justice Warren Burger. As is the custom, the chief justice frequently assigns the writing of opinions to a particular associate. Others then either "join" with the majority, or draft their own minority dissents. An associate typically welcomes the task of writing an important majority opinion, but may feel victimized when asked to deal with arcane cases.

Brennan felt that he got terrible assignments from the Chief. One decision he was assigned to write (*Antoine* v. *Washington*) addressed the question of whether Indians in Washington state could hunt and fish in the off season. . . . Brennan seethed at having to write this "chickenshit case." He had a solid majority of six, including the Chief, but typically, the Chief had not sent in his join memo, even though Brennan's draft had been in circulation for several weeks.

Late one afternoon at about four o'clock, just before Brennan planned to leave for home to see his ailing wife, the phone rang. The Chief wanted to see Brennan on the Indian case. . . .

At Burger's chambers, Burger showed Brennan several words he wanted added to a long paragraph in the draft. Brennan said he would consider the addition. Then he stomped back to his chambers and summoned his clerks. They had never seen him so angry. "Here is the change," Brennan said. "What the fuck does it mean?"

The clerks and Brennan examined the paragraph. It made no sense. Brennan concluded that it was just another of the Chief's niggling and arbitrary changes, made perhaps only to prove that he had read the draft. . . . Swallowing resentment, he told the Chief that he would be happy to make the addition.[17]

For many readers the book was a stunning revelation, if only in showing the ordinariness of the most honored of federal institutions. Many experts still wonder how the traditionally shrouded court suddenly came to be so transparent to two outsiders. But even with remaining questions about the authenticity of its details.

The Brethren presents a highly plausible account of the bureaucratic politics and human motivations that we know must exist in any institution—even one as special as the Supreme Court.

Woodward and Armstrong's book ended the long-standing tradition of secrecy and circumspection by members of the court. After its publication, and possibly because of its portrayal of ordinary people in an extraordinary setting, Justices began making more comments on the routines of the court, and more speeches with pointed reference to current issues. Within the last few years, for example, Justices Scalia and Rehnquist have offered mildly negative observations about the lack of give-and-take in conferences designed to formulate decisions. Others have gone even further. In a 1985 speech, Justice Stevens criticized Attorney General Edwin Meese for his comments about recent decisions affecting the states, and in 1987 he took the unprecedented step of endorsing Reagan-nominee Robert Bork to the high court. Similarly, Justices Blackmun and Marshall have commented to the press about the dangers of a court turning to the political right.[18] All of this unusual outspoken partisanship has led legal scholar David O'Brien to consider the obvious rhetorical fallout: "When you have sitting members of the Court roasting the President of the United States on television and endorsing a Supreme Court nominee, the danger is that the public will view the Justices as no different from any other Washington politicians."[19]

THE PUBLICITY FUNCTIONS OF COURT ACTIONS

By far the vast majority of the nation's courts go about their work without the attention of the mass media and general public. But the exceptions are important to consider. Even routine court cases, ranging from the divorce of a celebrity to a suit brought by one large corporation against another, may become the subject of public awareness and discussion. The higher the visibility of a court case, the greater the likelihood that its details will seem to raise questions or doubts about public policy. Conflicts that go to trial under the scrutiny of the press usually touch on evolving legislative issues or issues of political competency. This section briefly explores three kinds of trial settings that illustrate this principle.

The Politics of Prosecution

The process of determining who will become a defendant in a criminal trial is partly selective, as it is in every complex society. Justice in the United States is frequently pursued at the discretion of ordinary citizens, police, prosecutors, judges, and regulators. At various times all of these interested parties may function as gatekeepers in the reporting and prosecuting of crime. Using a wide variety of crime reports and general population surveys, for instance, criminal justice experts estimate that over half of all assaults and rapes go unreported by their victims; most burglaries go unsolved; and the vast majority of "victimless crimes" such as gambling, drug dealing, and prostitution remain concealed.[20]

It is probably obvious to most Americans that the criminal justice system has neither the capacity nor resources to follow through on most forms of lawbreaking. As Kenneth Davis has documented in extensive detail, government attorneys often have an extraordinary range of choices about whether or how to prosecute, even when prima facie evidence exists that laws have been broken. The ideal of "a government of laws and not of men" is, at best, a well-intentioned wish. "No government has ever been a government of laws and not of men in the sense of eliminating all discretionary power.[21] As Davis notes, the prosecution of cases involving anti-trust violations or tax evasion are almost entirely up to the investigators in whose jurisdiction they fall.[22] An especially shocking murder case may create public expectations that preempt the selectivity of a prosecutor, but far less visible forms of illegal behavior may provide more options. To cite a notorious case, there was perhaps no way investigators charged with locating the kidnapper of the child of Charles Lindbergh could not have found a suspect. Many questions remain about the 1935 trial and conviction of Bruno Hauptmann, especially the role of the press in exploiting the entire episode.[23] Arguably, mass media attention to a crime involving the child of a national celebrity probably made someone's arrest and eventual conviction a near certainty. By comparison, a federal tax audit that uncovers questionable accounting practices by an important American corporation generally carries no similar mandate for action.

Individual prosecutors from county to federal levels must weigh a number of priorities in determining whether evidence provided to them will be developed into a case. A wide range of reasons may explain why some potential cases are dropped and others are pursued. Shortages of staff, the known preferences of individual judges who would hear cases, a heavy workload, and countless other organizational facts could play a role.

In addition, important political and public relations criteria may become relevant in making a decision play about whether to pursue a case. Prosecutors must regularly navigate through the traffic of political issues and legal demands that regularly cross through their jurisdictions. Because crime in its many forms is a political as well as legal issue, and because they often use their offices to launch themselves into the political world, prosecutors are likely to be very responsive to the exigencies of public opinion. One case study of the pragmatic and political factors that figured into decisions to prosecute in the Seattle area points out a number of key variables. Observers found that a number of pragmatic factors were weighed in decisions of how to approach particular cases. How much public exposure will a prosecutor have in the courtroom by going forward? Could a case put him or her in an embarrassing situation; for instance, by forcing a confrontation with a popular leader or party ally?[24] In addition, victimless and victim-centered crimes can each have their rhetorical virtues. Personally prosecuting in behalf of a victim who is certain to be the beneficiary of public empathy may override the fact that evidence in the case leaves something to be desired. Similarly, the decision to go forward with trials of prostitutes or adult bookstore owners may have more to do with the public relations needs of a county or district attorney than the protection of the relatively contented "victims" of these offenders.

A high position in the criminal justice system can provide a fast track to someone with an eye on a political career. Theodore Roosevelt was hardly the first to discover that being a flamboyant enemy of crime—as New York's police commissioner—could pay enormous political dividends. Large numbers of state and national legislators have followed similar paths, using constant attention to news of crime as a way to create high local recognition as the first step in seeking elective office. One of Pennsylvania's senators, Arlen Specter, first became a district attorney in Philadelphia, specializing in the prosecution of sensational cases ranging from widely reported rapes to the structural failure in the roof of a newly constructed arena. As one observer of his career noted, "Hardly a day went by during Specter's stint in which he didn't hold a news conference, announce some new investigation, or release a statement to the press."[25] His work in the state's largest city was a perfect place to begin a successful 1980 campaign for the United States Senate.

A different but equally interesting pattern is evident in the career of Rudolph Giuliani, who served until early 1989 as the highly regarded United States attorney for the Southern District of New York. The young and photogenic Giuliani became as much a television celebrity as the governors of states adjacent to New York City. Known especially for his frequent press conferences announcing drug-related or mafia crime arrests, he gained recognition as the "crimebuster" interested in protecting "the little guy." Part of the obvious objective of his 130-lawyer office was to make sure that the public was aware of his law enforcement efforts. As one listener noted after hearing him give a speech to high school principals, "I saw you on TV five nights this week." "Actually it was only two nights," Giuliani demurred. "Last week it was five."[26]

His first national notoriety began some years before, as associate attorney general in the early years of the Reagan administration. He personally interceded in ongoing plans in the Justice Department in order to change key priorities. The previous Carter administration had built a new "white collar crime" unit within the F.B.I. to gather evidence about illegal business practices and corruption within federal contractors. McDonnell Douglass and E. F. Hutton were two firms that were nearly in the net of Justice Department prosecution at the end of the Carter years. Over the strenuous objections of many professionals who had been working on these cases, Giuliani dropped or settled them, favoring instead a more publicized 130-million-dollar enlargement of federal drug enforcement efforts.[27]

The Politics of Litigation

Another important way the courts function as extensions of the political process is in the way civil litigation can be used to generate favorable publicity. Many groups use legal action as a way to activate public opinion. Civil suits may be brought against corporations by individuals or consumers, against one corporation by another, or by private groups against an agency of government. Many use these suits to seek financial damages, changes in the conduct of one of the parties, or a combination of both. But the most tangible benefit may lie in the favorable publicity created when the suit is first filed. Litigation attracts attention, and sometimes taps into considerable public sympathy for the victims portrayed in widely reported news stories. For instance, the decision by an environmental group to seek damages in behalf of the residents near a corporation's factory carry the kind of credibility that simple charges might not have. The filing of a suit binds the corporation to respond, and potentially sets up a David and Goliath encounter that can have dramatic publicity value. This pattern helps explain why many more suits are filed than actually result in court actions. Once the threat of a public trial has been made, the prime objective of the plaintiff has sometimes been achieved. Both parties to the conflict may find that the uncertainty of a verdict is less desirable than an out-of-court settlement that allows each side to save face.

One such interesting environmental case developed in 1981. A conservation organization in Western Australia led by Neil Bartholomaeus took the unusual step of filing suit in U.S. District Court in Pittsburgh against the Alcoa Corporation. The class action suit sought to enjoin Alcoa from continuing its strip mining in a region where the practice was thought to have an adverse effect on the local water supply. The large-scale mining in the area was thought to have radically raised the salinity of Perth's drinking water. Under federal environmental laws, such suits may be filed, even if the alleged damage occurs outside of the United States. The group employed an American attorney, Victor Yannacone, who had successfully initiated highly visible class action suits in behalf of other consumer groups, including Vietnam veterans exposed to the toxic defoliant known as Agent Orange. For its part, Alcoa mobilized its own public relations personnel in both countries to try to counter the negative effects of the case. That the Australian environmentalists eventually failed to prevail in court is probably less important than the political gains they scored. As Michael Sherer notes,

While the plaintiffs lost the legal battle, they may have won the publicity war. The Australian government was embarrassed, Bartholomaeus achieved considerable domestic and international publicity, the aluminum companies were caught napping, and Yannacone enhanced his reputation as an environmental attorney.[28]

In libel cases a variation on this approach occurs when someone who claims to have been falsely defamed in a published or broadcast story uses a suit in part to regain lost stature. To sue for libel is to make a highly visible gesture that one's own reputation has been unfairly harmed. Even when the medium has practically no credibility—such as the tabloid *National Enquirer*—a suit may be brought against it, as actress Carol Burnett did, in order to focus attention on its low standards.[29] For more prestigious media the stakes are much higher. General William Westmoreland's highly publicized 120-million-dollar suit against CBS for their alleged falsification of his management of the military during the Vietnam War made almost daily headlines for nearly four months. The same was true of Israeli Defense Minister Ariel Sharon's suit against *Time* magazine, also being heard in the same New York courthouse at the same time. Sharon charged that he was incorrectly and carelessly identified in a February 1983 issue of *Time* as the instigator of a massacre that took place in two Palestinian refugee camps. The story occurred against the backdrop of the assassination of Bashir Gemayel in Lebanon, and reports of the murder of several hundred civilians living in camps in the villages of Sabra and Shatila. *Time* suggested that in a condolence visit to Gemayel's family, Sharon had urged the Christian Phalangist faction to retaliate by going into the Palestinian camps.

There was no doubt that some of CBS's conclusions in "The Uncounted Enemy" were serious and partly inaccurate. Among other things, Westmoreland was inaccurately portrayed as deceiving President Johnson about numbers of the enemy. His expensive legal effort against CBS gave his attorney and the press a two-year opportunity at vindication by bloodying the image of CBS and exploiting public suspicions about unbridled media power. In the end, CBS found some fault in its documentary production procedures and took heavy criticism for the program in a widely read *TV Guide* article entitled "Anatomy of a Smear." But they conceded little error and no money in the out-of-court settlement that was eventually reached before the end of the trial.[30] Similarly, *Time* later admitted in its own settlement with Sharon that it had been in error. Its own internal investigation revealed that they had no solid evidence for the accusation. Both cases raised a number of troubling questions about editorial control processes in the prestigious and well financed branches of the national media.[31] Even so, the legal issues and endless hours of confusing testimony that unfolded in both cases were ultimately of less consequence than the simpler fact that both men sought vindication of their public careers.

Legal Action on Status Issues: Race, Equal Treatment, and Bakke

One of the notable ironies of modern political life is that the same legal institutions charged with guaranteeing "equal protection under the law" have unintentionally become agents for conferring legitimacy to factions locked in volatile status disputes. Communication in all of its varieties typically defines hierarchical relationships.[32] Especially in the political world, certain issues evolve into potent symbols with vital significance for particular groups or social movements. Political issues become status issues when concerned advocates come to believe that a pending decision by an important political body will also have the effect of passing judgment on their core values. They come to see a decision as either endorsing or rejecting the fundamental legitimacy of their group's deeply felt convictions. Any governmental decision on the issue has the effect of making one side in a status conflict feel like its in-group honor has been rebuffed, forcing it through law or policy to yield to the hostile values of others. The victorious side will usually claim that its own priorities have been vindicated and given new social legitimacy. The suffrage and civil rights movements, the temperance movement, and efforts to pass an equal rights amendment all clearly involved such stakes. As Joseph Gusfield notes, even John Kennedy's Catholicism in the 1960 presidential campaign became a status issue to many Protestant Americans. "At stake . . . was the relative prestige of being Protestant in American life."[33]

In both of his campaigns, Ronald Reagan was extremely sensitive to the status ramifications of supporting prayer in public schools and federal restrictions on the widespread availability of abortion services. Reagan knew that for large numbers of supporters these issues were tied up with their own sense of political enfranchisement or alienation. To his and their deep frustration, however, the courts had at least partly defined federal policy on these questions. In *Roe* vs. *Wade*, for example, the Supreme Court declared that states cannot prohibit an abortion sought by a woman in the early stages of a pregnancy. And in a series of cases that began in 1962, it ruled that public school boards cannot require specific prayers or recitations of the Bible in classes. These and other decisions brought a storm of protest to the court and mobilized hundreds of groups who have continued to press for legislative redress of these rulings. Lacking massive state and congressional support needed for constitutional amendments, the most Reagan could promise was to use his power to appoint "strict constructionist" judges who would be less "activist" and more sympathetic to a conservative social agenda.

The presence of status issues that are woven into many appeals to higher courts accounts for much of the public and press attention they receive. Since *Brown* vs. *Board of Education*, for instance, desegregation cases that have followed have become defined by civil rights groups as representative of American commitments to racial equality. Even though virtually every school case heard by the court since Brown has specified only limited change in specific jurisdictions, its decisions have been widely presented as a symbol of American resolve to end racial divisions.[34]

A far more complex instance that placed several courts in the middle of a status dispute occurred in 1978, when the Supreme Court issued an opinion in *Regents of the University of California* vs. *Bakke*.[35] The case involved a relatively simple complaint, but became widely publicized because of the sensitive issue of racial quotas that it raised. In 1972 Allen Bakke applied to and was turned down by the University of California for admission to its new medical school in Davis. He was not admitted in part, he later discovered, because a certain number of positions at the university were held for candidates in an affirmative action program intended for minority candidates. It was true, he was told, that his high "B" average was better than some of the affirmative action candidates, but the university remained committed to hold some spaces for minority students who had suffered from years of racial prejudice and second-rate schooling in the United States.

Bakke's suit brought little national attention when it was raised in the quiet Sacramento Valley town of Woodland. But the decision to appeal to the California Supreme Court brought quick responses from a number of groups and their constituencies. There was deep irony in this case; a white middle-class man charged that his civil rights had been violated by the admissions personnel at the university. In some ways his complaint was a mirror image of desegregation cases in the 1960s and early 1970s that were brought against schools and colleges in Mississippi and Alabama and, later, against schools in many northern states as well. The difference, of course, was that Bakke's suit against the university split apart two civil rights principles that had usually been aligned. His attorneys raised the issue of whether protections against discrimination weren't by themselves discriminatory. Was Bakke the victim of reverse discrimination, or a dangerous threat to hard-won programs to finally redress the imbalance in educational opportunity within the United States? The Anti-Defamation League, other Jewish organizations, and the American Federation of Teachers spoke out in his defense and attacked race "quotas" that, they argued, unfairly excluded Bakke. On the other side of the issue the NAACP and various university associations supported the university's affirmative action plan.[36]

Far less visible but less important was the clear evidence that news about the case struck a raw public nerve. Building on the latent resentments of many whites, reports of Bakke's complaint provided tangible proof to large numbers of Americans that civil rights cases had "gone too far." For those who already harbored the suspicion, the case made it easy to conclude that minorities were using the law to achieve what they could not attain by merit. The phrases "reverse discrimination" and "less qualified minorities" were constantly featured in press reports at the time, giving subtle vent to the view that Bakke was the true victim in this case.[37]

The Supreme Court eventually upheld most of the findings of the California Supreme Court, but the decision was itself testimony to the status issues surrounding the case. In a five-to-four decision, the high court held that rigid quotas for minorities applying for admission to these kinds of programs were unconstitutional. However, it also noted that race was one of several factors that *could* be considered when admitting students. The justices were careful to not overturn the idea of affirmative action. But members of the court partitioned the case in such a way so that they could also vote five-to-four in favor of a lower court judgment that Bakke had been unfairly excluded. In other words, Bakke was admitted because of the vagaries in the way the university conducted its admissions program, yet at the same time the tribunal affirmed the key principles that traditional civil rights groups sought to protect. The decision was a clear compromise concealed in the highest of legal jargon. As Joel Dreyfuss and Charles Lawrence have noted in their exhaustive study of this case, "The Supreme Court had attempted to find a neutral ground for a political decision . . . "[38] What they settled on was a solution that would moderate tensions and resentments on a highly provocative status issue.

TELEVISED TRIALS AND THE POLITICAL AGENDA

The large majority of those who administer the courts in the United States have usually viewed the publicity value of mass media coverage with skepticism and occasional hostility. Former Chief Justice Warren Burger's legendary contempt for television journalism became one of the most identifiable features of his tenure before his 1987 retirement. He repeatedly cautioned clerks and staff in the Court to avoid talking to the press, or engaging in conversation about court business in any setting where members of the press could eavesdrop. It was not unusual for Burger to specify that he would speak to a group outside Washington only if broadcasters were prohibited from attending their meeting.[39] His reactions were extreme, but they reflect what have been the feelings of many who control the judiciary—that publicity is not a constructive force in the administration of justice.

The clearest evidence of this wary relationship is evident in continuing concerns about the effect that extensive press coverage of a crime has on potential jurors. Since crime news generates large numbers of readers and viewers, it pits two important constitutional principles against each other. On one hand, the First Amendment protects the rights of journalists, but at the same time the Sixth Amendment promises defendants a fair and impartial trial.[40] Extensive coverage of arrests and pretrial proceedings have sometimes made it difficult to find jurors who have not already formed opinions about a defendant's guilt based on what has been reported.

The issue of the press's role may be further complicated when a trial actually begins and judges and journalists may have to grope with the issue of privacy. For example, to what extent should the victims of crimes, especially profoundly wounding ones like rape or incest, have the protection of the courts to keep their names and faces from public view? And are witnesses to be given any protection if their testimony could place them in possible danger? It is easy for most people to accept a judge's decision to restrict the reporting of the names of children and other vulnerable victims. But members of the press are suspicious of any court proceedings that give weight to "gag rules" issued from the bench which could also be used to exclude information the public may have a right to know.

The kidnapping trial of Bruno Hauptmann mentioned earlier remains the classic case of journalistic excess. The normally placid farming town of Flemington New Jersey, was inundated with hundreds of reporters, photographers, and telegraph messengers. Scores of angry citizens filled the courthouse area, many hoping to see the alleged kidnapper of Charles and Ann Lindbergh's child. Others circulated pamphlets showing Hauptmann's earlier criminal record in Germany. Newspapers from all over reported the opinions of famous attorneys about his probable guilt, and the state's prosecutors freely spoke to reporters about the case. Through all of this the presiding judge only halfheartedly sought to maintain order. He prohibited photographs while the court was in session, but allowed pictures to be taken at other times, and even permitted after-session tours of the courthouse. It did not take long for several enterprising photographers to figure out how to hide their cameras, eventually taking pictures and recording some of the testimony of the trial.[41]

This media circus embarrassed many in the legal community by eroding the central ideal of impartiality that gives the judiciary its special status. Soon after the trial the American Bar Association adopted Judicial Canon 35, prohibiting photographic coverage of formal court proceedings.[42]

In the last decade this official hostility toward the mass media has been changing, especially with regard to the use of television in the courtroom. One of the key reasons more courts are now open to television is the 1981 decision reached by the Supreme Court in *Chandler* vs. *Florida*.[43] To the surprise of many, the justices unanimously ruled that television coverage of a court trial did not automatically violate the guarantees of the Sixth Amendment. To be sure, the court did not endorse television coverage, but it left the door open for states to experiment with the coverage of state court proceedings. As of early 1989, about 45 states allowed television cameras to cover some kinds of trials, subject to the restrictions of particular legislatures, courts and judges. Supporters of this new openness to television have generally agreed with mass media lawyer Floyd Abrams that "The more exposure the public has to the judicial process, the better we'll be as a society and the better our courts will become."[44]

In 1987, for example, the New York legislature set up an 18-month period to test the effects of television cameras in the courtroom. The experiment produced a steady flow of television news clips in testimony, most of them taking the form of short "sound bites" from well publicized murder and rape trials.[45] The most extensively covered case was the 1988 Manhattan trial of disbarred attorney Joel Steinberg who was charged with and convicted of beating his adopted six-year-old daughter to death. The case was made even more grisly by the fact that Steinberg's live-in companion, Hedda Nussbaum, was herself both a victim of Steinberg's abuse and a possible accomplice. Both were allegedly in a cocaine-induced fog while young Lisa lay comatose on the floor of their bathroom.[46] Goaded perhaps by extensive coverage of the case in the city's newspapers, CBS's flagship station in New York even went so far as to suspend some of its regular daytime programming to cover portions of the testimony live. Broadcasters explained their unusual attention to the case by noting that its horrors were symptomatic of an epidemic of child abuse. It also did not hurt to note that Steinberg and Nussbaum were professionals living a comfortable middle-class life. Their actions were news in part because they confounded the view that violent crime and flagrant drug abuse are maladies of the poor.

Critics of such television coverage have tended to discount the altruistic motives expressed by broadcasters. Writers covering the Steinberg case noted the tendency of television journalists to go for the most dramatic moments in the long flow of a trial. "Cameras are rapid, out-of-context untruths," noted one print journalist covering the proceedings. "Whatever justice is, it's a culmination of a long, thoughtful process. A process that requires privacy and cool deliberation."[47] Similar charges against television coverage were also made when Cable News Network and other broadcasters carried large portions of the 1984 trial of six men who were accused of the gang rape of a Massachusetts woman in a local bar. ABC's Betsy Aaron even conceded that "these trials have become spectator sport."[48]

In spite of increasingly dramatic coverage of sensationalistic trials in city and state courts, their federal counterparts still refuse to allow cameras. One accidental effect of this differential treatment is the prominence it gives to crimes of abuse and violence as opposed to the kinds of cases often heard in federal courts. Federal courts handle cases when more than one state is involved, or when lines of jurisdiction within a region are unclear. These are typically cases involving "paper" rather than physical crime, for example: bribery, fraud, espionage, obstruction of justice, and civil rights violations. Defendants tend to be corporations and their officers, heads of institutions, or major political officials. The net effect of this unequal access is that public attitudes are more susceptible to the voyeuristic pleasures of trials dealing with physical crimes than the less photogenic instances of lawbreaking that occur in the bureaucratic layers of social institutions. If those who administer the federal courts continue to hold out against the presence of cameras, the effect will probably be to heighten the already pronounced national tendency to view crime in its stereotypical forms: largely in terms of assaults and thefts. While cameras focused on key moments in the Steinberg trial, for example, they could not gain equal access to a corruption trial of three city officials that unfolded at the same time in a federal courtroom across the street.[49]

If this differential between federal and criminal courts remains, the long-term effects could significantly affect the news agenda that exists in any region. One reason is that television transforms almost any subject that it covers; a good case can be made that television involves its audiences at a more superficial level than the print media. As countless observers have pointed out, television content creates a kind of visceral contact between its subjects and viewers that is quite unlike more discursive forms of communication.[50] As we noted in Chapter 6, it personalizes almost any subject it deals with. Because its content always comes through someone, it invites the emotions to actively participate in the mapping of responses and attitudes.

Perhaps Woody Allen provided the perfect metaphor for television's place in the emotional life of individuals in his futuristic comedy, *Sleeper*. In the film a hapless healthfood store owner wakes up from a long coma, only to discover that he is now in a world that has only partly rebuilt itself after a devastating war. One of the few pleasures of this sterile place is the existence in most households of something called an "orb." For anyone who holds it, this silver ball induces a momentary but complete emotional "high," a mixture of instant ecstasy and self-involving arousal. As an important household appliance, the "orb" requires no intellectual effort, only the willingness to let its simple magic work on the brain's pleasure centers.

Allen's silver globe is a good metaphor for television. Whatever its content, television "connects" especially well with feelings and latent attitudes that are not as easily tapped in print. As the old television courtroom drama yields more and more to the courtroom of the broadcast journalist, it seems plausible to expect that future politicians will have to learn to live with a new agenda partly shaped by the highly publicized prosecution of criminal defendants—most of them poor—whose incomprehensible actions replayed and described in a televised trial will offend and anger all over again. Print reports of crime have a way of taking some of the sting out of its uglier details, of reducing a case to a series of less evocative verbal codes. The same code can also be used to condense the sequential nature of a trial. Television under stronger commercial and time constraints usually offers no such buffer against letting one or two moments stand for the whole. It can make outrage an instant pleasure available to everyone, a response that does not have to be confirmed by the disembodied facts of a written narrative. We already know that crime news can create a public fury from which no political institution is immune. The televised court trial may yet bring the process full circle to the sensationalism of the Hauptmann case—to a final denouement that minimizes details and emphasizes rituals of public retribution.

NOTES

1. Alexis de Tocqueville, *Democracy in America* ed. J. P. Mayer, trans. George Lawrence (New York: Doubleday, 1969), p. 99.

2. Quoted from the majority opinion in *National Association for the Advancement of Colored People* vs. *Button*, in Walter F. Murphy and C. Herman Pritchett, *Courts, Judges, and Politics*, 2d Ed. (New York: Random House, 1974), p. 300.

3. Alexander Hamilton, James Madison, and John Hay, *The Federalist Papers*, Paper No. 78 (New York: Mentor, 1961), p. 465.

4. Herbert Jacob, *Justice in America*, 3d Ed. (Boston, MA: Little, Brown, 1978), p. 118.

5. Jerome Frank, *Courts on Trial: Myth and Reality in American Justice* (Princeton, NJ: Princeton University, 1950), pp. 256–57.

6. Articles in popular media such as *Time* magazine reflected the power of a court case to raise larger political considerations, for example: "Is the Womb a Rented Space?," September 22, 1986, p. 36, and "Whose Child Is This?," January 19, 1987, pp. 56–58.

7. Charles Winick and Mariann Pezzella Winick, "Courtroom Drama on Television," *Journal of Communication* (Autumn 1974): 72.

8. Walter B. Jaehing, David H. Weaver, and Frederick Fico, "Reporting Crime and Fearing Crime in Three Communities," *Journal of Communication* (Winter 1981): 88–96.

9. For background on this case see Pete Axthelm and David L. Gonsalez, "A Death Wish Vigilante," *Newsweek*, January 7, 1985, pp. 10–11.

10. Bob Woodward and Scott Armstrong, *The Brethren: Inside the Supreme Court* (New York: Simon and Schuster, 1979), pp. 95–112.

11. David L. Horowitz, *The Courts and Social Policy* (Washington, D.C.: Brookings Institution, 1977), pp. 4–5.

12. See, for example, Stephen Cohen, "It's a Mad Mad Verdict," *The New Republic*, July 12, 1982, pp. 13–18; Lincoln Caplan, "Annals of Law," *The New Yorker*, July 2, 1984, pp. 45–78; and Bruch J. Ennis, "Straight Talk About the Insanity Defense," *The Nation*, July 24, 1982, p. 70–72.

13. For representatives of this debate see Michael S. Moore, *Law and Psychiatry: Rethinking the Relationship* (New York: Cambridge University Press, 1984), and Thomas S. Szasz, *The Myth of Mental Illness* (New York: Hoeber-Harper, 1961).

14. Cyrus R. Vance, "Now, Party Bosses Decide the 'Elections,' " *The New York Times*, May 22, 1988, p. E30.

15. Jacob, pp. 103–4.

16. Thurman Arnold, *The Symbols of Government*, Harbinger Edition (New York: Harcourt, Brace and World, 1962), p. 46.

17. Woodward and Armstrong, pp. 359–60.

18. Stuart Taylor Jr., "Lifting of Secrecy Reveals Earthy Side of Justices," *The New York Times*, February 22, 1988, p. A16.

19. Taylor, p. A16.

20. Jacob, p. 169; Howard Abadinsky, *Crime and Justice: An Introduction* (Chicago, IL: Nelson Hall, 1987), pp. 68–73.

21. Kenneth Culp Davis, *Discretionary Justice: A Preliminary Inquiry*, (Baton Rouge: Louisiana State University, 1969), p. 17.

22. Davis, pp. 195–205.

23. See, for example, Ludovic Kennedy, *The Airman and the Carpenter* (New York: Viking, 1985).

24. George F. Cole, "The Decision to Prosecute," in *American Court Systems*, ed. Sheldon Goldman and Austin Sarat (San Francisco, CA: W. H. Freeman, 1978), p. 100.

25. Murray Waas, "Media Specter," *The New Republic*, September 30, 1985, pp. 13–15.

26. Michael Winerip, "High Profile Prosecutor," *The New York Times Magazine*, June 9, 1985, p. 37.

27. Winerip, p. 50.

28. S. E. Rada, "A Class Action Suit as Public Relations," *Journalism Quarterly* (Spring 1985): 154. See also Frances Kahn Zemans, "Legal Mobilization: The Neglected Role of the Law in the Political System," *American Political Science Review* (September 1983): 690–703.

29. Ralph L. Holsinger, *Media Law* (New York: Random House, 1987), p. 119.

30. Peter J. Boyer, *Who Killed CBS?* (New York: Random House, 1988), pp. 182–92.

31. For an excellent study of these cases see Renata Adler, *Reckless Disregard: Westmoreland v. CBS et al.; Sharon v. Time* (New York: Knopf, 1986).

32. For a broad treatment of this view see Hugh Dalziel Duncan, *Communication and Social Order* (New York: Oxford, 1962), especially Chapters 20 and 21.

33. Joseph R. Gusfield, *Symbolic Crusade: Status Politics and the American Temperance Movement* (Urbana, IL: University of Illinois Press, 1963), p. 22.

34. Murphy and Pritchett, pp. 626–27.

35. Our summary of this case is drawn from Joel Dreyfuss and Charles Lawrence's *The Bakke Case: The Politics of Inequality* (New York: Harcourt Brace Jovanovich, 1979).

36. Dreyfuss and Lawrence, p. 69.

37. Dreyfuss and Lawrence, pp. 158–59.

38. Dreyfuss and Lawrence, p. 233.

39. William L. Rivers, *The Other Government: Power and the Washington Media* (New York: Universe, 1982), pp. 95–96.

40. Don R. Pember, *Mass Media Law*, 4th Ed. (Dubuque, IA: Wm. C. Brown, 1987), pp. 363–98; Alfred Friendly and Ronald L. Goldfarb, *Crime and Publicity* (New York: Vintage, 1968), pp. 9–53.

41. Friendly and Goldfarb, pp. 11–12.

42. Robert L. Hughes, "Chandler v. Florida: Cameras Get Probation in Courtrooms," *Journal of Broadcasting* (Winter 1982): 433.

43. Hughes, pp. 439–43.

44. Patricia Volk, "The Steinberg Trial: Scenes from a Tragedy," *The New York Times Magazine*, January 15, 1989, p. 25.

45. David A. Kaplan, "The Camera Is Proving Its Case in the Courtroom," *The New York Times*, December 18, 1988, p. 37.

46. Volk, pp. 22–25.

47. Volk, pp. 24–25.

48. Quoted in William A. Henry III, "When News Becomes Voyeurism," *Time*, March 26, 1984, p. 64.

49. Kaplan, p. 37.

50. For a well-developed statement of this argument see Joshua Meyrowitz, *No Sense of Place: The Impact of Electronic Media on Social Behavior* (New York: Oxford, 1985), pp. 93–114.

Chapter Ten

Political Communication and the Legislative Function

Congress is a verbal culture. . . . [1]

Nowhere else in Washington does one more keenly sense the cyclical movement of policy and publicity.[2]

The men and women who serve in the nation's legislatures are at the center of the nation's political life. The 535 members of Congress and their counterparts in the states must attempt to master the full range of political arts. In a routine day a senator or representative may meet with ordinary constituents in the morning, lunch with a lobbyist at noontime, question expert witnesses in an afternoon meeting of a House or Senate committee, and receive an evening phone call from a cabinet official soliciting support on a close upcoming vote. In between these events he or she may consult with a dozen colleagues, plan strategy on the introduction of a piece of legislation, tape a radio report to constituents back home, and edit a speech for a busy upcoming weekend of campaigning. In Washington the member's cramped offices a block or so away from the Capitol building often overflow with a staff involved in activities ranging from tracking down a lost Social Security check to preparing remarks for delivery on the House floor against a pending bill. With an eye on reelection, and the demands of an upcoming campaign a thousand miles away, the member of Congress must still concentrate on cherished committee assignments, on the need to "court" interests with powerful friends back home, and the need to work with colleagues who have favors to be repaid.

The prime communication activity of legislators is not speech making, nor single-minded attention to office work, but lobbying. *Lobbying* is the exchange of views—one-on-one or in small groups—for the purpose of winning the support of listeners. Its diverse characteristics are at the heart of many of the points we wish to raise. The member is both the object and practitioner of much of it: to and from colleagues, constituents, business groups, other governmental agencies, and even the press. The process of legislating involves an endless series of exchanges in which support is sought from others or solicited by them.

This chapter examines some of the major relationships and patterns that account for how power is communicated and how legislative support is won. Our primary focus is on the Congress, but much of what we note applies to other deliberative bodies as well. Members of state assemblies and senates, as well as those serving in city councils, share many of the same processes and institutional obligations. Like members of the federal legislature, they must learn to work as one among many, destined to organize their efforts around the ironic fact that their vote is probably the least of their powers. A legislator's power springs most clearly from important committee assignments, on the ability to form blocks of alliances, and from the power to influence other colleagues where a convincing claim can be made on one's own special credibility or expertise.

EXTERNAL AND INTERNAL ROLES

Members of legislatures serve two broad types of audiences in their work. They must maintain visibility in their own districts, while at the same time working to gain access to the power structure of state or federal agencies under the control of the executive branch. To some extent most legislators are forced to give one of the two worlds a higher priority. But neither can be totally ignored.

As with all elective politics, the home constituency provides the member's ticket to the capitol. A member of the House, for example, can never really afford to think of the District of Columbia as "home" in the way it is for other high-level government employees. The congressional district is a source of a large chunk of the member's workload, particularly in the first few terms of service when the skillful exploitation of incumbency can pave the way for easier reelection. For many members of Congress and most state legislatures the local constituency is the prime reason for being in politics. Former House Speaker Thomas "Tip" O'Neill's observation that "all politics is local politics" is a simple reminder that constituents are ignored at a representative's peril. Even if the member's attentions and interests turn increasingly to national issues, he or she will rarely feel secure enough to neglect constituents back home. Everything else a member undertakes depends upon the building and mending of bridges to the local community. The methods for doing this involve the prime tools of electoral politics: speeches, letters, press interviews, questionnaires, and appearances at countless meetings. Combined with the use of at least one district office, these tools serve to nurture sufficient local support.[3]

But if members of legislatures get there by "retailing" their politics to the average voter, success in influencing the political agenda depends upon mastering the considerable structural and rhetorical demands that exist in the capital city. Constituents may be one important audience to address, but members who are potential allies and opponents are also vital.

LEGISLATIVE AND COMMUNICATION FUNCTIONS

Legislatures have two primary functions: to provide oversight in the administration of the government and to pass laws. These two objectives are naturally related. The *oversight* of governmental operations—which today takes in nearly every facet of American life—leads to the revision, repeal, or enactment of laws designed to remedy evident problems. The "textbook" model for such processes is fairly straightforward. Various standing committees regularly (and sometimes with great fanfare) review problems and issues of public concern and the agencies responsible for the enforcement of relevant laws. Such hearings frequently serve an "educational" function, providing the committee or its leadership with the opportunity to orchestrate public opinion as a prerequisite to the introduction of new legislation. On many occasions oversight of particular agencies consumes the attention of the entire body. The resulting publicity may be used to create public pressure for change, as when the Republican Governor and his allies in the Pennsylvania legislature intensified public indignation over the failures of the state-owned liquor stores regulated by an unresponsive Liquor Control Board. At other times oversight may entail the more sensitive consideration of an alleged breach of ethics by a member, such as a 1988 inquiry into the questionable financial dealings raised against House Speaker Jim Wright.

The legislative function is equally complex, although the basic procedures and traditions are well-known. Bills are introduced by members, usually because they have a special interest in it, or because they serve the needs of a prime constituency. In what is usually a proposal's first critical test, it is routed to an appropriate committee according to what are sometimes unclear jurisdictional lines. The committee holds hearings, "marks up" the bill, votes it out to the floor, votes it down, or simply lets it die (as most do). A bill reported out of committee is considered by the whole body, usually reshaped by key amendments, and voted on. It, or one similar to it, is considered by the other house, and likewise voted on. Then differences between the two passed versions are then worked out in a conference committee composed of members from both the lower and upper houses.

Few bills actually move through the Congress in such a straight sequence. Most are tabled, defeated, and amended in what is often a multiyear process. Final passage often comes only after repeated attempts over several sessions. When a bill is passed, it is usually far different from what its initial sponsors had in mind. Its adoption occurs only after a good deal of private bargaining and carefully negotiated compromises between party leaders on key amendments. In all of this process a vigorous floor debate, airing the great issues of the question before well attended sessions, may have never occurred. But that is not to say that the legislative cycle did not involve a good deal of debate and discussion. The most widely reported summaries of the merits of bills are constructed by members of the press out of the variegated fabric of press statements made by interested parties during hearings in committees, and from presession publicity generated of lobbyists and members with financial or ideological stakes in their approval.

What emerges as central to the heart of the modern legislature is the vital role played by the standing committees and subcommittees. Most of the 15,000 or so bills that are introduced in a session of Congress, for example, will never be passed, but some may still get an initial hearing in a committee concerned with hunger, airline safety, industry regulation, water distribution, taxes, drug abuse, medical insurance, banking policy, and other substantive issues. Both Houses must approve all bills that become law, although measures that raise funds must originate in the House, and through a series of powerful committees. The task of passing on high level non-Civil Service presidential appointees goes to committees in the Senate.

Committees are a primary source of rhetorical and legislative work. Chosen to reflect party strengths, and promoted in accordance to overall seniority, House and Senate members generally hope to serve on several major committees and subcommittees, using their gatekeeping role as centerpieces of their own legislative activity and bargaining clout. The specialization that a member develops is usually based on committee work and the knowledge that comes with years of research on its issues. The Senate, for example, has 18 regular standing committees, with almost 150 subcommittees. The number is similar for the House. As a member of the Senate's prestigious Foreign Relations committee, or the House's Appropriations committee, a member gets an opportunity to become one of a limited number of voices in the discussion of vital national interests.[4]

THE BUILT-IN DILEMMAS OF LEGISLATIVE COMMUNICATION

From a communications standpoint legislatures present their occupants with a series of troubling contradictions. In comparison to the President, for example, members of Congress are—at best—cast into the role of subordinate players. Except for a few select leaders in the House and Senate—notably the speaker, the minority leader, and a handful of committee leaders in the House and Senate—the individual's personal political clout is severely limited. Moreover, the limits that apply to a member of Congress are even more evident for legislators in Lansing, Atlanta, Sacramento, or Albany. Legislators retain an important place in the state or district constituency, but their ability to be a voice on state and national issues ranges from minimal to nonexistent. There are two primary reasons for this. One is simply a result of the sheer numbers involved. Any topic of general public interest creates heavy competition for the chance to be heard by a wider public. In the search for an elusive (and illusory) ''Senate opinion'' or ''the feeling of the House,'' a key leader may be sought out by members of the news media. However, most are left to seek attention for their views in the local press within their districts. Even at the federal level representatives complain that they are overlooked, sometimes receiving practically no requests for comments or quotes from even the mass media in their states or districts.[5] A publicity blackout can even include high-ranking Senate leaders, many of whom have expressed frustration at having to engage in sensational stunts to get an opportunity to express a view.[6]

The problem is that the member usually can claim no permanent and reliable connection with any one institution as the basis for establishing credibility. Public communication is inherently viewed as a personal act, even when the communication itself flows from organizational needs. A corporate president speaks for the corporation; a union leader speaks for the membership. Even the President of the United States is accepted in the essentially untenable role of speaking for the nation as whole, in spite of the fact that the diversity of the population makes a national consensus highly unlikely. Such reductions are psychologically satisfying because they assign human motives to complex organizations. They give unseen and frequently incomprehensible institutions a personal voice and a human dimension. But who does the member of legislature represent? What formal and official structure is symbolized in his or her communication? There is no simple answer because legislative roles are so varied, and because deliberative bodies were set up to make representation intentionally diffuse. A legislator may be viewed as a mouthpiece for a party, for a set of interests, or for a home constituency. Every new legislative and oversight demand subtly shifts the realignment of these and other alliances. The party that is abandoned on one vote may be defined on another. A bipartisan coalition urging a particular tax package in one session may be hopelessly split when the issue arises again in the next session. And "speaking up" for the district plays well at home, but often seems like special pleading to the rest of a state or nation.

The price the member pays for being a part of an institution with ever-shifting coalitions is heavy. The fickle nature of these alliances cuts against the grain of news gatherers conditioned to regard advocates as carriers of one point of view in a narrative. By contrast, the organized defenses of governors or presidents seem hierarchical and orderly. An administration attempts to appear unified, an impossibility in the organized anarchy of a diverse legislative body. As several recent observers of press coverage of Congress note, "Searching for a single voice beggars the media. Covering all the conflicting subcommittees' and committees' mark up sessions, overlapping hearings, the floor deliberations, is an expensive proposition."[7] Most do not do it, or simply graft a reference to congressional debate onto a report centered on the more personalized executive.

A second dilemma is that party influence in Congress has declined in spite of the fact that congressional politics seem to require some sense of party discipline. There is a general but unmistakable trend—at least since World War II—away from the member's sense of party identification. In contrast to F.D.R.'s assured party support in the first two terms of the New Deal, for example, Jimmy Carter found that neither the Democratic leadership nor individual Democratic members could be lined up and counted on for a consistent "party-based" legislative approach. He had problems with his programs, in spite of the fact that his party had a sizable majority in the House. As Carter noted in his memoirs, he began to "commiserate" with the Speaker Tip O'Neill "about the almost anarchic independence of the House."[8]

In the age of the well bankrolled congressional candidate, the professional political consultant, and the heavy dependency on television campaigning, there is less and less dependency on party organization. Members are not inclined to wait to be selected as official advocates for a point of view representing the party or the caucus. They are more apt to take advantage of communications opportunities on an ad-hoc basis. "People get elected right off the street," lamented a Massachusetts congressman. "They don't have any political loyalties or i.o.u.'s."[9] The tendency is to view one's own political fortunes less in terms of the general successes of the party, and more in terms of the more ambitious objective of making a personal reputation that will sustain a career. Among some members in the House there is a sense of near desperation to find a way to make a lasting imprint on the voter's consciousness in order to win re-election. The fluid politics brought on by an independence of party places increased emphasis on the member's ability to communicate his own abilities. In 1978, for example, even though the Democrats had a two to one edge over Republicans, the leadership lost several key votes because of defections by many primarily young "non-team" players. "At one time you'd blow a whistle and say this is what the party wants and the members would line up and say, Yes sir . . . ," a Democratic whip recalled. "Today they get elected on Monday and they are giving a [floor] speech on Tuesday."[10]

An additional problem facing all legislatures is that their structure usually casts their members into a reactive role. In the popular aphorism, the President proposes, and the Congress disposes. Presidential leadership in the setting of major legislative objectives became commonplace during the New Deal,[11] and governors as its counterparts in many states are the sources of most initiatives. This arrangement naturally contributes to the general ambivalence Americans feel when questioned on the effectiveness of legislatures, especially Congress.[12] Unless it contains a high degree of support, a reactive response in politics is almost automatically perceived in negative terms. The Presidency provides an endless range of opportunities for its occupants to take bold initiatives, propose necessary actions, and generate what appear to be innovative new forms of legislation. A member of congress may be equally bold in proposing solutions, but the member's efforts will occur in what is, comparatively speaking, an information vacuum. Ultimately, he or she is left with the necessity to deal with the initiatives of the White House. This fact itself does not represent a flaw in the organization of deliberative bodies. After all, parliamentary democracies are supposed to examine and weigh the consequences of proposed legislation. But three factors work against earning the sympathy of the electorate in a reactive communication role.

One is that Americans generally expect that legislatures will cooperate with strong executives, that members will not use partisan differences as bases from which to fight a powerful and popular leader.[13] Presidents exploit this presumption repeatedly, as Truman did in his famous diatribes against the "do nothing" Congress in 1948. Another is that legislators are handicapped generally by the fact that they must be more cautious and more deferential to an executive than the executive must be to them. The potent symbolism behind a single head of state works against those who disregard its inherent appeals for unity. Woodrow Wilson's analysis of this aspect of the Presidency still seems valid today:

His is the only national voice in affairs. Let him once win the admiration and confidence of the country, and no other single force can withstand him, no combination of forces will easily overpower him. . . . If he rightly interpret the national thought and boldly insist upon it, he is irresistible; and the country never feels the zest of action so much as when its President is of such insight and caliber. Its instinct is for unified action, and it craves a single leader. It is for this reason that we often prefer to choose a man rather than a party.[14]

Perhaps the most interesting communication problem facing the legislator is that reactive and frequently critical communication often has the effect of casting its source as a pessimist, if not villain. All things being equal, it is easier to take an affirmative position than to hold back and deny the affirmations of someone else. It is more socially useful to seem to be reaching for new solutions and new ideas than to be attacking the proposals of others. To be sure, presidents and governors may also play the role of dissenter. The key difference is that they tend to exercise this power privately. Their surrogates within the legislature are sometimes successful in tabling or killing a bill proposed by others, all without the need to make a sharp public attack on it. In contrast, the public criticism of an executive's proposal may be the only significant way a representative can deal with an unwanted piece of legislation. A member may rightly judge that since his vote will make little difference, his criticism may be the only chance he has to have some impact. One of the few paths into the heady world of the op-ed page or 30 seconds of television news time may come with a concerted attack on the executive Goliath. The audacity of a far weaker legislative David may be enough to give the attack a certain notoriety. But part of the skill of a president or governor is to maintain the grace and equilibrium that makes would-be attackers appear all the more insensitive. In recent years the ability to show such grace under pressure has not been limited to the Teflon-coated Ronald Reagan, but a number of other executives ranging from New Jersey's Tom Kean to New York's Mario Cuomo. Such executive skill forces the legislative attacker to weigh the political and public relations costs of breaking with a popular executive on aspects of that leader's program.

Finally, it should be noted that some facets of legislative life are simply out of fashion today. So much of what goes on in legislative deliberation seems either troublesome to the average citizen or at odds with the needs of modern technology. Except for private constituency service, there is no general public admiration for legislative craftsmanship or coalition building: for the ability to write and modify legislation, or for the mastery of the politics of interparty and intraparty factions. Legislative skill is unlikely to be portrayed favorably in most forms of popular journalism. The reasons are many, but the most important may be that personalized Presidency has also personalized most of the rest of our politics. Of all the branches of government the executive is most easily adapted to the superficialities of television news. It is an office occupied by a personality with at least generally understood managerial responsibilities. The Congress, in contrast, is more a place of arguments, political negotiation, and compromise. Its institutionalized conflict produces the troubling sensation that political actions are not unanimous, and are often based on imperfect motives and incomplete facts. It takes little insight to realize that the mediation that represents the essential work of lawmaking will never fire the ordinary imagination in the same way that a "visionary" executive does. The latter dramatizes the affirmation of universal goals; the former carries on the essential task of finding pragmatic bases for making actual decisions.

CONGRESSIONAL ANONYMITY AND STARDOM: HIGH AND LOW PROFILES

With notable exceptions in populous states such as New York and California, state legislators who are not party leaders have little hope of gaining widespread public recognition for their work. Members of Congress, however, usually begin their careers with higher expectations of having a voice in national affairs. By the standards of state legislators, members of Congress have tremendous opportunities to influence public discussion on a number of issues. They have free mailing privileges, access to radio and television studios paid for in large part by the taxpaying public, sufficient staff research to explore the intricacies of most issues, a wealth of standing invitations to speak, and the opportunity to cross-examine the leaders of countless agencies, businesses, and institutions doing business with or for the government. In addition to these considerable advantages, members of the more exclusive Senate have even greater access to the national press, and to the prestigious forums (e.g., national news shows, and the nation's best op-ed pages) which reach millions at a time.

But even serving in the highest legislature has its limitations, as Harry McPherson recalls on one occasion when he was sitting next to Vice-President Lyndon Johnson, who was responsible for presiding over the Senate. The Kennedy administration was encountering heavy opposition to its legislative program, and Johnson remained grim even as two senators rose to speak in behalf of an administration proposal. "I asked Johnson what was wrong. 'We've got all the minnows,' he said. 'We've got none of the whales.' "[15] The former majority leader (himself a "whale") was characteristically direct in his constant effort to locate the centers of political power. Not all members of Congress are equal.

Senators get far more attention from the White House, the press, and each other than members of the House. Many chair important committees; others have the persuasive skills and knowledge of parliamentary procedure to salvage or block bills. For Johnson the "whales" were those in a position to make things happen. They were able to get votes. For us these people represent a special and small substratum in both Houses, because their communication activities are most likely to yield results affecting the course of legislation, and perhaps the fortunes of a president in need of solid legislative accomplishments. Leaving Johnson's prosaic metaphor, we prefer to identify legislative power in parallel parliamentary terms: "backbenchers" and "national" members of Congress.

Every parliamentary democracy can be thought of as having two general types of members. *Backbenchers* are generally loyal to their party, but to various degrees removed from the government and the center of parliamentary power. Their votes are sought by the legislative leadership and usually won. They are rarely consulted by the national press, and frequently do not wish to be. They enjoy the security and prestige of their surroundings, and are usually proud of the "case-work" load they carry on behalf of their local constituents. Most members of Congress and state deliberative bodies fall into this general category. Shunted to the less important committees, infrequently consulted by the leadership, and content to let others play the trump cards in the game of legislative politics, these members seek to pursue limited personal or political objectives. Primary concerns may include attracting home-based media attention for their work, and concentration on how votes will affect their districts. In Britain and other "party government" systems, their loyalty to government "front-benchers" is rarely in doubt. In the United States, as we have seen, the member is more independent. Essential priorities include service to the district and state, and deep interest in federal policy that directly affects that home base. If Washington reminds them of their limits, the local constituency offers a sense of accomplishment. As one member of the House told Richard Fenno,

My lack of confidence is still a pressure which brings me home. This is my political base. Washington is not my political base. I feel I have to come home to get nourished, to see for myself what's going on. It's my security blanket—coming home.[16]

Backbenchers get little attention from the national press. In a town where egos are measured in column inches of newsprint, prestige is closely tied to the importance the press attaches to your career. There are exceptions, of course. Members of Congress in "safe" seats may actually welcome the freedom that a low profile gives them. Or they may seek only to secure coverage in local media within their home district. But for many others the lack of mass media interest translates into the lack of power, or into potential reelection problems. One recent study of House members, for example, indicated that about 75 percent felt that the national mass media—the television networks, newsweeklies, and "prestige" press—paid no attention to them.[17] As Michael Robinson has noted,

"The fact is the nationals ignore members and pick on the institution—unless there is a scandal to cover."[18]

The pattern is only slightly different for the congressman's local home district media. Many papers are willing to run brief stories based on a steady flow of press releases for a Congress member's Washington offices. But the reporting is usually second-rate, with many papers and broadcasters contributing little time or thought to the issues and questions that may be intensely important to the legislator. As a new member of the House once noted,

The role of the newspaper is usually passive, and occasionally hostile. Their news staffs are overworked and understaffed, have very limited budgets, and receive a never-ending flood of materials from all sides. The congressman gets his due along with a thousand other competing interests. . . .

Newspapers at home usually see no need to check with their congressmen on facts or on his position. The number of times that I have been contacted by *any* newspaper in my district in two years can be counted on the fingers of one hand.[19]

A far smaller group in both Houses can be truly called "national" front-benchers. They differ from backbenchers in that they usually have an opinion-leading function both within the chamber in which they serve, and to special interest constituents well beyond the borders of their own state or district. Publicity powers sufficient to influence national debate on a question are sometimes within their grasp.

The political muscle of the national figure is usually based on a formal party or leadership role: as a chairman, subcommittee chairman, whip, minority or majority leader. Committee leadership especially provides at least grudging respect. In the recent history of the Senate, for example, the names of Hubert Humphrey, Russell Long, Lyndon Johnson, Howard Baker, Robert Byrd, and Robert Dole have become synonymous with effective leadership. Johnson proved to be a master negotiator in the late 1950s as Senate minority leader, managing an uneasy coalition of southern and liberal Democrats, while maintaining good relations with the popular Eisenhower regime at the other end of Pennsylvania Avenue.[20] As chairman of the powerful Senate Finance Committee, Russell Long controlled an enormous range of taxing and revenue-raising proposals with the equal respect of Republicans and members of his own party.[21] And as majority leader, Republican Robert Dole salvaged a number of crucial Reagan administration programs, including its controversial support for the Contra rebels attempting to overthrow the government of Nicaragua. Their counterparts in the House—reflected in the recent leadership of Robert Michael, Dan Rostenkowski, and Jim Wright—have played an equally vital role in forming well publicized positions with or in opposition to the President.

In addition, a smaller number of House and Senate members are able to stake out prominent positions for themselves by virtue of externally derived sources of power. A small number of members have always been able to build on a previous reputation, or a special relationship with a national clientele. They command rhetorical if not formal power. Aside from his considerable talents as a senator, for example, Edward Kennedy has carefully nurtured the Kennedy *ethos* to develop his role as a major spokesman for the "liberal" political agenda. Oregon's Wayne Morse did much the same in the late 1960s, using his sharp tongue and celebrated independence as a basis for challenging the power of several presidents. During the Reagan Presidency the ideologically conservative Jesse Helms has done much the same. By vocally criticizing Reagan for lapses in completing the conservative agenda on school prayer, abortion, and federally mandated school desegregation plans, Helms achieved a visibility and importance that made him a political force equal to that of entire committees.[22]

VITAL CHANNELS: COMMUNICATION NETWORKS IN CONGRESS

Two major dimensions shape our understanding of congressional communication. One involves the elaborate informational networks *within* the Congress, and between it and the executive agencies beyond Capitol Hill. The other involves channels of communication that radiate out to the mass media and constituencies beyond the beltway. The former might be symbolized by the private lobbying that might take place in a Senate cloakroom between a bill's sponsor and an undecided colleague. The latter is typified by the more familiar responses given to the press by the House speaker near the White House gate after a bargaining session with the President. In all, we think that there are four primary routes of private communication within the structure of official and unofficial Washington, and four public channels that are intended to reach the general population.

Internal Channels

Member to Staff

Packed into a few rooms in one of the enormous office buildings that ring the Capitol, the congressional staff labors to make a member of the House or Senate not just a representative, but a source of local or even national power. There really is no "typical" staff. Every office reflects the priorities of its member. Some put portions of their personal staff allowances into nonpersonal items, such as computing. Others in the House finds ways to go over the 22-person ceiling by utilizing part-time or "intern" help. In 1986, for example, Representative Patricia Schroeder used her $296,010 office allocation to hire over 20 employees to work in her offices in Washington and Denver.[23] Senators may have as many as 70 employees working in their offices.

Personal staffs are occupied with office functions ranging from the routine of typing letters to far more specialized work such as preparing and researching legislation. There can be no doubt about the importance of the staffs. They perform the vital functions of communicating with the rest of the bureaucracy within the Congress (especially the staff of particular committees), and the executive branch agencies spread out over the rest of Washington. Like the representative's staff, the "senator's personal office staffs are important" notes Donald R. Matthews. Indeed, "on routine matters they *are* the senators."[24]

The most common division that is made in the office is between the political side of congressional business, and the legislative side. Every member has several counterparts to the "AA," or administrative assistant, and the "LA," or legislative assistant. At various times a number of people may take up part of the work in these two broad areas. The first is responsible for the enormous logistical job of making the office responsive to the routine obligations of answering constituent requests and questions, perhaps 2000 to 5000 per week. They also schedule the member's time, coordinate the member's efforts in various committees, and run the office.[25] A legislative assistant is involved in helping a member deal with the hundreds of bills that are introduced. The job requires research on upcoming votes, or on bills in one of the member's committees.[26]

Most constituent requests, correspondence, scheduling, and office management functions do not require close consultation with a representative or senator. In classifying staff roles, Harrison Fox and Susan Hammond have found many duties that are essentially self-contained office tasks, for example: "writing letters of congratulations," "handling opinion ballots," "mailing government publications," and "visiting with constituents in Washington." A much smaller range of responsibilities requires close interpersonal communication with the member. These tasks include direct support of the member in a public setting—for example, accompanying a member in committee—or preparation of important messages that require the full knowledge and understanding of the member: "writing floor remarks and speeches," "bill drafting," and "writing magazine articles, books, and speeches other than those for Senate floor use."[27] Other tasks may be far more mundane, such as making sure the member's nameplate is removed when he leaves a highly publicized hearing, just in case cameras happen to dwell on the empty seat.

The member's relationship with the staff can vary greatly. Some in the House and Senate prefer to work alone without close ties to those in their offices. Others are just the reverse, looking to the staff for good intelligence, thoughtful advice, and emotional support. Theodore Sorensen's recollection of the Senate office of John F. Kennedy is probably representative of the middle ground.

The Senator was not always satisfied with his staff's work. He disliked complainers and procrastinators. He wanted the thought and both sides of an argument, but he had a special distaste for those who brought him only bad news. . . .

The employer, like the man, was patient with his employees, but impatient with any inefficiency or incompetence. He was always accessible and ready to listen, quick to grasp a recommendation and disappointed only when there was none. He never raised his voice when expressing disagreement with our work. Indeed, he was rarely and then only briefly angry at any staff member.[28]

As Fox and Hammond note, staffs "may have positive, neutral, negative, symmetrical or asymmetrical relationships with their boss."[29] There are few guidelines. The only apparent certainty is that there is little room for independence from the thinking and actions of the member. Individuals of course do have private attitudes that differ markedly from the member's. But staffers must learn that their relationships with the member are governed by an unvarying hierarchical relationship.

At the state level administrative support is far more limited and varied. The legislators of some western states, such as Oregon and South Dakota, are in session only a few months a year, making their members truly "citizen politicians" without much professional support. New Hampshire is unique in a different way; the modest area of the state belies the fact that its lower house is enormous. Its 400 members are almost enough to represent nearly every neighborhood in the state. With these arrangements staff members tend to be shared by many members. In more populous states legislators are provided with staff who perform many of the same tasks assigned to employees working in Congress. For example, larger states often allow the generous use of funds to hire public relations professionals that work for both of the major parties in the upper and lower houses. Pennsylvania employs staffs in four separate legislative press offices, helping to produce video and audio tapes for legislators to distribute to their home districts.[30]

Member to Member

A brief *Congressional Quarterly* description of some casual moments surrounding a routine budget vote readily points to the key nature of colleague-to-colleague contact in the legislative process. The occasion was a budget vote in the Ninety-fifth Congress. The ostensible issue was whether an amendment cutting money from the President's budget would be approved. The hidden issue was the prestige of the Democratic leadership in the House, and the Democratic President. The majority party had a two-to-one edge on the Republicans.

Freshman Rep. Leon E. Panetta, D-Calif., was having a tough time finishing his phone call in the House cloakroom.

First, Majority Leader Jim Wright, D-Texas, interrupted. Wright was followed by several other Democrats, who took turns breaking in. Then a page brought Panetta a note saying Speaker Thomas P. O'Neill Jr., D-Mass., wanted to see him. Panetta found no escape on the House floor. As he left the cloakroom and strode down the aisle into the crowded chamber, Jim Mooney, chief aide to Majority Whip John Brademas, D-Ind., spotted him. Mooney grabbed Norman Y. Mineta, D-Calif., and steered him toward Panetta.

"Can you give us a vote on this?" asked Mineta. Panetta said no, resisting his friend's plea to change the vote he had just cast in favor of an amendment by Joseph L. Fisher, D-Va., to cut about $7 billion from the first fiscal 1979 budget resolution.

Undaunted by the rejection, Mineta turned to court other Democrats who had voted for the amendment—and against the wishes of the Democratic leadership.

Meanwhile, Wright wove his way through a crowd of younger members in the well of the chamber, urging them to switch their votes by signing little red cards stacked on a nearby table. O'Neill and Bradamas stalked up the aisle, looking like hunters in search of prey. They, too, sought vote switchers. By the time the leaders stopped stalking—10 minutes after the House scoreboard showed that time had elapsed on the roll-call vote— 16 Democrats had trooped down to the well to change their votes. The amendment, which had been a sure winner when time ran out, instead was defeated, 195–203.[31]

It is probably not an accident that all of the renovations of the Capitol building have left unchanged the many private and quiet places out of public view. A deliberative body always functions with both private and public levels of discussion. No talk of "opening up" the legislative process will ever reduce the need for private talk among colleagues. The House and Senate floors are theatres to *demonstrate* commitment. The committees and cloakrooms are backstage places to bargain for it. The vital process of educating oneself in preparation for a vote or a floor debate must go on in the many anterooms, offices, and meeting rooms off of the floor. Only private discussion can create an atmosphere that preserves the possibility of a personal change of heart. Some 60 unmarked "hideaway" offices are scattered within the labyrinth of the Capitol[32]—off limits to the press and the public, but vital to the private communication that oils the public legislative machinery.

Communication among colleagues in the Senate and House has many permutations. The member sponsoring legislation may spend an enormous amount of time seeking cosponsors, votes from colleagues to get his bill out of committee, or a supporting vote in an upcoming close vote. Caucuses, committee hearings, votes on highly contested bills, disputes over legislative or party leadership, are but a few of the events that spur the member to consult with colleagues. The importance of such contact is obvious. A member of the House may have to "vote his district" on a bill, meaning he must represent what have perhaps been their vocal interests. He may also vote out of a deep conviction or a well defined principle. A bill may correspond with his sense of justice, or violate it. But on many floor votes the attitudes of colleagues matter most. Even a member that has been heavily lobbied by a variety of special interests may finally satisfy himself by seeking out the opinions of colleagues. "I try, and I think most other senators try to read the report on a bill before voting on it," notes a member, "but I must admit that I have voted on many hundreds of bills solely on the basis of what other senators told me about them."[33] Another longtime observer of the Congress comes to the same conclusion about the importance of other members' opinions:

[D]espite all the high-powered lobbyists, the constituent mail, and the briefs, brochures, and broadsides that might engulf Capitol Hill over a particularly controversial issue, the most important influence on an undecided Senator is usually the personal appeal of another Senator. . . . Most members of the U.S. Senate are more likely to listen to their peers on the inside than to an outsider, no matter how imposing his or her credentials.[34]

Members come to identify strongly with the institution. Most share the same general patriotic feelings toward the Senate or House, and frequently against its loudest critics. It is not unusual for members to feel closer to colleagues in the other party "across the aisle" than to their own party leader downtown at the White House.

This emphasizes on cooperation has strong task-oriented objectives. Most obviously, in an institution that requires *formal* opposition, interpersonal contact reduces disruptive conflict. There are, in Donald Matthew's phrase, "folkways" that require courtesy and tolerance for conflict.[35] The gulf that separates opposing forces on a pending bill often does not extend to future debates because there is an obvious need to keep the door open for future alignments. A willingness to talk, to bargain, serves to remind all participants that the public posturing common to debate on the House or Senate floor is to be viewed as policy-centered, not as an extension of destructive personal animosities.

Additionally, there is obviously a strategic need to build as broad a network of allies and contacts within the House or Senate as is possible (though rarely between them). The rule of reciprocity is one of the oldest and best known of political life. There may be simple vote swapping (for example, support for a public works project in Alabama in exchange for a new military installation in Georgia). But it is more likely that the member simply seeks to keep as many lines of communication open to colleagues as possible. A reservoir of goodwill can be tapped as needed.

There are two rhetorical/interpersonal dimensions of legislative life that require a fully developed network of interpersonal contacts beyond the glare of publicity. The most important is that private discussion provides an opportunity to use a range of appeals and arguments on a reticent colleague that would be taboo if spoken in a public forum. An advocate seeking a convert can explain his or her own reservations on a bill—caveats that perhaps could never be expressed in the defensive environment of the House or Senate floor. In private, it is also possible for a hold-out to explain his reasons without needlessly alienating other members, or to express regrets for having to "vote my district." It is evident that in the combative environment of debate total candor is impossible.

A second vital element in this private form of communication is the fact that comments made to one other person are far easier to alter than those made on the official record. Members who are ambivalent on a particular piece of legislation are not likely to give speeches, thereby revealing their own uncertainties. They are likely instead to seek the private counsel of members whose judgment they respect, usually retaining the option to switch positions if pressures from any one of a wide range of sources become significant. For example, countless acquaintances of Lyndon Johnson have contrasted the formal and somewhat awkward public persuasion of the Senate majority leader with their memory of the private master tactician. The notorious "Johnson treatment" was far more aggressive and sensitive to the political needs of the victim than was ever apparent from the "public" Johnson. In public he found most of his ideals in the rhetorical images of the New Deal. In private, he was far more inclined to strike all of the notes of personal interest to mobilize a legislative hold-out. Performing the role he played best, as manager of the Senate in a competitive but cooperative environment, Johnson knew how to utilize persuasive arguments that could never be touched in a Senate speech, and how to reassure another senator looking for some indication that a vote of support would not go unforgotten.[36]

Member to Reporter: "On Background"

In its idealized form, the Washington press is viewed as the "advocate of the people." It is often said that the journalistically proper relationship between a politician and a reporter is a courteous but distinctly wary form of mutual respect. And it often is. But one of the results of the "professionalizing" of political reporting, and of the increased dependency of congressmen on favorable press for reelection, is what can become a special interdependence that is cultivated by both newsmakers and newsgatherers. Journalist and professor William Rivers has called this a "sweetheart" relationship.[37] More bluntly, television commentator Harry Reasoner has characterized these ties as "incestuous."[38]

Reporters representing regional papers may seem to establish friendships with members of Congress from the same geographical area. Such contacts help justify the considerable expense of placing a reporter in Washington on a full-time basis. The arrangement gives the paper the best of both worlds: it has an additional source of information, but it also has the option of presenting it from a local angle. The "background" condition placed on information given to a reporter means only that he or she cannot specifically associate what has been gathered with a particular member. But it still allows the information to be used in writing a story.

The willingness of a member to give a reporter a candid "not for attribution" look at an unfolding issue has the twin effects of giving the reporter a special insider status, and providing the politician a chance to influence favorably the way a story is reported. The journalist gains new information that can give his reporting a special perspective. The politician, of course, gains a national forum that translates into an opportunity to alter public opinion. As Donald Matthews has noted with regard to the Senate,

Both senators and reporters have it in their power to build each other up. A senator, by giving a reporter preferential treatment, can enhance [a] newsman's prestige among the press corps, his standing with his employers and readers, and his earning power. A reporter, by giving the senator a good break, can contribute substantially to the success of the senator's career. This kind of "back scratching" is far more profitable to both sides than conflict.[39]

These mutual benefits are so attractive that, as Rivers notes, "the news business in Washington has developed an exceedingly high percentage of 'ins'—and far from enough 'outs.' "[40]

Stewart Alsop recalls a fairly typical example of this pattern in off the record meetings held between members of the press and Senator Lyndon Johnson:

In his Senate days, most of the reporters who covered Johnson were personal friends or at least friendly acquaintances. Most of them liked him, and even those who didn't were heavily dependent on the Majority Leader for news. . . . Several days a week, after the Senate adjourned, eight or ten reporters would crowd into Johnson's small, impressive, Brumidi-decorated office suite off the Senate floor, or later, into the vast unimpressive Texas-decorated office suite off the Senate floor, known as "the Taj Mahal," which Johnson co-opted for himself in 1959. Drink would flow generously, courtesy of the Majority Leader . . . amidst much talk, almost all of it Johnson's.[41]

"Internal" communication between members of the press and members of Congress also serves as a kind of mutual protection. The politician views his friendship with an influential columnist or correspondent as a possible guarantee against an unwelcome story. The journalist gains the assurance that an emerging story that should have been seen will not show up first in a competitor's paper. The information that flows between them includes an enormous amount of intelligence gathered in two parallel information networks. The press, with sources in many executive agencies, for example, may be in a position to pass on intelligence that a member's informal congressional network might miss. Conversely, a member with knowledge about a pending deal between two factions within the Congress may be able to fill in details vital to a journalist's efforts to piece together an elaborate political puzzle.

There is also a tangible lure to the power that is implicit in the friendship that a reporter may be able to "cultivate" with a key figure on Capitol Hill. The urge to be more than a spectator to the shaping of national laws would appeal to almost anyone's vanity. Reporters are not immune from the desire to influence the course of American legislative life, even in some small way. Serving as a source of information, as an ad hoc adviser, or even as a supporter of legislation under consideration, has its psychological rewards. Columnist Drew Pearson, for example, took an active interest in the Senate leadership of Lyndon Johnson, and the presidential candidacy of Hubert Humphrey in 1959. Jack Anderson was likewise predisposed to the candidacy of Senator John Kennedy.[42] And Bert Andrews, a reporter for the *New York Herald Tribune*, won a Pulitzer Prize in part for his work with Senator Richard Nixon in prosecuting alleged spying by Alger Hiss.[43]

Member to Lobbyists and Agency Officials

Members of Congress create many communication liaisons for convenience. Two channels of special interest are those that flow from Capitol Hill to various agencies in the executive branch, and from various special interests to the member. In the first case the flow is primarily from the Hill to the agencies, as when a member asks for help from the Veterans Administration in solving a constituent's specific problems. In the latter case the arrows are reversed; it is obviously the lobbyist who seeks support from the member. But as we shall see, even in exchanges with lobbyists, the member gains something in the transaction.

The men and women in any legislature obviously have a profound interest in the work of bureaucrats controlled by the executive. Ranging from housing, transportation, education, land management, and hundreds of similar concerns, the thick blanket of agencies spread over Washington and various state capitals collectively have the power to affect their political fortunes. The agencies are responsible for executing policy, and are subject to the oversight of legislatures and their specialist committees. These structural ties create an obvious need for executive-legislative communication.

Taken as a whole, members of federal agencies are responsive to the Congress because the legislative branch has a power that at times even surpasses that of the White House. Congress controls spending, and thus can exert enormous control over an agency. A department that is unresponsive to requests for help from a senior senator, for example, may find that it has lost a crucial ally on future appropriations or tax issue votes. For this reason most executive departments have a legislative liaison staff oriented to giving quick responses to members in need of information or help. The data that is supplied may include straightforward help in behalf of a member's constituent, or information that satisfies his or her own legislative research or committee needs. Many such staffers are former congressional employees, and are chosen for their ability to forge alliances with members and their staffs on Capitol Hill.[44]

From the agency's perspective the inherent pluralism of the Congress makes the fence-mending process difficult. Keeping a key member of Congress happy can tax the political skill of even a veteran administrator. Joseph Califano recalls the conflicting signals he got from the Congress as the cabinet official responsible for enforcing some of the nation's civil rights laws:

The Congress has too often been hypocritical—there is no more kind or accurate word for it—in proclaiming glorious rights through authorizing statutes, and subverting the ability to enforce those rights through the appropriation process. . . . I cannot remember a call from a member of Congress to set up civil rights enforcement action in the racial area; I recall scores of pleas to slow down or blunt such enforcement.[45]

Officials in state agencies often complain of the same difficulties. Bills passed by legislatures promising to produce better housing, better health care, and similar improvements are often not adequately funded, leaving the agencies with the impossible task of implementing popular legislative initiatives without enough money. The need to come up with "paper solutions" to the implementation of impressive legislative schemes is compounded by the fact that legislatures usually have control over the annual appropriations made available to an agency.[46] The burden is obviously placed on the hard-pressed agency officials to keep channels of communication open if they want to keep whatever funding they have been given.

But this is not to suggest that the agencies do not have legislative allies. There is a natural tendency for members to become advocates for phases of administrative action in which they have special interests. Specialization encourages the member to become an agency advocate. As a result, members may lobby *each other* in behalf of agencies with whom they have come to identify. For some it may be the Pentagon; for others the favored fields may be programs or agencies tied to veterans affairs, environmental protection, education, banking, small businesses, housing, the fishing industry, health care, or countless other concerns.

Lobbyists also represent an important link to persons serving terms in Congress and the state legislatures, although the role that special interests play is at least partially misunderstood. Virtually every organized group with a large financial or social stake in legislation has a full-time staff in Washington and at least some part-time lobbyists in the state capitals. The primary goal of these groups is obvious: to make their feelings known on any legislative or direct oversight activity within the legislature. At a more subtle level their presence is also a reminder to the member that a vote will not go unnoticed. Much of their work is essentially indirect, encouraging supporters to communicate via mail to their members. A smaller part of their time involves actual visits to congressional offices to lobby legislative assistants or members.[47] In a typical 1987 day for House Republican John Hiles, contact with lobbyists occurred in both formal and informal settings. His membership on the Banking and Small Business committees were good predictors of who would seek him out. Among those he saw on one September day were representatives of the manufactured housing industry, a delegation from the Coin Dealers Association, and another delegation from the International Council of Shopping Centers. In the evening he attended receptions held by the Mississippi Bankers Association and the National Restaurant Association.[48]

Most lobbyists concentrate their efforts on members who they believe are already sympathetic to their viewpoints. Their goal is frequently to "backstop" a member by providing information that can be used to persuade fellow colleagues. This support can come in the form of prepared speech inserts, "fact sheets," information on how a bill will affect a local area, and "head counting" to help determine a bill's prospects.[49] Some of the discussion occurs during arranged meetings, either with a member or with his staff. At other times lobbyists will seek the help of an intermediary who has the respect of a representative.[50]

Many special interests hire former members who can utilize their "insider" status to get a favorable hearing. An interesting use of such channels of friendship was evident to Senator Pete Domenici during his protracted effort to legislate user fees for river barge operators in 1977. The legislation was designed to make the users of America's navigable rivers partially liable for the enormous maintenance costs involved. The barge owners lobbied intensively against the issue. The barge competitors, the railroads, lobbied for it. As T. R. Reid noted, the barge operators recruited former Florida Senator George Smathers for their fight against the fees. He had formerly worked for the railroads, but switched, and became a powerful force in behalf of the barge companies. "As a former Senator, he was allowed to prowl the Senate floor and the cloakrooms just off it, where Senators congregate and where most outsiders are not admitted."[51] Lobbyists working for Domenici's bill could not produce the same effective personal kind of persuasion. By necessity they took a different approach:

The railroads and their allies, lacking a prominent individual lobbyist who had personal connections with Senators, concentrated, on the whole, on the Senator's staffs. . . . This staff strategy was a proven winner; one of the great victories in lobbying lore—the civil rights lobby's defeat of the nomination of G. Harrold Carswell to the Supreme Court— had been won by convincing staff members, who in turn convinced their Senators, that Carswell was unfit for the Court. Since Senators were even more likely to rely on staff advice on a relatively unfamiliar issue like the waterway bill, the railroad tactic seemed eminently sensible.[52]

Overall, it is probably the case that we overestimate the effect that lobbying has on the legislative process. From a communications prospective Congress is preeminently a place *for* persuasion. As we have already argued, in an extended sense "lobbying" occurs all of the time. It is not confined to just a few, but to an enormous range of "registered" and unofficial interests, including both groups, individuals, and members themselves. What is often overlooked is that lobbying is often a "protective" rather than an "offensive" activity. Like television advertisers who want to hold their share of a market, representatives of specific interests know their powers of persuasion are limited. The process of influencing others almost never occurs in a vacuum. Members spend a good deal of time persuading each other. Constituents offer their own assessments. Friendly reporters—in their unofficial roles as friends—may give their advice as well. The balance of interests may in fact be so close that they cancel each other out. When that occurs, it may be surprisingly easy for a member to render a decision on how to vote. Like former Iowa Senator John C. Culver, the member may see a no-win situation as one that frees him to vote on a bill's merits: "if it makes a lot of people unhappy in the process, so be it."[53]

External Communication

Up to this point we have discussed basic communication patterns between the members of legislatures and their interested observers. Obviously, however, members seek to exercise influence well beyond the highly politicized worlds of the District of Columbia, Richmond, Austin, or Madison. Whether they are communicating with individuals or groups, legislators seek to reach external publics for whom politics is not a profession, but an intermittently observed process of resolving problems and distributing resources. We start with one of the most basic forms of external contact.

Member to Constituents

If legislators have staff support, they will probably spend a significant portion of their time helping residents in the district or state make contact with various layers of the governmental bureaucracy. Only members of legislatures from small states avoid constituency service, largely because they meet infrequently and have virtually no office staff. By contrast, in some large cities such as Chicago or New York, the norm is still for officeholders in city government to attempt to intervene in behalf of citizens with complaints about services provided by the city. The old-style "ward heeler" is especially a fixture in large cities like Chicago, where ties between office holders, specific neighborhoods, and political factions remain very tight.[54] In Congress the percent of time devoted to constituent work varies, but averages to about 18 percent of the typical workweek, and about 65 percent of the personal staff's time.[55] Most of this constituency contact is relatively impersonal, involving mail or phone correspondence handled primarily by a member's staff. Lost Social Security or civil service checks, disputes over veteran's benefits, and requests for information regarding state or federal policy rank high on the list of topics. As a percent of the member's total effort, constituency work can range from one of many equally important roles (i.e., particularly for a senior senator or a major party or legislative leader) to *the* single most important activity. Particularly for members elected every two years, it is a form of insurance that enhances their electability in the district.

Many members of Congress maintain several offices in the home districts, visiting them regularly and providing opportunities for constituents to meet them personally, or consult with their staff. This kind of activity has a special attraction for a number of backbenchers. Compared with the snail's pace of activity in Congress, casework offers the possibility of gaining relatively fast results. In addition, a relatively weak backbencher may regain a sense of importance and "mission" in face-to-face encounters with constituents who are genuinely impressed with his ability to "get something done."[56]

Members also meet constituents for other reasons than casework. Some may try to routinely greet visitors from the home district. And most plan frequent trips to their districts or states for appearances and "town meetings" before constituents. It is not unusual for a representative to attempt to keep a dozen appointments and make a half dozen speeches in a one-day trip back in the district.[57] Quite a few seem to believe that no form of activity is as certain to produce support as the contact that comes in a personal appearance before constituents. As one representative with an upcoming campaign on his mind told Richard Fenno, "The best way to win a vote is to shake hands with someone. You don't win votes by the thousands with a speech. You win votes by looking individuals in the eye, one at a time, and asking them [for their vote]."[58]

Another common way to reach ordinary constituents is direct mail. Congressional newsletters and opinion polls cascade out of Washington and the state capitals every year, paid for by the generous postal frank available to members. Some of the newsletters take advantage of increasingly sophisticated computer technology that can "target" mail to specific groups. Cross-referenced lists of addresses can produce mailings for minorities, the elderly, veterans, or countless other groups who may be interested in particular pieces of legislation, or the member's latest statement on a specialized area. At least one senator won re-election in 1972 by using such a cross-referenced system to target an antibusing message to white middle-class voters in Michigan. His message deliberately excluded blacks, and eventually resulted in the imposition of tighter standards on selective public-financed mailings.[59]

Few members believe that such mail does much more than provide a fleeting reminder that their representative is active. While recognizing it as a basic tool for remaining in the consciousness of voters, most seem reluctant to depend too heavily on such mailings as a way to communicate with constituents. One aid to a senator noted that "once they get the newsletter, they read it between the mailbox and the living room."[60]

Member to the Press: "For Attribution"

In the late 1950s Douglass Cater called the Congress "a happy hunting ground of journalistic enterprise."[61] In some ways it still is. But it is also a troubled preserve, and one in which it is not entirely clear who is the hunter and who is the prey. Beginning in the 1970s a number of political writers advanced the theory that the balance of power had significantly shifted: that it was now the press that determined the fortunes and set the agenda of key political institutions such as the Congress. Conservative thinker Kevin Phillips asserted that we now had a national "mediacracy," a liberal, press "affluentsia with substantial control over the knowledge and information functions" of the society.[62] Others saw different trends. Press critic Ben Bagdikian described members of Congress who were attempting to maintain their political power by using print and television stories "to propagandize their constituents at the constituent's expense with the cooperation of the local news media."[63] More recently the widely respected British journalist Henry Brandon expressed the view that the press now has the upper hand in Washington, thriving on a confrontational style that has made the process of governing all the more difficult.[64]

No questions raise more interesting and varied answers than those which address the relationships between news gatherers and news makers. It can be said with some certainty that it is too simple to depend heavily on the model of the press as "adversary," or even the more enlightened model of the press as part of a relationship based solely on mutual benefits.[65] Dan Nimmo's extensive 1964 study of the relationships between public information officers and the press in Washington still contains valid conclusions. The press and those being covered have goals in common, but they also have divergent goals. Neither publicists nor press have a decisive upper hand:

The attitudes uncovered in the present day do not indicate either a willingness or an ability on the part of either the information establishment or the news media to exert leadership in the opinion process. Both the newsman and the [public information] officer defer to the political official as the primary articulator of issues for public debate. To information officers, conflict was inherently an evil to be avoided in favor of agreement. To publicize agreement is good; to publicize controversy is bad. The newsman views the whole process differently. The publicizing of agreement, although not bad, is also not news. To publicize controversy is the essence of news.[66]

The annual *Congressional Directory* lists more than 4000 national and international reporters accredited to cover Congress, but only several hundred are assigned on a full-time basis.[67] In the States the numbers are obviously much smaller, with only a handful of full-time correspondents—usually representing newspapers in the capital or the state's biggest cities—assigned to the legislature. Television stations frequently do even less, often limiting their coverage to wire service reports or temporary assignments to cover only the most controversial of legislative votes. Nearly all reporters in the States and many of their Washington counterparts have other duties and beats. A Washington correspondent for a midwestern daily, for example, may cover her state's congressional delegation. But she may be additionally responsible for covering committees and other executive agencies all over town. These various groups are likely to include those that are traditionally important to the cornbelt—such as the Departments of Agriculture or Interior.

The range of stories produced by journalists covering "the Hill" can be vast. Committee hearings, votes, news of trips by members, scandals, veto-override votes, House-Senate conferences, oversight hearings, interviews of presidential nominees, presidential messages, and campaign news are all fair game for comment and reporting. Newspapers and television stations from the distant provinces report these events in capsule form, sometimes with information from their own stringers or correspondents. More often than not they receive such stories from the wire services or one of the broadcast networks. A paper with modest means may be almost totally dependent on such reports for most Washington news. They can also count on receiving a steady flow of press releases identifying a local member's contributions to legislative action with a local dimension.

There is a significant gap between local and national coverage of Congress. Most members feel like they must seek out the press in order to gain publicity for their work. For the large majority of the 435 members of the House it is a fact of life that if they are sought out at all, it is by a representative of their own district's press. The major national networks and the "prestige" dailies have so many compelling news sources, that it is a fact of life that they need any one congressional source less than the source needs them. David Paletz and Robert Entman have succinctly summarized the problem:

Unfortunately for the legislators, the national press needs any single member of Congress less than members desire the press. The opportunity to broadcast unmediated speeches and invitations to participate in television panel discussions rarely accrue to ordinary members of Congress. In practice, Congressmen and -women court the press as the press courts the president. Their problem is the relative lack of interest of the mass media in most of their activities and the reporters' belief that the information released by legislators is even more self-interested than that coming from the White House.[68]

The *tone* of press coverage also differs markedly between national and local mass media. Although they have pointed out many exceptions, a number of analysts have noted that local broadcast and print coverage of individual members is far more sympathetic than the reporting that comes from national sources. Magazines such as *Time* and *Newsweek*, dailies such as the *New York Times* or the *Los Angeles Times*, all tend to focus on the collective nature of the institution, or the House and Senate leadership. The networks act similarly. In contrast, local papers and broadcasts tend to emphasize the activities of specific members.

It comes as no surprise that Congress fares poorly when coverage is reduced to its characteristics as a collection of diverse interests. Very little empathy is aroused for any organization described in terms of its decision-making processes. As we have noted earlier, compared to the simplicity and clarity of an individual's actions, a group's work will always appear more sluggish and less coordinated. The broadcast commentary of NBC's David Brinkley that "it would take Congress thirty days to make instant coffee"[69] is typical of the public frustration that is commonly expressed about Congress as a body. The remarks of former ABC commentator Howard K. Smith are even more revealing—and probably unfair—in their explicit comparison of the deliberative branch with the less ambiguous leadership found in the Presidency:

When Congress dominates, it's a mess, as after the Civil War when it created regional hatreds that are dying only now. The past year the Congress has been mostly in the saddle and among the results—a tax reform that didn't reform, an energy act that in no way meets the fuel crisis. . . .

Granted, recent presidents have abused power and have had to be checked. Still, we shan't see effective government again till the pendulum swings back to give the executive more leverage.[70]

The national media themselves have an institutional problem in covering Congress. Because they address the nation as a whole, they seem reluctant to focus on the work of "typical" members. Their vantage points tend to be on the committee, the leadership, and relations with other segments of the Washington establishment. Michael Robinson and Kevin Appel have looked at these and other instances, concluding that Congress—especially with regard to television—is in "a uniquely vulnerable position."

[L]egislatures in liberal secular societies abound in philosophical contradictions, intense political bargaining, and what some might call the amorality of democracy. This makes for "bad" news, which is, of course, "good" copy.

By contrast,

In most circumstances the president is covered too personally, too directly, to be maligned by the networks day to day. The networks need the president, and *generally* they need him. Congress is less personal and hence more subject to attack.[71]

The absence of any single official voice in Congress hurts it, and fights the tide of television's fascination with interesting pictures. To be sure, the luxury of space in a few nationally read journals may guarantee a reasonably accurate portrayal of the legislative process, and the impact of individuals who are affecting it. But television network news coverage is more typical, and its superficial coverage provides no such basis for understanding. As a former press secretary to the house speaker has noted, the networks have largely written Congress off. Correspondents must be "very adept" to convince their editors that a legislative struggle is worth coverage."[72] For all of its sources of information and helpful staff, laments the *Washington Post*'s David Broder, it is "the worst reported part of our government," largely because "Most of us are a lot more comfortable thinking about and writing about individuals than about institutions."[73]

Ironically, it is only on the local level that readers may see congressional activity from the vantage point of the individual member. Part of the member's role is to cultivate contacts with reporters tied to the home districts.[74] As we have already noted, papers want to emphasize the local angle of a congressional story, and members are more than happy to oblige, sometimes explaining how a bill will impact on their district, and occasionally getting the opportunity to release information that has been routed through them by a sympathetic committee or agency. From the average member's standpoint, such contacts are too infrequent, but satisfying, because they help to maintain the goodwill at home needed to gain reelection. In journalistic terms, the reporting done by local media may be superficial. "Some of the congressmen and staff I interviewed," Robinson recalls, "rejected the premise that the local press is softer than the national press, but most saw a fairly clear split between the two worlds of news."[75] There is a general feeling that many members of the local media—because of time constraints, and perhaps because of less of an adversarial edge—are more willing to be "spoon fed."

Sympathetic treatment by the local press is often cited as a reason for the puzzling differences of opinion Americans express between "Congress" as an institution, and *their* own congressman. Studies of public attitudes point out a general "nationwide contempt for Congress" on one hand, "and district-wide esteem for its members" on the other.[76] As Robinson indicates, this paradox is at least partially attributable to the combined effect of the more hostile national media and the more sympathetic local press.[77]

The publicity machinery that is available to Congress and some state legislatures includes a number of physical and staff resources. Virtually every deliberative body provides a press gallery in both Houses which is available to credentialed reporters. In addition, in Washington and most of the states reporters have access to some of the anterooms, eating areas, and elevators that are closed to the rest of the general public. They may also enjoy the comfort and prestige that comes with invitations to socialize with leaders in their private offices. In Washington and some states broadcasters may also make use of audio and video studios located in the legislative office buildings, as long as the object of their attention is a member of one of the two houses. The interviews taped in such locations usually feature a local television or radio reporter, but the true producer is actually the member being interviewed.[78]

In Congress the most important press resource is usually the member's staff. Any number of individuals may be variously involved in press-related work, the most common of which is the preparation of news releases for distribution in Washington and back home. Press relations specialists are responsible for translating a member's activities into stories that have at least a semblance of "news." Their job is essentially to find a way to meet the publicity goals of the member. Those goals may range from simply keeping local media at home "informed" so that the ground is laid for an easy reelection, to the more elaborate objective of gaining national recognition for a member's interests. But they must also sell their favorable releases as something that can be taken as serious (and not totally self-serving) information. Because these staff specialists are so common, and because congressional reporting is left to so few, these staffs gain a kind of bogus journalistic responsibility by default. They write "news" items about their employers that are often used uncritically by many home district newspapers and broadcasters. As press critic Ben Bagdikian notes,

Hundreds of press releases, paid for by the taxpayers, are sent to the media by members of Congress, and hundreds are run verbatim or with insignificant changes, most often in medium-sized and small papers, with only rare calls to check facts and ask questions that probe beyond the pleasant propaganda.[79]

Press releases remain the key piece of press member communication in the Congress. Among the 14 members of the New Jersey congressional delegation in 1983 there was an average of 86 news releases per member, with a low of ten from one, and a high of 175 from another.[80] "I think the public should know where you stand on issues," noted one member of the group. "You use the mail, press contacts, any way you can get visibility."[81] Others may arrange for private interviews with members of the press, and for scheduling of the television studios to record a broadcast interview. The latter may have much the same quality of a press release, but it is an important adaptation to an age that is increasingly dependent on television. As a representative from North Carolina has observed, "television and radio communication are the 20th-century version of the postal frank."[82]

Member to Press and Public: Hearings and Investigations

From a rhetorical standpoint, perhaps the most important forum in Washington outside of the White House is the congressional committee. Numerous observers have pointed out that more and more of the substantive work of the Congress is carried out in the standing committees, the subcommittees, and in special investigations.[83] Almost every item of legislation, every high level executive appointee, and most problems of general national concern will at some point be the subject of public hearings on Capitol Hill.

The propensity for Congress to divide itself into small committees has both a political and constitutional base. By constitutional right, members are charged with the responsibility to oversee the functioning government and—when necessary—to investigate areas where government has failed to perform properly. Between 1941 and 1944, for example, Harry Truman chaired the Senate Special Committee to Investigate the National Defense Program. As the name suggests, it was asked to certify that defense contracts were economically and fairly made. By most accounts, it did a good job in the course of its work with 1798 witnesses and 432 public hearings.[84] Equally spectacular was the unexpected 1989 grilling of George Bush's nominee for Secretary of Defense, former Texas Senator John Tower. In an unusual step, members of Tower's former committee on Armed Services turned what most thought would be a routine confirmation hearing into a prolonged and embarrassing look at Tower's former work as a $750,000-a-year consultant to contractors doing business with the Department of Defense.[85] More typically, individual House and Senate committees regularly meet to consider new bills or hear testimony on proposed legislation. Routine hearings by a committee may run for several hours over a number of days. Very few sessions are closed, but public and press attendance may be low anyway, depending on the gravity of the issues under consideration. Typically, the witnesses include other interested legislators, representatives from businesses or institutions who have a stake in the outcome, and academics who present themselves as nonpartisan experts.[86]

Many hearings are designed primarily to attract attention for a proposal, or investigations intended to shed light on a "national problem" suggest their own problems and advantages. Historian Arthur Schlesinger, Jr. notes that the power to investigate is often well used by the Congress. He believes that "while the conventional assumption is that the strength of legislative bodies lies in the power to legislate, a respectable tradition has long argued that it lies as much or more in the power to investigate."[87] But nearly every study of hearings and investigations also cites Walter Lippmann's searing judgment that the average congressional investigation is a "legalized atrocity . . . in which Congressmen, starved of their legitimate food for thought, go on a wild and feverish manhunt, and do not stop at cannibalism''[88] Lippmann had little faith in the motives or the expertise of the average legislator. Others, such as evidence analysts Robert and Dale Newman, have found that the truth is frequently abused at the hands of politically motivated committee chairs and members. The Newmans list a veritable catalogue of abuses which regularly occur in committee settings:

Hostile witnesses can be grilled, friendly ones babied. Third-rate authorities can be called, first-rate ones neglected. What matters, from a political standpoint, is headlines of the moment. Few will pore over the record to register a judgment of truth or falsehood, and even if they do, events have moved past the moment of relevance.[89]

Even granting that the quality of individual sessions varies greatly, there is little doubt that the committees of Congress serve several key groups in extremely important ways. From the member's point of view, the committee is a way to stand out and apart from their larger body. The specialist committee system encourages the member to develop two or three fields of expertise. Ideally, his knowledge grows as seniority within a particular committee increases. This pattern has several important effects. For the nation, it produces legislative experts equal to, and in some cases better than, those who work in the executive agencies. The specialist also approaches national problems with a greater understanding of the political consequences of governmental solutions. He may have a better sense of the workability of a bill than other experts who are beyond the reach of public opinion. Representatives and senators may become shrewd students of federal tax laws, farm subsidy programs, the banking or broadcasting industries, rural medical facilities, military procurement procedures, and many other important areas. Their expertise makes them able to offer effective public arguments that can challenge the natural rhetorical supremacy of the executive.

In addition, for the member/specialist there is the advantage of being able at least momentarily to seize attention as an individual rather than as just a small part of the heterogeneous legislature. Harry Truman, J. William Fulbright, Sam Ervin, Jr., William Proxmire, John Pastore, Joe Biden, Edward Kennedy, and Sam Nunn are but a few senators in the nation's recent past who have gained national recognition for their roles in hearings and investigations. With their counterparts in the House and in the state legislative bodies they have been able to carve out loyal constituencies with interests in their special areas of competence. Dealing with subjects as diverse as the effects of television violence on children, Korean government influence peddling, the Watergate affair, judicial appointments, environmental issues and countless other topics, members of committees are able to magnify their impact on legislation and—sometimes in the process—command a few seconds of precious airtime or a few columns of print. Hearings give members the opportunity to compete with the executive on his own terms: as *personal* and *committed* advocates rather than merely faceless members of deliberative bodies engaged in political brokerage.

Another rhetorically attractive feature of hearings is that they offer a refreshingly different set of roles to the member. Normally the work of Congress is associated with the need for a member to grasp detail and the fine points of legislative compromise. However, in the committee setting members are not only able to demonstrate their expertise, but they can use it in a way that ingratiates themselves to the general public. In examining the objections that a professional lobbyist may have to a new bill, for example, the member may represent himself as the champion of the public interest, counterpoised against the "special pleaders." His committee role allows him to enact a more heroic public interest–centered approach to politics than might be reflected alone in an examination of recent voting patterns. By performing as a public trustee, by protecting the federal coffers against those who would unfairly drain them, the representative is able to shake off some of the role-related liabilities that go with the incremental and pragmatic nature of legislative politics.

Reporters love such moments of drama. In an investigation or hearing members of Congress can be far more direct and accusatory than most other public officials. They can create the kind of legislative conflict that is deemed newsworthy. Just such debate was produced in the early 1970s when Rhode Island's feisty John Pastore challenged the executives of the three television networks. Pastore used his membership on the Senate's Subcommittee on Communications to press for less televised violence. The patient lecturing that Pastore gave the media moguls was something that could have come from a Frank Capra film. They were in his territory, and he was enacting the role of a man on a crusade. The fatherly senator with simple wire-framed glasses was appalled by the slickness and violence of Saturday morning cartoons, and other television fare directed to children. The politics of the moment were perfect: the decent "everyman" challenging the six-figure salary executives to be less concerned about profits and more concerned about the welfare of the nation's children.[90]

It was similarly said that the Watergate hearings did much the same for the chairman of the House Judiciary Committee, Representative Peter Rodino. A quiet man, Rodino had languished in public obscurity for years. Coming from the tough and often corrupt politics of Newark, New Jersey, no one expected much beyond the stereotype of a back-slapping ethnic-Italian politician. To those who knew only his name and his district, he was perhaps stereotyped as the kind of member who was only useful to like-minded folks in Newark's Democratic working-class wards. The Rodino persona presented in the widely televised hearings was quite different: seemingly fair-minded, cautious, serious, and genuinely saddened by the prospect of overseeing the impeachment of Richard Nixon.[91]

Another important element in the hearings process is what has been called the "safety valve" function. Hearings and investigations are a way to "let off steam" harmlessly, but with some symbolic effect.[92] In what might be a nearly complete symbolic gesture, groups may testify, members may offer bills, and social and governmental problems may be discussed without legislative action ever being taken. The resulting hearings may have publicity value, and may provide comfort to their participants by laying the groundwork for future action. Such hearings permit members to give what amounts to symbolic service to those for whom legislative action is all but impossible. They also permit the statements and tracts of dissidents to find their way into the official record. In the late 1970s, for example, all of these functions were performed by Edward Kennedy, who frequently held hearings in the Senate Labor and Public Welfare Committee urging the passage of a national health insurance plan. Even as the political divide between Jimmy Carter and Kennedy widened, and even though it became obvious that there was little or no chance of producing a bill the Congress could accept, Kennedy pressed ahead. Hearings became an important rhetorical exercise. His purpose, of course, was to keep the health care issue alive, to reassure political allies, and to put pressure on the Carter administration to accept his plan.[93] At the state level committee hearings on insurance reform, solid waste disposal, and reform of eligibility rules for welfare recipients have provided the same public relations functions.

From a communications perspective, nothing quite equals the effectiveness of hearings to attract press attention. Because they are conducted in a semi-judicial manner, with testifiers, examination, and cross-examination, they provide an ideal mix of personalities and issues. In some ways congressional hearings come the closest to producing real debate on Capitol Hill. Indeed, as was the case in 1966 when J. William Fulbright used the Senate Foreign Relations Committee to examine Vietnam policy, hearings may be designed to create a dialogue in what is otherwise a stillborn public debate. Fulbright's hearings gained national attention. They also created severe pangs of conscience within the networks, forcing one of them to decide between reruns of "I Love Lucy" and the televised discussions of America's escalating commitment in Southeast Asia.[94] Fulbright called the hearings "an experiment in public education," noting that "by bringing before the American people a variety of opinions and disagreements pertaining to the war and perhaps by helping to restore a degree of balance between the Executive and the Congress, [they] strengthened the country rather than weakened it."[95]

Arguably, the 1987 Iran-Contra hearings before a joint Senate-House panel had much the same effect. For six days in July the nation's routine news agenda was all but suspended during televised testimony offered by Colonel Oliver North. In a scheme worthy of an epic spy thriller, North revealed that he and members of the CIA used their positions within the White House to sell military hardware secretly to Iran and others to fund the Nicaraguan Contras favored by the Reagan administration. The hearings were tense and dramatic, focusing attention on the deep conflict between the Congress and the White House, and forcing Americans to consider the sharp differences between official rhetoric and secret actions.[96] Less anticipated, perhaps, was also the fact that the photogenic North was not about to become a willing villain. Members of the committee largely failed in their attempts to make Congress rather than their star witness the symbol of what was right with American policy in Latin America.

Press coverage of hearings is also aided by the fact that the rules on audio and video coverage are more lenient than in any other formal congressional settings. Many committee chairmen will go to great lengths to accommodate the equipment and personnel necessary for live or recorded reporting of statements, questions, and answers.

Robinson and Appel's survey of network news coverage of Congress shows that the member's emphasis on committees is not misplaced. In 1976 by far the largest single type of news story from the networks was on committee work. Other kinds of stories, such as those dealing with constituent work, scandals, or travel junkets, were infrequently aired. Almost half of all of the reports dealt with committee reports, "committee action," and hearings. It is particularly the latter, they note, that "are the *sine qua non* of network news coverage of Congress."[97] "So struck were we with the emphasis on committees, we recorded all 'committee action' stories to get some insight into what was actually going on."[98] What they found was that hearings can be placed in a dramatic context that is well suited to the needs of television:

A substantial proportion of those committee stories with testimony (20 percent) were "fights," fights between congressmen and bureaucrats or between congressmen and corporate executives. But the most "representative" network news story takes place on film, in a Senate committee hearing room, where senators and testifiers talked back and forth on some policy issues.[99]

Member to Public, via the Set Speech

No survey of the forms of congressional communication would be complete without briefly discussing the formal addresses by senators and representatives. Two settings for planned speeches are normal. One is on the floor of the House or Senate. The other is back in the member's district or state.

There is no precise way to assess the impact of floor speeches. They obviously allow the member the opportunity to clarify a position before a key vote. They also provide the means to establish a durable printed and video record of a position, a record that becomes part of the political legacy of the member. For these reasons many members are content to make remarks to a virtually empty chamber, even though their impact is negligible. At other times remarks made on the floor can have some impact—usually when key amendments to a highly controversial bill are debated, or when a member's public comments on an earlier bill are recalled favorably or unfavorably by other colleagues. A revealing instance of how speeches contribute to the institutional memory of legislators is cited by Reid on Senator Pete Domenici's waterway users' fee:

A few days before the waterway bill came up, Domenici had delivered a strong floor speech criticizing one of [Senator] Mike Gravel's pet legislative projects. Gravel was livid: "You just lost me on that user charge, Pete," he snapped, and Domenici was powerless to win him back.[100]

Few would argue with Barry Goldwater's comment that "speaking in the Senate has degenerated to such a point that it is almost impossible to get anyone to listen."[101] But floor speeches can be important, at least for what they potentially signify. An eloquent floor defense of a bill a member has cosponsored, for example, has the effect of reassuring colleagues that the speaker can be trusted, and is articulate enough to represent the party or a caucus. A member does not have to be an excellent orator to rise to a leadership position, but it is unlikely that an inarticulate person will be selected for major leadership roles, such as speaker of the House, committee chair, or majority or minority leader. Speaking in the Senate and House has the same symbolic objective that it has for other organizations. It signals an ability to handle public pressure, to comprehend the flow of arguments and refutations. Even the least likely member of the House of Representatives will need to use a speech not only to defend a position, but to demonstrate sensitivity and mental agility to colleagues who may be paying more attention than they appear to be. As we shall see, the relatively new use of television in the Congress and many state legislatures has made giving a floor speech something of a lottery. Most remarks will be quickly forgotten; but precious seconds in a few will go from obscurity to prominence as television news "sound bites."

The other major venue for speeches is in the district, particularly during reelection campaigns. As Richard Fenno has pointed out, there are many rhetorical objectives that can be met in meetings with constituents outside of Washington.[102] They may range from defending their votes on great national issues, to the more mundane but vital task of relating specific congressional or executive action to local community needs and problems. Most members seem to enjoy local appearances. Their status in the community is larger than it is in Washington. Constituents and the local press are generally more deferential. Many audiences are simply flattered to be the recipients of the member's attention.

BROADCASTING FROM CONGRESS: NEW VISIBILITY?

Television came to the House of Representatives in 1979 and the Senate in 1986 for at least some of the same reasons that microphones and cameras have gradually appeared in the parliaments of Britain, Canada, Australia, and state legislatures. Legislators worldwide have sensed the need to compete with other national institutions for access to the airwaves.

The Need for Change

Members of legislatures who have been raised in the television age realize that the personalizing nature of broadcasting can probably never restore the imbalance in access that favors presidents and party leaders. "Television," writes Michael Novak, "fixes on the President and makes him the main symbolic representative of the government. Symbolically it dwarfs the Congress and the courts."[103] Even so, to do nothing to deal with television's influence would probably have been inconceivable. By the mid–1970s many states had made some provision for radio and television coverage of debates, with Florida and Connecticut leading the way.[104] In Washington the House soon followed.

The House of Representatives system offers little variety to viewers: shots are largely confined to the "well" of the chamber containing the podium from which members speak. Cameras practically never include reactions of members, or pictures of the remainder of the House floor. A member may thus read the paper, leave the floor, or even sleep with impunity. By contrast, the Senate uses a greater variety of shots, including split screens featuring various debaters, and pictures of the entire chamber during roll call votes.[105] The cameras themselves are in control of each body, with broadcasters free to use whatever they wish from this television "feed."

The only channel making extensive use of coverage is C-SPAN, whose House coverage reached an impressive 25 million cable television households in 1987. An estimated 9 million homes receive its newer Senate channel, C-SPAN II.[106] On both services virtually all floor action is presented, along with extensive coverage of committee hearings. In one recent year C-SPAN presented over 237 hours of hearings held by various Senate and House committees.[107] To be sure, these channels seem to present no threat to other cable television programmers, but one study revealed that about 8 percent of C-SPAN's households viewed congressional activity for more than 30 minutes a week.[108] Regular viewers of the service may watch the service as many as 12 hours a month.[109]

Obviously, most commercial broadcasters have also welcomed having full access to congressional debates and hearings. But they rarely make extensive use of this resource. There are many reasons, some already noted. Television in particular is not a natural companion for any legislature. In fundamental ways each cuts against the grain of the other. The nature of legislative debate seems fundamentally antithetical to the pace and diversity of the entertainment-oriented networks. While debate can be lively and theatrical, the norm is usually quite different. Long and extended arguments are more typical. Full coverage of floor debates would not only be difficult to justify as complete commercial network broadcasts, but are difficult to edit for quick summarizing. Debate is a linear event which unfolds (if at all) only over a significant amount of time. With exceptions, such as the Iran-Contra hearings, network gatekeepers have had neither the patience or budgets to provide extensive coverage.

Another problem is that television has emerged in this decade as the undisputed merchant of effortless leisure. Its commercial outlets have made the medium less suitable to almost all but the most superficial forms of politics. There is a sense, particularly among politicians and newsgatherers generally, that "serious" political debate is best presented in the print media, and often is only exploited for superficial effects by commercial television. It grates on members of the

House, for example, that one of the few times the networks led their newscasts with House television pictures was when a member was formally expelled for corruption.[110]

Real and Imagined Effects

Only 15 years ago, broadcasting in most legislatures was a controversial issue. Perhaps the most highly debated decision on whether broadcasters should be allowed was in Britain's House of Commons, a full year before the House of Representatives set up its own experiment. The decision to first start with radio carried considerable importance because—as in all parliaments—cabinet-level members of the government continue to sit as members of the legislature as well. This fact has great significance because it means that the Prime Minister and his or her government must at times face questioning from the opposition party. The weekly institution of "Question Time" is a moment of high drama in the House of Commons. It is often the single biggest political news story of the day, comparable in some ways to a presidential press conference where members of the political opposition—not the press—get to ask the tough questions. The Prime Minister must face questions with an almost continual rumble of chants and jeers that would intimidate even the coolest of presidents. In 1978 the BBC began weekly broadcasts of "Prime Minister's Questions," (PMQs) providing a kind of running "play by play" of who was yelling to whom. Public reaction was dramatic and negative. Britons were genuinely shocked at what they heard from the "mother of parliaments" along the Thames. The negative response was not totally unexpected, but few anticipated the discredit brought on by "the faithful transmission of the jeers, insults, cat-calls, impromptu witticisms, interruptions, baying, howling, ranting, point-scoring and general nonsense which characterize PMQs."[111]

The results in Congress and the states have been more muted, perhaps because there is less direct debate in American legislatures than in most parliaments. The lack of dramatic impact on proceedings in the United States is evident in the comparative absence of public response. Indeed, one of the most notable changes broadcasting has brought to Capitol Hill has little to do with the public at all. The system has made it possible for members and the 14,000 staffers employed by members of the Congress to keep an eye on floor debate while attending to other House-related business back in their offices.[112] This "closed circuit" use has been much praised.

In discussions about whether to admit cameras the most commonly expressed fears were that members would "grandstand," "play to the cameras" and in other ways disrupt the flow of legislative work. Some in the Senate, such as Jake Garn, claim that this has happened.[113] But they seem to be in a very small minority. The reactions of J. Bennett Johnston, a former critic of Senate television, seem more typical of reactions inside and outside the institution. "It makes senators careful not to wander in their speeches," he noted after the first year of television coverage. "They are more disciplined and more succinct. They may make more speeches, but they're shorter and to the point." CBS's Phil Jones made the same point, arguing that the presence of television encouraged the senate to "clean up its act" with better preparation for debates and speeches.[114] "Our fears," Bennett conceded in 1987, "were unfounded."[115] A similar conclusion was reached by a Connecticut official responsible for arranging broadcasts of various sessions in Hartford. He dismissed concerns that some legislators would use television to promote themselves, or that some members would "enjoy a special advantage because they are more photogenic, more articulate, more flamboyant, or more colorful." "These fears are sometimes realized, but it cuts both ways. Compensating mechanisms come into play with comments during debates, and from peer pressure or leadership pressure."[116]

One conclusion seems certain. Legislatures will continue to compete with the proliferation of broadcasts devoted to political conventions, the courts, state legislatures, the Presidency, and even school board meetings carried by local cable companies. A few may dislike the modest demands television superimposes over the traditional political structure. But as the 1990s begin, there seems little chance that the Congress and the states will reverse their support for live coverage.

As we have seen, Congress and its sister institutions remain archetypal forums for fostering a wide variety of political discourse. No Washington institution has as large or as varied a need for constant publicity about its work than Congress. Television has been, and will continue to become, but one part in a matrix of communication networks that radiate from Capitol Hill. Just as L'Enfant's city plan placed the Capitol at the center of the District of Columbia's road network, so too the Congress will continue to act as a source of influence in almost every other phase of American political communication.

NOTES

1. Harrison W. Fox Jr. and Susan Webb Hammond, *Congressional Staffs: The Invisible Force in American Lawmaking* (New York: Free Press, 1977), p. 103.

2. Douglass Cater, *The Fourth Branch of Government* (New York: Vintage Books, 1959), p. 51.

3. See, for example, Donald G. Tacheron and Morris Udall, "Keeping in Touch with the People, Getting Along with the Press . . . " in *Congress and the News Media*, ed. Robert O. Blanchard (New York: Hastings House, 1974), pp. 370–83.

4. Douglass Cater, *Power in Washington* (New York: Vintage Books, 1964), pp. 144–60; Abner J. Mikva and Patti B. Harris, *The American Congress, The First Branch* (New York: Franklin Watts, 1983), pp. 123–54.

5. Clem Miller, "A Newcomer's View of the Press," in Blanchard, p. 160.

6. Newton N. Minow, John Bartlow Martin, and Lee M. Mitchell, *Presidential Television* (New York: Basic Books, 1973), pp. 115–16. See also Stephen Hess, *The Ultimate Insiders: U.S. Senators in the National Media* (Washington, DC: Brookings,

1986). As Hess has noted, "the average senator is irrelevant to the national media . . ."
(p. 8).

7. David L. Paletz and Robert M. Entman, *Media Power Politics* (New York: Free Press, 1981), p. 80.

8. Jimmy Carter, *Keeping Faith: Memoirs of a President* (New York: Bantam, 1982), p. 73.

9. Steven V. Roberts, "Slow Pace of Congress," *The New York Times*, October 5, 1979, p. A20.

10. Congressional Quarterly, "House Democratic Whips: Massing Support" in *Inside Congress*, 2d Ed. (Washington, DC: Congressional Quarterly, 1979), pp. 29–30.

11. John S. Saloma, 3rd., *Congress and the New Politics* (Boston, MA: Little Brown, 1969), pp. 94–96.

12. Ibid., p. 5.

13. Ibid., p. 6.

14. Wilson quoted in *The American President* ed. by Sidney Warren (Englewood Cliffs, NJ: Prentice Hall, 1967), p. 29.

15. Harry McPherson, *A Political Education* (Boston, MA: Atlantic–Little Brown, 1972), p. 48.

16. Richard F. Fenno, Jr. *Home Style: House Members in Their Districts* (Boston, MA: Little, Brown, 1978), pp. 217–18.

17. Michael J. Robinson, "Three Faces of Congressional Media" in *The New Congress*, ed. Thomas E. Mann and Norman J. Ornstein (Washington, DC: American Enterprise Institute, 1981), p. 87.

18. Robinson.

19. Miller, p. 160.

20. Merle Miller, *Lyndon: An Oral Biography* (New York: Ballentine, 1980), pp. 247–48.

21. *Inside Congress*, p. 74.

22. See, for example, R. Ajemian, "Ideologue with Influence," *Time*, May 4, 1982, pp. 20–21, and "Helms Plays Hardball," *Newsweek*, January 3, 1983, p. 11.

23. Jill Lawrence, "Frenzied World of the Hill, Where Everyone Has a Job," *San Francisco Examiner*, August 17, 1986, p. A6.

24. Donald R. Matthews, *U.S. Senators and Their World* (Chapel Hill, NC: University of North Carolina, 1960), p. 85.

25. Fox and Hammond, p. 89.

26. Ibid., p. 90.

27. Ibid., pp. 93–94.

28. Theodore Sorensen, *Kennedy* (New York: Harper & Row, 1965), p. 56.

29. Fox and Hammond, p. 149.

30. Dan Meyers, "A Giant Publicity Mill Grinds in Harrisburg," *The Philadelphia Inquirer*, April 28, 1985, pp. 1B–4B.

31. *Inside Congress*, p. 29.

32. Warren Weaver, Jr. *Both Your Houses: The Truth About Congress* (New York: Praeger, 1972), p. 39.

33. Matthews, p. 251.

34. T. R. Reid, *Congressional Odyssey: The Saga of a Senate Bill* (San Francisco, CA: W. H. Freeman, 1980), p. 60.

35. Matthews, pp. 97–101.

36. Miller, *Lyndon*, pp. 212–18.

37. William Rivers, *The Adversaries: Politics and the Press* (Boston: Beacon Press, 1970), pp. 91–133.

38. Quoted in Herbert J. Gans, *Deciding What's News* (New York: Vintage Books, 1980), p. 136.

39. Matthews, p. 214.

40. Rivers, p. 77.

41. Stewart Alsop, "Senator Lyndon Johnson: A Correspondent's View" in Blanchard, p. 285.

42. Jack Anderson and James Boyd, *Confessions of a Muckraker* (New York: Random House, 1979), pp. 313–15.

43. Bert Andrews, "Correspondents as Participants: Case I," in Blanchard, pp. 300–8.

44. Fox and Hammond, pp. 117–18.

45. Joseph A. Califano, Jr., *Governing America: An Insider's Report from the White House and the Cabinet* (New York: Simon and Schuster, 1981), p. 267.

46. Saloma, 3rd., pp. 145–52.

47. Lester W. Milbrath, *The Washington Lobbyists* (Westport, CT: Greenwood Press, 1963), pp. 214–27.

48. Fred Barnes, "The Unbearable Lightness of Being a Congressman," *The New Republic*, February 15, 1988, p. 20.

49. Matthews, pp. 176–83.

50. Milbrath, pp. 241–44.

51. Reid, p. 55.

52. Reid, p. 54.

53. Quoted in Elizabeth Drew, *Senator* (New York: Touchstone, 1979), p. 89–90.

54. See, for example, "I was a Chicago Ward Heeler," *The Washington Monthly*, March, 1988, pp. 10–17.

55. Saloma, p. 185.

56. Fenno, pp. 217–18.

57. Associated Press, "Jersey Pols Differ in Approach to Reaching Voters," *Trenton Times*, January 30, 1984, p. A8.

58. Fenno, p. 85.

59. Robinson, p. 61.

60. "Jersey Pols . . . ," p. A8.

61. Cater, *Fourth Branch of Government*, p. 52.

62. Kevin P. Phillips, *Mediacracy: American Parties and Politics in the Communication Age* (Garden City, NY: Doubleday, 1975), p. 29.

63. Ben H. Bagdikian, "Congress and the Media: Partners in Propaganda" in Blanchard, p. 398.

64. Henry Brandon, *Special Relationships: A Foreign Correspondent's Memoirs from Roosevelt to Reagan* (New York: Atheneum, 1989).

65. See, for example, Jay G. Blumer and Michael Gurevitch, "Politicians and the Press: An Essay on Role Relationships" in *Handbook of Political Communication*, ed. Dan D. Nimmo and Keith R. Sanders (Beverly Hills, CA: Sage, 1981), pp. 467–89.

66. Dan Nimmo, *Newsgathering in Washington* (New York: Atherton Press, 1964), p. 225.

67. Estimates range from a low of one hundred full-time reporters (Hess, p. xv) up to four hundred (Paletz and Entman, p. 80).

68. Paletz and Entman, p. 84.

69. Michael J. Robinson and Kevin R. Appel, "Network News Coverage of Congress," *Political Science Quarterly* 94 (Fall 1979): 413.

70. Quoted in Robinson and Appel, p. 414.

71. Ibid., p. 415.

72. "Network News Underplays House, According to Study," *Broadcasting*, August 24, 1987, p. 74.

73. David Broder, *Behind the Front Page* (New York: Simon and Schuster, 1987), pp. 208, 215.

74. Tacheron and Udall, pp. 370–383.

75. Robinson, p. 77.

76. Ibid., p. 88.

77. Ibid.

78. Martin Tolchin, "TV Studio Serves Congress," *The New York Times*, March 7, 1984, p. C22.

79. Bagdikian, p. 390.

80. "Jersey Pols . . . ", p. A8.

81. Ibid.

82. Tolchin, "TV Studio," p. C22.

83. Roger H. Davidson, "Subcommittee Government: New Channels for Policy Making" in Mann and Ornstein, pp. 99–107.

84. See Theodore Wilson, "The Truman Committee," in *Congress Investigates: 1792–1974*, ed. Arthur M. Schlesinger Jr. and Roger Bruns (New York: Chelsea House, 1975), p. 336.

85. Steven V. Roberts, "In Confirmation Process, Hearings Offer a Stage," *The New York Times*, February 8, 1989, p. B7.

86. Reid, p. 24.

87. Arthur M. Schlesinger Jr., "Introduction" in Schlesinger and Bruns, p. xii.

88. Ibid., p. xiv.

89. Robert P. Newman and Dale R. Newman, *Evidence* (Boston, MA: Houghton Mifflin, 1969), p. 97.

90. For a brief summary of these hearings see Harry J. Skornia, "The Great American Teaching Machine—of Violence," in *Mass Media Issues: Analysis and Debate*, ed. George Rodman (Chicago: S.R.A., 1977), pp. 153–54.

91. For a survey of the participants in the Watergate congressional investigations see Elizabeth Drew, *Washington Journal: the Events of 1973–1974* (New York: Vintage, 1976).

92. William J. Keefe and Morris S. Ogul, *The American Legislative Process: Congress and the State*, 4th Ed. (Englewood Cliffs, NJ: Prentice Hall, 1977), p. 204.

93. For one view of Kennedy's motives see Califano, pp. 88–119.

94. Fred W. Friendly, *Due to Circumstances Beyond Our Control* (London: McGibbon and Kee, 1967), pp. 213–35.

95. J. William Fulbright, *The Arrogance of Power* (New York: Random House, 1966), p. 56.

96. For a chronology and summary of these events see "Iran-Contra Events Span the Reagan Era," *The New York Times*, January 6, 1989, p. B4.

97. Robinson and Appel, p. 415.

98. Ibid., p. 411.

99. Ibid., p. 412.

100. Reid, p. 102.

101. Quoted in Dudley D. Cahn, Edward J. Pappas, and Ladene Schoen, "Speech in the Senate: 1978," *Communication Quarterly* (Summer 1979): 52.

102. Fenno, pp. 136–58.

103. Michael Novak, *Choosing Our King* (New York: Macmillan, 1974), p. 259.

104. Congressional Research Service, "Broadcast Coverage of State Legislatures," in *Congress and Mass Communications*, an Appendix to Hearings before the Joint Committee on Congressional Operations, Ninety-third Congress (Washington, DC: U.S. Government Printing Office, 1974), pp. 949–50.

105. "TV in the Senate: One Year After," *Broadcasting*, June 1, 1987, p. 36.

106. "Senate Adapts to Television," *Congressional Quarterly Almanac, 1987* 43, p. 47.

107. David Burnham, "A Channel that Focuses on Government," *The New York Times*, February 8, 1984, p. C21.

108. Ibid., p. C21.

109. Broder, p. 220.

110. Robinson, "Three Faces," p. 68.

111. David Leigh, "MPs Worried About Radio Image," *The Guardian*, May 30, 1978, p. 2.

112. Robinson, p. 69.

113. Nathaniel C. Nash, "A Tale of Two Legislators and How They View Their Institution," *The New York Times*, December 21, 1987, p. B10.

114. "TV in the Senate," p. 36.

115. "Senate Adapts to Television," p. 47.

116. Frank V. Donovan, "Accountability for the Legislature: The Impact of Extended Television Coverage," in *Congress and Mass Communications*, p. 752.

PART III

EPILOGUE

Chapter Eleven

Politics, Communication, and Public Trust

A diplomat learns to suppress his shame about small deceptions, if they serve a larger goal. In Saudi Arabia, I once heard a visiting American dignitary tell Saudi princes about the "deep similarities" between his nation and theirs. I maliciously hoped that someone would ask him for examples ... but I recognized the motive behind his fib. If he'd been gratuitously honest—"our societies have nothing in common"—he would have made no one any happier and would only have undermined his real purpose: securing a supply of oil.[1]

Q. Well, what do you make, General [Maxwell D. Taylor], of the principle of the people's right to know ... ?
A. I don't believe in that as a general principle.[2]

ETHICS AND COMMUNICATION: THE PROBLEM OF STANDARDS

No study of political discourse can escape its considerable ethical dilemmas. We started this book by noting that for many Americans it is nearly synonymous with deception and obfuscation. The low esteem in which political address is held flows from the belief that its practitioners routinely corrupt the relationship that should exist between thought and action. The assumption carried in this view seems to be that most other forms of goal-oriented communication are immune from similar lapses.

Our approach here has been different. We believe that political discourse has often been misunderstood, criticized for what it cannot be, and overburdened by criticism that precedes rather than follows sound analysis. Kenneth Burke's caution to critics ready to condemn the evil rhetoric in Hitler's *Mein Kampf* is still a useful reminder. A feeling of moral superiority is, by itself, an inadequate basis for understanding:

If the reviewer but knocks off a few adverse attitudinizings and calls it a day, with a guaranty in advance that his article will have a favorable reception among the decent members of our population, he is contributing more to our gratification than to our enlightenment.[3]

Politics naturally invites negative and positive judgment. Because the exercise of power involves the distribution of rewards, money, and sanctions, and because we must necessarily consider the motives of political agents, informed criticism is to be expected and encouraged. To talk about "value free" or "nonpartisan" politics is as futile as searching the calendar for a weekend with two Saturdays. There can really be no such thing as an all-encompassing and nonjudgmental "political science." The language and subject matter of politics prohibits that. Because politics is inherently about attitudes, it requires the assessment of individual motives, priorities and values. "The essence of a political . . . situation," argues John Bunzel, "is that someone is trying to do something about which there is no agreement."[4]

Even though the imposition of values and norms comes with the territory, it still remains appropriate to search for standards that can be invoked in the name of reasonableness. For example, if a presidential candidate—George Bush, to be specific—campaigns for a "kinder, gentler nation" while at the same time making harsh and inaccurate statements about his opponent, or if he says he "will not raise taxes," but may impose new "tariffs" and "user fees,"[5] is there some fair-minded basis for calling the veracity of his discourse into question? Does such rhetoric violate some universal code of reasonableness? With some exceptions, we think there *are* standards upon which individuals of different political persuasions can agree. But a number of misconceptions need to be reviewed first.

Because political communication is an audience-centered activity, universal rules of conduct are illusive. Any standards that we articulate are subject to exceptions imposed by different kinds of audiences. No system of a priori standards—including lists of logical fallacies—can be imposed on political discourse with anything more than the hope for widespread assent. Guidelines for assessing how issues should be presented can be asserted and argued. But they cannot be rendered unchallengeable.[6] It may be possible to gain nearly universal agreement on what constitutes a "bribe," illegal payoff, or some other form of corrupt political *act*. But we think it is far more difficult to judge the ethics of what someone *says*. A bribe to a legislator from a special interest group, for example, clearly violates a widely understood code governing the conduct of public officials. To secretly take money in exchange for political favors is an undeniable abuse of the public's trust. But there are few precise rhetorical equivalents. Short of deliberate lying, we expect that communication naturally permits a greater diversity of rhetorical means to achieve political ends. Communication always involves adjustments to an audience and, to some extent, the *construction* of realities. Language usage is always selective. Just as no group of individuals would describe the same scene in exactly the same way, so are political realities open to a diversity of interpretations. Realities are not discovered by political advocates; they are at least partly created. Such constructions may be widely shared, but not universally accepted.

This is perhaps one reason Ronald Reagan's penchant for providing examples and anecdotes of suspect validity did not harm his credibility with vast numbers of Americans in his first term. In his 1980 campaign, he regularly referred to a Chicago "welfare queen" who had supposedly become rich through the abuse of state and federal "handouts."[7] Apparently no such person existed. But the failure of the example to tally with the facts probably did not matter. For his strongest supporters, and even for some of his critics, it was recognized that such rhetoric had an expressive rather than instrumental role. Accuracy of communication is important. But even bowdlerized "examples" can have their own internal validity. As Reagan knew well, political discussion has more in common with the fabrications of drama than with the objective descriptions of the hard sciences.

THE RECIPROCAL OBLIGATIONS OF POLITICAL DISCOURSE

It is so common to focus on the obligations of political communicators that we often overlook the fact that democratic life carries responsibilities for audiences as well. Electoral politics in particular links the fortunes of advocates to the competencies of audiences. Advocates can never be very far out in front of their constituencies. What they say must strike chords of recognition in the audiences that have the power to approve or disprove of their actions. In an important sense, members of the polity are cocreaters of the messages they hear. Walt Whitman's observation that "to have great poets there must be great audiences, too" is as fitting for politics as for poetry.

The polity must also share the praise or blame that it heaps on its leaders. In the course of a political campaign it is a common ritual for the press to lament the low quality of discourse coming from the competing candidates and parties. The implication is usually that the candidates are too inept or devious to address the tough issues facing the electorate. But the reciprocal nature of communication should force us to reverse the direction of the arrows as well. A public that tolerates mediocre discourse gets not only what it probably deserves, but also what it no doubt *requires* of the candidate. For instance, one cannot review film footage from the 1952 or 1956 presidential campaign without sensing the quiet agony of Dwight Eisenhower and his challenger, Adlai Stevenson, as they tried to reduce their campaign themes to 30-second television commercials. Like so many before and after them, they were forced to take the voters where they found them. And in the 1950s the electorate was increasingly in front of the television set, learning to be intolerant of program interruptions that exceeded more than a minute.

The paradox in all of this is that accusations about political incompetence are almost always directed to the wrong audience: to political professionals rather than to their indifferent audiences. Popular portrayals of the venality of political life usually ignore references to the quiescent majorities that allow it to happen. We wish more discussions of demagoguery—for example, of notorious figures such as Boston's James Curley, Louisiana's Huey Long, or New Jersey's Frank Hague—included consideration of the failures in public competence that the successes of demagogues collectively imply.[8] The point is not necessarily to affix blame to any particular side of the equation, but to indicate that "the people" have largely been removed from too many popular discussions of political morality.[9] To cite but one discomforting case: Richard Nixon was reelected by a landslide in 1972 *after* substantial information about the Watergate break-in was before the public. That fact should give us pause for what it implies about the reciprocity of political transactions. It is widely thought that the Watergate affair and its aftermath demonstrated the strengths of our political institutions. There was a sense of collective relief when Nixon eventually resigned prior to probable impeachment. Outwardly, it appeared that the "system had worked"; Congress had prevailed in using its powers to investigate executive malfeasance. But few observers publicly questioned the lack of wisdom in the American electorate that gave the Nixon administration its ill-fated second term.[10]

The problem, of course, is that journalists and authors are not immune to the blandishments of a market economy. They, too, must win the support of their readers and viewers, but with circulation figures rather than votes. Few journalists want to alienate their audiences with any sort of collective guilt for the quality of political discourse. The far safer scapegoat is the incompetent politician who somehow fooled or misled the electorate. There is little future for a writer in the commercial media who equates the failings of the electorate with failures in society. It was a special courage that led television's Edward R. Murrow to end his famous program on the red-baiting tactics of Senator Joseph McCarthy with a gentle accusation. The rise of the demogogic McCarthy, Murrow suggested, was our doing:

The actions of the Junior Senator from Wisconsin have caused alarm and dismay amongst our allies abroad and given considerable comfort to our enemies. And whose fault is that? Not really his. He didn't create this situation of fear, he merely exploited it; and rather successfully. Cassius was right. "The fault, dear Brutus, is not in our stars, but in ourselves."[11]

POLITICS, TRUST, AND THE "CRISIS OF AUTHORITY"

The severest test facing any political system is probably when it must communicate its basic legitimacy through a period of sustained national adversity.

A government that has lost the respect of the citizens faces its toughest communication challenge. As Claus Mueller has noted, "There is no political system that does not need to legitimate itself . . . "[12] The perception that politics are unjust or failed, that corruption is common, or that levels of government have lost touch with popular sentiments, are common conditions in industrialized nations. Such periods have routinely cycled through the history of the United States. The Civil War, Reconstruction, the Great Depression, the Watergate affair, and to a lesser extent, the taking of American hostages in Iran and the Iran-Contra scandal, are only a few of the more obvious tests of governmental legitimacy. After Watergate in 1973, for example, over 65 percent of a cross section of Americans agreed with the negative conclusions that "Government is for the benefit of a few" and "You cannot trust government to do right." By contrast, only about 25 percent agreed with these statements in the relatively benign year of 1958.[13] Similarly, the last year of the Carter administration stands as a symbol for the idea of governmental powerlessness. The humiliating capture of Americans in the Iranian Embassy, and the administration's inability to win their release, left Americans bitter about the impotence of what we want to believe is the most powerful office in the free world.[14]

These events reflect a basic American ambivalence about political institutions. Decisive action by an executive faced with an apparent crisis is often supported. But long-term distrust of more routine governmental processes also runs deep. Political institutions function against a permanent backdrop of public skepticism that is as old as the nation. As John Dewey has written, "the events that finally culminated in democratic political forms were deeply tinged by fear of government, and were actuated by a desire to reduce it to a minimum so as to limit the evil it could do."[15] A Jeffersonian suspicion of centralized government is still imbedded in the American *ethos*, at least among those for whom government is seen as taker rather than giver.

A crisis of authority is reached when suspicion gives way to hostile dissent. France and the United States faced such fears of social disintegration in the 1960s, as agitation for domestic and foreign policy reforms first initiated by political activists caught hold on college campuses and spread through labor unions and activists. Similar fears of chaotic change brought on by widespread convulsions of public attitudes now regularly strike at the heart of the once unchallengeable one-party systems of Eastern Europe. Even in the Soviet Union, the anger that has surfaced in the non-Russian republics tests the limits of *glasnost* in ways that would have been unthinkable just a few years ago.

In most periods of intense political unrest, even factions which have limited political representation usually find ways to work within the existing political framework—sometimes through contacts with sympathetic legislators, interest groups, or other like-minded partisans who have access to the public media. Yet there clearly is a level beyond which the loss of credibility becomes lethal to institutions of the state. Vietnam policy and the deaths of Martin Luther King and Robert Kennedy produced the perception of political disintegration in 1968.

Thousands of alienated Americans became witnesses or victims to sustained periods of destructive urban violence. Millions more became spectators to this bitterness, much of it directed to the eroding legitimacy of the Johnson administration, the Congress, and social institutions in general. Whatever mending of the social fabric that took place slowly after that tumultuous year fell largely to the only national institution to come through the period with its credibility more or less intact—the press. The major networks and wire services grudgingly mediated the disorder by giving greater access to alienated and unofficial voices. Skepticism about war objectives filtered into war reporting. Documentaries elevated Martin Luther King from the level of political dissident to the higher realm of national idealist. Johnson, however, felt obliged to leave the scene, thereby avoiding the monumental task of repairing his image as the engineer of the "Great Society."[16]

TELEVISION AND COMMUNICATION ETHICS

As we noted in Chapter 6, assessments of the quality of politics in American life are routinely linked to the effects of the mass media. One belief common to politicians and spectators alike is that the advent of television has distorted the roles and objectives of political institutions. No single change in American political life has provoked more discussion than the role of political television.[17] It is thought to have placed another layer of bureaucracy between rulers and the ruled by supplanting the political parties as the primary network for public communication. While extending the power of executive offices such as the Presidency and governorships, it has obscured the Congress and the legislatures. And it has emphasized the role of affect in politics; the joining of advocates with issues changes the ways we think about politics. Especially in synoptic television news, the presence of specific personalities will often eclipse attention on the details of substantive issues.

Our discussion here is limited only to a final look at some general trends in the uses of television, trends that seem to have a direct bearing on the general quality of public discussion. In some cases these patterns provide grounds of optimism; in other cases, for pessimism.

Distaste for a Public Fight: Television and the Search for the Political Middle

By its nature, television delivers generally nonspecific and nonpolitical audiences to its users. A specific convention or meeting may provide the opportunity to sharpen partisan differences, but the very structure of commercial television offers no such incentives. Viewers are heterogeneous. The skillful user of television realizes that little can be gained by faithfully serving as an advocate for a sharply defined point of view. There are potentially more benefits to an approach that mimics the logic of prime-time television—namely to find the safe ideological center, and to broaden appeals to include as many in the audience as possible. The massive size of the television audience suggests that there is more to be gained by substituting agreement in place of argumentation, by identifying the broadest possible clientele rather than ideological compatriots. Television is not the only force working against the nondelineation of positions. But as the "massest" of the mass media, it most clearly offers risks to those striving for some kind of doctrinal purity. This fact results in an output that represents a strange kind of nonpartisan partisanship. With some exceptions, such as PBS's "MacNeil-Lehrer Report" or ABC's "Nightline," its audiences are thought to be too big and inert to be instructed. Genuine clarification of hard choices is thus frequently replaced by a truncated recital of "both sides" of a dispute. We often witness heated "debates" that are packaged more for their expressive content than their communication value.

Nowhere has this trend been more evident than in the conduct of the political parties and television networks during political conventions. The conventions of both parties in the 1980s—but especially those convened by the G.O.P.—were notable for an almost complete absence of convention debate on platform planks, the seating of delegations, and the merits of opposing candidates. To be sure, part of the change cannot be blamed on television. The presidential primary system has irrevocably replaced the convention as the basis for selecting presidential standardbearers. What is less acceptable is the shifting of natural intraparty differences away from the televised convention and into less public venues. The parties now recognize that the conventions provide the possibility of presenting the imagery of unity. Television debates that might lessen such highly contrived images are not given prominence, or are relegated to hours when many Americans are no longer viewing.[18] Convention time is increasingly taken up with patriotic ceremonies and filmed eulogies of party icons (with lights out in the convention hall, thus encouraging the networks to relent on their floor coverage in favor of the film). What are now euphemistically called the "streamlined" rules of the conventions largely prohibit floor debate on issues that divide the membership within the parties.

Consistency and the Mass Audience

National distribution of political messages—especially speeches and press conferences—has placed a greater premium on consistency, even as specific audiences change from one location to another. Television dramatizes political continuity, or the lack of it, in ways that are more vivid than is possible with print. Remarks and addresses now routinely travel statewide or nationwide— well beyond their original audience. What is said must be rectified for two audiences. The immediate audience for a political address seeks some recognition of its status and importance to the politician. The larger electronic audience must be assured that policy has not shifted, and that previous alliances and commitments have not been abandoned. At best, the existence of these twin groups lessens the opportunity for capricious changes for short-term gain. At worse, advocates may seek refuge in the vaguest forms of discourse, or may find themselves unexpectedly constrained by an ill-planned promise.

In very different periods of America's recent history Richard Nixon and George Bush faced the problem of rectifying the values of two audiences. During a 1959 tour of the Soviet Union, then Vice-President Nixon was invited to give a national television address to citizens of that country. In *Six Crises* he claims that he approached the task "solely with the Russian people in mind."[19] But the future presidential candidate was undoubtedly conscious of the Americans back home who would wonder what he had told America's ideological competitors. His address had to be—and largely was—conciliatory to the Soviets, but essentially consistent with his reputation as a determined anti-Communist.[20] Thirty years later George Bush inherited the need to deal with a very different Soviet Union, but still with some of the same complications that were part of Nixon's dilemma. The broadening of personal freedoms under Mikhail Gorbachev's "glasnost" were easy for the Reagan and Bush administrations to admire. What became troublesome in the spring of 1989 was the presence of ethnic unrest against "Russian imperialism" in Armenia, Georgia, and Eastern Block nations such as Poland. A few of these newly sanctioned protests produced demonstrations and violence of unprecedented scope, especially in the Caucasus region along the southern tier of the Soviet border. Some administration officials thought that too much domestic unrest might give Moscow's conservative hardliners new ammunition to counter Gorbachev's liberal reforms. They urged Bush to show patience with the Soviet leader's long-term goals, and to downplay attempts by the military to restore order. Suddenly Bush had to walk a fine rhetorical line between the conventional and the innovative: between traditional American criticism of Soviet repression, and the more novel view that an embattled Gorbachev needed the sympathetic support of an American president.[21]

Even the passing of time may not diminish the requirement for consistency. A president, a candidate, a legislator is not free to arbitrarily abandon commitments and attitudes that have been publicly asserted. Scores of national politicians have been confronted with television news accounts that dramatically juxtapose statements made years ago with newer utterances that are in sharp variance. The split-second "jump cut" that diminishes time by mixing old and new footage has the effect of heightening the viewer's distaste for political hypocrisy. More than ever, it is a fact of political life that commitments made in face-to-face televised encounters may lay down tracks of obligations that can lock in a leader to a predetermined course of action.

Consultants, Speechwriters, and the Distancing of Messages from Their "Sources"

Speechwriters, consultants, staff assistants, and researchers compose an important stratum within the political hierarchy. While the politician is still the most important source of his or her statements, we know that much of the routine preparation of the vast remainder of messages is often relegated to an extensive support system. As we noted in Chapter 8, the more powerful the official or institution, the more likely the burden for routine message preparation will fall to support staff. The tasks of communications experts are not just limited to the forming and wording of ideas. They are also increasingly used to make sense of the vagaries of polling, to locate appropriate audiences for messages, and even to oversee television lighting and makeup.

The intervention of so many of these specialists between audiences and communicators naturally raises questions about the speaker's autonomy and authenticity. When does such a person cease being an independent agent? Is there a point at which the "best" politician is the one that is the most malleable?

The "image" problem facing Ronald Reagan during his entry into both state and national politics involved just such issues. The pundits bombarded the nation with questions implying the inauthentic nature of a politician trained to be a mouthpiece for others. Would an actor be able to play the public role of chief executive better than he could actually perform its administrative duties? Was he—like others before him—essentially the product of the marketing expertise of others? Over his career Reagan was a spokesman for a number of groups with either political or commercial objectives. He worked in a radio station, perhaps the ultimate case of serving as a mouthpiece for others. He represented the Screen Actor's Guild in Hollywood. After he left films, he represented a soap company on television and an electrical conglomerate in hundreds of personal appearances. In short he had acquired the facility to assume the attitudes of those he served. Among his close advisers at various times in his administration were advertising consultant Stuart Roberts, pollster Robert Teeter, market researcher Richard Wirthlin, public relations expert Michael Deaver, and writers David Gergen and Pat Buchanan.[22] How much of the President that Americans saw was *their* creation? And how much was the "real" Reagan?

The President's widely reported dependence on consultants was obviously not unique. Aides wise in the arts of presentational cosmetics have been around at least since the Eisenhower years. Every administration has had its counterparts to the Reagan public relations team. The lessons they have imparted have not been lost on officeholders in major cities, the states, the Congress, and the cabinet. There can be little doubt that the rise of the consultant has changed politics, especially video politics. The unresolved issue is whether or not teams of mass media specialists have intervened in a way that is detrimental to the political process. More and more, presidential politics seem to come to the public with a marketing objective of eliciting a feeling reassurance rather than mastery of the arguments.[23] The public relations mentality rarely allows hard policy choices to be described as they are: difficult decisions that weigh personal costs against public benefits. Woodrow Wilson and Theodore Roosevelt reveled in presenting elaborate and detailed arguments in defense of policy, often to audiences less intellectually prepared for such discussions than their better-educated contemporaries. The approach to issues today seems far more personalistic, represented most concretely in the 1980 Reagan campaign strategy of focusing almost exclusively on personal prosperity and "happiness" rather than on policy.[24]

Television and the Dominance of the Executive

When the print press was still the prime source of political information for most Americans it was easier to communicate intragovernmental tensions in a way that would give equal weight to the various factions. The views of leaders in Congress and the legislatures could successfully compete with those offered by presidents and governors. Well into the twentieth century, for example, the Senate was more than just an equal match for the Presidency. Its titans admired by John Kennedy in *Profiles in Courage* were as well known as the chief executive. Various papers had their favorites among the Vandenburgs, Bryans, and LaFollettes. No one national figure dominated public attention. Many factors have since tipped the scales in favor of the executive. For several reasons the balance began to change under F.D.R.: because of his desire for strong leadership after the Presidency of Herbert Hoover, but mostly because Roosevelt was willing to exploit newer means of communication. First came popular newsreels and then radio. Both were better able to focus issues onto a single person rather than a less photogenic movement or organization. Television further developed the need for visual conciseness, making presidents, a few senators, dozens of movie stars, and scores of professional athletes the centerpieces of their stories. Where presidents Truman and Eisenhower viewed intense television exposure as a mixed blessing, later presidents—notably Johnson and Nixon—saw it as a source of new power.

The old tensions between Congress and the President have not been reduced by television's fascination with the single leader. But they have been muted. At least since the Nixon years, the dominant strategy of the consultant-oriented communication offices in the White House has been to *contain* rather than *engage* disputes. Television is the single most important tool of the Presidency, and "crisis management" is arguably its most valued use. In all of its many forms television news provides the vehicle for the management and containment of negative public opinion. Straightforward debate is frequently avoided in favor of televised appeals that can minimize the negative impressions raised by a controversy. A common goal is to deflect public criticism onto political institutions such as Congress, which are usually unable to muster any kind of decisive collective response. In parliamentary democracies, where government leaders also sit as elected members of the national deliberative body, there is an enforced dialogue between major political factions. In Britain, for instance, the Prime Minister personally responds to questions in parliament once a week. With the exception of some city governments, no similar mechanism exists in the American political system. Debates featuring the major parties to a political crisis (e.g., the Watergate affair in 1973, the Iran-Contra affair in 1986) are thus never quite joined. Surrogates end up representing the President in Congress and before the courts. And presidents almost always choose a set speech in the Oval Office or before carefully managed audiences to deal with the demands for political dialogue.

FOUR CORRUPTIONS OF POLITICAL DISCOURSE

As described throughout this book, political discourse is shaped by many needs and motives. In specific instances it rarely conforms to the rational ideals of decision making that are implied in constitutional or textbook models of government. We have noted, for example, that political communication involves many legitimate expressive functions. Preaching to the converted, evoking shared values, and providing a basis for official legitimacy are only the most common. But there are limits. While the enormous range of objectives of audiences described elsewhere in this book make any kind of moralizing difficult, we are not unmindful of the range of corruptions to which political language is prone. In politics, as in every community of shared disourse, there are thresholds of communication beyond which the public trust is violated. We close with a brief overview of four common abuses of political language. In what we describe as coercion, deception, mystification, and redefinition are some of the excesses to be found in the rhetoric of civil life.

Coercion

Coercion is the application of force instead of argument to change the behavior of someone else.[25] It differs from persuasion in several important ways. The individual's freedom to decide (i.e., to form an opinion) is taken away because of threats which directly or indirectly imply that his safety and well-being is at stake. Although coercion may connote impending harm, it is often enough to suggest the *possibility* of harm as the result of noncompliance.

In a free society political discourse invites the consideration of costs and consequences, positive as well as negative. But it is a different matter when the arguer reduces the issue to only negative personal consequences. To imply or state that dire effects on an individual will follow from an action can signal an advocate's intention of taking away the option of a freely made choice. For example, if the politicly appointed head of a city agency tells his staffers that "You are free to work for whichever mayoral candidate you like, but you ought to remember the incumbent has been pretty good to us," the freedom that is implied in the first clause is effectively negated by the second. Even the least political of workers would realize that any campaigning done against the incumbent will jeopardize his or her job. The possibility of making a decision based on the candidates' merits is foreclosed by the implied threat.

The television networks and their staffs believed they faced this problem after remarks made in 1969 by Vice-President Spiro Agnew. Agnew gave two speeches within a few weeks that were sharply critical of television and print press coverage. Among other things, he criticized the three networks for basing their reporting too extensively on the East and West Coasts, and not enough in America's "middle America." He also strongly criticized the "instant analysis" that followed the Nixon administration's explanations of Vietnam policy, expressing anger at the networks for filling out the remaining time after Nixon's addresses with brief summaries and analyses of his remarks.[26] For its part, the regulation-sensitive broadcast industry professed shock that a spokesman for the President would argue that control of the industry was falling into "fewer and fewer hands."[27]

Taken by themselves, Agnew's speeches contained some fair criticism. A wide spectrum of journalistic and academic critics had made many of the same points for years. But the vehemence of the comments hit a raw nerve. The key assets of any news source are its public credibility and institutional independence. The administration had been uncharacteristically bold in implying that both were in jeopardy. The threats were made even more ominous by the fact that others, close to the administration, such as Office of Telecommunications Chairman Clay Whitehead, were voicing similar concerns to receptive audiences. In concert with Agnew, Whitehead advocated stronger monitoring of the broadcasters' content.[28] Were these speeches about "fair play" and "letting viewers decide for themselves" simply the complaints of a frustrated administration? Or were darker coercive motives at work? To broadcasters, the timing and force of the addresses suggested a planned administration campaign of intimidation. At stake were the lucrative federal licenses that television stations need in order to remain on the air. No less a figure than Walter Cronkite noted that "this Administration ... has conceived, planned, orchestrated and is now conducting a program to reduce the effectiveness of a free press, and its prime target is television."[29]

In fact, soon after Agnew's remarks, CBS ended its policy of "instant analysis" of presidential speeches. If goading the networks to back off from their criticism was a goal of the administration, it had partially succeeded.

This example indicates how difficult it can be to separate coercive from non-coercive communication. As we noted at the beginning of this study, political power is inherently about the control of rewards and punishments. It is difficult to conceive of any extended piece of political discourse that does not include appeals to the hearer's sense of jeopardy. Such appeals may be considered an essential form of leverage. In intragovernmental communication these kinds of coercive power plays are common and expected. A Senate or House committee may seek information from a president under the threat of a subpoena to a cabinet member. Journalists may be "convinced" that it is in their best interests to give up a planned investigative article, if it becomes obvious that a "freeze out" by valuable sources will make their work impossible. Legislators may find that their sponsorship and advocacy of one bill requires an exchange of support with colleagues who have different legislative priorities. In each case the grounds for defeat and triumph can be measured in personal as well as ideological terms.

Deception

The idea of deception is so basic to the discussion of political persuasion that it is useful to approach it first by describing what it is not. There can be little doubt that the international misrepresentation of information is unethical, although advocates of covert government activity may justify official lies, or defend a campaign of *disinformation* that is intended to confuse an enemy. But it is not always easy to see the threshold that separates partial descriptions of reality from deliberate falsifications of it. As Kenneth Burke has noted, what amounts to the selective representation of events is frequently the consequence of legitimate motives:

Imagine that you, as President, were about to put through Congress some measure that would strongly alienate some highly influential class. What would be the most natural way for you to present this matter to the public? Would you try, as far as is stylistically possible, to soften the effects of the blow? You would try to be as reassuring as possible.
. . .
Imagine, on the other hand, that the public had been clamoring for such a measure, but you as President did not want to be so drastic. . . . In this case, you would try to put through a more moderate measure—but you would make up the difference stylistically by thundering about its startling scope. One could hardly call this hypocrisy; it is the normally prayerful use of language, to sharpen up the pointless and blunt the too sharply pointed.[30]

Language, notes Burke, is a "corrective" instrument. Its users cannot be *ipso facto* condemned for using it "artfully" to guide thought. In his view it is unrealistic to expect that language can be used to correspond exactly to a singular reality. Because man is an interactor, not a recorder, advocacy that is selective and idiomatic is to be expected. It is part of the human condition rather than indisputable evidence of deception.

In general, we think rhetorical deception often can be recognized, and should be condemned. But we also think that lying for political ends is less common than is widely perceived. One reason for this mistaken perception is the belief—to put it simply—that if two people disagree, one is probably concealing an important truth. But the deeper reality is probably that the analyst has misperceived that nature of the controversy. It is axiomatic to politics that disputes cannot be invariably tied to the expectation that there must be "true" and "false" sides. Policy questions that deal with issues of merits, costs, and benefits necessarily provide for a plurality of legitimate but different conclusions. There may be a certain degree of psychological satisfaction to assert that one side in a dispute is bankrupt of good reasons, and that advocates representing it are engaged in a colossal form of deception. But the more accurate view is that each side in a controversy carries presumptions that preclude the kind of empathy that would be necessary to "see" the other side. For example, Ralph K. White's study of North Vietnamese and American perceptions toward the war noted what is easy for a neutral observer to see, but a committed advocate to overlook: that both sides enhanced their own self-image at the other's expense. Such a state of mind is probably necessary to engage in war. The construction of a "diabolical enemy-image," a "virile self-image," and "a moral self-image" was enough to build up an impenetrable facade of moral and rational certainty on each side.[31]

Another problematic concept in the labeling of deception resides in the very idea of "political propaganda." Ominous connotations cling to this overworked phrase. It carries an enormous amount of negative weight. At times it is used as a synonym with lying and hypocrisy in politics—a convenient put-down label. It is common to characterize one's political enemies as masters of deceptive and manipulative propaganda, and one's own discourse as more fair and open. "The Soviets propagandize, but we simply inform" represents a common but unreflective use of the term. What is ignores is the presence of highly refined forms of political and commercial propaganda—for example, product advertising in the United States—which fuel virtually every nation's political and commercial life.

Part of the problem is that the very term connotes more than it denotes. The company that the term keeps teaches us to dislike it. More often than not, "propaganda" is little more than a convenient net into which we can place all of our anxieties about the nature of political discourse. It stands for the vague sense of betrayal that comes with the perception that we have been victims of untruths and manipulation. Carl Friedrich gets closer to its essence when he describes it in terms of the intentions of its users. The propagandist is "a person who hands out information in order to gain benefits, material or nonmaterial advantages, for himself or more typically for the group he is acting for."[32] The message involves an advocate with a financial or ideological interest in the success of the message—hardly an ominous or unique trait. Moreover, as Friedrich notes, it is too simple to prejudge propaganda as merely a collection of lies. "While lying may at times be a method of propagandists, it often is not."[33] Propaganda is another form of advocacy, neither better nor worse than past forms of public persuasion.[34]

Are we left, therefore, to declare that we have no basis for assessing (or condemning) "deceptive" political discourse? Of course not. Political advocates do lie: less often, perhaps, than the conventional wisdom about political morality would lead us to believe. But often enough.

One form of deception that is much discussed in all modern democracies is that which seems to be sanctioned by the national interest. The Eisenhower administration's denial that a spy plane had been shot down over Russia in 1960 was a bold but obvious attempt at deception. The President knew of the missions, since he had personally approved the use of the high-altitude plane. Only when the captured pilot and wreckage were displayed on Russian television did he finally admit the existence of the flights.[35] Lt. Colonel Oliver North's protests that he had no choice but to deceive congressional questioners probing the arms-for-hostages agreement with Iran became equally fascinating. In testimony before a special congressional committee, and in his own 1989 criminal trial, the former member of the National Security Council sought to vindicate himself and a broad plan of covert action expressly prohibited by Congress. The plan was apparently initiated by CIA Director William Casey, with some knowledge of President Reagan. North defended himself by claiming that what he told various senators and representatives might also be heard by America's enemies, and could have harmed the hostages. The deception of Congress and others was, he argued, a matter of national duty.

The Iran-Contra affair was one of many instances where officials argued that deception could sometimes be justified. For example, in 1974 a variety of congressional investigations studies made it increasingly evident that CIA Director Richard Helms had misled the Congress in explaining covert CIA actions. Members of Congress and reporters Seymour Hersh and Daniel Schorr received leaked information from former CIA operatives that left little doubt that Helms had deceived members of Congress engaged in oversight hearings. There was hard evidence that the organization had encouraged the overthrow and assassination of Chile's President Salvador Allende, had organized surveillance of members of the antiwar movement within the United States, and had ties to some of the Watergate burglars. Helm's earlier testimony before the Senate Foreign Relations Committee included a number of false denials. On America's role in overthrowing Chile's Allende, for example, Helms was explicit when asked questions by Senator Stuart Symington:

Symington: Did you try in the Central Intelligence Agency to overthrow the government of Chile?

Helms: No, sir.

Symington: Did you have any money passed to the opponents of Allende?

Helms: No sir?[36]

The CIA's own information painted a different picture. In Schorr's words,

He had denied passing money to Allende's opponents to Chile. He had denied any domestic spying. He had denied any pre-Watergate involvement with Howard Hunt. Now he blamed "misunderstood questions for previous contradictions," saying that he "had no intention of lying. . . ."[37]

Could Helms have *not* known what his agency was doing? It seems unlikely. Could he have felt that—by definition—covert acts cannot be communicated, even to the Congress? Probably. But members of Congress have security clearances for such information: a claim of exclusive rights to secrecy could not stand against that body's preeminent right to oversight.

A larger problem represented by the legacies of Oliver North and Richard Helms is that a secret intelligence service is, by definition, a paradox in an open society. Lies are automatically a part of a clandestine organization's business. But they are lies nonetheless. One of the less savory dilemmas faced by governments in open societies is how the executive's penchant for covert activity against foreign powers can be squared with democratic ideals. If open societies have secrets, when does the public's much vaunted "right to know" end and the secrecy begin? And what if the secrecy label is used to cover-up mistakes? The complexity of these questions defies glib and simple answers. The consideration of secrecy as a guise for deception must usually be considered on a case by case basis. What is apparent is that there has been widespread abuse of "national security" and "executive privilege" as reasons to give false information. The result is a residue of profound public cynicism.[38]

Another kind of deception goes beyond the rationale for the need for official secrets. These involve what Chaim Perelman calls "bad faith" statements.[39] A bad faith act violates the trust and respect that is implicit in most kinds of communication. The speaker engages in such communication cynically. Excessive promise keeping, exaggerated appeals to fear, oversimplification of complex issues, the raising of false two-sided dichotomies, are representative forms. All reflect a failure of the speaker to enter into dialogue with an audience on equal terms: to hear as well as assert, to risk at least as much as is asked of the audience, and to imply no more than is justified by arguments and evidence.

There are a number of bad faith ploys that not only deceive an audience, but also signal the speaker's fundamental contempt toward those in it. One involves the stereotypical political act of appearing to be all things to all people. The speaker who wears attitudes and values only to please an audience is engaging in an age-old form of deception. For him, values and attitudes can be exploited for their convenience as strategic tools to win them over. "The hypocrite," notes Perelman, "gives the appearance of adopting a rule of conduct in agreement with that of others in order to avoid having to justify some action which he prefers and which he adopts in reality." In this way, "hypocrisy is the homage that vice plays to virtue . . . "[40] The speaker's vice is his bad faith desire to succeed with an audience by fraudulently passing himself off as one of their own. Hearers are given false grounds for trust, and are asked to give more than they get in return.

Such were the origins of the downfall of Spiro Agnew in 1972. As Vice-President the former Governor represented himself in the eulogistic image of the self-made man. Agnew made his vice-presidential career by preaching the "silent majority's" gospel of hard work, common decency, and law and order. As the son of Greek immigrants, he was the enactment of the American dream. But his plea of "no contest" to charges that he had once accepted illegal kickbacks proved to be too much. This defender of "hard work" and "respect for the law" was suddenly accused of illegal graft. His fall was at least partially attributable to what many perceived to be a gross misrepresentation of his values.

Mystification

Another form of corruption to which political communication is vulnerable involves a different kind of deception. Mystification is more than omission or denial. It denotes the camouflaging of motives in language, sometimes cynically and sometimes naively. For Karl Marx and Thomas Carlyle, as Kenneth Burke has brilliantly pointed out, mystification was the process of using ideas to justify hierarchical distinctions that protect class prerogatives. Threads of status-protecting values that have been subtly woven into the fabric of the language provide a basis for mystification. Ideas that seem altogether natural, in actual fact, may work to benefit the privileged at the expense of the poor. Such ideas are presented "as primary where they should have been treated as derivative."[41] Religion as the "opium of the masses" was Marx's most infamous example of this process. It was his view that religious beliefs drained off the motive for social change by promising the poor a better life in the hereafter.

In their most insidious political forms, mystifications appeal to eulogize values or ideas that essentially contradict the speaker's private beliefs. Such appeals are laid out in a thin veneer which barely covers interests that would be unpalatable if known. Mystifying rhetoric involves the evoking of images and impressions that give listeners some basis for believing that they should defer to the superior wisdom or judgment of someone else. It is not simply deception, but the manipulation of appeals in a respectable language that implies no self-gain. The political communicator exercises his own form of bad faith by couching private objectives in a rhetoric of high-minded public good. Even so abhorrent a policy as nineteenth-century American slavery could be successfully represented to slaves and slave owners alike as an institution of enlightenment:

> Taught by the master's efforts, by his care
> Fed, Clothed, protected many a patent year
> From trivial number now to millions grown
> With the white man's useful arts their own
> Industrious, docile, skilled in wood and field,
> To guide the plow, the sturdy axe to wield,
> The Negroes schooled by slavery embrace
> The highest portion of the Negro race. . . .[42]

Mystification does *not* depend on exact understanding of what is said, but on a more generalized impression that the listener has no grounds from which to challenge the speaker. For example, in the techno-jargon that is now common to medicine, physics, and other specialized areas, there is the implicit connotation that decisions which will affect us are still best left to others. Thus, when a doctor uses a Latinate word to describe his diagnosis of an ailment, and prescribes a drug with an equally impressive name, his rhetoric has given the patient grounds for giving in to his expertise. Power and authority are communicated by impressions rather than full understanding.

Political mystifications play upon the credulity of audiences. They present advocates to be what they are not. In his study of political demogogues in the earlier part of this century, Reinhard Luthin noted that most of them successfully cultivated a public persona that was fundamentally in conflict with their private actions. For example,

The demogogues, while preaching and posing as "men of the people," are not averse to "doing business" with the "interests" whom they blisteringly assail on the stump. While they make dramatic displays of distributing milk to the poor, they all too often in a sense—skim the cream off for themselves.[43]

To be sure, no public official is ever quite as simple as the cultivated image that is offered to the public. The threshold that defines the corruption of the political process is when the public imagery conceals individual attitudes and investments that are seriously at odds with public statements. It is perhaps a harmless charade for a member of Congress to misrepresent himself as a lover of music in the presence of musicians. But it is quite another matter when the same figure presents himself as an altruistic advocate for legislation from which he or close friends will receive financial gain. Such advocacy is dishonest because motives are misrepresented on important ideas and principles. Like deadly weapons concealed in a child's doll, the mystification uses a legitimate vehicle for illegitimate gain, eventually making even the most honored of objects suspect. Such deception erodes the whole idea of political discussion because it appears to use the sacred— the wealth of shared values and beliefs—to conceal what is later discovered as profane.

Mystification by Redefinition

General semanticists have noted for decades that there is little to be gained by complaining about the "misuse" of language.[44] Language is a dynamic rather than static form of exchange. Dictionaries and grammarians notwithstanding, words and meanings change in nonuniform ways—not by plan or prescription, but by happenstance. Because words and meanings are plastic, their everyday use as instruments of public discussion cannot be frozen in time.

And yet, having said it, we still recognize that there are verbal constructions that impair our abilities to grasp the essentials of political events. It is one thing to extend an audience's understanding of an idea by evoking a term or a phrase in a new way. It is quite another to place the description of events in a fog of misused terms. Consider two examples that illustrate both possibilities. In a radio "Fireside Chat" in 1940, Franklin Roosevelt called on America to be the "arsenal for democracy."[45] The phrase was one of a number of suasory tools used by Roosevelt to prime American public opinion for entry into the European war, as an ally to Britain and France. This simple image aptly met two political necessities. One was to shape opinion on the importance of arms production and the consumer sacrifices that would be necessary. The other necessity was to create a linkage between what was happening in Europe and American values. Far more pragmatic reasons could have been cited by Roosevelt. But it was not hypocritical to claim that the protection of Western European democracies was essential. The United States' arsenal could and did "save" those countries from permanent Nazi domination. In contrast, Ronald Reagan's reference to a nuclear-armed missile on many different occasions as the "MX Peacekeeper" seemed to involve a fundamental corruption of terms.[46] President Carter had also favored the program, but referred to it by its basic designation: the "MX Missile." But President Reagan routinely added "peacekeeper" to its name, probably on the advice of staffers who found it a convenient way to deflect criticism of the extensive military expansion undertaken in his first term. Though it can hardly be classified as a serious form of political malfeasance, the use of the term stretches a word beyond its reasonable limits. A missile is designed to kill personnel and destroy property. One might credibly argue that a strong military helps "keep the peace" or "makes the world safe for democracy"—two common phrases in the presidential lexicon. But it seems to be a violation of reasonable usage when the term "peacekeeper" becomes the name for a weapon with awesome destructive power.

George Orwell's *1984* is undoubtedly best known for its study of mystification by redefinition. Orwell's book was both a warning and a prophecy. The concentration of power and communication in modern states, he felt, could be easily misused, much to the detriment of the ordinary citizen's freedom. The fictitious "Oceania" not only centralized all government, but the control and the wording of all information as well. His description of "Vocabulary B" of the official "Newspeak" language suggests the most oppressive kind of mind control. The goal of the language was not only "to make all other forms of thought impossible," but to use euphemisms to cover up the fundamental venality of the state.[47] The book opens with its famous description of three slogans put forth by the "Ministry of Truth":

WAR IS PEACE

FREEDOM IS SLAVERY

IGNORANCE IS STRENGTH[48]

What Orwell described in 1948 had already come to pass with perverse efficiency in the Third Reich. Claus Mueller cites a number of "language regulations" that were handed down to the German press from Hitler's government in the late 1930s. The following guidelines from the Office of the Press subverted thought by turning meaning on its ear. In the words of the office,

July 27, 1937   "According to the new government, the term 'propaganda' is a legally protected one, so to speak, and cannot be used in a derogatory sense. . . . In short, 'propaganda' only if it serves us; 'agitation' for those who are against us."

December 13, 1937   ''The urgent directive has been given that the term 'League of Nations' can no longer be used by the German press as of today. This word no longer exists. . . . ''

September 1, 1939   ''The word 'war' has to be avoided in all news coverage and editorials. Germany is repulsing a Polish attack.''

September 11, 1939   ''The word courageous can only be used for German soldiers.''[49]

To conclude that Orwell's predictions about the rhetorical manipulation of attitudes has come true is too simplistic. No era has had a monopoly on the corruption of meaning. Patterns of redefinition are as old as politics itself. What is apparent is that redefinition continues to be a common form of political abuse, particularly when agencies and bureaucracies rank their public relations requirements higher than their public information objectives.

Military press briefings during the Vietnam War have emerged as the archetypal instances of such abuse. To some extent the entire war was plagued with misinformation, beginning in 1964 with the ground war in Laos, and ending in the early 1970s with bombing raids in neighboring Cambodia. Throughout this period various campaigns of calculated misnaming became known. The credibility of the Johnson and Nixon administrations, the Pentagon, and field staff eroded in the face of what seemed like systematic attempts to cover up casualties, troop movements, and joint South Vietnamese–American objectives. Ordinary descriptive language was shunned in favor of mystifying technical terms. In routine briefings held for the press in Saigon a special language of doublespeak emerged: napalm became ''selective strike''; jails became ''pacification centers''; killing became ''termination''; and off-target bombs became ''incontinent ordinance.''[50] Irate over vocal objections by the press at these attempts at redefinition, one military press officer lashed back, ''You always write it's bombing, bombing, bombing. It's *not* bombing! It's air support.''[51]

No amount of etymological juggling could establish a tradition of usage for such terms. They were employed because of what they did *not* imply. By giving clinical meanings to events involving human misery of staggering proportions, those conducting the war built up a facade of respectability that finally could not conceal the hideous stalemate.

All jargons are prone to similar misuse. they may originate as specialized languages intended to lend precision to a narrowly focused subject area. But special terms may slowly become more expressive than instrumental, useful more for the image of competence that they suggest than what they specifically communicate. Such language frequently ends its useful life by functioning in what is essentially a prostituted role—serving the suasory interests of the user better than the informational needs of the listener.

A FINAL THOUGHT

All of what has been said here may seem to confirm the view that politics is a lowly calling. We think it is not. The abuses we have cited are replicated in every form of structured setting: in the politics of business, law, the arts, and probably even among two authors sharing the burden of writing a book. Compared to the relative anonymity of most forms of organizational life, the exposure that normally comes with public service makes it likely that politicians will be among the *most* deserving of the public's trust. It is common for citizens to assume that their disagreement with a politician is a sign that something is wrong. But as long as pluralism exerts contradictory demands, we must accept the fact that no one official can possibly assent to one "correct" position. Political leadership imposes the nearly impossible task of coaxing consensus out of conflict.

It is a gift to be able to function at the center of institutions which must serve diverse constituencies. Attempting to do it requires a search for common denominators that tax both the mind and soul. Those who honorably undertake public office—and there are many—deserve the forbearance of the rest of us. One wonders how many of even the strongest critics American political life could begin to produce the energy and empathy required for public service. Most of us intuitively know that it is a far easier life to serve the interests of a comparatively small group of company stockholders, professional colleagues, clients, or readers, than to serve a diverse constituency whose individual members identify with specialized rather than unitary goals. It is fairly common to hear reporters, campaign consultants and constituents express their admiration for individual political leaders. No one says much that is positive about them in the aggregate. This fact should be a clue to us that our political attitudes are often better reflections of our particular circumstances than our collective ideals.

There is nothing new in this. The nation's political institutions are deliberately structured so that many of those who hold elective office are serving interests other than our own. One intention that the designers of the Constitution had in mind was to take some of the efficiency *out* of government, while at the same time protecting the rights of a multitude of conflicting factions. George Washington was to be no king on the European model. He was to have less power than is presently the case for his modern successors. His limited formal role was proof of the willingness of the nation's creators to let debate within Congress and between the branches of state mediate conflict. The diffusion of power that defines nearly every form of government, from Washington DC down to the local town council, still requires the same respect for shared power and the opportunity of public debate. The structure, in short, replaces peremptory rule with rule that flows from agreements.

If there are risks to this system today, we think that the most serious lie within the public. Many citizens no longer equate the sound of political talk with the sound of a machine at work. In our time the inherently discordant nature of public dispute is often mistaken as a sign of the corruption or failure in politics. Today political conflict falls too painfully on the ear. Conflict has been widely equated with inaction, defeat, and the victory of special interests over the larger public interest. As Robert Bellah has noted,

What is paradoxical in . . . American politics is that in an individualistic culture that highly values diversity and "pluralism," it is consensus that is appreciated and the conflict of interests that is suspect.[52]

The greatest threat to an open society is not from the friction of dispute, but from neglect of the public forum. In truth, the more ominous sign of a state in trouble is when governance occurs in silence, when rhetoric is preempted by an enforced or manipulated consensus. Our concern is that audiences and speakers will find shorter and more surreptitious routes to their own objectives. In the long run a nation is well served when its civil life is sustained by contentious advocates. It is endangered when they have found means to power that are more efficient than those based on public communication.

NOTES

1. James Fallows, "Containing Japan," *The Atlantic Monthly*, May, 1989, p. 40.

2. Taylor quoted in David Wise, *The Politics of Lying: Government Deception, Secrecy, and Power* (New York: Random House, 1973), p. 53.

3. Kenneth Burke, *The Philosophy of Literary Form*, 3d Ed. (Berkeley, CA: University of California, 1973), p. 191.

4. John Bunzel, *Anti-Politics in America* (New York: Vintage, 1970), p. 7.

5. Elizabeth Drew, "Letter from Washington," *The New Yorker*, February 27, 1989, p. 85.

6. See Stephen Toulmin, *The Uses of Argument* (Cambridge, England: Cambridge University, 1964), pp. 146–69.

7. For similar examples see Howell Raines, "Reagan, in Speeches, Doesn't Let the Truth Spoil a Good Anecdote or Effective Symbol," *The New York Times*, October 19, 1980, p. 38.

8. For a slightly dated but complete study of demagogues see Reinhard Luthin, *American Demagogues* (Boston, MA: Beacon, 1954).

9. John Dewey and Walter Lippmann remain as two important exceptions. See Dewey, *The Public and Its Problems* (Chicago, IL: Swallow Press, 1954), and Lippmann, *The Good Society* (New York: Grosset and Dunlap, 1943) and *The Public Philosophy* (Boston, MA: Little, Brown, 1955).

10. For a discussion of the relationship between the Watergate break-in and the 1972 elections see Theodore H. White, *The Making of the President 1972* (New York: Atheneum, 1973), pp. 297–98.

11. Murrow quoted in A. M. Sperber, *Murrow: His Life and Times* (New York: Freundlich, 1986), pp. 438–39.

12. Claus Mueller, *The Politics of Communication* (New York: Oxford, 1973), p. 179.

13. Norman H. Nie, Sidney Verba, and John R. Petrocik, *The Changing American Voter*, Enlarged Edition (Cambridge, MA: Harvard University, 1979), p. 278.

14. A telling account of the administration's dilemma is given by Hamilton Jordan in *Crisis: The Last Year of the Carter Presidency* (New York: Putnam, 1982).

15. Dewey, p. 86.

16. Doris Kearns, *Lyndon Johnson and the American Dream* (New York: Signet, 1976), pp. 324–50.

17. Classic studies on television and politics include Newton N. Minow, John Bartlow Martin, and Lee M. Mitchell, *Presidential Television* (New York: Basic, 1973); Sig Mickelson, *The Electric Mirror: Politics in an Age of Television* (New York: Dodd and Mead, 1972); Kurt and Gladys Lang, *Politics and Television* (New York: Quadrangle, 1968); and Edwin Diamond, *The Tin Kazoo: Television, Politics and the News* (Cambridge, MA: MIT Press, 1975).

18. The extent to which conventions are scripted is revealed in Tim Crouse, *The Boys on the Bus* (New York: Ballentine, 1972), pp. 176–77.

19. Richard Nixon, *Six Crises* (New York: Pyramid, 1968), p. 301.

20. Nixon, pp. 472–80.

21. See, for example, Michael R. Gordon, "Bush Urged to Find a Middle Course on Soviet Changes," *The New York Times*, April 9, 1989, pp. 1, 20, and Esther B. Fein, "Soviet Georgians Continue Protest for More Autonomy," *The New York Times*, April 9, 1989, p. A20.

22. Sidney Blumenthal, "Marketing the President," *New York Times Magazine*, September 13, 1981, pp. 43, 110, 112, 114.

23. This is a central point in the scholarship of Murray Edelman. See, for example, his *Politics as Symbolic Action* (Chicago, IL: Markham, 1971), pp. 31–52, and *The Symbolic Uses of Politics* (Urbana, IL: University of Illinois, 1967), pp. 22–43.

24. Transcript of the presidential debate between Jimmy Carter and Ronald Reagan in Cleveland, Ohio, October 28, 1980, *The New York Times*, October 30, 1980, p. B19.

25. For a formal definition of one kind of coercion, see Dwight Van de Vate, Jr., "The Appeal to Force," *Philosophy and Rhetoric* (Winter 1975): 43.

26. Spiro T. Agnew, *Frankly Speaking* (Washington, DC: Public Affairs Press, 1970), pp. 62–85.

27. Presidential Assistant Patrick Buchanan wrote Agnew's speeches with the president's full knowledge. See William Safire, *Before the Fall* (New York: Doubleday, 1975), p. 352.

28. Marvin Barrett, ed. *The Politics of Broadcasting, 1971–1972* (New York: Thomas Crowell, 1973), pp. 39–48.

29. Cronkite quoted in Barrett, p. 49.

30. Kenneth Burke, *A Grammar of Motives* (New York: Prentice Hall, 1954), p. 393.

31. Ralph K. White, "Misperception and the Vietnam War," *The Journal of Social Issues*, July, 1966, pp. 1–156.

32. Carl J. Friedrich, *The Pathology of Politics* (New York: Harper & Row, 1972), p. 193.

33. Friedrich, p. 176.

34. For a broader and more disturbing description of propaganda see Jacques Ellul, *Propaganda: The Formation of Men's Attitudes*, trans. Konrad Kellen and Jean Lerner (New York: Vintage, 1973), pp. 3–32.

35. Wise, p. 34.

36. John M. Orman, *Presidential Secrecy and Deception: Beyond the Power to Persuade* (Westport, CT: Greenwood, 1980), p. 138.

37. Daniel Schorr, *Clearing the Air* (New York: Berkley, 1978), p. 143.

38. This problem is common in many Western nations where there is a presumption in favor of "free flow of information." For a study of British government deception, and the misuse of Britain's Official Secrets Act, see James Margach, *The Abuse of Power* (London: W. H. Allen, 1978), pp. 115–84.

39. The term is Chaim Perelman's and L. Olbrechts-Tyteca's in *The New Rhetoric: A Treatise on Argumentation*, trans. John Wilkinson and Purcell Weaver (Notre Dame, IN: University of Notre Dame, 1969), pp. 200–1.

40. Ibid., p. 199.

41. Kenneth Burke, *A Rhetoric of Motives* (New York: Prentice Hall, 1953), p. 104.

42. William J. Grayson, "The Hireling and the Slave," in *Slavery Defended: The Views of the Old South*, ed. Eric L. McKitrick (Englewood Cliffs, NJ: Spectrum, 1963), pp. 66–67.

43. Luthin, p. 308.

44. For a summary of this view see John C. Condon, Jr., *Semantics and Communication*, 2d Ed. (New York: Macmillan, 1975), pp. 33–53.

45. Franklin D. Roosevelt, Radio Address, Washington, DC, December 29, 1940, in *Contemporary Forum: American Speeches on Twentieth-Century Issues*, ed. Ernest J. Wrage and Barnet Baskerville (New York: Harper and Brothers, 1962), 246–54.

46. Reagan, Radio Address to the Nation, July 16, 1983, p. 1008; and Reagan, Remarks to the 65th Annual Convention of the American Legion, Seattle, Washington, August 23, 1983, in *Weekly Compilation of Presidential Documents*, Vol. 19, August 26, 1983, pp. 1160–61.

47. George Orwell, *1984* (New York: Signet, 1961), pp. 246–56.

48. Ibid., p. 7.

49. Quoted in Mueller, pp. 31–32.

50. Quoted in Howard Kahane, *Logic and Contemporary Rhetoric*, 3d Ed. (Belmont, CA: Wadsworth, 1980), p. 127.

51. Kahane, p. 128. See also David L. Altheide and John M. Johnson, *Bureaucratic Propaganda* (Boston, MA: Allyn and Bacon, 1980), pp. 210–27.

52. Robert N. Bellah, Richard Madsen, William M. Sullivan, Ann Swidler, and Steven M. Tipton, *Habits of the Heart: Individualism and Commitment in American Life* (Berkeley: University of California, 1985), p. 203.

Selected Bibliography

BOOKS

Abadinsky, Howard. *Crime and Justice: An Introduction*. Chicago, IL: Nelson Hall, 1987.

Adams, Sherman. *Firsthand Report: The Story of the Eisenhower Administration*. New York: Harper, 1961.

Agronoff, Robert. *The New Style in Election Campaigns*, Second Edition. Boston, MA: Holbrook, 1977.

Altheide, David and John Johnson. *Bureaucratic Propaganda*. Boston, MA: Allyn and Bacon, 1980.

Aristotle. *The Rhetoric*. Translator, Rhys Roberts. New York: The Modern Library, 1954.

Arlen, Michael. *Living Room War*. New York: Viking, 1969.

Armstrong, Richard. *The Next Hurrah*. New York: William Morrow, 1988.

Barber, James David. *Choosing the President*. Englewood Cliffs, NJ: Prentice Hall, 1974.

———. *The Pulse of Politics*. New York: Norton, 1980.

Barilleaux, Ryan. *The Post-Modern Presidency*. New York: Praeger, 1988.

Barnouw, Erik. *The Sponsor: Notes on a Modern Potentate*. New York: Oxford, 1978.

———. *Tube of Plenty: The Evolution of American Television*. New York: Oxford, 1975.

Barrett, Marvin. *Rich News, Poor News*. New York: Thomas Crowell, 1978.

———. *The Politics of Broadcasting*. New York: Thomas Crowell, 1973.

Bartels, Larry. *Presidential Primaries and the Dynamics of Public Choice*. Princeton, NJ: Princeton University Press, 1988.

Bell, Daniel. *The End of Ideology*. New York: The Free Press, 1960.

Bellah, Robert, Richard Madsen, William Sullivan, Ann Swidler, and Steven Tipton. *Habits of the Heart: Individualism and Commitment in American Life*. Berkeley, CA: University of California, 1985.

Bennett, Lance. *News: The Politics of Illusion*, Second Edition. New York: Longman, 1988.

Bitzer, Lloyd and Edwin Black. *The Prospect of Rhetoric*. Englewood Cliffs, NJ: Prentice Hall, 1971.

Blanchard, Robert. *Congress and the News Media*. New York: Hastings House, 1974.
Bloom, Melvyn. *Public Relations and Presidential Campaigns: A Crisis in Democracy*. New York: Thomas Crowell, 1973.
Blumenthal, Sidney. *Our Long National Daydream: A Political Pageant of the Reagan Era*. New York: Harper & Row, 1988.
———. *The Permanent Campaign*. New York: Touchstone Books, 1982.
Blumer, Herbert. *Symbolic Interactionism*. Englewood Cliffs, NJ: Prentice Hall, 1969.
Boorstin, Daniel. *The Americans: The Democratic Experience*. New York: Vintage, 1974.
———. *The Image*. New York: Atheneum, 1962.
Brandon, Henry. *Special Relationships: A Foreign Correspondent's Memoirs from Roosevelt to Reagan*. New York: Atheneum, 1989.
Broder, David. *Behind the Front Page*. New York: Simon and Schuster, 1987.
Buchanan, Bruce. *The Presidential Experience*. Englewood Cliffs, NJ: Prentice Hall, 1978.
Bunzel, John. *Anti-Politics in America*. New York: Vintage, 1970.
Burke, Kenneth. *Attitudes Toward History*. Boston, MA: Beacon, 1957.
———. *A Grammar of Motives*. Berkeley, CA: University of California Press, 1969.
———. *A Rhetoric of Motives*. New York: Prentice Hall, 1953.
———. *Language as Symbolic Action*. Berkeley, CA: University of California Press, 1966.
———. *Permanence and Change*. New York: Bobbs-Merrill, 1965.
———. *The Philosophy of Literary Form*, Third Edition. Berkeley, CA: University of California, 1973.
———. *The Rhetoric of Religion*. Berkeley, CA: University of California Press, 1970.
Burns, Roper. *America's Watching: Public Attitudes Toward Television*. New York: Television Information Office, 1987.
Califano, Joseph. *Governing America: An Insider's Report from the White House and the Cabinet*. New York: Simon and Schuster, 1981.
Carter, Jimmy. *Keeping Faith: Memoirs of a President*. New York: Bantam, 1982.
Cater, Douglass. *The Fourth Branch of Government*. New York: Vintage, 1959.
Chaffee, Steven. *Political Communication: Issues and Strategies for Research*. Beverly Hills, CA: Sage, 1975.
Chagall, David. *The New King-Makers*. New York: Harcourt, Brace, Jovanovich, 1981.
Charon, Joel. *Symbolic Interactionism: An Introduction, an Interpretation, an Integration*. Englewood Cliffs, NJ: Prentice Hall, 1979.
Cirino, Robert. *Don't Blame the People*. New York: Vintage, 1971.
Combs, James. *Dimensions of Political Drama*. Santa Monica, CA: Goodyear, 1980.
Corcoran, Paul. *Political Language and Rhetoric*. Austin, TX: University of Texas Press, 1979.
Corwin, Edward. *The President: Office and Powers*, Third Edition. New York: New York University Press, 1948.
Cronin, Thomas. *The State of the Presidency*. Boston, MA: Little, Brown, 1975.
Crouse, Timothy. *The Boys on the Bus*. New York: Ballatine, 1972.
Davis, Kenneth Culp. *Discretionary Justice: A Preliminary Inquiry*. Baton Rouge: Louisiana State University, 1969.
Deaver, Michael and Mickey Herskowitz. *Behind the Scenes*. New York: William Morrow, 1987.

DeFleur, Melvin and Everette Dennis. *Understanding Mass Communication*, Third Edition. Boston, MA: Houghton Mifflin, 1988.

Demac, Donna. *Keeping America Un-informed*. New York: Pilgrim Press, 1984.

Denton, Jr. Robert E. *The Primetime Presidency of Ronald Reagan*. New York: Praeger, 1988.

―――. *The Symbolic Dimensions of the American Presidency*. Prospect Heights, IL: Waveland Press, 1982.

Denton, Jr. Robert E. and Dan Hahn. *Presidential Communication: Description and Analysis*. New York: Praeger, 1986.

de Tocqueville, Alexis. *Democracy in America*. George Lawrence, translator. New York: Doubleday, 1969.

Devlin, Patrick. *Contemporary Political Speaking*. Belmont, CA: Wadsworth, 1971.

Diamond, Edwin. *The Tin Kazoo: Television, Politics and the News*. Cambridge, MA: MIT Press, 1975.

Diamond, Edwin and Stephen Bates. *The Spot*. Cambridge, MA: The MIT Press, 1984.

Drew, Elizabeth. *Senator*. New York: Touchstone, 1979.

Duncan, Hugh Dalziel. *Communication and Social Order*. New York: Oxford University, 1962.

―――. *Symbols in Society*. New York: Oxford University Press, 1968.

Edelman, Murray. *Constructing the Political Spectacle*. Chicago, IL: University of Chicago Press, 1988.

―――. *Politics as Symbolic Action*. Chicago, IL: Markham Publishing, 1971.

―――. *The Symbolic Uses of Politics*. Urbana, IL: University of Illinois, 1967.

Edwards, George. *The Public Presidency*. Ithaca, NY: Cornell University Press, 1985.

Efron, Edith. *The News Twisters*. New York: Manor Books, 1971.

Eisenhower, Dwight. *Mandate for Change, 1953–1956*. New York: Doubleday, 1963.

Epstein, Edward Jay. *News from Nowhere: Television and the News*. New York: Vintage, 1974.

Erickson, Paul. *Reagan Speaks*. New York: New York University Press, 1985.

Faules, Don and Dennis Alexander. *Communication and Social Behavior: A Symbolic Interaction Perspective*. Boston, MA: Addison-Wesley, 1978.

Fenno, Richard, F. *Home Style: House Members in Their Districts*. Boston, MA: Little, Brown, 1978.

Fisher, Walter. *Human Communication as Narration*. Columbia, SC: University of South Carolina Press, 1987.

Ford, Gerald. *A Time to Heal*. New York: Harper & Row, 1979.

Fox, Harrison and Susan Hammond. *Congressional Staffs: The Invisible Force in American Lawmaking*. New York: Free Press, 1977.

Frank, Jerome. *Courts on Trial: Myth and Reality in America*. Princeton, NJ: Princeton University, 1950.

Friedrich, Carl. *The Pathology of Power*. New York: Harper & Row, 1972.

Friendly, Fred. *Due to Circumstances Beyond Our Control* . . . . London: McGibbon and Kee, 1967.

Galbraith, John. *The Affluent Society*, Third Edition. Boston, MA: Houghton Mifflin, 1976.

Gans, Herbert. *Deciding What's News*. New York: Vintage, 1980.

Ginsberg, Benjamin. *The Captive Public: How Mass Opinion Promotes State Power*. New York: Basic Books, 1986.

Gitlin, Todd. *Inside Prime Time*. New York: Pantheon, 1983.

———. *The Whole World Is Watching: Mass Media in the Making and the Unmaking of the New Left*. Berkeley, CA: University of California, 1980.

Glad, Betty. *Jimmy Carter: In Search of the Great White House*. New York: W. W. Norton, 1980.

Goffman, Irving. *The Presentation of Self in Everyday Life*. New York: Doubleday, 1959.

Graber, Doris. *Mass Media and American Politics*. Washington, DC: Congressional Quarterly, 1980.

———. *Media Power and Politics*. Washington, DC: Congressional Quarterly, 1984.

———. *Processing the News*. New York: Longman, 1984.

———. *The President and the Public*. Philadelphia: Institute for the Study of Human Issues, 1982.

Grassmeichk, George. *Before Nomination: Our Primary Problems*. Washington, DC: American Enterprise Institute, 1985.

Grossman, Michael and Martha Kumar. *Portraying the President*. Baltimore, MD: Johns Hopkins University Press, 1981.

Halberstam, David. *The Powers That Be*. New York: Knopf, 1979.

Hart, John. *The Presidential Branch*. New York: Pergamon, 1987.

Hart, Roderick. *The Sound of Leadership*. Chicago, IL: University of Chicago Press, 1987.

———. *Verbal Style and the Presidency*. Orlando, FL: Academic Press, 1984.

Hartmann, Robert. *Palace Politics: An Inside Account of the Ford Years*. New York: McGraw-Hill, 1980.

Head, Sydney and Christopher Sterling. *Broadcasting in America*, Fourth Edition. Boston, MA: Houghton Mifflin, 1982.

Heath, Jim. *Decade of Disillusionment: The Kennedy-Johnson Years*. Bloomington, IN: Indiana University, 1975.

Heineman, Ben and Curtis Hessler. *Memorandum for the President*. New York: Random House, 1980.

Hess, Stephen. *The Ultimate Insiders: U.S. Senators in the National Media*. Washington, DC: Brookings Institution, 1986.

Hodgson, Godfrey. *All Things to All Men*. New York: Touchstone, 1980.

Horowitz, David. *The Courts and Social Policy*. Washington, DC: Brookings Institution, 1977.

Hughes, Emmet John. *The Living Presidency*. New York: Coward, McCann and Geoghegan, 1972.

———. *The Ordeal of Power*. New York: Atheneum, 1963.

Iyengar, Shanto and Donald Kinder. *News That Matters: Television and American Opinion*. Chicago, IL: University of Chicago, 1987.

Jacob, Herbert. *Justice in America*, Third Edition. Boston, MA: Little, Brown, 1978.

Jamieson, Kathleen. *Packaging the Presidency*. New York: Oxford University Press, 1984.

———. *Presidential Debates*. New York: Oxford University Press, 1988.

Janis, Irving. *Victims of Groupthink*. Boston, MA: Houghton Mifflin, 1972.

Janowitz, Morris and Paul Hirsch. *Readings in Public Opinion and Mass Communication*. Third Edition. New York: Free Press, 1981.

Johnson, Lyndon. *The Vantage Point: Perspectives on the Presidency*. New York: Holt, Reinhart, and Winston, 1971.

Jordan, Hamilton. *Crisis: The Last Year of the Carter Presidency*. New York: Putnam, 1982.

Kahane, Howard. *Logic and Contemporary Rhetoric*, Third Edition. Belmont, CA: Wadsworth, 1980.

Kaid, Lynda, Dan Nimmo and Keith Sanders. *New Perspectives on Political Advertising*. Carbondale, IL: Southern Illinois University Press, 1986.

Kearns, Doris. *Lyndon Johnson and the American Dream*. New York: Signet Books, 1976.

Keeter, Scott and Cliff Zukin. *Uniformed Choice: The Failure of the New Presidential Nominating System*. New York: Praeger, 1983.

Kellerman, Barbara. *The Political Presidency*. New York: Oxford University Press, 1984.

Kernell, Samuel. *Going Public*. Washington, DC: Congressional Quarterly Press, 1986.

Kissinger, Henry. *The White House Years*. Boston, MA: Little, Brown, 1984.

Klapp, Orin. *Symbolic Leaders*. Chicago, IL: Aldine, 1964.

Klapper, Joseph. *The Effects of Mass Communication*. New York: Free Press, 1960.

Kraus, Sidney. *The Great Debates: Carter Versus Ford*. Bloomington, IN: University of Indiana Press, 1976.

————. *The Great Debates: Kennedy Versus Nixon*. Bloomington, IN: University of Indiana Press, 1962.

Kraus, Sidney and Dennis Davis. *The Effects of Mass Communication on Political Behavior*. University Park, PA: Pennsylvania State University, 1976.

Lang, Kurt and Gladys Engel Lang. *Politics and Television*. Chicago, IL: Quadrangle Books, 1968.

Lasky, Victor. *Jimmy Carter: The Man and the Myth*. New York: Richard Marek, 1979.

Lasswell, Harold. *Power and Personality*. New York: Viking, 1962.

Lazarsfeld, P., B. Berelson, and H. Gaudet. *The People's Choice*. New York: Columbia University Press, 1984.

Lippmann, Walter. *Public Opinion*. New York: Macmillan, 1930.

————. *The Public Philosophy*. Boston: Little, Brown, and Co., 1955.

Lowi, Theodore. *The Personal President*. Ithaca, NY: Cornell University Press, 1985.

Machiavelli. *The Prince*. Mark Musa, translator. New York: St. Martin's Press, 1964.

MacNeil, Robert. *The People Machine: The Influence of Television on American Politics*. New York: Harper & Row, 1968.

McCartney, Laton. *Friends in High Places: The Bechtel Story*. New York: Simon and Schuster, 1988.

McClure, Robert. *The Unseeing Eye: Myth of Television Power in National Politics*. New York: G. P. Putnam, 1976.

McConnell, Grant. *The Modern Presidency*. New York: St. Martin's Press, 1976.

McDonald, Forrest. *The Presidency of George Washington*. New York: W. W. Norton, 1974.

McGinniss, Joe. *The Selling of the President: 1968*. New York: Trident Press, 1969.

McPherson, Harry. *A Political Education*. Boston, MA: Atlantic–Little, Brown, 1972.

McQuaid, Kim. *Big Business and Presidential Power*. New York: William Morrow, 1982.

Mann, Thomas and Norman Ornstein. *The New Congress*. Washington, DC: American Enterprise Institute, 1981.

Marshall, Thomas. *Presidential Nomination in a Reform Age*. New York: Praeger, 1981.

Martel, Myles. *Political Campaign Debates*. New York: Longman, 1983.

Mauser, Gary. *Political Marketing*. New York: Praeger, 1983.

Mayo, Earl. *The Great Debates*. Santa Barbara, CA: Center for the Study of Democratic Institutions, 1962.

Mead, George H. *Mind, Self, and Society*. Chicago, IL: University of Chicago Press, 1972.

Medved, Michael. *The Shadow Presidents*. New York: Times Books, 1979.

Meyrowitz, Joshua. *No Sense of Place: The Impact of Electronic Media on Social Behavior*. New York: Oxford University Press, 1985.

Mickelson, Sig. *The Electric Mirror: Politics in an Age of Television*. New York: Dodd and Mead, 1972.

Mikva, Abner and Patti Harris. *The American Congress, the First Branch*. New York: Franklin Watts, 1983.

Milbrath, Lester. *The Washington Lobbyists*. Westport, CT: Greenwood Press, 1963.

Miller, Mark. *Boxed In: The Culture of TV*. Evanston, IL: Northwestern University Press, 1988.

Miller, Merle. *Lyndon: An Oral Biography*. New York: Ballantine, 1980.

Minow, Newton, John B. Martin and Lee Mitchell. *Presidential Television*. New York: Basic Books, 1973.

Moore, Michael S. *Law and Psychiatry: Rethinking the Relationship*. New York: Cambridge University, 1984.

Mueller, Claus. *The Politics of Communication*. New York: Oxford University, 1973.

Mullen, William. *Presidential Power and Politics*. New York: St. Martin's Press, 1976.

Murphy, Walter and C. Herman Pritchett. *Courts, Judges, and Politics*. Second Edition. New York: Random House, 1974.

Napolitan, Joseph. *The Election Game and How to Win It*. New York: Doubleday, 1972.

Nelson, Michael. *The Elections of 1988*. Washington, DC: Congressional Quarterly Press, 1989.

Nessen, Ron. *It Sure Looks Different from the Inside*. Chicago, IL: Playboy Press, 1978.

Newcomb, Horace. *Television: The Critical View*, Third Edition. New York: Oxford, 1982.

Nie, Norman, Sidney Verba, and John Petrocik. *The Changing American Voter*. Cambridge, MA: Harvard University, 1979.

Nimmo, Dan. *Political Communication and Public Opinion in America*. California: Goodyear, 1978.

———. *The Political Persuaders*. Englewood Cliffs, NJ: Spectrum Books, 1970.

Nimmo, Dan and James E. Combs. *Mediated Political Realities*. New York: Longman, 1983.

———. *Subliminal Politics*. Englewood Cliffs, NJ: Spectrum Books, 1980.

Nimmo, Dan and Keith Sanders. *Handbook of Political Communication*. Beverly Hills, CA: Sage, 1981.

Nixon, Richard. *Six Crises*. New York: Pyramid, 1968.

Novak, Michael. *Choosing Our King*. New York: Macmillan, 1974.

Orman, John. *Presidential Secrecy and Deception: Beyond the Power to Persuade*. Westport, CT: Greenwood, 1980.

Paletz, David and Robert Entman. *Media Power Politics*. New York: Free Press, 1981.

Patterson, Thomas. *The Mass Media Election*. New York: Praeger, 1980.

Pember, Don. *Mass Media Law*, Fourth Edition. Dubuque, IA: William C. Brown, 1987.

Peters, Charles. *How Washington Really Works*. Reading, MA: Addison-Wesley, 1980.

Peters, Charles and James Fallows. *The System: The Five Branches of American Government*. New York: Praeger, 1967.

Perelman, Chaim and L. Olbrechts-Tyteca. *The New Rhetoric*. John Wilkinson and Purcell Weaver, translators. Notre Dame, IN: University of Notre Dame Press, 1969.

Perry, Roland. *The Programming of the President*. London: Aurum Press, 1984.

Phillips, Kevin. *Mediacracy: American Parties and Politics in the Communication Age*. Garden City, NY: Doubleday, 1975.

Plato, *Great Dialogues of Plato*. W. D. Rouse, translator. New York: E. P. Dutton, 1947.

Pomper, Gerald, et al. *The Election of 1984*. Chatham, NJ: Chatham House, 1985.

Reagan, Ronald and Richard Hubler. *Where's the Rest of Me?* New York: Dell, 1965.

Reedy, George. *The Twilight of the Presidency*. New York: World, 1970.

Reeves, Richard. *A Ford, Not a Lincoln*. New York: Harcourt Brace Jovanovich, 1975.

———. *The Reagan Detour*. New York: Simon and Schuster, 1985.

Reid, T. R. *Congressional Odyssey: The Saga of a Senate Bill*. San Francisco, CA: W. H. Freeman, 1980.

Regan, Donald. *For the Record*. New York: Harcourt, Brace, Jovanovich, 1988.

Rivers, William. *The Adversaries: Politics and the Press*. Boston: Beacon, 1970.

———. *The Other Government: Power and the Washington Media*. New York: Universe, 1982.

Robinson, Michael and Margeret Sheehan. *Over the Wire and on TV: CBS and UPI in Campaign '80*. New York: Russell Sage, 1983.

Rockman, Bert. *The Leadership Question*. New York: Praeger, 1984.

Rodman, George. *Mass Media Issues: Analysis and Debate*. Chicago, IL: SRA, 1977.

Rose, Richard. *People in Politics*. New York: Basic Books, 1970.

Rosenman, Samuel and Dorothy Rosenman. *Presidential Style: Some Giants and a Pygmy in the White House*. New York: Harper & Row, 1976.

Rossiter, Clinton. *The American Presidency*. New York: Mentor Books, 1962.

Rueckert, William. *Critical Responses to Kenneth Burke*. Minneapolis, MN: University of Minnesota Press, 1969.

Sabato, Larry. *Campaigns and Elections*. Glenview, IL: Scott, Foresman, and Co., 1989.

———. *The Rise of Political Consultants*. New York: Basic Books, 1981.

Safire, William. *Before the Fall*. New York: Doubleday, 1975.

Schiller, Herbert. *The Mind Managers*. Boston, MA: Beacon Press, 1973.

Schlesinger, Arthur. *The Imperial Presidency*. Boston, MA: Houghton-Mifflin, 1973.

Schorr, Daniel. *Clearing the Air*. New York: Berkeley, 1978.

Schram, Martin. *The Great American Video Game*. New York: William Morrow, 1987.

Schramm, Wilbur and Donald Roberts. *The Process and Effects of Mass Communication*, Revised Edition. Chicago, IL: University of Chicago Press, 1971.

Schwartz, Tony. *The Responsive Chord*. New York: Doubleday, 1972.

Sennett, Richard. *The Fall of Public Man: On the Social Psychology of Capitalism*. New York: Vintage Books, 1978.

Sennett, Richard and Jonathan Cobb. *The Hidden Injuries of Class*. New York: Knopf, 1973.

Simons, Herbert and Aran Aghazarian. *Form, Genre and the Study of Political Discourse*. Columbia, SC: University of South Carolina Press, 1986.

Simpson, Smith. *Anatomy of the State Department*. Boston, MA: Beacon Press, 1967.

Smith, Carolyn. *The '88 Vote—ABC News*. New York: Capital Cities/ABC, 1989.

Smith, Hedrick. *The Power Game*. New York: Random House, 1988.

Sorensen, Theodore. *A Different Kind of Presidency*. New York: Harper & Row, 1984.

————. *Kennedy*. New York: Harper and Row, 1965.

Speakes, Larry and Robert Pack. *Speaking Out: The Reagan From Inside the White House*. New York: Avon, 1989.

Spero, Robert. *The Duping of the American Voter*. New York: Lippincott and Crowell, 1980.

Stockman, David. *The Triumph of Politics*. New York: Harper & Row, 1986.

Swerdlow, Joel. *Presidential Debates*. Washington, DC: Congressional Quarterly Press, 1987.

Thack, Charles. *The Creation of the Presidency*. Baltimore, MD: The Johns Hopkins Press, 1969.

Toulmin, Stephen. *The Uses of Argument*. Cambridge, England: Cambridge University Press, 1964.

Trent, Judith and Robert Friedenberg. *Political Campaign Communication*. New York: Praeger, 1984.

Truman, Harry. *Memoirs: Years of Decision*. Garden City, NY: Doubleday, 1955.

Tuchman, Gaye. *Making News: A Study in the Construction of Reality*. New York: Free Press, 1978.

Tugwell, Rexford and Thomas Cronin. *The Presidency Reappraised*. New York: Praeger, 1974.

Tulis, Jeffrey. *The Rhetorical Presidency*. Princeton, NJ: Princeton University Press, 1987.

Watson, Richard. *The Presidential Contest*. New York: John Wiley & Sons, 1980.

Waxman, Chaim. *The End of Ideology Debate*. New York: Funk and Wagnall, 1968.

Weaver, Richard. *The Ethics of Rhetoric*. Chicago, IL: Henry Regnery, 1953.

Weaver, Warren. *Both Your Houses: The Truth About Congress*. New York: Praeger, 1972.

Westin, Av. *Newswatch: How TV Decides the News*. New York: Simon and Schuster, 1982.

White, Theodore. *The Breach of Faith*. New York: Atheneum, 1975.

————. *The Making of the American Voter*. New York: Atheneum, 1973.

Windt, Theodore. *Presidential Rhetoric*. Second Edition. Dubuque, IA: Kendall-Hunt, 1980.

Wildavsky, Aaron. *The Presidency*. Boston, MA: Little, Brown & Co., 1969.

Wills, Gary. *Reagan's America*. New York: Doubleday, 1987.

Wise, David. *The Politics of Lying*. New York: Random House, 1973.

Woodward, Bob and Scott Armstrong. *The Brethren: Inside the Supreme Court*. New York: Simon and Schuster, 1979.

Wooten, James. *Dasher: The Roots and Rising of Jimmy Carter*. New York: Warner Books, 1978.

Zimbardo, Philip, Ebbe Ebbesen, and Christina Maslach. *Influencing Attitudes and Changing Behavior*, Second Edition. Boston, MA: Addison-Wesley, 1977.

ARTICLES/BOOK CHAPTERS

Becker, Samuel. "Rhetorical Studies for the Contemporary World." *The Prospect of Rhetoric*. Lloyd Bitzer and Edwin Black, eds. Englewood Cliffs, NJ: Prentice Hall, 1971.

Bitzer, Lloyd. "Political Rhetoric." *Handbook of Political Communication.* Dan Nimmo and Keith Sanders, eds. Beverly Hills, CA: Sage, 1981.

Blumer, Jay and Michael Gurevitch. "Politicians and the Press: An Essay on Role Relationships." *Handbook of Political Communication.* Dan Nimmo and Keith Sanders, eds. Beverly Hills, CA: Sage, 1981.

Brooks, Richard. "The Self and Political Role: A Symbolic Interactionist Approach to Political Ideology." *The Sociological Quarterly* 10 (Winter 1969): 23–32.

Burke, Kenneth. "Dramatism." *Communication: Concepts and Perspectives.* Lee Thayer, ed. New Jersey: Hayden, 1967.

———. "Interaction-Dramatism." *International Encyclopedia of the Social Sciences.* New York: International Encyclopedia of the Social Sciences, 1967, 445–52.

Ceaser, James, et al. "The Rise of the Rhetorical Presidency." *Essays in Presidential Rhetoric,* Theodore Windt, ed. Dubuque: Kendall-Hunt, 1983.

Cobb, Roger and Charles Elder. "Individual Orientations in the Study of Political Symbolism." *Social Science Quarterly* 53 (June 1972): 79–90.

Cook, Rhodes. "The Nominating Process." *The Elections of 1988.* Michael Nelson, ed. Washington, DC: Congressional Quarterly Press, 1989.

Cundy, Donald. "Political Commercials and Candidate Image." *New Perspectives on Political Advertising.* Lynda Kaid, Dan Nimmo, and Keith Sanders, eds. Carbondale, IL: Southern Illinois University, 1986.

Devlin, Patrick. "An Analysis of Presidential Television Commercials: 1952–1984." *New Perspectives on Political Advertising.* Lynda Kaid, Dan Nimmo, and Keith Sanders, eds. Carbondale, IL: Southern Illinois University Press, 1986.

———. "Contrasts in Presidential Campaign Commercials of 1988." *American Behavioral Scientist* 32, no. 4 (March/April 1989): 389–414.

Diamond, Edwin and Adrian Marin. "Spots." *American Behavioral Scientist* 32, no. 4 (March/April 1989): 382–88.

Diamond, Edwin and Kathleen Friery. "Media Coverage of Presidential Debates." *Presidential Debates.* Paul Swerdlow, ed. Washington, DC: Congressional Quarterly Press, 1987.

Elshtain, Jean. "Issues and Themes in the 1988 Campaign." *The Elections of 1988.* Michael Nelson, ed. Washington, DC: Congressional Quarterly Press, 1989.

Fisher, Walter. "Romantic Democracy, Ronald Reagan, and Presidential Heroes." *The Western Journal of Speech Communication* 46 (Summer 1982): 299–310.

Gallup, George. "The Impact of Presidential Debates." *Presidential Debates.* Paul Swerdlow, ed. Washington, DC: Congressional Quarterly Press, 1987.

Gitlin, Todd. "Prime Time Ideology: The Hegemonic Process in Television Entertainment." *Television: The Critical View,* Third Edition. Horace Newcomb, ed. New York: Oxford University Press, 1982.

Graber, Doris. "Personal Qualities in Presidential Images: The Contribution of the Press." *Midwest Journal of Political Science* 16 (February 1972): 46–76.

———. "Political Languages." *Handbook of Political Communication.* Dan Nimmo and Keith Sanders, ed. Beverly Hills, CA: Sage Publications, 1981.

Gregg, Richard and Gerald Houser. "Richard Nixon's April 30, 1970 Address on Cambodia: The Ceremony of Confrontation." *Speech Monographs* (August 1973): 167–187.

Gronbeck, Bruce. "Functional and Dramaturgical Theories of Presidential Campaigning." *Presidential Studies Quarterly* 14 (Fall 1984): 487–98.

———. "The Functions of Presidential Campaigning." *Communication Monographs* 45 (November 1978): 268–80.

———. "Mythic Portraiture in the 1988 Iowa Presidential Caucus Bio-ads." *American Behavioral Scientist* 32, no. 4 (March/April 1989): 351–64.

———. "Ronald Reagan's Enactment of the Presidency in His 1981 Inaugural Address." *Form, Genre, and the Story of Political Discourse.* Herbert Simons and Aran Aghazarian, eds. Columbia, SC: University of South Carolina Press, 1986.

Hale, Myron. "Presidential Influence, Authority, and Power and Economic Policy." *Toward a Humanistic Science of Politics.* Dalmas Nelson and Richard Sklar, eds. Lanham, MD: University Press of America, 1983.

Hall, Peter. "A Symbolic Interactionist Analysis of Politics." *Sociology Inquiry* 42 (1972): 35–73.

Halperin, Morton. "The Presidency and its Interaction with the Culture of Bureaucracy." *The System: The Five Branches of American Government.* Charles Peters and James Fallows, eds. (New York: Praeger, 1967).

Herzik, Eric. "The President, Governors and Mayors: A Framework for Comparative Analysis." *Presidential Studies Quarterly* 15, no. 2 (Spring 1985): 353–66.

Herzik, Eric and Mary Dodson. "The President and Public Expectations: A Research Note." *Presidential Studies Quarterly* 12 (Spring 1982): 168–73.

Hirsch, Paul. "The Role of Television and Popular Culture in Contemporary Society." *Television: The Critical View.* Third Edition. Horace Newcomb, ed. New York: Oxford University Press, 1982.

Hughes, Robert L. "Chandler versus Florida: Cameras Get Probation in Courtrooms." *Journal of Broadcasting* (Winter 1982): 433–50.

Joslyn, Richard. "Political Advertising and the Meaning of Elections." *New Perspectives on Political Advertising.* Lynda Kaid, Dan Nimmo, and Keith Sanders, eds. Carbondale, IL: Southern Illinois University Press, 1986.

Kaid, Lynda. "The Neglected Candidate: Interpersonal Communication in Political Campaigns." *Western Journal of Communication* (Fall 1977): 245–52.

Kaid, Lynda and Dorothy Davidson. "Elements of Videostyle." *New Perspectives on Political Advertising.* Lynda Kaid, Dan Nimmo, and Keith Sanders, eds. Carbondale, IL: Southern Illinois University Press, 1986.

Keeter, Scott and Cliff Zukin. "New Romances and Old Horses: The Public Images of Presidential Candidates." *The President and the Public.* Doris Graber, ed. Philadelphia: Institute for the Study of Human Issues, 1982.

Kellner, Douglas. "TV, Ideology, and Emancipatory Popular Culture." *Television: The Critical View,* Third Edition. Horace Newcomb, ed. New York: Oxford University Press, 1982.

Kennedy, Patrick and Tom Rice. "The Contextual Determinants of Presidential Greatness." *Presidential Studies Quarterly* 18, no. 1 (Winter 1988): 161–68.

Lang, Kurt and Gladys Engel Lang. "The Mass Media and Voting." *Readings in Public Opinion and Mass Communication,* Third Edition. Morris Janowitz and Paul Hirsch, eds. New York: Free Press, 1981.

Manheim, Jarol. "Can Democracy Survive Television?" *Journal of Communication* (Spring 1976): 84–90.

McCombs, Maxwell. "The Agenda Setting Approach." *Handbook of Political Communication.* Dan Nimmo and Keith Sanders, eds. Beverly Hills, CA: Sage, 1981.

McCombs, Maxwell and D. L. Shaw. "The Agenda Setting Function of the Mass Media." *Public Opinion Quarterly*. (Summer 1972): 176–87.

McDonald, Lee. "Myth, Politics, and Political Science." *Western Political Quarterly* 22 (1969): 141–50.

McLeod, Jack and Lee Becker. "The Uses and Gratifications Approach." *Handbook of Political Communication*. Dan Nimmo and Keith Sanders, eds. Beverly Hills, CA: Sage, 1981.

Meadow, Robert. "The Political Dimensions of Nonproduct Advertising." *Journal of Communication*. (Summer 1981): 69–82.

Moore, Raymond. "The Constitution, the Presidency and 1988." *Presidential Studies Quarterly* 18, no. 1 (Winter 1988): 55–60.

O'Keefe, Garrett. "Political Campaigns and Mass Communication Research." *Political Communication: Issues and Strategies for Research*. Steven Chaffee, ed. Beverly Hills, CA: Sage, 1975.

O'Keefe, Garrett and Edwin Atwood. "Communication and Election Campaigns." *Handbook of Political Communication*. Dan Nimmo and Keith Sanders, eds. Beverly Hills, CA: Sage, 1981.

Osborn, Michael. "Rhetorical Depiction." *Form, Genre, and the Study of Political Discourse*. Herbert Simons and Aran Aghazarian, eds. Columbia, SC: University of South Carolina Press, 1986.

Patterson, Thomas. "The Press and Its Missed Assignment." *The Elections of 1988*. Michael Nelson, ed. Washington, DC: Congressional Quarterly Press, 1989.

Payne, Gregory, et al. "Perceptions of the 1988 Presidential and Vice Presidential Debates." *American Behavioral Scientist* 32, no. 4 (March/April 1989): 425–35.

Quirk, Paul. "The Election." *The Elections of 1988*. Michael Nelson, ed. Washington, DC: Congressional Quarterly Press, 1989.

Ratzan, Scott. "The Real Agenda Setters." *American Behavioral Scientist* 32, no. 4 (March/April 1989): 451–64.

Robbin, Jonathan. "Geodemographics: The New Magic." *Campaigns and Elections*. Larry Sabato, ed. Glenview, IL: Scott, Foresman and Co., 1989.

Robinson, John. "Mass Communication and Information Diffusion." *Readings in Public Opinion and Mass Communication*, Third Edition. Morris Janowitz and Paul Hirsch. New York: Free Press, 1981.

Robinson, Michael. "Three Faces of Congressional Media." *The New Congress*. Thomas Mann and Norman Ornstein, eds. Washington, DC: American Enterprise Institute, 1981.

Robinson, Michael and Kevin Appel. "Network News Coverage of Congress." *Political Science Quarterly* 94 (Fall 1979): 413–36.

Roiphe, Anne. "Ma and Pa and John-Boy in Mythic America: The Waltons." *Television: The Critical View*, Third Edition. Horace Newcomb, ed. New York: Oxford University Press, 1982.

Sanders, Keith and Lynda Kaid. "An Overview of Political Communication Theory and Research: 1976–1977." *Communication Yearbook II*. Brent Rubin, ed. New Brunswick, NJ: Transaction Books, 1978.

Savage, Robert. "Statesmanship, Surfacing, and Sometimes Stumbling: Constructing Candidate Images During the Early Campaign." *Political Communication Review* 11, (1986): 43–57.

Searing, Donald. "Models and Images of Man and Society in Leadership Theory." *Journal of Politics* 31 (1969).

Simon, Dennis and Charles Ostrom. "The Politics of Prestige: Popular Support and the Modern Presidency." *Presidential Studies Quarterly* 18, no. 4 (Fall 1988): 742–55.

Smith, Craig. "Addendum to 'Contemporary Political Speech Writing.' " *Southern Speech Communication Journal* (Winter 1977): 191–94.

———. "Speechwriting: An Acquired Art." *Campaigns and Elections*. Larry Sabato, ed. Glenview, IL: Scott, Foresman and Co., 1989.

Swerdlow, Joel. "History of Presidential Debates in America." *Presidential Debates*. Joel Swerdlow, ed. Washington, DC: Congressional Quarterly Press, 1987.

Tiemens, Robert. "Television's Portrayal of the 1976 Presidential Debates." *Communication Monographs* 45 (November 1978): 362–70.

Trent, Judith. "Presidential Surfacing: The Ritualistic and Crucial First Act." *Communication Monographs* 45 (November 1978): 281–92.

Underwood, Doug. "The Boeing Story and the Hometown Press." *Columbia Journalism Review* (November/December 1988): 50–60.

Zukin, Cliff. "Mass Communication and Public Opinion." *Handbook of Political Communication*. Dan Nimmo and Keith Sanders, eds. Beverly Hills, CA: Sage, 1981.

Index

Abrams, Floyd, 271
Adams, Sherman, 216, 234
administrative rhetoric, 111–38; assessing roles of, 119–23; backchannels and leaks, 136–38; control, 112–19, 127–28; disinformation, 134–36; leadership styles, 117–19; manipulation, 123–28; mystery and, 127–28; policy advocacy 115; policy formation, 114–15; speaking with one voice, 132–34; strategies and tactics, 128–38; using surrogates, 131–32
advertising, political, 56–61, 166–70; direct mail, 64–66; functions of, 59; negative, 60–61; types, 57–59; videostyles of, 59
agenda setting, 29, 149–51
Agnew, Spiro, 3, 131, 238, 330, 334
Ailes, Roger, 60
Alexander, Dennis, 25
Alsop, Stewart, 293
Andrews, Bert, 293
Appel, Kevin, 300, 307
Apple, R.W., 8
Aristotle, 12, 121
Arlin, Michael, 151
Armstrong, Richard, 56, 60, 64
Armstrong, Scott, 262, 263
Arnold, Thurmond, 127, 128, 261
art and politics. *See* nonpolitical forms
Arthur, Chester, 231

Babbitt, Bruce, 59
Bagdikian, Ben, 298, 302
Bailey, Doug, 52
Baker, Howard, 286
Bakke, Allen, 268, 269
Barabba, Vincent, 170
Barber, James David, 34, 89, 214
Barilleaux, Ryan, 199
Barnouw, Eric, 167, 182
Bartels, Larry, 79, 85
Bates, Stephen, 59
Becker, Samuel, 76
Bellah, Robert, 339
Bennett, Lance, 150, 153
Bennett, William, 132
Berelson, Bernard, 171
Bernays, Edward, 49, 50
Bevan, Tim, 184
Biden, Joseph, 6–8, 9, 10, 17, 250, 304; issue of honesty, 6–8
Bitzer, Lloyd, 13
Blackmun, Harry, 263
Blumenthal, Sidney, 35, 51, 52
Blumer, Herbert, 23–25, 42
Boorstin, Daniel, 115, 151, 152, 201, 211
Bork, Robert, 6, 8–9, 263
Bormann, Ernest, 40, 250–51; fantasy themes, 40–41
Bowen, Jerry, 156

About the Authors

ROBERT E. DENTON, Jr., has degrees in political science and communication from Wake Forest University and Purdue University. He teaches and writes in the areas of the American presidency, political communication, mass media, and contemporary rhetorical theory. Denton is the author of *The Symbolic Dimensions of the American Presidency*, *The Primetime Presidency of Ronald Reagan* (Praeger), and coauthor of *Presidential Communication* (Praeger), *Persuasion and Social Movements*, and *Persuasion and Influence in American Life* (with Gary Woodward). In addition, he has published articles in the fields of political science, advertising, and communication. Denton is currently head of the Department of Communication Studies at Virginia Polytechnic Institute and State University.

GARY C. WOODWARD has degrees in communication and rhetorical theory from California State University at Sacramento and the University of Pittsburgh. He has taught in England as well as in the United States. He teaches and writes in the areas of politics, the mass media, and contemporary issues. He is the author of *Persuasive Encounters* (Praeger) and coauthor of *Persuasion and Influence in American Life*. In addition, he has published articles in the areas of communication and rhetorical theory. Woodward is currently an associate professor in the Department of Speech Communication and Theatre Arts at Trenton State College.